PENGUIN  CLASSICS

WOMEN WHO DID

Angelique Richardson is Senior Lecturer in English at the University of Exeter. She has published widely on nineteenth-century fiction and is the author of *Love and Eugenics in the Late Nineteenth Century: Rational Reproduction and the New Woman* (Oxford University Press, 2003). She is also co-editor of *The New Woman in Fiction and in Fact: Fin-de-Siècle Feminisms* (Palgrave, 2001).

Women Who Did

Stories by Men and Women, 1890–1914

Edited with an Introduction and Notes by
ANGELIQUE RICHARDSON

PENGUIN BOOKS

PENGUIN BOOKS

Published by the Penguin Group
Penguin Books Ltd, 80 Strand, London WC2R ORL, England
Penguin Group (USA) Inc., 375 Hudson Street, New York, New York 10014, USA
Penguin Group (Canada), 10 Alcorn Avenue, Toronto, Ontario, Canada M4V 3B2
(a division of Pearson Penguin Canada Inc.)
Penguin Ireland, 25 St Stephen's Green, Dublin 2, Ireland
(a division of Penguin Books Ltd)
Penguin Group (Australia), 250 Camberwell Road, Camberwell, Victoria 3124, Australia
(a division of Pearson Australia Group Pty Ltd)
Penguin Books India Pvt Ltd, 11 Community Centre, Panchsheel Park, New Delhi – 110 017, India
Penguin Group (NZ), cnr Airborne and Rosedale Roads, Albany, Auckland 1310, New Zealand
(a division of Pearson New Zealand Ltd)
Penguin Books (South Africa) (Pty) Ltd, 24 Sturdee Avenue, Rosebank 2196, South Africa

Penguin Books Ltd, Registered Offices: 80 Strand, London WC2R ORL, England

www.penguin.com

First published 2002
Published in Penguin Classics with minor revisions 2005

4

Editorial material copyright © Angelique Richardson, 2002, 2005

The Acknowledgements on pp. ix–x constitute an extension of this copyright page

Set in 10/12.5 pt PostScript Adobe Caslon
Typeset by Rowland Phototypesetting Ltd, Bury St Edmunds, Suffolk
Printed in England by Clays Ltd, St Ives plc

ISBN-13: 978-0-141-44156-6

www.greenpenguin.co.uk

CONTENTS

CONTENTS

vi

For my friends

ACKNOWLEDGEMENTS

I would like to thank Laura Barber, Gillian Beer, the late Chris Brooks, Walter Stetson Chamberlin, the faculty members of the Dickens Project at the University of California at Santa Cruz, David Doughan, Peter Faulkner, Regenia Gagnier, Nick Gingell, Lee Grieveson, Ann Heilmann, Huguette Henryson-Caird, George Levine, Colin MacCabe, Rupert Mann, Laura Marcus, Joss Marsh, Grace Moore, Dorothy Porter, Diane Purkiss, David Trotter, Lindeth Vasey, Marina Warner, the late Chris Willis, Charmaine Wyre, my parents and my wider family.

I am also grateful to the British Academy and the University of Exeter for financial support, and to the librarians and archivists of Bath Central Library, the Bodleian Library (especially the librarians of the Map Room), the British Library, the Fawcett Library, the History of Advertising Trust Archive, the Library of Congress, the National Library of Scotland, New York Public Library, University College London and the Wellcome Library for the History and Understanding of Medicine, London, for their time and assistance.

ACKNOWLEDGEMENTS

The Society of Authors as the Literary Representatives of the Estate of Katherine Mansfield.

George Moore, 'The Wedding Feast' is reproduced by permission of Colin Smythe Literary Agents.

Edith Wharton, 'The Reckoning' is reprinted by permission of the Estate of Edith Wharton and the Watkins/Loomis Agency.

Virginia Woolf, 'Phyllis and Rosamond' from *The Complete Shorter Fiction of Virginia Woolf*, ed. Susan Dick, copyright © 1985 by Quentin Bell and Angelica Garnett, is reprinted by permission of Random House for the executors of the Virginia Woolf Estate and Hogarth Press and by permission of Harcourt, Inc.

CHRONOLOGY

Centring on events in Britain and the United States, this chronology provides a political, social and cultural framework for this anthology. Beginning in 1875, with the official involvement of women with the British Trades Union Congress, it ends in 1928, with Universal Suffrage in Britain.

1875   British Trade Union Act allows peaceful picketing
British Public Health Act
House of Commons raises the age of consent to thirteen
Emma Patterson is first woman to be invited to British Trades Union Congress
US Supreme Court rules unanimously that citizenship does not automatically confer the right to vote

1876   Royal Titles Act makes Victoria Empress of India
British Mothers' Union, Anglican organization (developed into international body by 1890s)
Battle of Little Big Horn – Custer's Last Stand
Scottish-born Alexander Graham Bell introduces his telephone at the Centennial Exposition in Philadelphia
US Socialist-Labor Party
US Great Railroad Strike

George Eliot, *Daniel Deronda*
Mark Twain (Samuel L. Clemens), *The Adventures of Tom Sawyer*

1877   Royal Free Hospital, London, admits female students to clinical instruction

Trial of Charles Bradlaugh and Annie Besant for republishing Charles Knowlton's *The Fruits of Philosophy*, on birth control

End of Reconstruction (implemented by Congress in 1866 and aimed at reorganizing the Southern states after the Civil War, providing the means for readmitting them into the Union and defining the ways by which whites and blacks could live together in a non-slave society)

Henry James, *The American*

1878   London University admits women to degrees and University College London becomes coeducational

Matrimonial Causes Act gives magistrates' courts summary jurisdiction to make separation orders in cases of cruelty

Woman Suffrage Amendment introduced in Congress (not passed)

Anna Katherine Green, *The Leavenworth Case: A Lawyer's Story* (arguably the first woman-authored detective novel)

Thomas Hardy, *The Return of the Native*

James, *The Europeans*

1879   Anglo-Zulu War

Lady Margaret Hall and Somerville College, Oxford, opened

James, *Daisy Miller*

George Meredith, *The Egoist*

1880   Tories defeated under Disraeli; Gladstone's second Cabinet

Irish National Land League founded – organizes boycotting of unpopular landlords and their agents

Pedal and chain bicycle invented

Deaths of George Eliot and Gustave Flaubert

1881   Cambridge University allows women to sit the examination, but does not award degrees

Charles Stewart Parnell succeeds Isaac Butt as leader of Irish Home Rule Party

Ladies' Land League launched in Ireland

Rational Dress Society founded

Deaths of Disraeli and Thomas Carlyle

James, *The Portrait of a Lady* and *Washington Square*
Dante Gabriel Rossetti, *Ballads and Sonnets*

1882   Cambridge University authorizes issue of certificates to women, which state the class of their tripos
Married Women's Property Act – married women allowed to own and administer their own property; no longer considered husband's 'chattel' but separate and independent
State grant for cookery teaching to girls in elementary schools
Phoenix Park murders – Irish Chief Secretary assassinated
US Chinese Exclusion Act (renewed 1892, 1902) ends Chinese immigration

Death of Charles Darwin
Birth of Virginia Woolf

Walter Besant, *All Sorts and Conditions of Men*
Twain, *The Prince and the Pauper*

1883   Francis Galton coins the term 'eugenics' in *Inquiries into the Human Faculty and its Development*
Women's Co-operative Guild founded

Death of Karl Marx

Ladies' Home Journal (USA) founded
Andrew Mearns, *The Bitter Cry of Outcast London*
Friedrich Nietzsche, *Thus Spake Zarathustra* (–1892)
Olive Schreiner, *The Story of an African Farm*
Elizabeth Cady Stanton, *Raising Clio's Consciousness*
Robert Louis Stevenson, *Treasure Island*

1884   Gladstone's Third Reform Act enfranchises agricultural labourers
Matrimonial Causes Act
Social Democratic Federation founded by Henry Hyndman – members include Eleanor Marx and William Morris
Fabian Society founded by Beatrice and Sidney Webb,

George Bernard Shaw and H. G. Wells, as group promoting non-Marxist evolutionary socialism
US National Bureau of Labor

Friedrich Engels, *Origin of the Family*
Joris-Karl Huysmans, *A rebours*
Sarah Orne Jewett, *A Country Doctor* (heroine chooses a career in medicine over marriage)
George Moore, *A Mummer's Wife*
George Bernard Shaw, *An Unsocial Socialist*
Twain, *The Adventures of Huckleberry Finn*

1885   Salisbury's first cabinet; he begins policy of 'splendid isolation'
Criminal Law Amendment Act raises the age of consent from thirteen to sixteen, strengthens existing legislation against prostitution and proscribes all homosexual relations
Housing of the Working Classes Act, inspired by Andrew Mearns's *The Bitter Cry of Outcast London* of 1883 (further acts 1890, 1900, 1903)
Karl Pearson, leading British eugenist, forms the Men and Women's Club
Major-General Charles Gordon defeated by Sudanese at Khartoum, where he had been sent to evacuate the Egyptians
US Statue of Liberty erected (dedicated following year)
Bryn Mawr, Philadelphia, founded – first women's college to offer both graduate and undergraduate degrees

Births of D. H. Lawrence and Ezra Pound

Eleanor and Edward Marx Aveling, *The Woman Question*
W. S. Gilbert and A. Sullivan, *The Mikado*
Henry Rider Haggard, *King Solomon's Mines*
William Dean Howells, *The Rise of Silas Lapham*
Richard von Krafft-Ebing, *Psychopathia sexualis*
Meredith, *Diana of the Crossways*

1886   Liberals split on Home Rule
Gladstone's first Irish Home Rule Bill defeated

Salisbury's second cabinet, with coalition of Conservatives and Liberal Unionists (he remains Prime Minister until 1902)
Repeal of Contagious Diseases Acts (passed during the 1860s, requiring the registration and compulsory examination in garrison towns and ports of suspected female prostitutes – implied the state's support for the sexual double standard)
Edinburgh School of Medicine for Women founded
Charles Bradlaugh becomes the first avowedly atheist MP to take his seat
Chicago Haymarket Square Riot – protests against police brutality towards striking workers
American Federation of Labor (AFL) organized by Samuel Gompers
Coca-cola put on sale

Cosmopolitan (USA) and *Forum* founded
Henry Arthur Allbut, *The Wife's Handbook*
Frances Hodgson Burnett, *Little Lord Fauntleroy*
James, *The Bostonians* and *The Princess Casamassima*
Stevenson, *The Strange Case of Dr Jekyll and Mr Hyde*

1887   Victoria's Golden Jubilee
Independent Labour Party founded
Queen opens Queen's Hall, first part of the People's Palace, Mile End Road
Liberal Women's Suffrage Society founded
US Dawes Act dissolves communal land rights of Indians, except for Pueblo groups (provided for private ownership only)

Arthur Conan Doyle, *A Study in Scarlet*
Hardy, *The Woodlanders*

1888   British Imperial East African Company granted royal charter – encourages Indian immigration, primarily to provide indentured labour for railway construction
London Bryant & May 'match girls' and dockworkers' strikes
Jack the Ripper murders in London's East End

International Council of Women (ICW), founded by Susan B. Anthony, May Wright Sewell and Frances Willard, holds its first convention in Washington, DC – 49 delegates from England, Ireland, France, Norway, Denmark, Finland, India, Canada and the United States
Congress establishes Department of Labor
Eastman-Kodak's box camera invented

Death of Matthew Arnold
Births of Katherine Mansfield and T. S. Eliot

'Are We Degenerating Physically?' appears in *Lancet*
Edward Bellamy, *Looking Backward From 2000 to 1887*
Mona Caird, *Westminster Review* articles, 'Ideal Marriage' and 'Marriage', spark national debate: 'Is Marriage a Failure?', in *Daily Telegraph*
Henry Havelock Ellis, *Women and Marriage*
Sarah Grand, *Ideala: A Study from Life*
George and Weedon Grossmith, *The Diary of a Nobody* (serialized in *Punch*)
Rudyard Kipling, *Plain Tales from the Hills*
Mrs Humphry Ward, *Robert Elsmere*

1889 Women's Trade Union League formed
London dockers' strike
Oklahoma opened to white settlers

Patrick Geddes and J. Arthur Thomson, *The Evolution of Sex*
Henrik Ibsen, *A Doll's House* – first English production (performed in Norway 1879)
Jerome K. Jerome, *Three Men in a Boat*
Twain, *A Connecticut Yankee in King Arthur's Court*

1890 Housing of the Working Classes Act passed
Healthy and Artistic Dress Union founded
Cecil Rhodes becomes Prime Minister of Cape Colony
US Army shoots and kills over 250 unarmed Sioux women, men and children at the Battle of Wounded Knee in South Dakota

National Woman Suffrage Association and American Woman Suffrage Association (both founded 1869) unite as National American Woman Suffrage Association (NAWSA), under leadership of Elizabeth Cady Stanton

Jane Addams and Ellen Gates Starr found Hull House, a US settlement house project – part of a movement which propelled thousands of college-educated white women and a number of women of colour into careers in social work

National Society of Daughters of the American Revolution (NSDAR) founded

AFL announce their support for women's suffrage at their convention

Literary Digest (USA) and *Strand* founded

Ellis, *The Criminal* and *The New Spirit*

John Fiske, *The American Revolution*

James, *The Tragic Muse*

William Morris, *News from Nowhere* (serialized in *Commonweal*)

Jacob A. Riis, *How the Other Half Lives*

Elizabeth Sharp, *Women Poets of the Victorian Era*

Oscar Wilde, *The Picture of Dorian Gray*

1891   Free elementary education

Appeal court rules that no man has right to detain and imprison his wife (*R.* v *Jackson*)

First international copyright law

US Forest Reserve Act – beginning of conservation movement

Deaths of Parnell – hopes fade for Home Rule – and Herman Melville

George Gissing, *New Grub Street*

Grand, *A Domestic Experiment*

Hardy, *Tess of the D'Urbervilles*

Ibsen, *Hedda Gabler* performed

George Noyes Miller, *The Strike of a Sex*

Schreiner, *Dreams*

1892 Tories lose election; fourth Gladstone government
Emily Massingberd opens the Pioneer Club, for women to meet and debate – members include Caird and Grand
Almost 2 million acres of Crow Indian reservation in Montana opened to white settlers

Deaths of Alfred, Lord Tennyson and Walt Whitman

Stephen Crane, *Maggie: A Girl of the Streets (A Story of New York)*
Max Nordau, *Degeneration* (translated into English in 1895)

1892–5 Scottish universities admit women to degrees

1893 Independent Labour Party formed under Keir Hardie
House of Lords rejects second Irish Home Rule Bill
First two women factory inspectors appointed
Married women's property rights affirmed
New Zealand becomes first country to enfranchise women
Colorado becomes first US state to enfranchise women
Militant American Railway Union founded
Chicago World Fair
US Anti-Saloon League

Besant, *The Rebel Queen*
Hubert Montague Crackanthorpe, *Wreckage: Seven Studies*
George Egerton, *Keynotes*
Gilbert and Sullivan, *Utopia, Limited*
Gissing, *The Odd Women*
Grand, *The Heavenly Twins*
Emile Zola, *Doctor Pascal; or, Life and Heredity*

1894 Gladstone resigns; Rosebery's Liberal government
American railway strikes

Birth of e. e. cummings

First issue of *The Yellow Book* (–1897)
Emma Frances Brooke, *A Superfluous Woman*
Caird, *The Daughters of Danaus*

Edward Carpenter, *Marriage in a Free Society*
George du Maurier, *Trilby*
Egerton, *Discords*
Ellis, *Man and Woman: A Study of Human Secondary Sexual Characters*
Charlotte Perkins Gilman, 'The Yellow Wallpaper'
Sidney Grundy, *The New Woman: An Original Comedy in Four Acts*
Hardy, *Life's Little Ironies*
Anthony Hope, *The Prisoner of Zenda*
Henry Arthur Jones, *The Case of Rebellious Susan*
Kipling, *The Jungle Book*
Moore, *Esther Waters*
Arthur Morrison, *Tales of Mean Streets*
Karl Pearson, 'Woman and Labour'

1895   National Union of Women Workers founded
Scottish Council for Women's Trades founded
Oscar Wilde convicted of committing homosexual acts and sentenced to 2 years' hard labour; writes *De Profundis*
NAWSA develops 'Southern Strategy', arguing that woman suffrage with educational or property qualifications would disqualify most black women
New York Public Library founded
Lumière brothers invent cinematography

Birth of Enid Blyton

Grant Allen, *The Woman who Did*
Anton Chekhov, *The Seagull*
Joseph Conrad, *Almayer's Folly*
Ella D'Arcy, *Monochromes*
Ménie Muriel Dowie, *Gallia*
Sigmund Freud and Josef Breuer, *Studies on Hysteria*
George F. Hall, *A Study in Bloomers, or, The Model New Woman*
Hardy, *Jude the Obscure*
Arthur Wing Pinero, *The Notorious Mrs Ebbsmith*

Elizabeth Cady Stanton, *The Woman's Bible*
H. G. Wells, *The Time Machine*
Oscar Wilde, *An Ideal Husband* and *The Importance of Being Earnest*

1896   Alfred Harmsworth establishes *Daily Mail*, Britain's first tabloid
Klondike Gold Rush
US General Federation of Women's Clubs established – comprising over 500 white women's clubs with 150,000 members
US National Association of Colored Women (NACW), led by Mary Church Terrell, formed to work for racial 'uplift', to campaign against lynching and discrimination and to promote health and education in black communities
NSDAR incorporated by an Act of Congress
Thomas Edison introduces motion pictures in the US
Freud introduces the term 'psychoanalysis'

Edward Carpenter, *Love's Coming-of-Age: A Series of Papers on the Relations of the Sexes*
W. E. B. Du Bois, *The Suppression of the African Slave Trade*
A. E. Housman, *A Shropshire Lad*
Jewett, *The Country of the Pointed Firs*
George Santayana, *The Sense of Beauty*

1897   Victoria's Diamond Jubilee
National Union of Women's Suffrage Societies (NUWSS) formed
Commons passes second reading of Women's Suffrage Bill by 228 votes to 157

Caird, *The Morality of Marriage and Other Essays on the Status and Destiny of Woman*
Elizabeth Rachel Chapman, *Marriage Questions in Modern Fiction, and Other Essays on Kindred Subjects*
Egerton, *Symphonies*
Grand, *The Beth Book*

James, *What Maisie Knew*
Mary Kingsley, *Travels in West Africa*

1898 Spanish–American War
Rational Dress League founded – enjoys greater prominence
than the earlier society, and promotes bifurcated clothing for
cycling
Discovery of radium

Death of Gladstone
Birth of Bertolt Brecht

Egerton, *Fantasias*
Gilman, *Women and Economics*
Grand, *The Modern Man and Maid*
James, *The Turn of the Screw*
Wilde, *The Ballad of Reading Gaol*

1899 Second South African (Boer) War begins
International Congress of Women meets in London
US United Mine Workers organized

Everybody's Magazine (USA) launched
Charles W. Chesnutt, *The Conjure Man*
Kate Chopin, *The Awakening*
Freud, *The Interpretation of Dreams*
James, *The Awkward Age*
Frances Swiney, *The Awakening of Women, or Woman's Part
in Evolution*
Thorstein Veblen, *The Theory of the Leisure Class*
Edith Wharton, *The Greater Inclination*

1900 Labour Representation Committee founded
Commonwealth of Australia founded
US working-class women organize International Ladies
Garment Workers Union
US Socialist Party founded
Key co-ordinator of the suffrage movement Carrie (Lane)
Chapman Catt becomes NAWSA president (–1904)

Mendel's peas, and laws of heredity, rediscovered

Deaths of Wilde and John Ruskin

L. Frank Baum, *The Wonderful Wizard of Oz*
Joseph Conrad, *Lord Jim*
Theodore Dreiser, *Sister Carrie*
Gilman, *Concerning Children*
Jack London, *The Son of the Wolf*

1900–   Nearly 30,000 Lancashire women mill-workers petition for
1901   suffrage

1901   Death of Victoria; accession of Edward VII
           Women's commission of inquiry into conditions in South
           African concentration camps
           British Psychological Society founded
           Theodore Roosevelt becomes president (–1909)
           First transatlantic radio

           Freud, *The Psychopathology of Everyday Life*
           Kipling, *Kim*
           Arnold White, *Efficiency and Empire*

1902   Peace of Vereeniging ends South African War
           Catt co-organizes the International Woman Suffrage Alli-
           ance (IWSA) – eventually sympathetic association in 32
           nations
           Maryland enacts first state workmen's compensation law

           Samuel Butler, *The Way of All Flesh*
           Conrad, *Heart of Darkness*
           Thomas Dixon, *The Leopard's Spots: A Romance of The White
           Man's Burden, 1865–1900*
           Ellen Glasgow, *The Battle Ground*
           Henry James, *The Wings of the Dove*
           William James, *Varieties of Religious Experience*
           Riis, *The Battle with the Slum*
           Shaw, *Mrs Warren's Profession* performed
           Wharton, *The Valley of Decision*

1903   Alfred Harmsworth establishes *Daily Mirror*, a newspaper 'for gentlewomen'
Some members of NUWSS in Manchester form Women's Social and Political Union – led by Emmeline Pankhurst, it was not willing to restrict itself to constitutional methods
AFAFL convention, blue-collar and middle-class women unite to form the National Women's Trade Union League
US Department of Commerce and Labor established
Wright brothers make first powered aircraft flight

Du Bois, *The Souls of Black Folk*
Gilman, *The Home: Its Work and Influence*
James, *The Ambassadors*
London, *The Call of the Wild*
Shaw, *Man and Superman*
Kate Douglas Wiggin, *Rebecca of Sunnybrook Farm*

1904   Entente Cordiale between Great Britain and France
Russo-Japanese War begins
Royal Academy of Dramatic Art founded
Daily Mirror becomes a picture paper for men as well as women
Abbey Theatre opened in Dublin
American Academy of Arts and Letters founded
Pacific cable completed

J. M. Barrie, *Peter Pan*
Chekhov, *The Cherry Orchard*
Conrad, *Nostromo*
James, *The Golden Bowl*
Saki, *Reginald*

1905   First Russian Revolution
Alien Act passed
First militant action by WSPU at Free Trade Hall, Manchester
Industrial Workers of the World (IWW) organized in Chicago – led by William 'Big Bill' Haywood

Daniel De Leon, *Socialist Reconstruction of Society*
Dixon, *The Clansman: An Historical Romance of the Ku Klux Klan*
E. M. Forster, *Where Angels Fear to Tread*
Freud, *Three Essays on the Theory of Sexuality*
London, *The War of the Classes* – essays advocating socialism
Baroness Orczy, *The Scarlet Pimpernel*
Shaw, *Major Barbara*
Wharton, *The House of Mirth*

1906   Sweeping Liberal victory at General Election
Labour Party founded
Women's Labour League (WLL) founded – political pressure group active in suffrage and trade unionism
USA passes Naturalization Act
US Pure Food and Drug Act

Birth of Samuel Beckett

John Galsworthy, *The Man of Property* (first novel of *The Forsyte Saga*, –1921)
Edith Nesbit, *The Railway Children*

1907   Medical Inspection Act
Qualification of Women Act – County and Borough Councils open to women
Artists' Suffrage League formed
70 WSPU members form the Women's Freedom League (WFL), and use non-violent illegal methods
'Gentleman's Agreement' restricts Japanese immigration to USA

Votes for Women, WSPU newspaper, established
Crackanthorpe, *Population and Progress*
Edmund Gosse, *Father and Son*
James, *The American Scene*
J. M. Synge, *The Playboy of the Western World*
Wharton, *Madame de Treymes*

1908   Bosnia and Herzegovina annexed by Austria-Hungary
Old Age Pensions Act: non-contributory pensions for all citizens over 70
Women's National Anti-Suffrage League
Women Writers' Suffrage League (WWSL) founded by Betty Hatton and Cecily Hamilton
Fabian Women's Group founded
Actresses' Franchise League (AFL) founded
First international meeting of psychoanalysts (Salzburg)

Forster, *A Room with a View*
Kenneth Grahame, *The Wind in the Willows*
Grand, *Emotional Moments*
Cecily Hamilton, *Marriage as a Trade* and *Diana of Dobson's*
L. M. Montgomery, *Anne of Green Gables*
Gene Stratton-Porter, *A Girl of the Limberlost*

1909   Lloyd George's People's Budget introduces principle of progressive taxation; rejected by House of Lords and constitutional crisis ensues
First hunger strikes by imprisoned suffragettes; forcible feeding policy implemented
Women's Exhibition, WSPU, at Prince's Skating Rink, Knightsbridge, London
US coalition of blacks and whites form National Association for the Advancement of Colored People (NAACP)
Model-T Ford inaugurates car mass-production

Hamilton, *A Pageant of Great Women* and *How the Vote was Won* (with Christopher St John)
Shaw, *Press Cuttings*
Wells, *Ann Veronica* and *Tono-Bungay*

1910   Mexican Revolution
General Election in January serves as referendum on budget and peers; People's Budget passed in April
Edward VII dies; accession of George V (–1936)

Forster, *Howards End*

1911   Parliament Act destroys House of Lords' veto power
        Women's Coronation Procession
        Militant tactics increase by WSPU following failure of con-
        ciliation bill

        Freewoman launched (–1912; relaunched in 1914 as *New Free-
        woman*), edited by Dora Marsden – gives space to lesbianism,
        and is denounced as an 'immoral paper' in *Morning Telegraph*
        Max Beerbohm, *Zuleika Dobson*
        Burnett, *The Secret Garden*
        Gertrude Colmore, *Suffragette Sally*
        Gilman, *Man Made World: Our Androcentric Culture*
        Schreiner, *Woman and Labour*
        Wharton, *Ethan Frome*

1912   Balkan Wars start
        Peak activity of suffrage campaign (–1913)
        Theodore Roosevelt's Progressive Party first US national
        political party to adopt a women's suffrage plank
        Massachusetts establishes first minimum wage for women
        and children

        Grand, *Adnam's Orchard*
        James Weldon Johnson, *The Autobiography of an Ex-Colored
        Man*
        Thomas Mann, *Death in Venice*

1913   'Cat and Mouse' Act
        Emily Davison throws herself in front of the King's horse at
        the Derby, and dies four days later – her cortège is drawn
        through London
        Caird speaks out against eugenics at the Annual Speech of
        the Personal Rights Association
        Woodrow Wilson becomes President (–1921)
        Alice Paul returns to USA from England and, with Lucy
        Burns, organizes Congressional Union (from 1916, National
        Women's Party) – adopts tactics of the WSPU, and members
        participate in hunger strikes, picket the White House and
        engage in other forms of civil disobedience

US establishes separate Department of Labor
Willa Cather, *O Pioneers!*
Floyd Dell, *Women as World Builders*
D. H. Lawrence, *Sons and Lovers*
Christabel Pankhurst, *Plain Facts about a Great Evil (The Great Scourge and How to End It)*

1914   Outbreak of World War I
Cessation of militant suffrage activities in Britain
WLL becomes official voice of women in Labour Party
British Nationality and Status of Aliens Act confers status of British subject upon persons with specified dominion connections
US National Federation of Women's Clubs – membership of more than 2 million women of all colours – formally endorses the suffrage campaign

James Joyce, *Dubliners* and *A Portrait of the Artist as a Young Man* (–1915)
Shaw, *Common Sense About the War*

1915   Second Ku Klux Klan founded – nativism, anti-catholicism and anti-semitism now combine with white supremacy (first formed in 1866)
Catt returns to NAWSA presidency
Margaret Sanger publishes first issue of *Woman Rebel*, and is indicted for violating US postal obscenity laws – by distributing material relating to birth control

Clementina Black, *Married Women's Work*
John Buchan, *The Thirty-Nine Steps*
Caird, *Stones of Sacrifice*
Cather, *The Song of the Lark*
Ford Madox Ford, *The Good Soldier*
Gilman, *Herland* (serialized in *Forerunner*)
D. W. Griffith, *The Birth of a Nation* (based on Dixon's *Clansman*), the most controversial film in the history of cinema, premieres

Lawrence, *The Rainbow*
Edgar Lee Masters, *Spoon River Anthology*
W. Somerset Maugham, *Of Human Bondage*

1916   Battle of the Somme
Lloyd George becomes Prime Minister
Easter Rising in Ireland
Alice Paul and followers organize picketing of White House following Wilson's re-election and publicly burn his war-time speeches
Jeannette Rankin of Montana becomes the first woman elected to US House of Representatives

Grand, *The Winged Victory*

1917   Russian Revolution
US enters World War I

Clemence Dane, *Regiment of Women*
T. S. Eliot, *Prufrock and Other Observations*
Siegfried Sassoon, 'A Soldier's Declaration', in *The Old Huntsman*

1918   End of World War I
Women's Suffrage Act – property-owning women over the age of thirty given the vote
WLL becomes an integrated section of Labour Party, renaming itself Labour Party Women's Organization

Cather, *My Antonia*
Wyndham Lewis, *Tarr*
Wilfred Owen, 'Dulce et Decorum Est'
Sassoon, 'Glory of Women', in *Counter-Attack and Other Poems*
Marie Stopes, *Married Love*
Lytton Strachey, *Eminent Victorians*
Rebecca West, *The Return of the Soldier*

1919   Sex Disqualification Removal Act makes it illegal to exclude women from legal profession on grounds of sex

Thorstein Veblen, *The Place of Science in Modern Civilization*

1920   Congress grants women the right to vote
NAWSA becomes the nucleus of the League of Women Voters

Eugene O'Neill, *The Emperor Jones* and *Beyond the Horizon*
Lawrence, *Women in Love*
Stopes, *Radiant Motherhood: A Book for Those Who are Creating the Future*
Wharton, *The Age of Innocence*

1921   Anglo-Irish Treaty concluded

Thorstein Veblen, *The Engineers and the Price System*

1922   Cather, *One of Ours*
Johnson's *The Book of American Negro Poetry*
Katherine Mansfield, *The Garden Party and Other Stories*

1923   Matrimonial Causes Act – grants equality in divorce proceedings to women
Catt, *Women Suffrage and Politics: The Inner Story of the Suffrage Movement*
Margaret Sanger, *The Pivot of Civilization* – advocating birth control
Schreiner, *Stories, Dreams and Allegories* and *Thoughts on South Africa* (published posthumously)

1924   Ramsay MacDonald forms first Labour government

Forster, *A Passage to India*

1925   Scopes Trial, in Dayton, Tennessee, on whether evolution should be taught in schools (Jerome Lawrence and Robert E. Lee's play *Inherit the Wind* (1950) based on this)

Virginia Woolf, *Mrs Dalloway*

1926   Transatlantic wireless telephone

Carl Van Vechten, *Nigger Heaven*

1928   Universal suffrage in Britain
        Lawrence, *Lady Chatterley's Lover*
        Shaw, *The Intelligent Woman's Guide to Socialism and Capitalism*
        Woolf, *Orlando*

INTRODUCTION

The Shock of the New

'Did all these things happen, Jackson, or did you invent them?' asked George Bernard Shaw in 1913 after reading Holbrook Jackson's *The Eighteen Nineties*.[1] The *fin de siècle*[2] was an explosive cocktail of endings, beginnings and transitions, a remarkably dynamic time in which aesthetes, dandies and decadents rubbed shoulders with social purists, rational dressers, striking match-girls, smoking and cycling New Women – and alarmed reactionaries. It was a time of heightened self-consciousness, of confusion, uncertainty and questioning: the century was coming to its end, but what would follow in its wake? 'What shall be considered good tomorrow – what shall be beautiful – what shall we know tomorrow – what believe in? What shall inspire us? How shall we enjoy? So rings the question from the thousand voices of the people', recorded Max Nordau in *Degeneration*,[3] his panicked diagnosis of the *fin de siècle*.

In 'The Contemporary Novel' H. G. Wells echoed these thoughts:

> formerly there was a feeling of certitude about moral values and standards of conduct that is altogether absent today. It wasn't so much that men were agreed upon these things – about these things there have always been enormous divergences of opinion – as that men were emphatic, cocksure, and unteachable about whatever they did happen to believe to a degree that no longer obtains. This is the Balfourian age, and even religion seeks to establish itself on doubt. There were, perhaps, just as many differences in the past as there are now, but the outlines are harder ... all our social, political, moral problems are being approached in a new spirit, in an inquiring and experimental spirit.[4]

The new mood was everywhere. As Colonel Cazenove remarks in Sidney Grundy's West End hit, *The New Woman* (1894), 'everything's New nowadays!'[5] The cultural critic Henry Duff Traill opened *The New Fiction* with the words 'not to be "new" is, in these days, to be nothing'.[6] Emily Morgan-Dockrell, Irish social commentator and wife of a prominent London doctor, captured the spirit of the age in the *Humanitarian*:

The close of the nineteenth century marks an epoch of social revolutions! . . . The remnant of the old order stand aghast, clinging affrightedly to their traditions; meanwhile the new order hastens forth eagerly, heralding and welcoming the fuller entrance of the New Era. That very word, 'new', strikes as it were the dominant note in the trend of present-day thought, present day effort and aspiration. It sounds out from every quarter. The new art, the new literature, the new fiction, the new journalism, the new humour, the new criticism, the new hedonism, the new morality . . . Lastly, more discussed, debated, newspaper paragraphed, caricatured, howled down and denied, or acknowledged and approved, as the case may be, than any of them, we have the new woman.[7]

The following sections consider the appearance and flourishing of New Women on both sides of the Atlantic, and explore various expressions of protest and desire for social change, situating these within a wider social, economic and political framework. The influence of Victorian science on changing concepts of womanhood will also be examined. *Fin-de-siècle* Britain and the United States saw a dramatic rise in the popularity of the short story, which provided a fitting forum for exploration and experimentation, and I will explore the vital connections between this genre and the social and sexual turbulence of the late nineteenth century, concluding with the birth of psycho-analysis.

New Women in Britain and the United States

The New Woman, an emerging form of emancipated womanhood, marked a new departure in femininity: a subject, not an object, she was an icon of the 1890s. Smoking, cycling, defiant and desiring New Women were splashed across the press and entered the world of fiction with astonishing rapidity – more than a hundred novels and a far greater number of short stories were published about her before the century was out, and magazines studied and satirized her without respite. Endlessly debated in fiction and the media, New Women took many forms, both in fiction and in fact, and cannot be characterized by a single set of ideas. Nonetheless, New Women were united in their belief in the autonomy of women and in the need for social and political reform. While New Women have been associated primarily with British culture, their presence and popularity soon spread to other parts of the world, most notably the United States, and they became one of the most striking features of the late nineteenth century on both sides of the Atlantic. In 1911 Hardy thought about turning *Jude the Obscure* into a play called 'The New Woman'.[8] In 1917 George Sims recorded in *Glances Back*:

the young women of mid-Victorian days were chaperoned everywhere. Even married women would have hesitated to dine in a restaurant without male escort. Today our young women take each other out and puff their cigarettes in places of public resort. No wonder the surviving mid-Victorian rubs his eyes sometimes when he looks around him and wonders if he is still living in the London of his youth and young manhood.[9]

Smoking, a recurrent image in this collection, contravened images of Victorian femininity; in the 1890s it came to signal pleasure and independence and, like the bicycle, which became a craze at this time among the middle classes, was a hallmark of the New Woman. 'The New Woman will not continue long in the land', hoped the critic William Barry in the *Quarterly Review* in 1894. 'Like other fashions, she is destined to excite notice, to be admired, criticized, and forgotten.'[10] In fact, the social and political resonances embodied by the

New Woman persisted into the new century. In 1911, the year in which Olive Schreiner's landmark *Woman and Labour* was published, the polemical suffragette paper *Votes for Women* remarked: 'a straw shows the way of the wind, and the tendency in books and plays to introduce the characters of "new women" are signs of the triumphant intrusion of the woman question'.[11]

In 1883 the first New Woman novel, Schreiner's *The Story of An African Farm*, 'first clearly sounded the note of this revolt, as it has been called, against the old and hitherto sanctioned ideas regarding the closest and most exacting tie between man and woman'.[12] The word 'woman' was embraced as positive in the phrase 'New Woman', marking a shift in attitudes; it had been more usually considered derogatory, contrasting with 'lady': vestiges of this hierarchy, underpinned by conservative notions of respectability and sexual modesty, linger in the twenty-first century. The term 'New Woman' was introduced into popular transatlantic currency in 1894 through Sarah Grand's essay in the *North American Review*, 'The New Aspect of the Woman Question' (in the same year, 'feminist' made its first appearance in the *Daily News*, and 'feminism' in the *Athenæum* the following year). The *North American Review* published, in swift succession, Grand's 'The Modern Girl' and 'The Man of the Moment', and Ouida's sparring 'The New Woman', and Grand lectured in America and Britain on female emancipation. In 1893 Grand's infamous novel *The Heavenly Twins* took syphilis and the sexual double standard by the horns, and the public by storm, selling over 100,000 copies in the United States, and over 20,000 copies in Britain (where it was reprinted six times in its first year). In 1895 the American novelist George F. Hall published *A Study in Bloomers, or, The Model New Woman*, a lavishly illustrated exploration of this female phenomenon. The same year, Ella D'Arcy's Pleasure-Pilgrim made her brief and striking appearance: 'the newest development of the New Woman', an 'American edition' who is 'the pioneer of the army coming out of the West, that's going to destroy the existing scheme of things, and rebuild it nearer to the heart's desire'. As Christine Stansell writes in *American Moderns*: 'nowhere in Europe – or in the world, for that matter – did modern culture orient itself to the New Woman as its defining figure as it did in America'.[13] It is no surprise that Irene Adler, the only person to outwit Sherlock Holmes, is American. Best-selling novelist and biologist Grant Allen's Type-writer Girl, Juliet Appleton, is a feisty American-born Girton girl.[14]

The New Woman also made an appearance in *The American Scene*, in which Henry James stressed that America was unique, for its social life was 'constituted absolutely by women', and, observing that the very essence of the American New Woman was 'not to be threatened or waylaid', he declared 'the woman produced by a woman-made society alone has obviously quite a new story'. She had, he wrote, 'been grown in an air in which a hundred of the "European" complications and dangers didn't exist'.[15] This perception of the American New Woman as one step ahead of her British counterparts persisted in the press. It was because she had grown up in greater freedom that she set her sights higher than her British sisters. 'The American woman is regarded by many people as the highest development of modern feminism . . . as we see her on this side of the Ocean [she] is an exotic of the "orchidaceous type"', wrote Hugh E. M. Stutfield, British social critic and travel writer, in 1897;[16] the *North American Review* noted in 'Petticoat Government' that the New Woman was 'flourishing throughout the length and breadth of this huge continent'.[17]

Before the century was out, Kate Chopin wrote 'The Storm', which reveals the repression on which respectability can be predicated. A sexually-explicit adulterous encounter is presented not as the cause but as the resolution of domestic problems, and as a form of redemption. The following year (1899) she published her controversial exploration of female sexual desire, *The Awakening*, and in 1903 in George Moore's 'The Wedding Feast' Kate Kavanagh, married for a day, left her husband for America.

Punch seized upon the New Woman as an easy target for parody, exploiting her diversity, while simultaneously seeking to reduce her to man-hating, oversexed stereotypes. Egerton's 'A Cross Line' from *Keynotes* (1893) was parodied as 'She-Notes' by 'Borgia Smudgiton' (Owen Seaman) and illustrated with 'Japanese Fan de Siècle Illustrations' – Beardsleyesque portraits by 'Mortarthurio Whiskersly' (Edward Tennyson Reed) – of decadent, eroticized womanhood: such satires added to the confusion surrounding the Woman Question debates, and attempted to put a spoke in the wheel of social and political change.

The Woman Question

The second half of the nineteenth century was a time of accelerated change for women. The census of 1851 had revealed that nearly one-half of the adult women in Britain had no spouse to support them, giving a 'surplus', as it was termed, of 400,000;[18] some women waited endlessly for marriage, notably in the novels of Anthony Trollope. The census report of 1861 saw the unequal ratio as the result of male emigration. As single working-class women were employed in manufacturing or domestic service, they were not seen as a problem; the 'surplus' was middle class. Previously, middle-class women working outside the home had been engaged largely in charitable works, but now bread-and-butter considerations were forcing them into the work force, and the Woman Question into public prominence. What constituted the nature of woman? What was her status and role? What difference did class make? What was the relationship of women to men, to education, labour and citizenship? And what was her destiny? These questions came collectively to be known as the 'Woman Question'.

In 1850 the North London Collegiate School, a secondary day school for girls, was founded by Frances Mary Buss, and informally organized campaigns for educational reforms during the 1850s, culminating in a Royal Commission Report in 1858 which recommended the establishment of a national system of girls' secondary schools. Radicals such as Barbara Leigh-Smith and Bessie Rayner-Parkes used the 'surplus' to argue for the necessity of training and employment for women. Some girls' schools were set up in England by national organizations: the Girls' Public Day School Company, founded in 1872, was responsible for thirty-three schools by the end of the century, and in 1883 the Church Schools Company was founded. Other schools were financed through the Endowed Schools Act (1869) or resulted from local pressure groups. While the first reforms resulted in the provision of quality secondary education for middle- and upper-class girls, attendance at elementary schools, provided and controlled by the state, and intended for the working classes, became compulsory in 1880.[19] In Gissing's *The Odd Women* (1893), Rhoda Nunn declares 'so many *odd* women – no making a pair with them. The pessimists call them useless, lost, futile lives. I, naturally – being one of them myself – take another view. I look upon them as a great reserve.'[20] In 'Our Sisters Across the Sea' in the first issue of the *Young Woman*, Brother Jonathan Junior reported there were '250,000 women in New York City exclusive of the domestic service, who are breadwinners, who have no male protectors, and no means of support other than their own efforts'. He also noted that 'three hospitals in Philadelphia are conducted exclusively by women'.[21] Lady Jeune wrote in *The Modern Marriage Market* (1897):

in a community where the female element is largely in excess of the male, and where modern thought and education have raised them intellectually on a more equal basis, it was not possible for women to remain the colourless, dependent creatures of the past. And as they have become emancipated they have more or less chosen their own careers, and thousands of women are now living proofs of the advantages of a change that has given them an aim in life which they can pursue successfully.[22]

In Britain by 1891 4,500,000 (out of 13,000,000) women were in the work force: 2,000,000 in domestic service, 1,500,000 in textiles and clothing, 264,000 in the professions (teachers and nurses) and 80,000 in agriculture;[23] while most of these were working-class occupations, middle-class women entering the professions contravened middle-class domestic ideology, and were perceived as signs of the persisting 'surplus'. Women were also knocking on the doors of universities on both sides of the Atlantic. In the United States in the closing decades of the century women's colleges proliferated; in Britain Girton College, Cambridge, admitted women in 1869, and by the 1890s the 'Girton Girl' abounded in fiction, most notably in Grant Allen's *The Woman Who Did*, and in 1878 London University admitted women on the same grounds as men. The *Quarterly Review* lamented in 1894: 'women are now graduates in half a dozen professions, and disciples in all. They practise medicine as well as novel-writing; the forceps is familiar to them no less than the bicycle; even dress-cutting advertises itself as "scientific" at six guineas the course.'[24]

The Woman Question reached a head in the 1890s, with mounting campaigns for women's rights to education, property and the vote. The *Westminster Review* complained: 'it is not possible to ride by road or rail, to read a review, a magazine or a newspaper, without being continually reminded of the subject which lady-writers love to call the "Woman Question" . . . "The Eternal Feminine", the "Revolt of the Daughters", the "Woman's Volunteer Movement", Women's Clubs, are significant expressions and effective landmarks'.[25] Talk about ' "the ascent of man"!' breezed Herbert Jamieson in his upbeat study of the 'Modern Woman': 'the ascent of woman entirely overshadows it in importance'.[26]

Support for the emancipation of women did not fall neatly into gendered camps but persisted among freethinking radicals of both sexes. Some women would actively oppose female suffrage, and decry the break-up of time-hallowed social and sexual patterns, with the *Nineteenth Century* publishing, in June 1889, an all-female 'Appeal Against Female Suffrage'. The popular novelist and philanthropist Mrs Humphry Ward drafted the appeal, arguing that 'disabilities of sex' and habitual practices 'resting ultimately upon physical difference' were inflexible barriers to political equality for women. The petition declared that: 'the undersigned protest strongly against the proposed Extension of the Parliamentary Franchise to Women which they believe would be a measure distasteful to the great majority of the women of the country – unnecessary – and mischievous both to themselves and to the State'.[27] Supporters included public figures such as Lady Stanley of Alderley (wife of the Liberal MP Edward John Stanley), and, as they signed themselves, Mrs Leslie Stephen (Virginia Woolf's mother) and Mrs Matthew Arnold. The following month the journal published responses to the petition from the suffragettes Millicent Garrett Fawcett and Margaret Mary Dilke, with Fawcett arguing that the claim of women to representation was predicated on the different service they could provide the state, and Dilke pointing out that the dependence of women upon men for their rights and privileges had always had an 'extremely demoralizing effect' on men, who must, she argued, be aware that they were influenced more by 'personal charms' than abstract appeals to justice. Louise Creighton, anti-suffrage activist and historical writer, came back with a rejoinder, concluding that sex was a fact which no Act of Parliament could eliminate.[28] The August issue supplied in an appendix the names of more than two thousand women who had signed the appeal against suffrage (it ran to twenty-eight double-columned pages).

Other women were involved in the sexual oppression of their own sex, as Gertrude Colmore's insightful and politically topical 'The Woman in the Corner' demonstrates,[29] and those New Women who advocated eugenics were actively biased against the working classes of both sexes.

While suffrage was opposed by large numbers of women as well as men, the struggle for female emancipation and enfranchisement had had significant male support from early in the century. For example, during the 1820s and 1830s Owenite socialists, inspired by Mary Wollstonecraft and Robert Owen, argued that the abolition of private property would end the status of women as property. Mona Caird would publicly champion these views in the closing years of the century. The philosopher and left-liberal sex egalitarian John Stuart Mill introduced female suffrage to the Representation of the People Bill that would become the Second Reform Bill, in 1867, suggesting that the clause containing the term 'man' be amended to read 'person'. *Punch* was horrified.[30] The amendment was defeated by 196 votes to 73.

Nonetheless, the Second Reform Bill ushered in a new age. It brought in a (male) borough electorate of 44% in England and Wales; before 1832 it had been about 14%. By 1892 this had risen to 60% of adult males and under the 1884 household franchise counties in England and Wales had 73% of adult males registered.[31] In the United States in 1870 the Fifteenth Amendment to the Constitution prohibited federal or state governments from infringing a citizen's rights to vote 'on account of race, colour or previous condition of servitude', although this had little practical impact, especially in the South, until well into the twentieth century. With these changes the case for the female franchise seemed stronger than ever.

In 1869, Mill published *The Subjection of Women*, arguing that 'what is now called the nature of women is an eminently artificial thing – the result of forced repression in some directions, unnatural stimulation in others'.[32] In a letter to Millicent Fawcett in 1906, Hardy questioned whether the stereotyped household should be 'the unit of society'.[33] In 1907, Henry Nevinson (Evelyn Sharp's friend and, from 1933, husband), Laurence Housman and Henry Brailsford set up the Men's League for Women's Suffrage, and in the same year at a by-election in Wimbledon Bertrand Russell stood unsuccessfully as the suffragist candidate. There was also male support for female suffrage in the United States, with, for example, the American Federation of Labor (AFL) announcing their support for women's suffrage at their annual convention in 1890.

By including stories by men, *Women Who Did* testifies to male interest in the Woman Question, and suggests that points of view on the various issues of roles, rules and freedom could not be predicted or explained absolutely along lines of sex.

Freedom and Biology

The education of women was not without opposition. Shortly after *The Origin of Species* appeared, George Eliot's close friend and confidant Herbert Spencer, the evolutionary sociologist and philosopher who coined the term 'survival of the fittest' (frequently attributed to Charles Darwin), warned in *Education: Intellectual, Moral, and Physical* (1861) that the 'pale angular, flat-chested young ladies so abundant in London drawing rooms' were the product of excessive education, and were likely to be unable to reproduce.[34] Physical degeneracy was not the only danger: Spencer emphasized that 'by subjecting their daughters to this high-pressure system, parents frequently ruin their prospects in life. Besides inflicting on them enfeebled health, with all its pains and disabilities and gloom, they not infrequently doom them to celibacy.' Reprinted several times, with a cheap edition appearing in

1880 (with a print run of 4,000), *Education: Intellectual, Moral, and Physical* remained in print well into the twentieth century. The new scientific discourses, themselves heavily informed by prevailing social attitudes, lent new authority to traditional prejudice. In *The Descent of Man*, Darwin remarked that 'with woman the powers of intuition, of rapid perception, and perhaps of imitation, are more strongly marked than in man', powers which he considered inferior, while man, by contrast, was 'more courageous, pugnacious, and energetic' with 'a more energetic genius'.[35] In 'A Woman in Grey' Alice Meynell refuted the popular socio-scientific notion that mental and physical powers were determined by sex. The debates over the effects of education on the mental and physical well-being of women really got off the ground in 1874 with the publication of *Sex in Education* by the Harvard physician Edward H. Clarke, in which he gave an emphatic warning that girls were reaching breaking point on account of intellectual work. Clarke soon had a flock of followers in the periodical press, with the most vociferous being the psychologist Henry Maudsley, and the anti-feminist journalist Eliza Lynn Linton.[36] The United States was frequently referred to as exemplifying the ill effects of educating girls along the same lines as boys, and American medical men, notably Weir Mitchell, whose 'rest cure' forms the subject of Charlotte Perkins Gilman's 'The Yellow Wallpaper', were repeatedly cited as authorities.

The British physician Benjamin Ward Richardson remarked in 1886 that he had been taught that girls and women could not learn to play cricket because they could never throw a cricket ball with force or precision;[37] the exclusion of girls from cricket is an idea which Sharp gives a neat twist to in 'The Game that wasn't Cricket'. But campaigners for female education held their ground. Elizabeth Garrett Anderson, who qualified as a doctor in Paris in 1870, argued with characteristic wit that the 'evil physical results' of dullness were the ones to watch out for.[38] The debates intensified as the idea of the degeneration of the race provided a new language and framework for arguing that it was in the interests of the nation that women did not overtax themselves. In 1890 Grant Allen warned in the *Universal Review* that if she did not turn her hand to motherhood, the 'girl of the future' would soon be 'as flat as a pancake'.[39]

The Woman Question debates were underpinned by the same issues that lay at the heart of debates over heredity and evolution – how *fundamental* was biology to society and social change? If biology was all-determining, what implications did this have for the nature of freedom? Frederic Harrison declared: 'Women must choose to be either women or abortive men. They cannot be both women and men. When men and women are once started as competitors in the same fierce race, as rivals and opponents ... Woman will have disappeared.'[40] The arguments against the education of women gained considerable weight amid growing concerns that the white races were degenerating, an idea which fed British anxieties over the future of the imperial race. The term *fin de siècle* was itself born of a biologization of time; the idea of the human body, its energies sapped, its health failing, was everywhere. 'Are We Degenerating Physically?' asked the *Lancet* in 1888.[41] While the threat to health here is seen to be the squalid living conditions of the urban poor, the causes of ill health were increasingly being held as biological. Between 1893 and 1902, over two thousand men – more than one-third of the total – who were examined for military enlistment were turned away as unfit.[42]

Many middle-class British women advanced the idea that women were agents of regeneration. In doing so they began to draw on the ideas of fundamental sexual difference which had been in the ascendant over the course of the century,[43] and which found expression in Darwin and later, for example, in Patrick Geddes and J. Arthur Thomson in *The Evolution of Sex* (1889) and Havelock Ellis in *Man And Woman* (1894). Biological determinism would prove a powerful counter narrative to the emerging freedoms of the *fin de siècle*.

Sarah Grand was a strong supporter of eugenics – selective human breeding. In 1896 she declared: 'I hope we shall soon see the marriage of certain men made a criminal offence';[44] she also remarked: 'it is in the action of woman in this particular matter, i.e. in regard to the improvement of the race, – that the one hope lies of saving our present civilization from the extinction which has overtaken the civilization of all previous peoples; and all I write is for the purpose of spreading this opinion and opening up these subjects to discussion'.[45] In her sensational best-seller of 1897, *The Beth Book*, Beth declares medical help for the 'unfit' an unwelcome endeavour to hinder Nature's good work, arguing that society should 'take pains to prevent the appearance' of the unfit; 'by the reproduction of the unfit, the strength, the beauty, the morality of the race is undermined, and with them its best chances of happiness'.[46] By the closing decades of the nineteenth century, 'unfitness' – or degeneracy – came to signify a conflation of moral and physical weakness, and moral and physical traits were increasingly perceived as hereditary. It was as vague and embracing a term as 'the feeble-minded', another concept which became increasingly central to the politics and vocabulary of eugenics, culminating in the Mental Deficiency Act of 1913, which was known more generally as the Feeble-Minded Act.

The pioneering sexologist Edward Carpenter saw the narrowing of sexual difference in a more positive light. He opened his chapter on the 'intermediate sex', in *Love's Coming-of-Age* (1896):

> . . . in late years (and since the arrival of the New Woman amongst us) many things in the relation of men and women to each other have altered, or at any rate become clearer. The growing sense of equality in habits and customs – university studies, art, music, politics, the bicycle, etc. – all these things have brought about a *rapprochement* between the sexes. If the modern woman is a little more masculine in some ways than her predecessor, the modern man (it is to be hoped), while by no means effeminate, is a little more sensitive in temperament and artistic in feeling than the original John Bull.[47]

Carpenter, however, was unusual. The possibility of masculine women and feminine men contributed to the feeling of uncertainty and unrest experienced by men and women at the *fin de siècle*. In 'The Regeneration of Two', George Egerton referred to the new type of woman as a 'desexualized half-man' and the new man as a 'man-woman'.[48] She remarked: 'I am not greatly concerned in the social, so-called educational, or political advancement of women. They are *exotics* – what interests me is her development from within out as a female.'[49] Sarah Grand was horrified by the idea of effeminate men, as she reveals, for example, through her characterization of Alfred Pounce in *The Beth Book*, and she repeatedly emphasized the importance of motherhood and femininity. She argued that 'womanhood is a constitutional condition which cannot be altered',[50] remarking in 1900 that all she had meant by the term 'New Woman' was 'one who, while retaining all the grace of manner and feminine charm, had thrown off all the silliness and hysterical feebleness of her sex'; she concluded: 'woman was never meant to be developed man'.[51]

In 'Plain Words on the Woman Question', in *Popular Science Monthly*, Grant Allen urged: 'we are of two sexes: and in healthy diversity of sex, pushed to its utmost, lies the greatest strength of all of us. Make your men virile: make your women womanly.'[52] Allen had released Herminia Barton, The Woman Who Did, into the 1890s; as he saw it, a true woman would fulfil her maternal function outside marriage; feminists such as Sarah Grand and Margaret Oliphant were outraged,[53] and others came up with antidotes such as *The Woman Who Didn't* (1895), by Victoria Cross and *The Woman Who Wouldn't* (1895) by Lucas Cleeve. Allen warned that the emancipation of woman might leave her 'a dulled and spiritless epicene automaton', observing that healthy girls who embarked upon higher education ('mannish training') became unattractive and unsexed; 'both in England and America, the women of the cultivated classes are becoming unfit to be wives or mothers. Their sexuality (which lies at the basis of everything) is enfeebled or destroyed.'[54] By contrast, radical thinkers from Mary Wollstonecraft to John Stuart Mill, Eleanor Marx and Mona Caird saw separate-sphere ideology as the root cause of gender oppression, exposing nature, which was used to justify separate spheres and which conservative thinkers looked to for guidance on social and sexual codes, as a socially *constructed* cluster of ideas. They argued *against* the idea of fixed and fundamental sexual difference which historically had led to the belief that women were driven by intuition and instinct, while men were governed by reason, a superior form of knowledge which legitimized their rule, and which led invariably to social inequality. Hardy was numbered among those who opposed fundamental sexual difference. In *Desperate Remedies* (1871), his tale of lesbian and heterosexual love, he remarked: 'in spite of a fashion which pervades the whole community at the present day – the habit of exclaiming that woman is not undeveloped man, but diverse, the fact remains that, after all, women are Mankind, and that in many of the sentiments of life the difference of sex is but a difference of degree'.[55]

The Short Story and the Speeding up of Life

'Short Stories broke out everywhere', observed H. G. Wells in 1911, looking back at the 1890s.[56] And so they did. From Arthur Conan Doyle's Sherlock Holmes to George Egerton's enigmatic sirens and Evelyn Sharp's suffragette rebels, they lined the pages of a burgeoning number of monthlies, weeklies and sixpenny popular magazines,[57] and were met with an enthusiasm that had previously been reserved for the Victorian three-decker novel. While 1884 had seen the publication of one hundred and ninety-three triple-deckers in Britain, 1897 saw only four. Likewise, the serialized novel had had its day: in a speeded-up world, short stories offered immediate gratification; they did not necessarily bring closure, but neither did they leave their readers with the cliffhanger that had sold serialized novels. The new magazine culture – which encompassed a proliferation of women's magazines – and rapidly expanding reading audiences on both sides of the Atlantic provided the perfect conditions for the rise of the short story. In her address to the Women Writers' Dinner in 1894, Mrs H. R. Haweis, author, medievalist and designer of furniture, captured the new importance, the centrality of the periodical press, to everyday life: 'the press is taking the place of the pulpit, the rostrum, the judgment seat . . . Journalism, the shortest form of book, is therefore on the up-grade; its importance is growing for political, educative, and decorative purposes, and because women are the most interesting creatures alive, women are getting into journalistic posts all the time, and they serve those posts well.'[58] In Britain the last two decades of the nineteenth century saw the appearance of 48 new journals, and by 1910 there were 155 quarterlies in London and 797 monthlies.[59] In 1891 the first issue of the art journal *Black and White* set the new tone: 'there will be no serial stories: but a complete short story by an eminent writer, English or foreign, will appear in each number'. George Newnes's *Strand* for its first five years published no serials, only complete short stories. The first issue of the sixpenny *Lady's Realm* (1896) enticed readers with 'a long complete story by Marie Corelli' – an extremely popular writer into the early twentieth century. Conan

Doyle's Sherlock Holmes short stories began to appear from July 1891: they were an immediate and extraordinary success, and ushered in the detective story. In 1895 the social critic Blanche Crackanthorpe lamented in 'Sex in Modern Literature', in the *Nineteenth Century*: 'the three-volume novel is shortly to be condemned to the limbo where lie forgotten the crinoline, the bonnet, "curtain", and the four corner dishes of the early Victorian dinner table'.[60] By others, its demise was seen as an unequivocal good, a victory against the proprietors of circulating libraries who enjoyed a stranglehold over mid-Victorian writers and whose motives, in the words of *Fraser's Magazine*, were 'entirely mercenary': three-volumes could be charged by the volume and were thus essential to the livelihood of such librarians. *Fraser's Magazine* rejoiced in the thought that 'the dynasty of the circulating library novel will be assuredly overturned, at no very distant period, by the levellers of the railroad'; it hailed a 'revolution' through 'the indefatigable newsvendors' stands' and rejoiced in the advent of 'the Flying Stationer' whose 'heels are winged with steam'.[61]

In the United States it was the same story. The new international copyright agreement of 1891, which protected overseas works from piracy, combined with a rapidly growing magazine industry and, as Andrew Levy has shown in *The Cultural Commerce of the American Short Story*, led to a sharp rise of national interest in the short story.[62] Critical fascination with the local and national fruits of this rising genre proliferated. As the American writer and editor Henry Seidel Canby noted, 'new developments in literature do not arise or become popular without reason. There are causes, artistic and otherwise, for the present blossoming of the Short Story.'[63] What were these causes? Short stories were easier to handle for editors and writers, and more lucrative for writers. Most importantly, they captured, with their fragmented nature, their open-endedness, the spirit of the age. The short story arose at a time when social and moral outlines were blurring – it grew in new places, and flourished in the cracks of conventional morality. Previously, according to Wells, 'there was no such penetrating and pervading element of doubt and curiosity – and charity, about the rightfulness and beauty of conduct, such as one meets on every hand today'.[64] The short story, concerned with questions, rather than answers, was perfectly suited to give expression to the turbulence and uncertainties of the late nineteenth century. Bliss Perry, editor of the *Atlantic Monthly*, who had a keen interest in creating a vision of America which expanded its focus from the East Coast to include the West and Mexican and American Indian culture, observed that novels invariably had ' "a certain philosophy", "a chart or plan of human life". Consciously or unconsciously held or formulated, it is nevertheless there.' He proceeded: 'the reaction against the three-volume novel, and particularly against George Eliot, has been caused by the universal passion for the short story'.[65]

As the century came to an end, the pace of life accelerated; the railway bookstall and the short story triumphed together. Short stories could be read on short journeys. The *Ladies Gazette* kept itself small to be taken on trains – according to one correspondent in 1895 it was the 'ideal size for reading in the train as so many of us like to do'.[66] Railways also assisted the rise of the magazine culture in providing an efficient distribution network, and reaching a reading public in the provinces. And literature partook of the new, hurried existence which the railways had helped to create. Haweis sought to account for the rise of the short story:

it seems to me, since the tendency of modern literary form is in the direction of condensation, brevity . . . long books are giving way to short books, short books getting shorter, and smaller in every way but value, like the dear little old-fashioned standard works – the prospects of journalism, the daily and monthly press, are very bright. Because readers depend more on the journals, therefore journals are forming public taste and pushing public progress . . . it is a question of *time* – people are doing more, and therefore always discovering more to do, even in that haven of sleep and privacy the *House*. Therefore they must get over ground faster; they have not so much time for reading *long books*, but they digest the stronger stuff, they buy short books, and *précis* of short books, and they buy magazines because they contain short books.[67]

Canby echoed these thoughts. The short story was 'a precipitate of the important things from the general solution . . . In a time of much writing, tastes are quickly jaded, and the Short Story, because it is terse, striking, highly-colored, and somewhat new, meets with quick applause. Its brevity is of advantage, for many people can be made to swallow good literature in a pill who reject it in larger doses.'[68] The short story offered a writer the opportunity to be thought-provoking without wearying their audience. For some it was symptomatic of the nervous condition that characterized the *fin de siècle*:

it is a kind of writing perfectly adapted to our over-driven generation, which rushes from one task of engagement to another, and between times, or on the way, snatches up a story. Our habit of nervous concentration for a brief period helps us indeed to crowd a great deal of pleasure into the half-hour of perusal; our incapacity for prolonged attention forces the author to keep within that limit, or exceed it at his peril.[69]

Economic considerations played a significant part in the rise of the short story. It provided a way for women to enter the labour market which made greater practical, and economic, sense for many than novel writing. The huge expansion of advertising in the late Victorian period also enabled editors to pay their authors a reasonable sum; journals which came into being in the 1890s, such as the *Young Woman* and the *Young Gentlewoman*, were packed with advertisements from their birth. Explaining 'the present popularity of the short story with authors and public alike', the *Atlantic Monthly* declared: 'here is a form of literature easy to write and easy to read. The author is often paid as much for a story as he earns from the copyrights of a novel, and it costs him one tenth the labor. The multitude of magazines and other periodicals creates a constant market, with steadily rising prices . . . The public pays its money and takes its choice.'[70]

Women and the Short Story

It was easier to raise new subjects in a new form. Whatever their precise social and political agenda, women needed a new fiction if they were to break free from social no less than literary tradition. The social critic Edith Slater pointed out in 'Men's Women in Fiction' that the 'stock virtues and vices' of women had 'been carefully catalogued by the wisdom of ages in a thousand epigrams, plays, novels, and poems' written by men.[71] Women writers on both sides of the Atlantic began to experiment with short stories, breaking out of tired literary codes, outgrowing happily-ever-after romances and questioning existing relationship patterns and sexualities. The effect was striking, as this collection demonstrates. Various stories are concerned with forms of art; writing about writing is the subject of 'In Search of a Subject'; women write as men in 'A Nocturne' and 'The Undefinable'. Women detectives emerge, for example in 'The Stir Outside the Café Royal: A Story of Miss Van Snoop, Detective'; suffrage forms the focus of 'Filling the War Chest', which, along with 'Jimmy's Afternoon' and 'A Daughter of the Lodge', also explores class tensions. 'Miss McEnders' takes on middle-class hypocrisy; 'Virgin Soil', the sexual double standard. 'Tommy, the Unsentimental' and 'Leves Amores' explore same-sex relationships, free love is the subject of 'The Storm' and 'The Reckoning', while 'Ellen', 'The Yellow Drawing Room' and 'The Buddhist Priest's Wife' explore the desire to – and not to – have a child. The collection also explores illegitimacy ('A Cross Line', 'Jimmy's Afternoon'); the autonomy of the single life ('The Buddhist Priest's Wife', 'The Wedding Feast'); older women and female community ('Turned'); sexual fantasy, desire and cross-dressing ('George Lloyd' and 'If I were a Man'). The taboo subject of prostitution brings closure to 'The Woman in the Corner'; 'Désirée's Baby' and 'Talma Gordon' take race and racial prejudice as their subject, while marriage finds various treatments in 'When the Door Opened—', 'A New Sensation', 'A Warrior's Daughter', 'The Wedding Feast' and 'Phyllis and Rosamond'. The ideological complexities of feminism emerge in 'The Advanced Lady' – *who* is the advanced woman in this story? – while Saki adds a light touch to female rebellion in 'The Schartz-Metterklume Method', and Chopin celebrates the joys of shopping in 'A Pair of Silk Stockings'.

In *Modern Women* (1895), the pioneering German feminist Laura Marholm remarked: 'this is not only a new phase in the work of literary production, it is also a new phase in woman's nature'. Formerly, women had attempted 'to accommodate themselves to men's wishes. They were always trying to follow in the footsteps of the man. Man's ideas, interests, speculations, were to be understood and sympathized with.' Noting that Egerton's startling collection of short stories, *Keynotes*, sold three thousand copies in the course of a few months, Marholm praised her for making no attempt to imitate men.[72] In her landmark *Women and Economics* (1898), Charlotte Perkins Gilman observed:

in the fiction of today women are continually taking larger place in the action of the story. They are given personal characteristics beyond those of physical beauty. And they are no longer content simply to *be*: they *do*. They are showing qualities of bravery, endurance, strength, foresight, and power for the swift execution of well-conceived plans. They have ideas and purposes of their own; and even when, as in so many cases described by the more reactionary novelists, the efforts of the heroine are shown to be entirely futile, and she comes back with a rush to the self-effacement of marriage with economic dependence, still the efforts were there.[73]

There were practical reasons why women and the short story went together so well. In *A Room of One's Own* Virginia Woolf wrote: 'The book has somehow to be adapted to the body, and at a venture one would say that women's books should be shorter, more concentrated, than those of men, and framed so that they do not need long hours of steady and uninterrupted work. For interruptions there will always be.'[74] In 'A Keynote to Keynotes' Egerton stated: 'I still believe that Marriage, Motherhood and Writing are each whole time jobs', pointing out, 'I was a short story, at most a long short story writer. For years they came in droves and said themselves, leaving no scope for padding or altered endings; the long book was not my pigeon.'[75] Short stories, by virtue of their brevity, combined more easily with marriage and motherhood. In 'Women as Writers' Haweis observed: 'it is because women reveal themselves most in their books and articles, that women's books and articles are the most interesting reading of the present day'. But the new fiction wasn't only entertaining, it had the potential to change the world, she continued: 'in women's hands – in women writers' hands – lies the regeneration of the world . . .'[76]

From the New Woman to the Suffragette, the marriage of fiction and feminism was flourishing. In 1912 Elizabeth Robbins addressed the Women Writers' Suffrage League (founded in 1908):

Fellow members of the League, you are in such a field as never writers had known before. You are – in respect of life described fearlessly from woman's standpoint – you are in that position for which Chaucer has been so envied by his brother poets, when they say he found the English language with the dew upon it. You find woman at the Dawn . . . The Great Adventure is before her. Your great adventure is to report her worthily.[77]

It was the job of the feminist writer not only to report, but also to participate in the Great Adventure; not only to describe what she saw but to aim at what she desired; and, where she could, to bring about change.

In 1923, Beatrice Harraden gave a speech to the Votes for Woman Fellowship about her recent trip to the United States, and about American support for suffrage. She emphasized that what her American audiences and interviewers wanted to hear was 'not a statement of principles or reasons but just a story of life that would illustrate the truth and stick in their minds'.[78] Such stories had become vital to the suffragette cause, and *Votes for Women*, launched in 1907 by the Women's Social and Political Union, was quick to realize its powers. In April 1908, it went weekly, and its circulation of 5,000 trebled over the next six months; during this time the short story became a fixed feature, a political act.

The Marriage Question

The closing decades of the century witnessed significant changes in legislation relating to women. The passage of the Married Women's Property Acts of 1870 and 1882 eventually gave all married women the right to their own property.[79] The age of consent had been raised, in 1875, to thirteen; following W. T. Stead's campaign against juvenile prostitution, or 'white slavery', in the *Pall Mall Gazette*, the Criminal Law Amendment Act of 1885 raised it to sixteen. Following the 1884 Matrimonial Causes Act, women who left their husbands could no longer be imprisoned, and power was given to the court to make orders regarding the custody of the couple's children. In 1886 mothers gained the right to custody of their children upon the death of the father, and in 1891 the *R. v Jackson* case established that a husband did not have the right to detain and imprison his wife. It was hailed as a charter of personal liberty in the national press,[80] though for conservatives such as Eliza Lynn Linton, it marked the beginnings of 'universal topsyturvydom'.[81] However, these reforms only marked a beginning; the coercive element remained, and a husband could still force sexual intercourse upon his wife without being guilty of rape (this continued until 1991). Likewise, grounds for divorce were still different: adultery gave men sufficient grounds, but women had to prove cruelty as well. But social and legislative changes put marriage in the spotlight of public debate.

Debate peaked with Mona Caird's article, 'Marriage', in the *Westminster Review* (1888). She declared marriage in its present form 'a vexatious failure', remarking that 'in most cases the chain of marriage frets and chafes, if it does not make a serious wound' and 'the tyrannical spirit has little or no check under present conditions of married life ... except when the grievance is of such a nature as to come within the reach of the law'.[82] Caird argued that the habitual forms of oppression that characterized the present marriage relation would be difficult to bring into the courtroom, and noted that the reforms that were most needed were ones not merely of the penal system but of social convention. Sarah Grand placed more faith in state intervention, arguing for the divorce law to be applied equally to husband and wife.[83]

Caird's article inspired the most famous newspaper debate of the century, when in response Edwin Arnold, editor of the *Daily Telegraph*, posed the question 'Is Marriage a Failure?' At this time the paper boasted average daily sales of 'in excess of 500,000', and could claim the 'largest circulation in the world';[84] during August and September 1888 it received 27,000 responses to the question. In the words of the editor, 'wives and mothers, maids and bachelors, spinsters and husbands, clerks and curates, priests and publicans, saints and sinners, gathered themselves into one compact mass of respondents, and hurled their woes, their joys, their experiences, their doctrines, and themselves at the head of the *Daily Telegraph*'.[85] In *The Diary of a Nobody* Mr and Mrs Pooter, who made their first appearance in *Punch* this year, remarked: 'we had a most pleasant chat about the letters on "Is Marriage a Failure?" It has been no failure in our case.'[86]

As Grand put it, 'the Woman Question is now the Marriage Question'.[87] In the words of Elizabeth Chapman, the conservative British author of *Marriage Questions in Fiction*: 'that the ferment of the century on the subject of marriage should penetrate, nay, should saturate fiction, was a matter of course ... the once sacred, the once theoretically indissoluble life-tie between husband and wife has become, in short, an open question'.[88]

The sexual double standard was another area of fierce debate. Social-purity campaigners had emerged victorious in 1886 with the repeal of the Contagious Diseases Acts which had been introduced during the 1860s. These acts, by demanding the registration and compulsory examination in garrison towns and ports of suspected female prostitutes, had given state backing to the double standard; Eleanor Marx, daughter of Karl, and her co-author and partner Edward Aveling had referred to them in *The Woman Question* as 'a monstrosity begotten of male cowardice and brutality'.[89] But there was still the pressing question of sex education. Florence in Egerton's 'Virgin Soil' berates her mother: 'I was fourteen when I gave up the gooseberry-bush theory as the origin of humanity.' Around the same time, Hardy's Tess questioned her mother: 'I was a child when I left this house four months ago. Why didn't you tell me there was danger? Why didn't you warn me? Ladies knew what to guard against, because they read novels that tell them of these tricks; but I never had the chance of discovering in that way, and you did not help me!'[90]

Victorian novels tended to end with happy marriages: George Eliot's *Adam Bede* (1859) is rung out by wedding bells, Charles Dickens's *Great Expectations* (1860–61) and Eliot's *Middlemarch* (1871–2) leave us with weddings and progeny. In 1856 a critic in *Fraser's Magazine* had pointed out that 'the interest of the novel terminates with marriage, where the real interest of the biography usually begins'.[91] Novels were beginning to break these constraints. Sarah Grand's social-purity novel *The Heavenly Twins* explores disastrous marriages to syphilitic men. On a lighter note, Evelyn Sharp's *At the Relton Arms* (1895) explores the love triangle of Lady Joan, the advanced, clever New Woman; Norah, the most ordinary woman; and Digby Raleigh, the indecisive musician; Sharp shows that rules and relationships don't really go together, resisting dogma and finding sanity in humour. But the short story was streets ahead of the novel in releasing writers from the codes of convention. It was concerned with biographical snapshots, moments of real life. As the American writer Brander Matthews observed, the short story was unusual because 'no love interest is needed to hold its parts together'.[92] Short stories could be plotless, and love and marriage could be omitted, or explored in new ways. Woolf's 'Phyllis and Rosamond' resign themselves to marriage: 'we are brought up just to come out in the evening and make pretty speeches, and well, marry I suppose . . . We are daughters, until we become married women', while Wharton's 'The Reckoning' suggests that alternatives can be or can become more oppressive, especially if they are underpinned by an inflexible ideology. Wharton's story demonstrates the complexity of human relations, and resists positing solutions.

Released from the strictures of the novel, of life histories, Grand adopted a more light-hearted approach in her stories. For example, in 'The Tenor and the Boy: An Interlude' (which was incorporated into *The Heavenly Twins*),[93] she toys with cross-dressing and an affair which is extramarital for one party, and homo-erotic for the other, and in 'The Undefinable' she again chafes at the boundaries of convention. By contrast, her novels, ranging over generation and community, are concerned with life as linear – and biological – narrative rather than as a series of moments, and offer, for example, worked-through expositions of race regeneration.

Separate Spheres and the Threat of the Bicycle

One of the fears of the *fin de siècle* was the idea that Victorian gendered ideology was in crisis; that 'separate spheres' were ceasing to be separate, as women entered the work force in increasing numbers; and that the Angel in the House, as Coventry Patmore had termed the ideal dutiful woman in his narrative poem of this name,[94] would escape. According to one short story by Charlotte Perkins Gilman, 'An Extinct Angel', she was already extinct – 'Poor dodo!'[95] In 'Professions of Women' (1931), Virginia Woolf would write: 'Killing the Angel in the House was part of the occupation of a woman writer . . . it was an experience that was bound to befall all women writers at that time.'[96] Separate-sphere ideology found its most emphatic exposition in John Ruskin's pronouncements on masculinity and femininity: 'Of King's Treasuries' and 'Of Queen's Gardens', in *Sesame and Lilies* (1865). In 'The Yellow Drawing Room' Mona Caird's defiant Vanora Haydon stands in direct opposition to mid-Victorian ideas of sexual difference. When the narrator warns her that 'The sacred realms where woman is queen will soon be forbidden to you if you consistently continue to think and act in disharmony with the feminine nature and genius', she responds, 'I rather prefer the realms where woman is *not* queen', adding 'My father never sought to arrange a "sphere" for me, and in my case instinct seems at fault'. This story, which, like many others, has received no critical attention for over a century, appeared in the same year as 'The Yellow Wallpaper' and both, with *The Yellow Book*, align 'yellow' with decadence and female emancipation.

Several men and women saw the collapse of separate spheres as leading to a collapse, or even reversal, of sex roles. In *The Psychology of Woman* Laura Marholm warned 'the great human and educational problem of all girls' schools is the rearing of women to sexlessness'.[97] Hall records in *A Study in Bloomers*: 'some of these public howlers will object to the bicycle for women unless it can be rigged with a side-saddle and its power for health and recreation practically destroyed. We have here a remnant of the old superstition about "woman's sphere" which ought to have no influence in this day of intelligent and broad-minded consideration of all social and moral questions.'[98]

Following the introduction in the late 1880s of the Rover safety bicycle by John Kemp Starley, and of the pneumatic tyre by John Boyd Dunlop, the bicycle took off among middle-class women, giving them unprecedented freedom of movement and equality. It was wheeled swiftly into fiction, featuring here in 'A Woman in Grey' and 'A Daughter of the Lodge'. In 1895 the trade unionist and social reformer Clementina Black stated:

I believe the bicycle is doing more for the independence of women than anything expressly designed to that end. It is perhaps a mark of the change of view which has come over us, that nobody expects a woman to go cycling escorted by a chaperon, a maid or a footman. It is an amusement – perhaps the first amusement – which woman has taken up to please herself, and not to please man, and it is one which can only be followed in a moderately comfortable and healthy kind of dress.[99]

The same year, the *Lady Cyclist* declared that the bicycle was responsible for 'a new dawn, a dawn of emancipation' and, looking backwards from her seventies, the headmistress Sarah Burstall, born in 1859, remarked: 'it is difficult for the modern woman . . . to realise what the bicycle meant to us who were in the prime of life in the 'nineties'.[100]

The bicycle also accelerated important changes in fashion. These had been introduced from the early 1880s, with the Rational Dress Movement calling for healthy clothing which would allow new freedom of movement. Tight corsets and layers of starched petticoats were ousted by new forms of underwear. The 1870s had seen the demise of the crinoline, and by the 1890s the bustle too was a thing of the past. Trousers for women, or 'Bloomers', first introduced by the American dress reformer Amelia Bloomer in the mid nineteenth century, had threatened to undermine the fabric of civilization; now they returned in the form of a knickerbockers outfit, a prerequisite for comfortable cycling. It was dramatically sported by sixteen-year-old Tissie Reynolds, who raced to London and back from Brighton in 1893.[101]

In *A Study in Bloomers* Hall charts the impact of the bloomer on womanhood. His Rev. Dr Charlton falls helplessly in love with Miss Thorne, the Model New Woman, who is attired in an 'offensive costume' which leaves exposed 'a plump calf and delicately moulded ankle, for the boots were low cut, and there were no leggings . . . I felt almost like apologizing for being in the presence of a woman who seemed only half dressed.' The Model New Woman's view is quite different; she looks to the time 'when men and women forget sex differences in the common comradeship which is possible between intellectual and social equals', concluding 'already the light is breaking. It will not be long till skirts are relegated to the garret.'[102]

Sarah Grand confessed to the *Hub* in 1896 that while she felt free to wear bloomers in Paris, 'here [in London] I conform to the usual custom, and don a skirt'; when asked if she cycled much in London she remarked: 'No; it makes my menfolk so nervous. I went about at first, but they endured such agonies on my behalf that I was forced to drop it in town.'[103] The bicyclist provided Hugh Stutfield with a useful analogy in his angry outburst, 'Tommyrotics' (a term which appeared first in the sedate *Spectator*), in 1895: the modern woman writer was 'a literary bicyclist'; 'sometimes her machine takes her along some sadly muddy roads, where her petticoats – or her knickerbockers – are apt to get soiled'.[104] A mass market for bicycles developed, and early in the new century *Votes for Women* began to offer them as prizes to those who could sell the most magazines; in 1907 *Tit-bits*, concerned for the failing health of Imperial Britain, began to offer free bicycles as prizes in its weekly competition on the number of weekly births.

Home Economics

As the Angel left the house, the Woman Question gained a new economic edge. Edith Ellis, partnered to the sexologist Havelock Ellis, opened her tract *A Noviciate for Marriage* (1894) with the words 'the problems of labour and of sex rule the century'.[105] While the industrial novels of mid century had engaged with class issues, the solutions they proposed were often ones of Christian benevolence and paternalism, and of sentimental reconciliation enacted through romantic cross-class liaison, as can be seen in Elizabeth Gaskell's *Mary Barton* (1848) and *North and South* (1855), and Benjamin Disraeli's *Sybil, or The Two Nations* (1845).

In *The Woman Question*, Eleanor Marx argued: 'the position of women rests, as everything in our complex modern society rests, on an economic basis . . . The Woman Question is one of the organization of society as a whole.' They lamented: 'the ideas of our "advanced" women are based either on property, or on sentimental or professional questions. Not one of them gets down through these to the bed-rock of the economic basis, not only of each of these three, but of society itself.'[106] But many were getting to this bed-rock. Letters to the *Daily Telegraph* debate on marriage, which came from Britain, the United States, Japan and various parts of Europe, gave economic inequality as a deciding factor in the failure of marriage. In *Women and Economics* Gilman wrote 'no sociological change equal in importance to this clearly marked improvement of an entire sex has ever taken place in one century. Under it all, the *crux* of the whole matter, goes on the one great change, that of the economic relation.'[107] She drew on the American socialist tradition which differs from Marx and Engels in its rejection of class antagonism in favour of co-operation.[108] Many of the women in Gilman's stories support themselves, often working in small-scale communities, and property-owning individuals with wealth and prestige are figured as sources of harmony rather than antagonism.

Several plays, short stories and essays were directly engaged with issues of women and economics. Henrik Ibsen had made money the stuff of *The Doll's House* (performed in 1879), and the relation between marriage – apparently the seal of respectability – and prostitution was forced into public notice, most candidly by Eleanor Marx and Edward Aveling in 'The Woman Question: from a Socialist Point of View' in the *Westminster Review* (1886), and by Cecily Hamilton in *Marriage as a Trade* (1907). The latter argued that only men could afford to be romantic – for women marriage was a means of earning a living. Olive Schreiner devoted the first three chapters of *Woman and Labour* to a malaise she termed 'parasitism': the condition of the unlabouring woman.

In the closing years of the century there was a dramatic increase in trade unionism among women. From 19,500 in 1876, by 1906 female trade unionists had risen to 166,425.[109] In 1874 the suffragist Emma Paterson founded the Women's Provident and Protection League (WPPL), later the Women's Trade Union League, to encourage the formation of women's trade unions. While it got off to a slow start, being predominantly a middle-class organization rather than an initiative by the workers themselves, it succeeded in establishing a national network of women's societies, enabling women workers to develop a shared identity separate from men, and to campaign for changes in working conditions in emergent female industries. By the 1880s, however, working women had become more involved with the League and it was to play an important part in the Bryant & May match girls' strike in London of 1888 – probably the most conspicuous example of working-class female militancy of the time. Between 1886 and 1906, small women's unions proliferated.[110] Various political pressure groups formed over the next two decades, such as the Women's Cooperative Guild (which D. H. Lawrence's mother joined) in 1883 and the National Union of Women Workers and the Scottish Council for Women's Trades in 1895. In the United States, working-class women organized the International Ladies Garment Workers Union in 1900, and founded the Women's Trade Union League in 1903.

The politicization of women culminated in militant suffragette activity. American and British feminist campaigners increasingly engaged in the same debates through the transatlantic press, and united in the fight for enfranchisement. In 1890 the two suffrage factions in America, the National Woman Suffrage Association and the American Woman Suffrage Association (both founded in 1869), united as the National American Woman Suffrage Association (NAWSA) under the leadership of Elizabeth Cady Stanton, women's rights activist and co-author of the three-volume *History of Woman Suffrage* (1881–6). In 1903 Emmeline Pankhurst set up the Women's Social and Political Union (WSPU) in Britain. In 'The New Sex Psychology' Edith Searle Grossman observed: 'the suffrage struggle has shown [women's] increased force of character. We are now in the midst of the widest sex-revolution yet known. There has never before been such a numerous body of women united for reform of their inequalities, and there never before has been such solidarity in their ranks.'[111]

British militant suffragette activity, which peaked in 1912–13, declined during World War I as women joined the war effort. In 1913 the American women's rights campaigner Alice Paul returned to the United States from England and, with Lucy Burns, organized the Congressional Union, known from 1916 as the National Women's Party. Adopting the militant tactics of the WSPU, American suffragettes participated in hunger strikes, picketed the White House and engaged in other forms of civil disobedience to publicize the suffrage cause. The term 'Rebel Girl' was popularized by the US-based Industrial Workers of the World (IWW), and in a show of cross-gender class solidarity it became the title of an American feminist and socialist popular song, composed in 1914 by Joe Hill.[112] The *Woman Rebel*, an American militant feminist monthly, was launched the same year. It was banned after three issues for advocating birth control and the editor Margaret Sanger was charged with violating postal obscenity laws for distributing material on the subject.

Questions of Class and Race

The Elementary Education Act 1870 (Forster's Act) required locally elected school boards to provide elementary schools, known as board schools, where existing facilities were inadequate. Popular instruction before 1870 had been catered for by a system of government-inspected voluntary schools partially state financed but otherwise independent. Provision was made for the transfer of voluntary schools to school-board control. In 1872 the Scottish Elementary Education Act made attendance compulsory, and in 1880 it became compulsory in England and Wales. These were factors in the birth of the new fiction: a new reading public flowed forth from the Board Schools. In 1892 the *Young Woman* declared:

We have now reached the point where the full effect of national education is being felt. Everyone can read. Books have become cheaper and cheaper. The entire intellectual life of the nation has received an enormous quickening. Hence journals play a part in national life wholly undreamed of in the days when the realm of letters was governed by the *Edinburgh Review* and *Quarterly*.[113]

Publishers and writers were quick to respond to these new readers. The plight of working-class women is highlighted in Kipling's 'Badalia of Herodsfoot', in *Many Inventions* (1893), Arthur Morrison's 'Lizerunt', in *Tales of Mean Streets* (1894), and, less sympathetically, Gissing's 'Lou and Liz', in *English Illustrated Magazine* (1893). Gissing addresses the cost of the bicycle, prerequisite of New Woman status, in 'A Daughter of the Lodge' (1901), and in so doing raises the issue of how many women could afford to be new women. Through the disjunction between wealthy consumers and an exhausted shopgirl, Katherine Mansfield's 'The Tiredness of Rosabel' dramatizes class tensions. The wealthy Harry addresses Rosabel with 'the slight tinge of insolence, of familiarity': 'Ever been painted?'

Seeing that the campaign for suffrage brought middle- and working-class women into contact, Evelyn Sharp, author of *Rebel Women* (1910), highlighted distinctions as much as commonalities between them. In 'To Prison while the Sun Shines' she dramatized the differences experienced by middle-class suffragettes and those born on the wrong side of the tracks, for whom crime was not only a way of life, but part of the struggle for life: these 'imperturbably serene young women' by 'the grace of God and the aid of a good cause, did not belong to the criminal classes'; 'These were not people whose spirit had been driven out of them by monotony and bad luck, as it had been driven out of the derelicts who stood in the dock before them . . . It may be a perilous business to hunt down the colour of life for other people; but it is a less hopeless kind of job than hunting it down for yourself.'[114] The suffragette's certain return to middle-class comforts, with new heroic status among her supporters, made her prison experience an immeasurably different one. In 'Filling the War Cabinet' a suffragette street seller begins to be accepted by her fellow workers as they share the frosts and fortunes of selling in the street, but she ceases to belong when she leaves at the end of a week. Class barriers are not easily surmounted. The story reveals that the women selling *Votes for Women* are middle class; they are sufficiently well-heeled to raise money for the cause, while their working-class counterparts sell in the streets in order to survive.

New Women such as Kate Chopin, Mona Caird and Evelyn Sharp spoke out in their fiction against racial and social prejudice. But the feminism of many New Women on both sides of the Atlantic co-existed with conservative thinking as they upheld racial and social hierarchies, drawing on the racial biases and prejudices of Victorian scientific discourse to further their social agendas. The term race could slip easily from signifying the human race to a national race, or even a social class or group. Within Britain, the idea of race was used of the white population to distinguish groups of varying social as well as ethnic backgrounds, as exemplified in the study of the ethnologist John Beddoe, *The Races of Britain: A Contribution to the Anthropology of Western Europe* (1885). As the new discourses on heredity and biological determinism gained popularity, the issues and languages of class and race bled into each other and class was increasingly biologized. Grand, for example, was concerned with questions of imperial strength, and saw a role for women in ensuring the fit reproduction of the British race, by which she meant the reproduction of the middle classes. In 'The Case of the Modern Married Woman' she urged middle-class women to 'learn to appreciate the value and weight of their own class, the great middle class' where 'the best breeding . . . the highest culture are now to be found'.[115] The term breeding implies a conflation of the social and the racial – of ideas of class and race – which is at work here. Much of Grand's writing gave expression to the concept of civic maternalism that was developing at this time as part of a new, gendered citizenship: the idea that motherhood might constitute a woman's first act of citizenship, her contribution to strengthening the imperial race. Equally, while George Egerton challenged forms of female oppression and social convention, her sustained interest in biological determinism and her emphasis both on the centrality of reproduction to womanhood, and on the need for 'race improvement', a widely used term in the late nineteenth century, complicates both her radical stance and her relationship to freedom.

In 'The Yellow Drawing Room', through the validation of reproduction as *choice* rather than duty, Mona Caird took an opposite view, arguing against an unreflective passage into domestic routine and motherhood. She would continue to expose repressive ideologies which lay behind the rhetoric of family and motherhood, and in her later novels, *Stones of Sacrifice* (1915) and *The Great Wave* (1931), she explicitly attacked racial thinking and the idea of eugenics.

While issues of class predominated in Britain in the nineteenth century, in the United States issues of race and ethnicity were far more central. Immigration was increasing steadily, and peaked at nearly one million in 1907 with most of the new arrivals coming from eastern and southern Europe (Russia, Poland, Austria-Hungary and Italy). These immigrants began to be figured as racially *other* and inferior to northern Europeans.[116] Grace Thorne, America's Model New Woman, lectured across America on 'the race question':

Whoever asks admission at our gates, East or West, and is unwilling to conform to our habits, learn our language and become naturalized and patriotic American citizens, should be unceremoniously dismissed. The springing up of immense foreign colonies in our midst, where our language is despised, our Bible scoffed at, our flag trailed in the dust, and our institutions generally demeaned, is a menace of mighty magnitude. No party should be so anxious for votes as to wink at these things. Strict immigration laws should be enacted and enforced to the letter. 'America for Americans' should be the watchword of all.[117]

In 1898 in *Women and Economics*, Charlotte Perkins Gilman wrote 'competition among males, with selection by the female of the superior male, is the process of sexual selection, and works to racial improvement'. *Herland*, her feminist Utopia of 1915, embraces eugenics as a solution to over-population. Motherhood is now 'the highest social service – a sacrament, really . . . it is only undertaken once, by the majority of the population . . . those held unfit are not even allowed that . . . and to be encouraged to bear more than one child is the very highest reward and honor in the power of the state'. As a result of these practices, 'sickness was almost wholly unknown among them, so much so that a previously high development in what we call the "science of medicine" had become practically a lost art. They were a clean-bred, vigorous lot.' In her sequel, *With Her in Ourland* (1916), Gilman delivers a diatribe against slavery through her sociologist heroine, Ellador. Having left her home country, Herland, for the United States – Ourland – Ellador declares to her American husband Vandyck Jennings: 'about the first awful mistake you made was in loading yourself up with those reluctant Africans. If it wasn't so horrible, it would be funny. A beautiful healthy young country, saddling itself with an antique sin every other civilized nation had repudiated.' However, her critique is underpinned by ideas of racial purity and fitness. Diagnosing America as 'bloated and verminous', she turns to the question of white immigration, arguing that democracy will never be achieved in the United States on the basis of an 'ill-assorted and unassimilable mass of human material . . . victims, poor ignorant people scraped up by paid agents, deceived by lying advertisements, brought over here by greedy American ship owners and employers of labor'. Democracy, she advises her husband, must 'pick and choose' its people, for races were at 'different stages of development'. She draws a comparison with Europe: 'you go to England, and the people are English. Only three per cent of aliens even in London, I understand. And in France the people are French – bless them! And in Italy, Italian.'[118]

A burgeoning of newspapers and periodicals in the United States began to cater for specific ethnic and immigrant audiences, and the short story became a vehicle for addressing racial issues. Importantly, it provided minority groups with an effective way of preserving the past, and expressing present protest, and it gained popularity and political resonance among Native Americans whose ancient oral culture was severely threatened by white colonization. The turn of the century saw the launch of the *Colored American Magazine*, one of the first major literary magazines targeted at a largely African-American audience; as editor-in chief, Pauline Hopkins used the magazine as a forum for writing African Americans into American history.

The writer of regional stories Bret Harte noted in the *Cornhill Magazine* in 1899 that the American short story developed alongside an appreciation of place; 'the secret of the American short story was the treatment of characteristic American life'.[119] Zitkala-Ša, a Sioux, was one of a number of Native Americans who sought to preserve their culture in the short story, while campaigning for the rights of American Indians. Women of all creeds shared an ambivalent and marginal relation to cultural hegemony, and, like British women, and her compatriots in America, Zitkala-Ša was drawn to a style and form which mirrored the liminal position of the people whose culture she was seeking to preserve and express.

Subjectivity

Fiction was turning inward. The narrator of George Eliot's *Adam Bede* had pledged to his readers: 'I aspire to give no more than a faithful account of men and things as they have mirrored themselves in my mind', going on to confess that 'the mirror is doubtless defective; the outlines will sometimes be disturbed; the reflection faint or confused.'[120] Over the course of the century, such 'defects' would become virtues; a transformation to which the short story, with its prevailing interest in the life of the mind, was pivotal. The nameless man in Katherine Mansfield's 'Psychology' (1921), speaking very fast, declares: 'I simply haven't got any external life at all. I don't know the names of things a bit – trees and so on – and I never notice places or furniture or what people look like.'[121] In 'Telling a Short Story' (1924), Edith Wharton wrote: 'it has been often, and inaccurately, said that the mind of a creative artist is a mirror, and the work of art the reflection of life in it. The mirror, indeed, is the artist's mind, with all his experiences reflected in it; but the work of art, from the smallest to the greatest, should be something projected, not reflected, something on which his mirrored experiences, at the right conjunction of the stars, are to be turned for its full illumination.'[122] Offering up snapshots, fragments, the short stories captured the essentially indefinable nature of identity. 'As long as the infinite complexities of modern emotion play about situations that are as old as the race, so long will there be an opportunity for the free development of the short story as a literary form', wrote Perry, for the story writer 'deals not with wholes, but with fragments; not with the trend of the great march through the wide world, but with some particular aspect of the procession as it passes.'[123]

For women, the short story opened up new opportunities to explore female subjectivity. As Stutfield put it in 'The Psychology of Feminism', they were turning themselves 'inside out'.[124] While it would be simplistic to read subjectivity along reductively gendered lines, or to neglect the effects of other social and bodily divisions such as class and race on perceptions of self and other, it is nonetheless clear that women at this time were exploring new spaces, new interiors which had previously been denied them, as they told their own stories and, in doing so, constructed *themselves*. Inconclusive, open-ended, evasive short stories were a perfect fit for the modern woman, as she released herself from repressive social codes, and tried out new identities. Why does the Pleasure-Pilgrim shoot herself? Why does the model in Grand's 'The Undefinable' walk out? Where is Florence in 'Virgin Soil' going, when she takes a train in the opposite direction from her home? In the words of Grand's model, 'I am altogether an outcome of the age, you will perceive, an impossible mixture of incongruous qualities, which are all in a ferment at present.' Stutfield wrote:

the Soul of Woman, its Sphinx-like ambiguities and complexities, its manifold contradictions, its sorrows and joys, its vagrant fancies and never-to-be-satisfied longing, furnish the literary analyst these days with inexhaustible material . . . to be subtle, inscrutable, complex – irrational possibly, but at any rate incomprehensible – to puzzle the adoring male, to make him scratch his head in vexation and wonderment as to what on earth she will be up to next – this is the ambition of the latter-day heroine. She is consumed with a desire for new experiences, new sensations, new objects in life.[125]

The unknowability of woman is reclaimed, and embraced, in Grand's 'The Undefinable', and given a novel twist by Wilde in 'The Sphinx without a Secret'. This increasing self-analysis was hailed by many as a sign of disease. Bemoaning the fact that 'self-sacrifice' has been supplanted by 'self-development', Stutfield wrote: 'this consciousness of the self is of recent growth; it was unknown to our mothers and grandmothers'. He drew parallels between the morbid form of self-obsession, or 'ego-mania' – which Max Nordau had held to be a major symptom of degeneration – and 'this newly aroused consciousness' which 'lies at the root of our modern introspectiveness, and accounts for many of the strange things that neurotic people do both in real life and in fiction'.[126]

Supporters of the short story stressed that one of its most novel, and defining, features was its privileging of one point of view and consequent exploration and validation of subjectivity, of what Mansfield would name 'the secret self' in 'Psychology'. Edith Wharton stressed that one of the main defining features of the short story was its observance of 'a modern and complex' unity, 'which requires that any rapidly enacted episode shall be seen through only one pair of eyes'.[127] In the case of Grand's nameless model, and D'Arcy's Pleasure-Pilgrim, it is a point of view that remains inaccessible to the reader. In other stories we are taken into the consciousness of the first-person narrator, but we are not told everything. As Canby noted, the single point of view was the distinguishing feature of the short story.[128] The short story dramatizes the uniqueness, the uniquely knowing and unknowing self. By undermining objectivity, the time-hallowed status of woman in fiction as an *object* was no longer a possibility, in the hands of either a male or female writer: she remained ultimately unreadable, a version of Joyce's Eveline in *Dubliners*. Perry remarked:

recall how George Eliot pictures Dorothea in *Middlemarch*, now in this position, now in that. If one scene does not present her vividly to us, the chances are that another will, and in the end, it is true, we have an absolutely distinct image of her. The short story writer, on the other hand, has but one chance. His task, compared with that of the novelist, is like bringing down a flying bird with one bullet, instead of banging away with a whole handful and having another barrel in reserve.[129]

With the short story, wholeness is sacrificed to intensity; as Canby said, 'the process is very artificial, but very powerful; it is like turning a telescope upon one nebula in the heavens'. The writer 'looks only for one episode, which, like the bubble on the stream, is part of, and yet distinguished from, the main current'.[130]

Plot was to be reduced in favour of psychological development. Whatever their political outlook women writers of the time participated in fiction's inward turn. W. T. Stead remarked: 'woman at last has found woman interesting to herself, and she has studied her, painted her, and analysed her as if she had an independent existence'.[131] George Egerton began to reclaim what she saw as women's essential illegibility, as something to be celebrated, embraced as proof of sexual difference. Sexual difference and equality feminists made women their subjects, and wrote from a woman's point of view. Eliot was considered old hat, even patriarchal. 'Keynotes is not addressed to men, and it will not please them . . . It is not written in the style adopted by other women Georges – George Sand and George Eliot – who wrote from a man's point of view with the solemnity of a clergyman, or the libertinism of a drawing-room hero.'[132] During the course of the 1890s Eliot was increasingly figured as an establishment figure from whose literary clutches new woman writers had to escape: Haweis pronounced in her speech to Women Writers that Eliot had written 'from the man's point of view, and under the influence of a man', while Sarah Grand, George Egerton and 'many other writers, English and American', wrote from 'the *woman's special point of view*' and were 'opening the new door'.[133]

Psychoanalysis

'Do you mean you feel that the . . . young writers of today' are 'trying simply to jump the psychoanalyst's claim?' asks the nameless woman in Mansfield's 'Psychology'. 'Yes, I do,' replies her interlocutor.[134] The relationship between the new fiction and the new discourse of psychoanalysis is summed up by Egerton: 'if I did not know the technical jargon current today of Freud and the psychoanalysts, I did know something of complexes and inhibitions, repressions and the subconscious impulses that determine actions and reactions. I used them in my stories.'[135] Freud published his first work, *Studies on Hysteria*, co-authored with Josef Breuer, in 1895, and *The Interpretation of Dreams* in 1899. The rise of the short story and the birth of psychoanalysis coincided; both are underpinned by a fascination with the workings, the knowing, and unknowability, of the mind. The titles of short stories, and collections, at this time signal self-consciously their relations to the mind, to moments; they suggest moods, emotions, situations rather than narratives: Egerton's *Keynotes*, *Discords* (1894), including 'A Psychological Moment', and *Symphonies* (1897), D'Arcy's *Monochromes* (1895) and Grand's *Emotional Moments* (1908). Stutfield complained: 'Psychology – word more blessed than Mesopotamia – is their never-ending delight; and modern woman, who, if we may believe those who claim to know most about her, is a sort of enigma, is their chief subject of investigation.'[136] In *The Psychology of*

Women, Marholm wrote that 'to comprehend the woman of today . . . to read the secrets of her inner and concealed experience . . . that were worth our pains! . . . But how read this hidden writing? – how open these concealed and locked chambers?'[137] Just as the analysand looks to the analyst to be read, so the short-story writer expects the reader to read actively, to work from fragments, traces, dreams even; the short story offers itself up for analysis. Like the analyst, the reader must work with the material they are given: William Dean Howells, writer, socialist and editor of the *Atlantic Monthly* from 1871–81, wrote in 1901: 'a condition that the short story tacitly makes with the reader, through its limitations, is that he shall subjectively fill in the details and carry out the scheme which in its small dimensions the story can only suggest'.[138] Through his systematic investigation of the unconscious, Freud developed the idea that active parts of the mind are not immediately open to inspection either by an onlooker or by the subject. He would define the task of the analyst as 'to make out what has been forgotten from the traces which it has left behind or, more correctly, to *construct* it'.[139]

Dreams were beginning to be perceived as the key to the secret self, both in psychoanalysis and in short stories. In *The Interpretation of Dreams*, Freud posited that the interpretation of dreams was 'the royal road to a knowledge of the unconscious activities of the mind'.[140] Olive Schreiner released a series of stories in 1890 under the collective title *Dreams*; later she published *Stories, Dreams, and Allegories*. Kate Chopin's 'The Story of an Hour' appeared first in 1894 as 'The Dream of an Hour', in *Vogue*, a bold new journal of the 1890s. In 1898 Egerton published a collection of short stories, *Fantasias*. One feature dreams shared with short stories was compression: as Freud put it in *The Interpretation of Dreams*, 'these phantasies, like any other component of the dream-thoughts, are compressed, condensed, superimposed on one another, and so on . . . as a rule one underestimates the amount of compression that has taken place, since one is inclined to regard the dream-thoughts that have been brought to light as the complete material, whereas if the work of interpretation is carried further it may reveal still more thoughts concealed behind the dream'.[141] What he called a 'pictographic script', in 'The Dream Work',[142] Schreiner referred to in 'A Dream of Wild Bees' (*Dreams*) as a 'brain picture'. In

'A Cross Line' Egerton makes her reader work to understand the new, psychoanalytic dimension she is giving the term 'picturesque'; she opens the story with the unidiomatic observation that 'Her mind is nothing if not picturesque; her busy brain, with all its capabilities choked by a thousand vagrant fancies, is always producing pictures and finding associations between the most unlikely objects'.

For Nordau, the *fin de siècle* was a time of darkness, in which dreams thrived. 'The day is over, the night draws on.' Dreams filled up 'the hours of darkness till the breaking of the new day', and 'in the artistic products of the age we see the form in which these dreams become sensible'.[143] Freud showed how waking fantasies could have consequences in the real world; this receives striking treatment in Gilman's 'The Yellow Wallpaper', where the protagonist's waking thoughts and movements, under the prescription of the 'rest-cure', express her madness: 'I lie down ever so much now. John says it is good for me, and to sleep all I can.' She knows this is bad for her, for it induces a waking madness: 'It is a very bad habit I am convinced, for you see I don't sleep'. The story dramatizes striking similarities between dreaming and madness; both give expression to desires that social rules would suppress. The story also warns that when fantasy is the only space for freedom, it risks turning in on the dreamer. The protagonist's thoughts take such a hold on her that she experiences an increasing disjunction from the external world: a disjunction which dramatizes the marginal position of women at the time. The internal world is projected outwards; the woman in the wallpaper is the ego. Just as the short story privileged one point of view, one subjectivity, so Freud remarked: 'dreams are completely egoistic';[144] in 'The Yellow Wallpaper' the dreamer identifies with the (imagined) woman behind wallpaper bars. Freud observed that the 'unconscious excitations' which emerged in dreams could, in cases of pathological intensification, obtain 'control over speech and actions' and 'to this state of things we give the name of psychosis'.[145] 'The Yellow Wallpaper' released the mad woman that the early Victorians had confined to the attic, and makes her its subject. It was for the reader to decide whether her mental state was the result of social oppression.

Dreams and waking thoughts opened up new possibilities in fiction, allowing women a language and form in which they could negotiate and express desire. Freud held that dreams were primarily of interest to the analyst because the 'critical watchman' censorship relaxes its activities during the night. Dreams give access to the desiring self: 'the reason why dreams are invariably wish-fulfilments is that they are products of the system unconscious, whose activity knows no other aim than the fulfilment of wishes and which has at its command no other forces than wishful impulses'.[146] Waking dreams provided women writers with a space to explore a sexual freedom that literature was not yet happy to take beyond the realm of fantasy. Stutfield remarked: 'it cannot be denied that women are chiefly responsible for the "booming" of books that are "close to life" – life, that is to say, as viewed through sex-maniacal glasses'.[147] In 'A Cross Line' the protagonist, known only as 'Gypsy', falls into a series of daydreams in which her 'thirst for excitement, for change, this restless craving for sun and love and motion' come to the fore, dramatizing the daydream as wish-fulfilment. Kate Chopin dramatizes through the eponymous Egyptian Cigarette the potential of dreaming to release, and to intoxify. Freud wrote that 'closer investigation of the characteristics of these day-time phantasies shows us how right it is that these formations should bear the same name as we give to the products of our thought during the night – the name, that is, of "dreams" . . . Like dreams, they are wish-fulfilments; like dreams, they are based to a great extent on impressions of infantile experiences; like dreams, they benefit by a certain degree of relaxation of censorship.'[148] In Mansfield's 'Leves Amores', it is not until night-time that desire is expressed, that the passion of youth returns.

Dreaming and fantasy offered release from the logic and constraints of the external world. In Hardy's 'An Imaginative Woman', Ella Marchmill's fantasies, the omnipotence of her thoughts, override external laws of causality. Hardy is careful to point out that her son bears the appearance of her dream lover, as a 'trick of Nature'; this is not the working of the supernatural. The world of dreams, of fantasy, opens up as a space for the expression of female desire, uninhibited by literary and social propriety. It also provides a space for the expression of desire unfulfilled, of opportunity missed. In Mansfield's 'The

Tiredness of Rosabel', the tiredness of the shopgirl allows her access to a world and to emotional fulfilment that she is denied in the real world. When an insensitive upper-class customer asks Rosabel to model a hat, she temporarily places Rosabel in a position of privilege. The moment dramatizes the gap between the real and the imagined which only the world of dreams can erase – or invert. In her waking dreams, back in the privacy of her dingy bedsit, the wealthy man becomes Rosabel's lover and she experiences the luxuries, the sensations of upper-class existence. Relations between the real world and the world of thoughts are reversed; reality and the real Rosabel are, literally, bracketed off: '(Rosabel realized that her knees were getting stiff; she sat down on the floor and leant her head against the wall.) . . . (The real Rosabel, the girl crouched on the floor in the dark, laughed aloud, and put her hand up to her hot mouth.)' The story itself has the non-linear quality of a dream: we begin with Rosabel's journey home, before we are told of an event in her day at the shop. And, even on the bus, she begins to daydream: 'Through her half-closed eyes the whole row of people on the opposite seat seemed to resolve into one, fatuous, staring face . . .' The fantasy world offers such respite, that Rosabel begins her dreaming at seven o'clock. Moved by the cold, Rosabel moves from daydreaming to dreaming: 'she slept and dreamed, and smiled in her sleep'. Elizabeth Bowen noted: 'recall that in 1908 the idea of writing a story *about* a daydream was in itself novel – a daring break with accepted pattern. And how many *Rosabel* tales today would have been written at all but for Katherine Mansfield?'[149]

It is perhaps fitting to end this sketch of the new fiction with an eyewitness account from the press. In 1901 Howells observed:

in the process of time the short story . . . has proved itself possibly the most flexible of all the literary forms in its adaptation to the needs of the mind that wishes to utter itself, inventively or constructively, upon some fresh occasion, or wishes briefly to criticize or represent some phase or fact of life. The riches in this shape of fiction are inestimable, if we consider what has been done in the short story, and is still doing everywhere.[150]

Embracing a multiplicity of themes and genres, from the detective story to the suffragette story, from realism to satire and experimentalist fiction, *Women Who Did* explores the outbreak of a rebellion that was social, sexual and literary.

NOTES

1. Holbrook Jackson, 1927 Preface to *The Eighteen Nineties: A Review of Art and Ideas at the Close of the Nineteenth Century* (1913; Penguin, 1939), p. 9.

2. The term *fin de siècle* (end of century) was used by contemporaries of the closing years of the nineteenth century: it was the title of a play first put on in April 1888 in Paris, which seems to have been the earliest usage.

3. Max Nordau, *Degeneration* (1892), trans. from 2nd German edn of *Entartung* (1895; University of Nebraska Press, 1968), p. 6.

4. H. G. Wells, 'The Contemporary Novel', title of serial and book publication of talk given to the Times Book Club in 1911; reprinted as 'The Scope of the Novel', in *An Englishman Looks at the World: Being a Series of Unrestrained Remarks upon Contemporary Matters* (Cassell and Company, 1914), p. 145. Arthur James Balfour (1848–1930), Conservative prime minister (1902–5), was also a philosopher, whose book *A Defence of Philosophic Doubt* (1879) argued that the scepticism of scientists with regard to religion should also logically be applied to science, and that, given that any set of beliefs must ultimately therefore be founded on faith rather than reason, a theistic model of the universe made more sense than one without god.

5. Sidney Grundy, *The New Woman: An Original Comedy in Four Acts* (1894; Oxford University Press, 1998), I.i. 547.

6. Henry Duff Traill, *The New Fiction: and Other Essays on Literary Subjects* (Hurst and Blackett, 1897), p. 1.

7. Emily Morgan-Dockrell, 'Is the New Woman a Myth?', *Humanitarian* 8 (1896), 339. David Rubinstein (*Before the Suffragettes: Women's Emancipation in the 1890s* (Brighton: Harvester, 1986), pp. 231–2n) notes that she was probably the Mrs M. Dockrell who was an Irish local councillor (*Englishwoman's Review*, 31 (1900), 194).

8. Michael Millgate, *Thomas Hardy: His Career as a Novelist* (1971; Macmillan, 1994), p. 312.

9. George Sims, *Glances Back* (Jarrolds, 1917), p. 253.

10. William Barry, 'The Strike of a Sex', *Quarterly Review* 179 (1894), 317.

11. *Votes for Women*, 6 October 1911, p. 6.

12. Thomas Bradfield, 'A Dominant Note of some Recent Fiction', *Westminster Review* 142 (1894), 541.

13. Christine Stansell, *American Moderns: Bohemian New York and the Creation of a New Century* (Henry Holt, 2000), p. 232.

14. Arthur Conan Doyle, 'A Scandal in Bohemia', *Strand* (1891). Grant Allen, *The Type-writer Girl* (1897); see p. xxxvii for further discussion of the Girton girl.

15. Henry James, *The American Scene* (1907; Penguin, 1994), pp. 255, 256.

16. Hugh E. M. Stutfield, 'The Psychology of Feminism', *Blackwood's Edinburgh Magazine* 161 (1897), 105.

17. Max O'Rell, 'Petticoat Government', *North American Review* 163 (July 1896), 102.

18. Judith Worsnop, 'A Re-evaluation of "the problem of surplus women" in 19th-century England: The case of the 1851 Census', *Women's Studies International Forum* 13 (1990), 21–31.

19. For useful contemporary discussion and perspective, see C. S. Bremner, *Education of Girls and Women in Great Britain* (Swan Sonnenschein, 1897), and Alice Zimmern, *The Renaissance of Girls' Education in England* (A. D. Innes, 1898).

20. George Gissing, *The Odd Women* (1893; Penguin, 1993), p. 41.

21. Brother Jonathan Junior, 'Our Sisters Across the Sea', *Young Woman* 1 (1892).

22. Marie Corelli, Flora Annie Steel, Lady Jeune and Susan, Countess of Malmesbury, *The Modern Marriage Market* (Hutchinson & Co., 1897), pp. 70–71.

23. Janet Howarth, 'Gender, Domesticity, and Sexual Politics', in Colin Matthew (ed.), *The Nineteenth Century: The British Isles 1815–1901* (Oxford University Press, 2000), pp. 184–5.

24. Barry, 'The Strike of a Sex', p. 294.

25. A. G. P. Sykes, 'The Evolution of the Sex', *Westminster Review* 143 (1895), 396.

26. Herbert Jamieson, 'The Modern Woman', *Westminster Review* 152 (1899), 69.

27. 'The Appeal Against Female Suffrage', *Nineteenth Century* 25 (1889), 781–8.

28. Millicent Garrett Fawcett, 'The Appeal Against Female Suffrage: A Reply. 1', *Nineteenth Century* 26 (1889), and Margaret Mary Dilke, 'The Appeal Against Female Suffrage: A Reply. 2', *Nineteenth Century* 26 (1889), 86–96, 97–103; Louise Creighton, 'The Appeal Against Female Suffrage: A Rejoinder', *Nineteenth Century* 26 (1889), 347–54.

29. See headnote to Gertrude Colmore's 'The Woman in the Corner'.

30. See, for example, 'Womanhood Suffrage', *Punch*, 30 March 1867; 'Shall Lovely Woman Vote?', *Punch*, 4 May 1867, and 'Mill's Logic; or Franchise for Females', *Punch*, 1 June 1867.

31. See Colin Matthew, 'Public Life and Politics', in Matthew, *The Nineteenth Century*, p. 96.

32. J. S. Mill, *On the Subjection Of Women* (1869; J. M. Dent, 1986), p. 238.

33. *The Collected Letters of Thomas Hardy*, ed. Richard Little Purdy and Michael Millgate (Clarendon Press, 1978–88), vol. 3, pp. 238–9.

34. Herbert Spencer, 'Elements of Feminine Attraction', *Quarterly Review* (1859); collected in *Education: Intellectual, Moral, and Physical* (Williams & Norgate, 1861), pp. 174, 176.

35. Charles Darwin, *The Descent of Man, and Selection in Relation to Sex*, 2 vols. (1871; Princeton University Press, 1981), vol. 2, pp. 326–7.

36. Henry Maudsley, 'Sex in Mind and Education', *Fortnightly Review* 15 (1874); Eliza Lynn Linton, 'The Higher Education of Woman', *Fortnightly Review* 40 (1886).

37. Benjamin Ward Richardson, 'Woman's Work in Creation', *Longman's Magazine* 8 (1886).

38. Elizabeth Garrett Anderson, 'Sex in Mind and Education: A Reply', *Fortnightly Review* 15 (1874), cited in *Gender and Science: Nineteenth-Century Debates on the Female Mind and Body*, ed. Katharina Rowold (Thoemmes Press, 1996), p. 64.

39. Grant Allen, 'The Girl of the Future', *Universal Review* 7 (1890), 57.

40. Frederic Harrison, 'The Emancipation of Women', *Fortnightly Review* 56 (1891), 451–2.

41. 'Are We Degenerating Physically?', *Lancet* (1 December 1888), 1076–7.

42. 'National Health and Military Service', *British Medical Journal* 25 (1903), 202, in Anthony S. Wohl, *Endangered Lives: Public Health in Victorian Britain* (Methuen, 1984), p. 332.

43. See Thomas Laqueur, *Making Sex: Body and Gender from the Greeks to Freud* (Harvard University Press, 1990), and Angus McLaren, 'The Pleasures of Procreation: Traditional and Biomedical Theories of Conception', in W. F. Bynum and Roy Porter (eds.), *William Hunter and the Eighteenth-Century Medical World* (Cambridge University Press, 1985), pp. 323–41.

44. Sarah A. Tooley, 'The Woman Question: An Interview with Madame Sarah Grand', *Humanitarian* 8 (1896), 162.

45. Letter from Sarah Grand to Professor Viëter, Nizza, Germany (15 December 1896), in Ernst Foerster, *Die Frauenfrage in den Romanen Englischer Schriftstellerinnen der Gegenwart* (N. G. Elwert'sche Verlagsbuchhandlung, 1907), pp. 55–8; reprinted in Ann Heilmann (ed.), *The Late Victorian Marriage Debate: A Collection of Key New Woman Texts* (Routledge and Thoemmes Press, 1998), vol. 5.

46. Sarah Grand, *The Beth Book, Being a Study from the Life of Elizabeth*

Caldwell Maclure, A Woman of Genius (1897; Thoemmes Press, 1994), p. 442.

47. Edward Carpenter, *Love's Coming-of-Age* (1896; Methuen & Co., 1914), p. 114. John Bull denotes a typical Englishman, from a character intended to be representative of the English nation in *The History of John Bull*, by John Arbuthnot (1712).

48. George Egerton, *Keynotes and Discords*, ed. Martha Vicinus (1893 and 1894; Virago, 1983), p. 199.

49. George Egerton, 'Women in the Queen's Reign: Some Notable Opinions, Illustrated with Photographs', *Ludgate* (1898), 216.

50. Letter from Sarah Grand to John Blackwood (5 December 1892), Letters of Frances Elizabeth McFall, National Library of Scotland.

51. Athol Forbes, 'My Impressions of Sarah Grand', *Lady's World* 21 (June 1900), 883.

52. Grant Allen, 'Plain Words on the Woman Question', *Popular Science Monthly* 36 (1889), 179.

53. Margaret Oliphant, 'The Anti-Marriage League', *Blackwood's Edinburgh Magazine* 159 (1896), 135–45, and Tooley, 'The Woman Question', pp. 168–9.

54. Allen, 'Plain Words on the Woman Question', p. 179.

55. Thomas Hardy, *Desperate Remedies* (1871; Penguin, 1998), vol. 2, chapter 2.

56. H. G. Wells, Preface to *The Country of the Blind and Other Stories* (Nelson, 1911), p. v.

57. The sixpenny magazine was half the price of existing middle-class monthlies such as *Cornhill*, and included *Woman at Home* and *Longman's Magazine* (both launched in 1892). The 'sixpenny public' was seen to represent the new mass readership, but in effect it catered to the middle classes, while weekly magazines such as George Newnes's *Tit-bits*, launched in 1881, and Alfred Harmsworth's *Answers*, launched in 1888, went on sale for only one penny, with circulations of over half a million each. Launched at Christmas 1890, George Newnes's *Strand* was marketed as 'A monthly magazine costing sixpence but worth a shilling', and by 1896 it was selling 392,000 copies a month (including 60,000 exported to the USA) (Richard Altick: *The English Common Reader* (University of Chicago Press, 1957), p. 396).

58. Mrs H. R. Haweis, 'Women as Writers', in *Words to Women: Addresses and Essays* (Burnet and Isbister, 1900), pp. 69–70.

59. Cynthia White, *Women's Magazines, 1693–1968* (Michael Joseph, 1970), p. 58; Philip Horne, 'Henry James and the Economy of the Short Story', in Ian Wallison, Warwick Gould and Warren Chernaik (eds.), *Modernist Writers and the Marketplace* (Macmillan, 1996), p. 3.

60. Blanche A. Crackanthorpe, 'Sex in Modern Literature', *Nineteenth Century* 37 (1895), 613.

61. 'The Art of Story-Telling', *Fraser's Magazine* 53 (1856), 726.

62. Andrew Levy, *The Cultural Commerce of the American Short Story* (Cambridge University Press, 1993), pp. 289–318.

63. Henry Seidel Canby, *The Short Story* (Henry Holt, 1902), p. 28.

64. H. G. Wells, in Henry James and H. G. Wells, *Henry James and H. G. Wells: A Record of Their Friendship, Their Debate on the Art of Fiction, and Their Quarrel* (R. Hart-Davis, 1958), p. 146.

65. Bliss Perry, 'The Short Story', *Atlantic Monthly* 90 (1902), 250. On Eliot, see also p. lxviii above.

66. White, *Women's Magazines*, p. 59.

67. Haweis, 'Women as Writers', pp. 69–70.

68. Canby, *The Short Story*, p. 28.

69. Perry, 'The Short Story', p. 251.

70. Ibid.

71. Edith Slater, 'Men's Women in Fiction', *Westminster Review* 149 (1898), 572.

72. Laura Marholm, 'Neurotic Keynotes', in *Modern Women*, trans. Hermione Ramsden (Bodley Head, 1896), pp. 81, 61, 62.

73. Charlotte Perkins Gilman, *Women and Economics: A Study of the Economic Relation between Men and Women as a Factor in Social Evolution* (1898; (University of California Press), pp. 150–51.

74. Virginia Woolf, *A Room of One's Own* (1929; Oxford University Press, 1992), p. 101.

75. George Egerton, 'A Keynote to Keynotes', in John Gawsworth (ed.), *Ten Contemporaries: Notes Towards their Definitive Bibliography* (Earnest Benn, 1932), p. 60.

76. Haweis, 'Women as Writers', pp. 69, 71.

77. *Votes for Women*, 30 June 1912, p. 639.

78. *Votes for Women*, 16 May 1923.

79. See Ann Sumner Holmes, ' "Fallen Mothers", Maternal Adultery and Child Custody in England, 1886–1925', in Claudia Nelson and Ann Sumner Holmes (eds.), *Maternal Instincts: Visions of Motherhood and Sexuality in Britain, 1875–1925* (St Martin's Press and Macmillan, 1997). Through an analysis of custody cases between 1886 and 1925 Holmes demonstrates that English judges began to recognize the significance of factors other than sexual purity in determining a woman's value as a mother.

80. E.g. *The Times* (3 April 1891).

81. Eliza Lynn Linton, 'The Judicial Shock to Marriage', *Nineteenth Century* 171 (1891), 700.

82. Mona Caird, 'Marriage', independent section, *Westminster Review* (1888), reprinted in *The Morality of Marriage and Other Essays on the Status and Destiny of Woman* (George Redway, 1897), pp. 105, 106; 'The Morality of Marriage' is reprinted in Heilmann, *The Late Victorian Marriage Debate*, vol. 1.

83. Tooley, 'The Woman Question', p. 167.

84. I am grateful to Phil Broad, *Daily Telegraph*, for providing me with this information for 1887.

85. Harry Quilter (ed.), *Is Marriage a Failure?* (Swan Sonnenschein, 1888), p. 2.

86. *Punch* 97 (17 November 1888), 233; George and Weedon Grossmith, *The Diary of a Nobody* (Penguin, 1999).

87. Sarah Grand, 'The New Aspect of the Woman Question', *North American Review* 158 (1894), 275.

88. Elizabeth Rachel Chapman, *Marriage Questions in Modern Fiction and Other Essays on Kindred Subjects* (John Lane, 1897), p. 10.

89. Edward and Eleanor Marx Aveling, *The Woman Question* (Swan Sonnenschein, 1886), p. 5.

90. Thomas Hardy, *Tess of the D'Urbervilles* (1891; Penguin, 1986), Phase the Second, chapter 12, p. 82.

91. Anonymous, 'On the Treatment of Love in Novels', *Fraser's Magazine* 53 (1856), 412.

92. Cited in Perry, 'The Short Story', p. 242.

93. Sarah Grand, *The Heavenly Twins* (1893; Ann Arbor Paperbacks, 1992), pp. 353–462.

94. Coventry Patmore, *The Angel in the House* (John W. Parker & Son, 1856).

95. Charlotte Perkins Gilman, *The Yellow Wall-Paper and Other Stories*, ed. Robert Shulman (Oxford University Press, 1995), p. 50.

96. Virginia Woolf, 'Professions of Women' (1931), in *Collected Essays*, 4 vols. (Hogarth Press, 1966), vol. 2, pp. 285–6.

97. Laura Marholm, 'The Women of Today', in *Psychology of Woman*, trans. Georgia A. Etchison (Grant Richards, 1899), p. 35.

98. George F. Hall, *A Study in Bloomers, or, The Model New Woman* (American Bible House, 1895), p. 41.

99. Clementina Black, *Women's Signal* (29 August 1895), p. 131.

100. Louise Jeye, *Lady Cyclist*, and Sarah Burstall, *Retrospect and Prospect: Sixty years of Women's Education* (Longman's, 1933), cited in Rubinstein, *Before the Suffragettes*, p. 217. For contemporary discussion of women and cycling, see 'Some Famous Lady Cyclists', *Lady's Realm* 2 (1897), and, for contemporary opposition, see 'How Cycling Injures Health', *Review of Reviews* 1 (1890) and 'Cyclomania Morbus', *Review of Reviews* 15 (1897). See also Sarah Wintle,

'Horses, Bikes and Automobiles: New Women on the Move', in Angelique Richardson and Chris Willis (eds.), *The New Woman in Fiction and in Fact: Fin de Siècle Feminisms* (Palgrave, 2001), pp. 66–78; and Patricia Marks, *Bicycles, Bangs, and Bloomers: The New Woman in the Popular Press* (University Press of Kentucky, 1990).

101. *Cyclist* (13 September 1893), p. 805, cited in Rubinstein, *Before the Suffragettes*, 218. For further discussion of dress reform see Kathleen Waldon, 'Clothes and the Woman', *Physical Culture* (later *Sandow's Magazine of Physical Culture*) 1 (1898), 92–8; C. Willett Cunnington, *English Women's Clothing in the Nineteenth Century* (Faber, 1937) and Elizabeth Ewing, *Fashion in Underwear* (Batsford, 1971).

102. Hall, *A Study in Bloomers*, pp. 32–3, 42.

103. 'Women of Note in the Cycling World: A Chat with Madame Sarah Grand', *Hub* 1 (1896), 419.

104. Hugh E. M. Stutfield, 'Tommyrotics', *Blackwood's Edinburgh Magazine* (1895), 837. Stutfield begins his article: 'A most excellent wag – quoted with approval by the grave and sedate *Spectator* – recently described modern fiction as 'erotic, neurotic and Tommyrotic' (p. 833). The *OED* gives the USA as the home of the word, its first recorded use in *Chicago Advance*, 4 July 1895: 'A whole school of what has been humorously called erotic and tommyrotic realists asserting that progress in art requires the elimination of moral ideas.'

105. Edith Ellis, *A Noviciate for Marriage* (Haslemere, 1894), p. 1.

106. Marx Aveling, *The Woman Question*, pp. 4–5. For an historical exploration of socialism in the context of the United States, see Seymour Martin Lipset and Gary Marks, *It Didn't Happen Here: Why Socialism Failed in the United States* (Norton, 2000).

107. Gilman, *Women and Economics*, p. 151.

108. See Naomi B. Zauderer, 'Consumption, Production, and Reproduction in the Work of Charlotte Perkins Gilman', in Jill Rudd and Val Gough (eds.), *Charlotte Perkins Gilman: Optimist Reformer* (University of Iowa Press, 1999).

109. Patricia Hollis, *Women in Public: The Women's Movement 1850–1900* (George Allen & Unwin, 1979), p. 53.

110. Barbara Drake, *Women in Trade Unions* (1920; Virago, 1984), p. 29. The all-female work force at the Bryant & May match factory in Bow went on strike for better conditions of work, supported by the radical socialist Annie Besant, who wrote an editorial on the subject 'White Slavery in London' for the *Law and Liberty League*'s weekly newspaper, *Link* (23 June 1888). The company conceded and the Union of Women Matchmakers was set up by the end of July 1888. See *Annie Besant: An Autobiography* (London: T. Fisher Unwin 1893), pp. 331–8.

111. Edith Searle Grossman, 'The New Sex Psychology', *Westminster Review* 172 (1909), 510.

112. See Stansell, *American Moderns*, p. 237.

113. White, *Women's Magazines*, p. 59.

114. Evelyn Sharp, 'To Prison while the Sun Shines', in *Rebel Women* (Women's Freedom League, 1910), pp. 24–5.

115. Sarah Grand, 'The Case of the Modern Married Woman', *Pall Mall Gazette* (1913), 209.

116. See John Higham, *Strangers in the Land: Patterns of American Nativism, 1860–1925* (Rutgers University Press, 1955; 2nd edn, 1988), and Richard Hofstadter, *Social Darwinism in American Thought*, rev. edn (Beacon Press, 1955). See also Mathew Frye Jacobson, *Whiteness of a Different Color: European Immigrants and the Alchemy of Race* (Harvard University Press, 1998). See also Daniel Kevles, *In the Name of Eugenics: Genetics and the Uses of Human Heredity* (1985; Harvard University Press, 1995 (with a new preface by the author)). For the emphasis on class within Britain, and the ways in which this informed feminism, see Angelique Richardson, *Love and Eugenics in the Late Nineteenth Century: Rational Reproduction and the New Woman* (Oxford University Press, 2003). For discussion of this preoccupation with class in relation to the British Empire, see David Cannadine, *Ornamentalism: How the British saw their Empire* (Penguin, 2001).

117. Hall, *A Study in Bloomers*, p. 196.

118. Charlotte Perkins Gilman, *Herland*, ed. Ann J. Lane (1915; Women's Press, 1979), p. 69, 72, and *With Her in Ourland*, ed. Mary Jo Deegan and Michael R. Hill (1916; Praeger Publishers, 1997), pp. 118–19; 120–21.

119. Bret Harte, 'The Rise of the "Short Story"', *Cornhill Magazine* 7 (1899), 8.

120. George Eliot, *Adam Bede* (1859; Penguin, 1980), p. 221.

121. Katherine Mansfield, 'Psychology', *The Collected Stories of Katherine Mansfield* (Penguin, 1981), p. 113.

122. Edith Wharton, 'Telling a Short Story', *The Writing of Fiction* (1924; Octagon Books, 1966), p. 58.

123. Perry, 'The Short Story', pp. 249, 250.

124. Stutfield, 'The Psychology of Feminism', p. 104.

125. Ibid., pp. 104–5.

126. Ibid., pp. 110–11.

127. Mansfield, 'Psychology', p. 111. Wharton, 'Telling a Short Story', p. 43.

128. Canby, *The Short Story*, p. 23.

129. Perry, 'The Short Story', p. 249.

130. Canby, *The Short Story*, p. 26.

131. W. T. Stead, 'Book of the Month: The Novel of the Modern Woman', *Review of Reviews* 10 (1894), 64.

132. Marholm, 'Neurotic Keynotes', p. 62.

133. Haweis, 'Women as Writers', p. 68.

134. Mansfield, 'Psychology', p. 115.

135. Egerton, 'A Keynote to Keynotes', p. 58.

136. Stutfield, 'The Psychology of Feminism', p. 104.

137. Marholm, 'The Woman of Today', pp. 33, 35.

138. William Dean Howells, 'Some Anomalies of the Short Story', *North American Review* 173 (1901), 423.

139. Sigmund Freud, 'Constructions in Analysis', *The Standard Edition of the Complete Psychological Works of Sigmund Freud*, trans. James Strachey (Hogarth Press, 1964), vol. 23, p. 268.

140. Sigmund Freud, *The Interpretation of Dreams* (1899), trans. James Strachey, Penguin Freud Library (Penguin, 1991), vol. 4, p. 769. Freud added this sentence in 1909. For the early circulation of Freud's ideas on dreams, see Frank J. Sulloway, *Freud: Biologist of the Mind: Beyond the psychoanalytic legend* (Fontana, 1980), pp. 346–50.

141. Freud, *The Interpretation of Dreams* (Penguin), pp. 634, 383.

142. Freud, 'The Dream-Work' forms chapter 6 of *The Interpretation of Dreams* (Penguin), p. 381.

143. Nordau, *Degeneration*, p. 6.

144. Freud, *The Interpretation of Dreams* (Penguin), p. 434.

145. Ibid., p. 722.

146. Ibid., pp. 722–3.

147. Stutfield, 'Tommyrotics', p. 844.

148. Freud, *The Interpretation of Dreams* (Penguin), p. 632.

149. Elizabeth Bowen, *Afterthought: Pieces about Writing* (Longman, 1962), p. 62.

150. Howells, 'Some Anomalies of the Short Story', p. 429.

FURTHER READING

Primary Sources

'The Higher Education of Women', *Westminster Review* 129 (1888), 152–62

Allen, Grant, *The Woman Who Did* (1895; Oxford: Oxford University Press, 1995)

Ammons, Elizabeth and Valerie Rohy (eds.), *American Local Color Writing, 1880–1920* (New York: Penguin, 1998)

Besant, Walter, *All Sorts and Conditions of Men* (1882; Oxford: Oxford University Press, 1997)

Biddis, Michael D. (ed.), *Images of Race* (Leicester: Leicester University Press, 1979)

Brooke, Emma Frances, *A Superfluous Woman* (London: Heinemann, 1894)

Butler, Josephine, *Social Purity: An Address* (London: Social Purity Alliance, 1879)

Caird, Mona, 'A Defence of the So-called "Wild Women"', *Nineteenth Century* 31 (1892), 811–29; reprinted in Heilmann, *The Late Victorian Marriage Debate*, vol. 1

—, *Romance of the Moors* (Leipzig: Heinemann and Balestier, 1892)

—, *The Daughters of Danaus* (London: Bliss, Sands & Foster, 1894)

—, *Stones of Sacrifice* (London: Simpkin, Marshall, Hamilton, Kent & Co. Ltd, 1915)

—, *The Great Wave* (London: Wishart, 1931)

—, *The Morality of Marriage and Other Essays*, in Heilmann, *The Late Victorian Marriage Debate*, vol. 1

Chapman, Elizabeth Rachel, *Marriage Questions in Modern Fiction and Other Essays on Kindred Subjects* (London and New York: John Lane, 1897)

Chopin, Kate, *Bayou Folk* and *A Night in Acadie*, ed. Bernard Koloski (1894 and 1897; New York: Penguin, 1999)

Dowie, Ménie Muriel, *Gallia*, ed. Helen Small (1895; London: J. M. Dent, 1995)

Eastwood, Mrs M., 'The New Woman in Fiction and in Fact', *Humanitarian* 5 (1894), 375–9

Egerton, George, *Keynotes and Discords*, ed. Martha Vicinus (1893 and 1894; London: Virago, 1983)

—, *Symphonies* (London and New York: John Lane, 1897)

—, *A Leaf from the Yellow Book: The Correspondence of George Egerton*, ed. Terence de Vere White (London: Richards Press, 1958)

Ellis, Henry Havelock, *Man and Woman: A Study of Human Secondary Sexual Characters* (London: Walter Scott, Ltd, 1894)

—, *The Problem of Race-Regeneration* (London, New York, Toronto and Melbourne: Cassell and Co., 1911)

Freud, Sigmund, *The Interpretation of Dreams*, trans. James Strachey (1899; Harmondsworth: Penguin, 1991), Freud Library, vol. 4

Fuller, Margaret, *Woman in the Nineteenth Century* (1845; Oxford: Oxford University Press, 1994)

Gilman, Charlotte Perkins, *Charlotte Perkins Gilman's Utopian Novels: 'Moving the Mountain', 'Herland' and 'With Her in Ourland'*, ed. Minna Doskow (Madison, NJ and London: Fairleigh Dickinson University Press, 1999)

Gissing, George, *The Odd Women*, ed. Elaine Showalter (1893; Harmondsworth: Penguin, 1993)

Grand, Sarah, *The Heavenly Twins* (1893; Michigan: Ann Arbor Paperbacks, 1992)

—, 'The Modern Girl', *North American Review* 158 (1894), 706–14

—, [with Thomas Hardy, Max Nordau et al.], 'The Tree of Knowledge', *New Review* 10 (1894), 675–90

—, 'Eugenia, A Modern Maiden and a Man Amazed', in *Our Manifold Nature* (London: William Heinemann, 1894)

—, 'Marriage Questions in Fiction', *Fortnightly Review* 63 (Jan.–June 1898), 378–89

—, 'On the Choice of a Husband', *Young Woman* 7 (1898–9), 1–9

—, [with Mona Caird et al.], 'Does Marriage Hinder a Woman's Self-Development?', *Ladies' Realm* 5 (1898–9), 576–86

—, *Emotional Moments* (London: Hurst and Blackett Ltd, 1908)

Greg, William Rathbone, 'Why are Women Redundant?', *National Review* 14 (1862), 434–60

Hall, George F., *A Study in Bloomers, or, The Model New Woman* (Philadelphia and Stockton: American Bible House, 1895)

Hardy, Thomas [with Sarah Grand et al.], 'Candour in English Fiction', *New Review* 2 (1890), 15–21

Harrison, Frederic, 'The Emancipation of Women', *Fortnightly Review* 56 (1891), 437–52

Heilmann, Ann (ed.), *The Late Victorian Marriage Debate: A Collection of Key New Woman Texts*, 5 vols. (London and New York: Routledge and Thoemmes Press, 1998)

Hogarth, Janet E., 'Literary Degenerates', *Fortnightly Review* 63 (1895), 586–92

James, Henry, *Daisy Miller* (1878; Harmondsworth: Penguin, 1986)

—, *The Bostonians* (1886; London: Penguin, 2000)

—, *The American Scene* (1907; London: Penguin, 1994)

Linton, Eliza Lynn, 'The Wild Women as Social Insurgents', *Nineteenth Century* 30 (1891), 596–605

Mansfield, Katherine, *The Collected Stories of Katherine Mansfield* (Harmondsworth: Penguin, 1981)

Mill, John Stuart, *The Subjection of Women*, ed. Mary Warnock (London: J. M. Dent, 1985)

Nordau, Max, *Degeneration* (1892), trans. from 2nd edn (1895; Lincoln and London: University of Nebraska Press, 1968)

Schreiner, Olive, *The Story of an African Farm* (1883; London: Century Hutchinson Ltd, 1987)

—, *Woman and Labour* (1911; London: Virago, 1978)

Sharp, Evelyn, *Rebel Women* (London: Women's Freedom League, 1910)

Stanton, Elizabeth Cady, *The Woman's Bible* (1895, 1898; New York: Prometheus Books, 1999)

Swiney, Frances, *The Awakening of Women, or Woman's Part in Evolution* (London: William Reeves, 1899)

Tooley, Sarah A., 'The Woman Question: An Interview with Madame Sarah Grand', *Humanitarian* 8 (1896), 161–9

Wollstonecraft, Mary, *A Vindication of the Rights of Woman* (1792; London: J. M. Dent, 1986)

Woolf, Virginia, *A Room of One's Own* (1929; Harmondsworth: Penguin, 1992)

Zitkala-Ša, *American Indian Stories* (1921; Lincoln and London: University of Nebraska Press, 1985)

Secondary Sources

Acocella, Joan, *Willa Cather and the Politics of Criticism* (Lincoln: University of Nebraska Press, 2000)

Ardis, Ann, *New Women, New Novels: Feminism and Early Modernism* (New Brunswick: Rutgers University Press, 1990)

Boumelha, Penny, *Thomas Hardy and Women: Sexual Ideology and Narrative Form* (Brighton: Harvester Press, 1982)

Bourne Taylor, Jenny, and Sally Shuttleworth (eds.), *Embodied Selves: An Anthology of Psychological Texts, 1830–1890* (Oxford: Oxford University Press, 1998)

Bremner, C. S., *Education of Girls and Women in Great Britain* (London: Swan Sonnenschein, 1897)

Burdett, Carolyn, *Olive Schreiner and the Progress of Feminism: Evolution, Gender, Empire* (Basingstoke: Palgrave, 2001)

Caine, Barbara, *Victorian Feminists* (Oxford: Oxford University Press, 1992)

Cott, Nancy, *The Grounding of Modern Feminism* (New Haven: Yale University Press, 1987)

Cunningham, Gail, *The New Woman and the Victorian Novel* (London: Macmillan Press Ltd, 1978)

David, Deirdre, *Rule Britannia: Women, Empire and Victorian Writing* (Ithaca: Cornell University Press, 1995)

Dutta, Shanta, *Ambivalence in Hardy: A Study of his Attitude to Women* (Basingstoke: Macmillan, 2000)

Dyhouse, Carol, *No Distinction of Sex? Women in British Universities 1870–1939* (London: UCL Press, 1995)

Fletcher, Ian, 'Some Aspects of Aestheticism', in O. M. Brock (ed.), *Twilight of Dawn: Studies in English Literature in Transition* (Tucson: Arizona State University, 1987)

Flexner, Eleanor, *Century of Struggle: The Woman's Rights Movement in the United States* (Cambridge: Harvard University Press, 1976)

Gagnier, Regenia (ed.), *Critical Essays on Oscar Wilde* (New York and Oxford: G. K. Hall and Maxwell Macmillan International, 1991)

—, *Subjectivities: A History of Self-Representation in Britain (1832– 1920)* (New York and Oxford: Oxford University Press, 1991)

Gallagher, Catherine, and Thomas Laqueur (eds.), *The Making of the Modern Body: Sexuality and Society in the Nineteenth Century* (Berkeley, Los Angeles and London: University of California Press, 1987)

Gardiner, Juliet (ed.), *The New Woman: Women's Voices 1880–1918* (London: Collins & Brown, 1993)

Gilbert, Sandra, and Susan Gubar, *The Madwoman in the Attic: The Woman Writer and the Nineteenth-Century Literary Imagination* (New Haven: Yale University Press, 1979)

Golden, Catherine (ed.), *The Captive Imagination: A Casebook on 'The Yellow Wallpaper'* (New York: Feminist Press at the City University of New York, 1992)

Gomersall, Meg, *Working-Class Girls in Nineteenth-Century England: Life, Work and Schooling* (Basingstoke and New York: Macmillan and St Martin's Press, 1997)

Harris, Wendell V., 'Identifying the Decadent Fiction of the Eighteen-Nineties', *PMLA* (1962), 1–13

Hunt, Felicity (ed.), *Lessons for Life: The Schooling of Girls and Women, 1850–1950* (Oxford: Basil Blackwell, 1987)

John, Angela V. (ed.), *Unequal Opportunities: Women's Employment in England 1800–1918* (Oxford: Blackwell, 1986)

Kersley, Gillian, *Darling Madame: Sarah Grand & Devoted Friend* (London: Virago, 1983)

Koloski, Bernard, *Kate Chopin: A Study of the Short Fiction* (New York: Twayne, 1996)

Lane, Ann J., *To 'Herland' and Beyond: The Life and Work of Charlotte Perkins Gilman* (New York: Pantheon, 1990)

Ledger, Sally, *The New Woman: Fiction and Feminism at the Fin de Siècle* (Manchester: Manchester University Press, 1997)

Levine, Philippa, *Feminist Lives in Victorian England: Private Roles and Public Commitment* (Oxford: Basil Blackwell, 1990)

Levy, Andrew, *The Cultural Commerce of the American Short Story* (Cambridge: Cambridge University Press, 1993)

Lewis, Jane (ed.), *Before the Vote was Won: Arguments For and Against Women's Suffrage 1864–1896* (London: Routledge, 1987)

Linehan, Katherine Bailey, '*The Odd Women*: Gissing's Imaginative Approach to Feminism', *Modern Language Quarterly* 40 (1979), 358–75

Marks, Patricia, *Bicycles, Bangs, and Bloomers: The New Woman in the Popular Press* (Lexington: University Press of Kentucky, 1990)

Meyering, Sheryl L., *Charlotte Perkins Gilman: The Woman and Her Work* (Ann Arbor: UMI Research Press, 1989)

Miller, Jane Eldridge, *Rebel Women: Feminism, Modernism and the Edwardian Novel* (London: Virago, 1994)

Nelson, Claudia, and Ann Sumner Holmes (eds.), *Maternal Instincts: Visions of Motherhood and Sexuality in Britain, 1875–1925* (New York and Basingstoke: St Martin's Press and Macmillan, 1997)

Papke, Mary E., *Verging on the Abyss: The Social Fiction of Kate Chopin and Edith Wharton* (Westport, CT: Greenwood, 1990)

Pick, Daniel, *Faces of Degeneration: A European Disorder, c1848–c1918* (Cambridge: Cambridge University Press, 1993)

Richardson, Angelique, 'The Eugenization of Love: Sarah Grand and the Morality of Genealogy', *Victorian Studies* 42 (1999/2000), 227–55

—, *Love and Eugenics in the Late Nineteenth Century: Rational Reproduction and the New Woman* (Oxford: Oxford University Press, 2003)

—, and Chris Willis (eds.), *The New Woman in Fiction and in Fact: Fin de Siècle Feminisms* (Basingstoke: Palgrave, 2001)

Roberts, Elizabeth, *A Woman's Place: An Oral History of Working-Class Women, 1890–1940* (Oxford: Basil Blackwell, 1984)

Rowold, Katharina (ed.), *Gender and Science: Nineteenth-Century Debates on the Female Mind and Body* (Bristol: Thoemmes Press, 1996)

Rubenstein, David, *Before the Suffragettes: Women's Emancipation in the 1890s* (Brighton: Harvester, 1986)

Rudd, Jill, and Val Gough (eds.), *Charlotte Perkins Gilman: Optimist Reformer* (Iowa City: University of Iowa Press, 1999)

Russett, Cynthia Eagle, *Sexual Science: The Victorian Construction of Womanhood* (1989; Cambridge and London: Harvard University Press, 1991)

Shanley, Mary Lyndon, *Feminism, Marriage and the Law in Victorian England, 1850–1895* (London: I. B. Tauris and Co., 1989)

Showalter, Elaine, *A Literature of Their Own, from Charlotte Brontë to Doris Lessing* (1977; London: Virago, 1982)

—, *The Female Malady: Women, Madness and English Culture, 1830–1980* (1985; London: Virago, 1993)

—, *Sexual Anarchy: Gender and Culture at the Fin de Siècle* (1990; London: Virago, 1992)

—, *Sister's Choice, Tradition and Change in American Women's Writing* (Oxford: Oxford University Press, 1994)

Smith-Rosenberg, Carol, *Disorderly Conduct: Visions of Gender in Victorian America* (New York: Knopf, 1985)

Stansell, Christine, *American Moderns: Bohemian New York and the Creation of a New Century* (New York: Henry Holt, 2000)

Stepan, Nancy Leys, *The Idea of Race in Science: Great Britain 1800–1960* (London: Macmillan, 1982)

Tate, Claudia, 'Pauline Hopkins: Our Literary Foremother', in *Conjuring: Black Women, Fiction, and Literary Tradition*, ed. Marjorie Pryse and Hortense J. Spillers (Bloomington: Indiana University Press, 1985), pp. 53–66

Taylor, Barbara, *Eve and the New Jerusalem* (London: Virago, 1983)

Vicinus, Martha, *Independent Women: Work and Community for Single Women 1850–1920* (London: Virago, 1985)

Zimmern, Alice, *The Renaissance of Girls' Education in England* (London: A. D. Innes, 1898)

NOTE ON THE TEXTS

The sources for the stories are given in the Notes. Because these sources follow different house styles, some standardization has been applied in this volume. For punctuation: single quotation marks (dialogue and emphasis), titles without a full stop (Mr, Mrs, Dr, St), numbering and spacing for internal divisions, and paragraphing in 'She-Notes'. Variations in spelling and hyphenation are smoothed out, e.g. grey/gray, enquire/inquire, drawing room/drawing-room, wallpaper/wall-paper (see also headnote in the Notes to 'The Yellow Wallpaper').

WOMEN WHO DID

Stories by Men and Women, 1890–1914

OSCAR WILDE

The Sphinx without a Secret

One afternoon I was sitting outside the Café de la Paix,[1] watching the splendour and shabbiness of Parisian life, and wondering over my vermouth at the strange panorama of pride and poverty that was passing before me, when I heard some one call my name. I turned round, and saw Lord Murchison. We had not met since we had been at college together, nearly ten years before, so I was delighted to come across him again, and we shook hands warmly. At Oxford we had been great friends. I had liked him immensely, he was so handsome, so high-spirited and so honourable. We used to say of him that he would be the best of fellows, if he did not always speak the truth, but I think we really admired him all the more for his frankness. I found him a good deal changed. He looked anxious and puzzled, and seemed to be in doubt about something. I felt it could not be modern scepticism, for Murchison was the stoutest of Tories, and believed in the Pentateuch[2] as firmly as he believed in the House of Peers; so I concluded that it was a woman, and asked him if he was married yet.

'I don't understand women well enough,' he answered.

'My dear Gerald,' I said, 'women are meant to be loved, not to be understood.'

'I cannot love where I cannot trust,' he replied.

'I believe you have a mystery in your life, Gerald,' I exclaimed; 'tell me about it.'

'Let us go for a drive,' he answered, 'it is too crowded here. No, not a yellow carriage, any other colour – there, that dark green one will do'; and in a few moments we were trotting down the boulevard in the direction of the Madeleine.

'Where shall we go to?' I said.

3

'Oh, anywhere you like!' he answered – 'to the restaurant in the Bois;[3] we will dine there, and you shall tell me all about yourself.'

'I want to hear about you first,' I said. 'Tell me your mystery.'

He took from his pocket a little silver-clasped morocco case, and handed it to me. I opened it. Inside there was the photograph of a woman. She was tall and slight, and strangely picturesque with her large vague eyes and loosened hair. She looked like a *clairvoyante*, and was wrapped in rich furs.

'What do you think of that face?' he said; 'is it truthful?'

I examined it carefully. It seemed to me the face of someone who had a secret, but whether that secret was good or evil I could not say. Its beauty was a beauty moulded out of many mysteries – the beauty, in fact, which is psychological, not plastic – and the faint smile that just played across the lips was far too subtle to be really sweet.

'Well,' he cried impatiently, 'what do you say?'

'She is the Gioconda[4] in sables,' I answered. 'Let me know all about her.'

'Not now,' he said; 'after dinner', and began to talk of other things.

When the waiter brought us our coffee and cigarettes I reminded Gerald of his promise. He rose from his seat, walked two or three times up and down the room, and, sinking into an armchair, told me the following story: –

'One evening,' he said, 'I was walking down Bond Street about five o'clock. There was a terrific crush of carriages, and the traffic was almost stopped. Close to the pavement was standing a little yellow brougham, which, for some reason or other, attracted my attention. As I passed by there looked out from it the face I showed you this afternoon. It fascinated me immediately. All that night I kept thinking of it, and all the next day. I wandered up and down that wretched Row, peering into every carriage, and waiting for the yellow brougham; but I could not find *ma belle inconnue*, and at last I began to think she was merely a dream. About a week afterwards I was dining with Madame de Rastail. Dinner was for eight o'clock; but at half-past eight we were still waiting in the drawing room. Finally the servant threw open the door, and announced Lady Alroy. It was the woman I had been looking for. She came in very slowly, looking like a moonbeam in grey lace, and, to my intense delight, I was asked to take her in to dinner. After we had sat down, I remarked quite innocently, "I think I caught sight of you in Bond Street some time ago, Lady Alroy." She grew very pale, and said to me in a low voice, "Pray do not talk so loud; you may be overheard." I felt miserable at having made such a bad beginning, and plunged recklessly into the subject of the French plays. She spoke very little, always in the same low musical voice, and seemed as if she was afraid of some one listening. I fell passionately, stupidly in love, and the indefinable atmosphere of mystery that surrounded her excited my most ardent curiosity. When she was going away, which she did very soon after dinner, I asked her if I might call and see her. She hesitated for a moment, glanced round to see if any one was near us, and then said, "Yes; tomorrow at a quarter to five." I begged Madame de Rastail to tell me about her; but all that I could learn was that she was a widow with a beautiful house in Park Lane, and as some scientific bore began a dissertation on widows, as exemplifying the survival of the matrimonially fittest, I left and went home.

'The next day I arrived at Park Lane punctual to the moment, but was told by the butler that Lady Alroy had just gone out. I went down to the club quite unhappy and very much puzzled, and after long consideration wrote her a letter, asking if I might be allowed to try my chance some other afternoon. I had no answer for several days, but at last I got a little note saying she would be at home on Sunday at four and with this extraordinary postscript: "Please do not write to me here again; I will explain when I see you." On Sunday she received me, and was perfectly charming; but when I was going away she begged of me, if I ever had occasion to write to her again, to address my letter to "Mrs Knox, care of Whittaker's Library, Green Street". "There are reasons," she said, "why I cannot receive letters in my own house."

'All through the season I saw a great deal of her, and the atmosphere of mystery never left her. Sometimes I thought that she was in the power of some man, but she looked so unapproachable that I could not believe it. It was really very difficult for me to come to any conclusion, for she was like one of those strange crystals that one sees in museums, which are at one moment clear, and at another clouded. At last I determined to ask her to be my wife: I was sick and tired of the incessant secrecy that she imposed on all my visits, and on the few letters I sent her. I wrote to her at the library to ask her if she could see me the following Monday at six. She answered yes, and I was in the seventh heaven of delight. I was infatuated with her: in spite of the mystery, I thought then – in consequence of it, I see now. No; it was the woman herself I loved. The mystery troubled me, maddened me. Why did chance put me in its track?'

'You discovered it, then?' I cried.

'I fear so,' he answered. 'You can judge for yourself.'

'When Monday came round I went to lunch with my uncle, and about four o'clock found myself in the Marylebone Road. My uncle, you know, lives in Regent's Park. I wanted to get to Piccadilly, and took a short cut through a lot of shabby little streets. Suddenly I saw in front of me Lady Alroy, deeply veiled and walking very fast. On coming to the last house in the street, she went up the steps, took out a latchkey and let herself in. "Here is the mystery," I said to myself; and I hurried on and examined the house. It seemed a sort of place for letting lodgings. On the doorstep lay her handkerchief, which she had dropped. I picked it up and put it in my pocket. Then I began to consider what I should do. I came to the conclusion that I had no right to spy on her, and I drove down to the club. At six I called to see her. She was lying on a sofa, in a tea gown of silver tissue looped up by some strange moonstones that she always wore. She was looking quite lovely. "I am so glad to see you," she said; "I have not been out all day." I stared at her in amazement, and pulling the handkerchief out of my pocket, handed it to her. "You dropped this in Cumnor Street this afternoon, Lady Alroy," I said very calmly. She looked at me in terror, but made no attempt to take the handkerchief. "What were you doing there?" I asked. "What right have you to question me?" she answered. "The right of a man who loves you," I replied; "I came here to ask you to be my wife." She hid her face in her hands, and burst into floods of tears. "You must tell me," I continued. She stood up, and, looking me straight in the face, said, "Lord Murchison, there is nothing to tell you." – "You went to meet someone," I cried;

"this is your mystery." She grew dreadfully white, and said, "I went to meet no one." – "Can't you tell the truth?" I exclaimed. "I have told it," she replied. I was mad, frantic; I don't know what I said, but I said terrible things to her. Finally I rushed out of the house. She wrote me a letter the next day; I sent it back unopened, and started for Norway with Alan Colville. After a month I came back, and the first thing I saw in the *Morning Post*[5] was the death of Lady Alroy. She had caught a chill at the Opera, and had died in five days of congestion of the lungs. I shut myself up and saw no one. I had loved her so much, I had loved her so madly. Good God! how I had loved that woman!'

'You went to the street, to the house in it?' I said.

'Yes,' he answered.

'One day I went to Cumnor Street. I could not help it; I was tortured with doubt. I knocked at the door, and a respectable-looking woman opened it to me. I asked her if she had any rooms to let. "Well, sir," she replied, "the drawing rooms are supposed to be let; but I have not seen the lady for three months, and as rent is owing on them, you can have them." – "Is this the lady?" I said, showing the photograph. "That's her, sure enough," she exclaimed; "and when is she coming back, sir?" – "The lady is dead," I replied. "Oh, sir, I hope not!" said the woman; "she was my best lodger. She paid me three guineas a week merely to sit in my drawing rooms now and then." – "She met someone here?" I said; but the woman assured me that it was not so, that she always came alone, and saw no one. "What on earth did she do here?" I cried. "She simply sat in the drawing room, sir, reading books, and sometimes had tea," the woman answered. I did not know what to say, so I gave her a sovereign and went away. Now, what do you think it all meant? You don't believe the woman was telling the truth?'

'I do.'

'Then why did Lady Alroy go there?'

'My dear Gerald,' I answered, 'Lady Alroy was simply a woman with a mania for mystery. She took these rooms for the pleasure of going there with her veil down, and imagining she was a heroine. She had a passion for secrecy, but she herself was merely a Sphinx without a secret.'

'Do you really think so?'

'I am sure of it,' I replied.

He took out the morocco case, opened it and looked at the photograph. 'I wonder?' he said at last.

OLIVE SCHREINER

The Buddhist Priest's Wife

Cover her up! How still it lies! You can see the outline under the white. You would think she was asleep. Let the sunshine come in; it loved it so. She that had travelled so far, in so many lands, and done so much and seen so much, how she must like rest now! Did she ever love anything absolutely, this woman whom so many men loved, and so many women; who gave so much sympathy and never asked for anything in return! did she ever need a love she could not have? Was she never obliged to unclasp her fingers from anything to which they clung? Was she really so strong as she looked? Did she never wake up in the night crying for that which she could not have? Were thought and travel enough for her? Did she go about for long days with a weight that crushed her to earth? Cover her up! I do not think she would have liked us to look at her. In one way she was alone all her life; she would have liked to be alone now! . . . Life must have been very beautiful to her, or she would not look so young now. Cover her up! Let us go!

Many years ago in a London room, up long flights of stairs, a fire burnt up in a grate. It showed the marks on the walls where pictures had been taken down, and the little blue flowers in the wallpaper and the blue felt carpet on the floor, and a woman sat by the fire in a chair at one side.

Presently the door opened, and the old woman came in who took care of the entrance hall downstairs.

'Do you not want anything tonight?' she said.

'No, I am only waiting for a visitor; when they have been, I shall go.'

'Have you got all your things taken away already?'

'Yes, only these I am leaving.'

The old woman went down again, but presently came up with a cup of tea in her hand.

'You must drink that; it's good for one. Nothing helps one like tea when one's been packing all day.'

The young woman at the fire did not thank her, but she ran her hand over the old woman's from the wrist to the fingers.

'I'll say goodbye to you when I go out.'

The woman poked the fire, put the last coals on and went.

When she had gone the young one did not drink the tea, but drew her little silver cigarette case from her pocket and lighted a cigarette. For a while she sat smoking by the fire; then she stood up and walked the room.

When she had paced for a while she sat down again beside the fire. She threw the end of her cigarette away into the fire, and then began to walk again with her hands behind her. Then she went back to her seat and lit another cigarette, and paced again. Presently she sat down, and looked into the fire; she pressed the palms of her hands together, and then sat quietly staring into it.

Then there was a sound of feet on the stairs and someone knocked at the door.

She rose and threw the end into the fire and said without moving, 'Come in.'

The door opened and a man stood there in evening dress. He had a great-coat on, open in front.

'May I come in? I couldn't get rid of this downstairs; I didn't see where to leave it!' He took his coat off. 'How are you? This is a real bird's nest!'

She motioned to a chair.

'I hope you did not mind my asking you to come?'

'Oh no, I am delighted. I only found your note at my club twenty minutes ago.'

He sat down on a chair before the fire.

'So you really are going to India? How delightful! But what are you to do there? I think it was Grey told me six weeks ago you were going, but regarded it as one of those mythical stories which don't deserve credence. Yet I'm sure I don't know! Why, nothing would surprise me.'

He looked at her in a half-amused, half-interested way.

'What a long time it is since we met! Six months, eight?'

'Seven,' she said.

'I really thought you were trying to avoid me. What have you been doing with yourself all this time?'

'Oh, been busy. Won't you have a cigarette?'

She held out the little case to him.

'Won't you take one yourself? I know you object to smoking with men, but you can make an exception in my case!'

'Thank you.' She lit her own and passed him the matches.

'But really what have you been doing with yourself all this time? You've entirely disappeared from civilized life. When I was down at the Grahams' in the spring, they said you were coming down there, and then at the last moment cried off. We were all quite disappointed. What is taking you to India now? Going to preach the doctrine of social and intellectual equality to the Hindu women and incite them to revolt? Marry some old Buddhist Priest, build a little cottage on the top of the Himalayas and live there, discuss philosophy and meditate? I believe that's what you'd like. I really shouldn't wonder if I heard you'd done it!'

She laughed and took out her cigarette case.

She smoked slowly.

'I've been here a long time, four years, and I want change. I was glad to see how well you succeeded in that election,' she said. 'You were much interested in it, were you not?'

'Oh, yes. We had a stiff fight. It tells in my favour, you know, though it was not exactly a personal matter. But it was a great worry.'

'Don't you think,' she said, 'you were wrong in sending that letter to the papers? It would have strengthened your position to have remained silent.'

'Yes, perhaps so; I think so now, but I did it under advice. However, we've won, so it's all right.' He leaned back in the chair.

'Are you pretty fit?'

'Oh, yes; pretty well; bored, you know. One doesn't know what all this working and striving is for sometimes.'

'Where are you going for your holiday this year?'

'Oh, Scotland, I suppose; I always do; the old quarters.'

'Why don't you go to Norway? It would be more change for you and rest you more. Did you get a book on sport in Norway?'

'Did you send it me? How kind of you! I read it with much interest. I was almost inclined to start off there and then. I suppose it is the kind of *vis inertiae* that creeps over one as one grows older that sends one back to the old place. A change would be much better.'

'There's a list at the end of the book,' she said, 'of exactly the things one needs to take. I thought it would save trouble; you could just give it to your man, and let him get them all. Have you still got him?'

'Oh, yes. He's as faithful to me as a dog. I think nothing would induce him to leave me. He won't allow me to go out hunting since I sprained my foot last autumn. I have to do it surreptitiously. He thinks I can't keep my seat with a sprained ankle; but he's a very good fellow; takes care of me like a mother.' He smoked quietly with the firelight glowing on his black coat. 'But what are you going to India for? Do you know anyone there?'

'No,' she said. 'I think it will be so splendid. I've always been a great deal interested in the East. It's a complex, interesting life.'

He turned and looked at her.

'Going to seek for more experience, you'll say, I suppose. I never knew a woman throw herself away as you do; a woman with your brilliant parts and attractions, to let the whole of life slip through your hands, and make nothing of it. You ought to be the most successful woman in London. Oh, yes; I know what you are going to say: "You don't care." That's just it; you don't. You are always going to get experience, going to get everything, and you never do. You are always going to write when you know enough, and you are never satisfied that you do. You ought to be making your two thousand a year, but you don't care. That's just it! Living, burying yourself here with a lot of old frumps. You will never do anything. You could have everything and you let it slip.'

'Oh, my life is very full,' she said. 'There are only two things that are absolute realities, love and knowledge, and you can't escape them.'

She had thrown her cigarette end away and was looking into the fire, smiling.

'I've let these rooms to a woman friend of mine.' She glanced round the room, smiling. 'She doesn't know I'm going to leave these things here for her. She'll like them because they were mine. The world's very beautiful, I think – delicious.'

'Oh, yes. But what do you do with it? What do you make of it? You ought to settle down and marry like other women, not go wandering about the world to India and China and Italy, and God knows where. You are simply making a mess of your life. You're always surrounding yourself with all sorts of extraordinary people. If I hear any man or woman is a great friend of yours, I always say: "What's the matter? Lost his money? Lost his character? Got an incurable disease?" I believe the only way in which anyone becomes interesting to you is by having some complaint of mind or body. I believe you worship rags. To come and shut yourself up in a place like this away from everybody and everything! It's a mistake; it's idiotic, you know.'

'I'm very happy,' she said. 'You see,' she said, leaning forwards towards the fire with her hands on her knees, 'what matters is that something should need you. It isn't a question of love. What's the use of being near a thing if other people could serve it as well as you can. If they could serve it better, it's pure selfishness. It's the need of one thing for another that makes the organic bond of union. You love mountains and horses, but they don't need you; so what's the use of saying anything about it! I suppose the most absolutely delicious thing in life is to feel a thing needs you, and to give at the moment it needs. Things that don't need you, you must love from a distance.'

'Oh, but a woman like you ought to marry, ought to have children. You go squandering yourself on every old beggar or forlorn female or escaped criminal you meet; it may be very nice for them, but it's a mistake from your point of view.'

He touched the ash gently with the tip of his little finger and let it fall.

'I intend to marry. It's a curious thing,' he said, resuming his pose with an elbow on one knee and his head bent forward on one side, so that she saw the brown hair with its close curls a little tinged with grey at the sides, 'that when a man reaches a certain age he wants to marry. He doesn't fall in love; it's not that he definitely plans anything; but he has a feeling that he ought to have a home and a wife and children. I suppose it is the same kind of feeling that makes a bird build nests at certain times of the year. It's not love; it's something else. When I was a young man I used to despise men for getting married; wondered what they did it for; they had everything to lose and nothing to gain. But when a man gets to be six-and-thirty his feeling changes. It's not love, passion, he wants; it's a home; it's a wife and children. He may have a house and servants; it isn't the same thing. I should have thought a woman would have felt it too.'

She was quiet for a minute, holding a cigarette between her fingers; then she said slowly:

'Yes, at times a woman has a curious longing to have a child, especially when she gets near to thirty or over it. It's something distinct from love for any definite person. But it's a thing one has to get over. For a woman, marriage is much more serious than for a man. She might pass her life without meeting a man whom she could possibly love, and, if she met him, it might not be right or possible. Marriage has become very complex now it has become so largely intellectual. Won't you have another?'

She held out the case to him. 'You can light it from mine.' She bent forward for him to light it.

'You are a man who ought to marry. You've no absorbing mental work with which the woman would interfere; it would complete you.' She sat back, smoking serenely.

'Yes,' he said, 'but life is too busy; I never find time to look for one, and I haven't a fancy for the pink-and-white prettiness so common and that some men like so. I need something else. If I am to have a wife I shall have to go to America to look for one.'

'Yes, an American would suit you best.'

'Yes,' he said, 'I don't want a woman to look after; she must be self-sustaining and she mustn't bore you. You know what I mean. Life is too full of cares to have a helpless child added to them.'

'Yes,' she said, standing up and leaning with her elbow against the fireplace. 'The kind of woman you want would be young and strong; she need not be excessively beautiful, but she must be attractive; she must have energy, but not too strongly marked an individuality; she must be largely neutral; she need not give you too passionate or too deep a devotion, but she must second you in a thoroughly rational manner. She must have the same aims and tastes that you have. No woman has the right to marry a man if she has to bend herself out of shape for him. She might wish to, but she could never be to him with all her passionate endeavour what the other woman could be to him without trying. Character will dominate over all and will come out at last.'

She looked down into the fire.

'When you marry you mustn't marry a woman who flatters you too much. It is always a sign of falseness somewhere. If a woman absolutely loves you as herself, she will criticize and understand you as herself. Two people who are to live through life together must be able to look into each other's eyes and speak the truth. That helps one through life. You would find many such women in America,' she said: 'women who would help you to succeed, who would not drag you down.'

'Yes, that's my idea. But how am I to obtain the ideal woman?'

'Go and look for her. Go to America instead of Scotland this year. It is perfectly right. A man has a right to look for what he needs. With a woman it is different. That's one of the radical differences between men and women.'

She looked downwards into the fire.

'It's a law of her nature and of sex relationship. There's nothing arbitrary or conventional about it any more than there is in her having to bear her child while the male does not. Intellectually we may both be alike. I suppose if fifty men and fifty women had to solve a mathematical problem, they would all do it in the same way; the more abstract and intellectual, the more alike we are. The nearer you approach to the personal and sexual, the more different we are. If I were to represent men's and women's natures,' she said, 'by a diagram, I would take two circular discs; the right side of each I should paint bright red; then I would shade the red away till in a spot on the left edge it became blue in the one and green in the other. That spot represents sex, and the nearer you come to it, the more the two discs differ in colour. Well then, if you turn them so that the red sides touch, they seem to be exactly alike, but if you turn them so that the green and blue paint form their point of contact, they will seem to be entirely unlike. That's why you notice the brutal, sensual men invariably believe women are entirely different from men, another species of creature; and very cultured, intellectual men sometimes believe we are exactly alike. You see, sex love in its substance may be the same in both of us; in the form of its expression it must differ. It is not man's fault; it is nature's. If a man loves a woman, he has a right to try to make her love him because he can do it openly, directly, without bending. There need be no subtlety, no indirectness. With a woman it's not so; she can take no love that is not laid openly, simply, at her feet. Nature ordains that she should never show what she feels; the woman who had told a man she loved him would have put between them a barrier once and for ever that could not be crossed; and if she subtly drew him towards her, using the woman's means – silence, finesse, the dropped handkerchief, the surprise visit, the gentle assertion she had not thought to see him when she had come a long way to meet him, then she would be damned; she would hold the love, but she would have desecrated it by subtlety; it would have no value. Therefore she must always go with her arms folded sexually; only the love which lays itself down at her feet and implores of her to accept it is love she can ever rightly take up. That is the true difference between a man and a woman. You may seek for love because you can do it openly; we cannot because we must do it subtly. A woman should always walk with her arms folded. Of course friendship is different. You are on a perfect equality with man then; you can ask him to come and see you as I asked you. That's the beauty of the intellect and intellectual life to a woman, that she drops her shackles a little; and that is why she shrinks from sex so. If she were dying perhaps, or doing something equal to death, she might . . . Death means so much more to a woman than a man; when you knew you were dying, to look round on the world and feel the bond of sex that has broken and crushed you all your life gone, nothing but the human left, no woman any more, to meet everything on perfectly even ground. There's no reason why you shouldn't go to America and look for a wife perfectly deliberately. You will have to tell no lies. Look till you find a woman that you absolutely love, that you have not the smallest doubt suits you apart from love, and then ask her to marry you. You must have children; the life of an old childless man is very sad.'

'Yes, I should like to have children. I often feel now, what is it all for, this work, this striving, and no one to leave it to? It's a blank, suppose I succeed . . . ?'

'Suppose you get your title?'

'Yes; what is it all worth to me if I've no one to leave it to? That's my feeling. It's really very strange to be sitting and talking like this to you. But you are so different from other women. If all women were like you, all your theories of the equality of men and women would work. You're the only woman with whom I never realize that she is a woman.'

'Yes,' she said.

She stood looking down into the fire.

'How long will you stay in India?'

'Oh, I'm not coming back.'

'Not coming back! That's impossible. You will be breaking the hearts of half the people here if you don't. I never knew a woman who had such power of entrapping men's hearts as you have in spite of that philosophy of yours. I don't know,' he smiled, 'that I should not have fallen into the snare myself – three years ago I almost thought I should – if you hadn't always attacked me so incontinently and persistently on all and every point and on each and every occasion. A man doesn't like pain. A succession of slaps damps him. But it doesn't seem to have that effect on other men . . . There was that fellow down in the country when I was there last year, perfectly ridiculous. You know his name . . .' He moved his fingers to try and remember it – 'big, yellow moustache, a major, gone to the east coast of Africa now; the ladies unearthed it that he was always carrying about a photograph of yours in his pocket; and he used to take out little scraps of things you printed and show them to people mysteriously. He almost had a duel with a man one night after dinner because he mentioned you; he seemed to think there was something incongruous between your name and —'

'I do not like to talk of any man who has loved me,' she said. 'However small and poor his nature may be, he has given me his best. There is nothing ridiculous in love. I think a woman should feel that all the love men have given her which she has not been able to return is a kind of crown set up above her which she is always trying to grow tall enough to wear. I can't bear to think that all the love that has been given me has been wasted on something unworthy of it. Men have been very beautiful and greatly honoured me. I am grateful to them. If a man tells you he loves you,' she said, looking into the fire, 'with his breast uncovered before you for you to strike him if you will, the least you can do is to put out your hand and cover it up from other people's eyes. If I were a deer,' she said, 'and a stag got hurt following me, even though I could not have him for a companion, I would stand still and scrape the sand with my foot over the place where his blood had fallen; the rest of the herd should never know he had been hurt there following me. I would cover the blood up, if I were a deer,' she said, and then she was silent.

Presently she sat down in her chair and said, with her hand before her: 'Yet, you know, I have not the ordinary feeling about love. I think the one who is loved confers the benefit on the one who loves, it's been so great and beautiful that it should be loved. I think the man should be grateful to the woman or the woman to the man whom they have been able to love, whether they have been loved back or whether circumstances have divided them or not.' She stroked her knee softly with her hand.

'Well, really, I must go now.' He pulled out his watch. 'It's so fascinating sitting here talking that I could stay all night, but I've still two engagements.' He rose; she rose also and stood before him looking up at him for a moment.

'How well you look! I think you have found the secret of perpetual youth. You don't look a day older than when I first saw you just four years ago. You always look as if you were on fire and being burnt up, but you never are, you know.'

He looked down at her with a kind of amused face as one does at an interesting child or a big Newfoundland dog.

'When shall we see you back?'

'Oh, not at all!'

'Not at all! Oh, we must have you back; you belong here, you know. You'll get tired of your Buddhist and come back to us.'

'You didn't mind my asking you to come and say goodbye?' she said in a childish manner unlike her determinateness when she discussed anything impersonal. 'I wanted to say goodbye to everyone. If one hasn't said goodbye one feels restless and feels one would have to come back. If one has said goodbye to all one's friends, then one knows it is all ended.'

'Oh, this isn't a final farewell! You must come in ten years' time and we'll compare notes – you about your Buddhist Priest, I about my fair ideal American; and we'll see who succeeded best.'

She laughed.

'I shall always see your movements chronicled in the newspapers, so we shall not be quite sundered; and you will hear of me perhaps.'

'Yes, I hope you will be very successful.'

She was looking at him, with her eyes wide open, from head to foot. He turned to the chair where his coat hung.

'Can't I help you put it on?'

'Oh, no, thank you.'

He put it on.

'Button the throat,' she said, 'the room is warm.'

He turned to her in his great-coat and with his gloves. They were standing near the door.

'Well, goodbye. I hope you will have a very pleasant time.'

He stood looking down upon her, wrapped in his great-coat.

She put up one hand a little in the air. 'I want to ask you something,' she said quickly.

'Well, what is it?'

'Will you please kiss me?'

For a moment he looked down at her, then he bent over her.

In after years he could never tell certainly, but he always thought she put up her hand and rested it on the crown of his head, with a curious soft caress, something like a mother's touch when her child is asleep and she does not want to wake it. Then he looked round, and she was gone. The door had closed noiselessly. For a moment he stood motionless, then he walked to the fireplace and looked down into the fender at a little cigarette end lying there, then he walked quickly back to the door and opened it. The stairs were in darkness and silence. He rang the bell violently. The old woman came up. He asked her where the lady was. She said she had gone out, she had a cab waiting. He asked when she would be back. The old woman said, 'Not at all'; she had left. He asked where she had gone. The woman said she did not know; she had left orders that all her letters should be kept for six or eight months till she wrote and sent her address. He asked whether she had no idea where he might find her. The woman said no. He walked up to a space in the wall where a picture had hung and stood staring at it as though the picture were still hanging there. He drew his mouth as though he were emitting a long whistle, but no sound came. He gave the old woman ten shillings and went downstairs.

That was eight years ago.

How beautiful life must have been to it that it looks so young still!

MONA CAIRD

The Yellow Drawing Room

I approach this episode in my life, which presents itself to my memory thus entitled, with dislike, mingled with fascination. I hate the whole subject, but I can't leave it alone. Those accursed three weeks, spent under the same roof with Vanora Haydon, seem to have deprived me of myself, unhinged me, destroyed the balance of my character. I feel as if I might, perhaps, throw off this absurd spell by calmly smoothing out the ruffled memories and studying them scientifically.

Vanora's aunt, Miss Clementina Thorne, was a nice appreciative old maiden lady, who thought me the most estimable and charming of men. I had long regarded her with warm affection, tempered only by a mild resentment at her perpetual attempts to get me married. In her pressing invitation to come once more to Fairfield, where the fresh air would be so good for me after my dusty and dingy office, I read at sight that another matrimonial scheme was fermenting in that most hymeneal brain. I knew that this time she had destined me for one of her nieces, as she mentioned that they had no visitors at present, and that Vanora would be at home. Though I had hovered about Clara with vague admiration for over a year, I had never yet seen Vanora. Her aunt mentioned, in her much underlined epistle, that her brother-in-law, since his dear wife's death, had let the girls have too much of their own way, and that Vanora (who had received permission to decorate and furnish the drawing room at Fairfield exactly as she pleased), had unworthily employed her liberty by producing a room of brilliant yellow.

I had a prejudice against Vanora, and this last freak made me think none the better of her. Evidently she was rather a headstrong and probably affected young person; everyone said that she liked to make herself conspicuous, and that you never knew what she was going to do next. I hate that sort of girl. The true woman is retiring, unobtrusive, indistinguishable even until you come to know her well, and then she is very much like what every other true woman would be under the same conditions. I had pronounced views in these matters.

As for the yellow drawing room –!

I was anxious to see just how far Vanora's mania to be out of the common had carried her in this instance.

Arrived at Fairfield, I was at once shown into the notorious drawing room. It *was* yellow! The colour had been washed out of the very daffodils, which looked green with jealousy; the sunshine was confronted in a spirit of respectful independence, brotherhood being acknowledged, but the principle of equality uncompromisingly asserted.

Miss Thorne sadly shook her head.

'We want my brother-in-law to have the room done over again, Mr St Vincent, but he won't hear of it. We did all we could with Vanora – we told her that *nobody* used such a brilliant colour, but she only said that she found Nobody, when you came to talk to him seriously, was a person quite open to reason. Dear Vanora is so quaint.'

'Her taste seems to be rather quaint,' I said.

Several visitors were passionately admiring the prospect, the pictures, the chairs and tables, anything to protect themselves against a threatening summons to say something about the general colouring. Miss Thorne seemed to be piteously endeavouring, by her manners, her attire, her sentiments, to atone for that unpardonable drawing room. The sisters also, Mary and Clara, were doing their best in the same direction. But hopeless was their protest. The room was in a glow of golden light; no ladylike antidote, however strong, could lead one to ignore it. It was radiant, bold, unapologetic, unabashed. It was not the room that my ideal woman would have created. My ideal woman would unfailingly choose a nice tone of grey-blue. Certain suspicions which I had harboured that Clara Haydon was my ideal woman grew stronger as I watched her quiet English face bent over the tea-tray. I liked the straightforward look of the girl, her blue eyes and fair complexion. If I *was* to give up my liberty, the reins should be handed over to a kind, sensible young woman like Clara, who would hate to make herself remarkable, or her drawing room yellow.

I think the hot afternoon sun, and the unceasing sound of Aunt Clementina's voice, must have made me drowsy, for I was thinking mistily what a wonderfully and conspicuously *clean* girl Clara Haydon was, when the door opened, and I found myself floundering (I cannot do more than describe these dreamy impressions) in an ocean of laughter.

In my efforts to keep my head above water, I discovered rather sharply that I had upset my tea, which Clara's exceedingly clean fingers had just poured out for me. This brought me to my senses.

'I appear to be graduating for an idiot,' I exclaimed, furious at my clumsiness and stupidity.

Vanora laughed in a friendly manner. 'We have all been yearning to get rid of this cup,' she said, 'and we really feel grateful to you for your opportune assistance.'

In the few bewildering moments of apology and reassurance, I found myself presented emphatically to Vanora, and lightly indicated to a dark and lank young man who followed her into the room. Vanora herself was simply radiant. She had a mass of glistening, golden hair, a colour full, varying, emotional, eyes like the sea (I lose my temper when people ask me to describe their colour). In figure she was robust, erect, pliant, firmly knit. Though her movements were so swift, there was nothing restless about her. A ground-tone of repose sounded up through the surface scintillations. She was vital, not galvanic. That was the revealing word: vital. In the human colour-spectrum, she took the place of the yellow ray.

This was all out of keeping. According to my doctrines it was even impossible. Women ought to take the place of the blue or violet rays. In my scheme of the universe they always did so, except in the case of a distinctly unwomanly woman. But this – in spite of offending against every canon I had ever set up – Vanora certainly was not. She was supremely, overpoweringly womanly. The womanhood of her sisters paled before the exuberant feminine quality which I could not but acknowledge in Vanora. Everything was wrong and contradictory. I seemed to be taking part in some comedy of errors, wherein Vanora played Columbine,[1] and I – the part of fool, I began grimly to suspect.

For already (I shrugged my shoulders at myself in contemptuous despair) I found that I hated the lank young man who had been introduced as Mr George Inglis, simply because and solely because I saw that he was head over ears in love with Vanora, and that she treated him with a sort of indescribable good-fellowship, mingled with a peculiar tenderness when she was moved that way.

'I hear, Miss Vanora,' I said, 'that the credit of this room is entirely yours.'

The lank admirer looked round. Vanora glanced at me alertly.

'You have every reason to be proud,' I continued, determined not to spare her; 'you must have surprised more people than you could easily count – though I have no wish to impugn your arithmetic. They will all be grateful to you for a new sensation.'

'Forgive me for disagreeing with you,' she said. 'It is so easy to surprise people; they are so amiable; they keep themselves always prepared for astonishment; they are like a sensitized plate which is ready at a moment's notice to be surprised into a photograph. You come with your dogma or your self-evident fact, or simply your pot of yellow paint, and, behold, forth spring the various amazements. Oh, no! (thanking you all the same) I am not proud!'

I raised my eyebrows witheringly. My ideal woman would consider it almost indelicate to play with words in this fantastic fashion. I glanced at my grey-blue goddess. How comfortably certain one felt with *her* of enjoying conversational repose! Dear Clara! With what admirable good taste she carried out one's cherished ideas; she fitted them like a glove. I completely, ardently, approved of Clara. To her I rather ostentatiously devoted myself for the rest of the afternoon, but I was furtively watching her sister.

And now I come to the disagreeable and inexplicable part of my broken and absurd episode. I know not to this day why or wherefore, but Vanora began to exercise over me an extraordinary fascination. If there were any other word I would use it, but I cannot find one. I fell into the strangest and most contradictory state of mind. Vanora's personality seemed to enwrap me as a garment; she was like some great radiating centre of light and warmth; I was penetrated with the glowing atmosphere. I never approved of the girl; I don't believe that

I then liked her. I know that I often hated her, and yet I felt miserable out of her sight. She became a necessity to me.

A feeling of misery, which I cannot describe, assailed me in her absence; a sick feeling of senseless despair. I used to pace the terrace among the peacocks (the boys impertinently insisted that they were unable on such occasions to distinguish me from those conceited birds), and as I thus worked off some of my restlessness, I tried to understand what had happened to me.

One morning, before breakfast, Vanora came out on to the terrace. She walked straight up to me and said, 'Good morning; I think you want to talk to me, don't you?'

I looked at her in despair. If she lived and improved for a thousand years she would never be an ideal woman!

'You disapprove of me,' Vanora continued calmly. 'I wish you would tell me why.'

'You really wish me to be frank?' I said, stopping and facing her.

'I really do,' she replied, offering crumbs of bread to a haughty peacock, who eyed them superciliously.

'Well, then, Miss Haydon, your blood be upon your own head (beautiful was that golden head in the morning light). You seem to have many qualities and ideas that are not suited to your sex. No doubt, I am old-fashioned about these things, but I confess that I cannot rejoice when I see our beautiful ideas of womanhood set scornfully at naught.'

'No?' said Vanora. 'Do go on.'

'I scarcely know how to approach a subject of which you do not seem to understand the rudiments,' I said severely.

'This interests me,' cried Vanora. 'I particularly desire to be awakened on this drowsy side of me; I can't bear to be blind and stupid. I want very much to be shown at least the gates of realms that are forbidden to me.'

'The sacred realms where woman is queen will soon be forbidden to you if you consistently continue to think and act in disharmony with the feminine nature and genius.'

'That is what Aunt Clementina and Mr Barnes so often tell me (Mr Barnes is our clergyman). But at present the threat of being excluded from the realms you mention does not terrify me. I rather prefer the realms where woman is *not* queen.'

'A mistake, a mistake!' I exclaimed.

'Yes, so I am told. But often people don't know what is good for them. I have heard of persons of mature judgement who had a chance of going straight off to Heaven to play on golden harps and wear a halo, hanging back and sending for the doctor in a strongly ill-advised manner. Of course we shall all have to go to the realms where woman is queen, but for myself I confess to a weak inclination to postpone, or let us say, not to anticipate, my royalty. The suspicion is clearly blameable, but what if I should happen to get tired of the everlasting harping?'

Vanora's face was perfectly serious.

'Miss Haydon,' I said, gravely and sadly, 'you may have a brilliant career in the future, but the more brilliant, the more complete will be your failure, the more I shall mourn the loss of a real woman from the spheres where she was intended to create and to maintain those sacred ties and sentiments, without which this world would be a howling wilderness.'

Vanora tossed another crumb to the supercilious peacock.

'Do go on,' she repeated.

'If women only realized where their true power lay, and how mighty was that power, they would never seek to snatch it in directions where they are inevitably weak, and – if I must say it – inevitably ridiculous.'

'I was born to be ridiculous,' said Vanora. 'My father never sought to arrange a "sphere" for me, and in my case instinct seems at fault. At one time I used to make a creditable number of antimacassars and sofa-cushions, and to this day my sisters do all that can possibly be required of a well-conducted family, – and what is especially satisfactory from a popular point of view, – they think a baby far more interesting than a grown-up creature with a soul, or even than a child who can think and feel. They are keeping up the feminine traditions admirably. Don't you think it would be a little monotonous if I were to go over exactly the same ground? It seems to me that that ground is getting rather trodden in.'

'I am sorry to hear you sneer at your good and charming sisters, and at the true instincts of your sex.'

Vanora burst out laughing.

'Oh! Mr St Vincent, you really are a little stupid sometimes,' she said. She turned, and I saw a change come into her face as George Inglis appeared from the wood at the far end of the terrace, and walked towards us. That filled me with unaccountable fury. My critical mood, which I had maintained with no little difficulty, fell off me, and I was swaying as a wind-tossed reed with strange, uncontrollable emotion.

'You don't know what it has cost me to speak to you thus,' I said, catching her hand. 'You interest me, you – yes, I must say it, you fascinate me, and it distresses me, maddens me to feel myself led away by qualities which ought to repel me – the attraction is morbid – unwholesome. I am angry with myself for even feeling it. Vanora, you must release me.'

'Release you,' she repeated; 'what do you mean?'

'I mean,' I replied crazily, 'that you must learn to love me and to be a woman in the old sweet sense, for my sake.'

'You are very naif,' she said, smiling; 'you seem just now to me like a nice, egotistical child.' I knew that George Inglis joined her, and that they walked down the terrace together. I suppose I must have been in love with her, yet all the time I seemed to hate her. I longed to make her yield to me; to love me with a lowly up-looking love. I had a burning desire to subdue her. She seemed to evade me and my theories as if she were a creature from another sphere. I cannot describe the irritation of mind which all this caused me. I set about my wooing as if I had been going to fight a duel.

Shortly after this, to my intense disgust, I found that George Inglis had discovered my accursed secret. I chanced to overhear him saying to Miss Thorne: 'The context is a typical one; if one could imagine the Eighteenth Century as a lover wooing the Nineteenth Century, this is the sort of angular labyrinthine courtship we should have!' I wondered what the chattering fool meant by it!

'She *shall* love me, and she *shall* learn, through love, the sweet lesson of womanly submission,' I said to myself, all the dominating instincts of my manhood roused into activity by this hateful experience. I felt that she was utterly wrong, that she had mistaken her own powers and her own noblest impulses. It was for me, through the might of an overwhelming affection, to set alight the true womanly flame within her heart. I would make her proud of her subordination; I would turn the splendid stream of her powers and affection into the true channel.

After a day or two of lover-like devotion, I began to slacken in my pursuit, and to transfer my attentions to Clara. Clara became a new creature. Her expression softened, her eyes brightened, but I was too absorbed in my own little drama to consider what part Clara might be likely to play in it. I watched Vanora secretly. She seemed depressed and restless. My heart bounded. Vanora was jealous; a woman after the old eternal pattern! – therefore to be won! Dear, erratic, foolish, brilliant Vanora, you shall be brought back safe and sound to your true destiny!

I followed her to the garden, whither I knew she had gone to gather flowers. Very lovely she looked in her white dress, with a bunch of daffodils in her belt.

I plunged headlong. 'Vanora, I love you; I want to know my fate.'

'*Me*,' she said, with a gasp of astonishment, 'I thought it was Clara!'

I clasped her hands; I protested; I told her how my love for her had overwhelmed and shattered me.

'And Clara?' she repeated in dismay.

Did she not understand? It was out of pique, to make her jealous –.

'When I become jealous of my sisters,' said Vanora, with a quiet and scornful aloofness, 'you can come and preach me your doctrines. I shall understand them then.'

'Vanora!'

'At present they seem to me like soap-bubbles; full of emptiness.'

'But you don't understand –'

'True,' she returned, 'they have never before assailed me in this stiff-backed fashion. I offend against them unconsciously. My father never constrained me to move in any particular direction because of my sex. He has perhaps spoiled me. I have hitherto had only a joyous sense of drawing in what was outside, and radiating out what was within me. When you describe your doctrines I seem to see the doors of a dark prison opening out of the sunshine; and, strange to say, I feel no divine, unerring instinct prompting me to walk in.'

'I offer you no prison but a home,' I cried excitedly.

'You would turn all homes into prisons,' she returned.

'Prisons whose bars are the golden bars of love and duty.'

'Yes, you take a woman's love and duty, and fashion out of them her prison bars. Is that generous? I fancy not, but it is most ingenious. It is Loyalaesque. But I don't like even *golden* bars, Mr St Vincent.'

'You have evidently not a spark of love for me,' I cried distractedly.

Her face suddenly changed. 'Ah! That is the horrible absurdity of it!' she exclaimed, colouring painfully. 'You enthral one part of me and leave the other scornful and indifferent. We have scarcely a thought in common, but I am miserable when you are absent – stop, don't misunderstand. Your Gods and Goddesses are to me creatures of pasteboard; your world of belief seems to me like a realm fashioned out of tissue paper.' She spoke with breathless rapidity and she was quivering from head to foot. 'To live with you would be like living in a tomb; I lack the sense of fresh air. And there is no sunshine within miles of you! Yet when I am not with you there is a sort of ache; your personality seems to fascinate me – I wish to heaven you had never come here. You have disturbed my happiness, destroyed my delight in life, left me miserably dependent on you; yet to the end of time I should continue to shock and irritate you, and you would stifle, depress and perhaps utterly unhinge me. I wish you would go – today, now.'

She looked white and distraught. I pleaded like a lunatic, argued, urged; for one supreme moment my arms were round her, and I thought that she would yield. But whether or not a triumph was in store for me I shall never know, for suddenly we both started in dismay. Before us, pausing abruptly as she came round the bend of the laurel shrubberies, stood Clara. I shall never forget the look on her face at that moment. It was like that of some gentle animal mortally and wantonly wounded. Without a word Clara turned away, and Vanora and I stood in silence.

At last, slowly moving away, Vanora spoke. 'I can forgive you the injury you have done to *me* – that you could not help, and the fault, after all, is my own – but I can never forgive what you have done to Clara.'

She passed out of sight, and I stood spellbound. I never saw Vanora again. I left Fairfield immediately, and I heard that she and her sister had gone abroad. I could not find out where they were, nor had I the temerity to think of following them. I knew that Fate had no reprieve for me.

The episode remains in my mind as a haunting, incomprehensible dream. Ponder as I may, I cannot understand what impulses of our nature Vanora and I had power mutually to set at variance; what irresistible attraction we had for one another, combined with what inevitable antipathy. We could never have lived together; I see that now. Yet, when the memory of those ten days returns to torment me, I feel that neither can we live apart. I have never been the same man since I met Vanora. I am neither my former self, complete and comfortable, nor am I thoroughly a new being. I am a sort of abortive creature, striding between two centuries. The spirit of a coming age has brushed me with his wing, but I resent and resist that which brings havoc into the citadel of my dearest beliefs; and I angrily pluck off the tiny feather which he dropped from those great ploughing pinions of his, that shadow – the firmament of the Future.

CHARLOTTE PERKINS GILMAN

The Yellow Wallpaper

It is very seldom that mere ordinary people like John and myself secure ancestral halls for the summer.

A colonial mansion, a hereditary estate, I would say a haunted house, and reach the height of romantic felicity – but that would be asking too much of fate!

Still I will proudly declare that there is something queer about it.

Else, why should it be let so cheaply? And why have stood so long untenanted?

John laughs at me, of course, but one expects that in marriage.

John is practical in the extreme. He has no patience with faith, an intense horror of superstition, and he scoffs openly at any talk of things not to be felt and seen and put down in figures.

John is a physician, and *perhaps* – (I would not say it to a living soul, of course, but this is dead paper and a great relief to my mind –) *perhaps* that is one reason I do not get well faster.

You see he does not believe I am sick!

And what can one do?

If a physician of high standing, and one's own husband, assures friends and relatives that there is really nothing the matter with one but temporary nervous depression – a slight hysterical tendency – what is one to do?

My brother is also a physician, and also of high standing, and he says the same thing.

So I take phosphates or phosphites – whichever it is, and tonics, and journeys, and air, and exercise, and am absolutely forbidden to 'work' until I am well again.

Personally, I disagree with their ideas.

Personally, I believe that congenial work, with excitement and change, would do me good.

But what is one to do?

I did write for a while in spite of them; but it *does* exhaust me a good deal – having to be so sly about it, or else meet with heavy opposition.

I sometimes fancy that in my condition if I had less opposition and more society and stimulus – but John says the very worst thing I can do is to think about my condition, and I confess it always makes me feel bad.

So I will let it alone and talk about the house.

The most beautiful place! It is quite alone, standing well back from the road, quite three miles from the village. It makes me think of English places that you read about, for there are hedges and walls and gates that lock, and lots of separate little houses for the gardeners and people.

There is a *delicious* garden! I never saw such a garden – large and shady, full of box-bordered paths, and lined with long grape-covered arbours with seats under them.

There were greenhouses, too, but they are all broken now.

There was some legal trouble, I believe, something about the heirs and co-heirs; anyhow, the place has been empty for years.

That spoils my ghostliness, I am afraid, but I don't care – there is something strange about the house – I can feel it.

I even said so to John one moonlight evening, but he said what I felt was a *draught*, and shut the window.

I get unreasonably angry with John sometimes. I'm sure I never used to be so sensitive. I think it is due to this nervous condition.

But John says if I feel so, I shall neglect proper self-control; so I take pains to control myself – before him, at least, and that makes me very tired.

I don't like our room a bit. I wanted one downstairs that opened on the piazza and had roses all over the window, and such pretty old-fashioned chintz hangings! but John would not hear of it.

He said there was only one window and not room for two beds, and no near room for him if he took another.

He is very careful and loving, and hardly lets me stir without special direction.

I have a schedule prescription for each hour in the day; he takes all care from me, and so I feel basely ungrateful not to value it more.

He said we came here solely on my account, that I was to have perfect rest and all the air I could get. 'Your exercise depends on your strength, my dear,' said he, 'and your food somewhat on your appetite; but air you can absorb all the time.' So we took the nursery at the top of the house.

It is a big, airy room, the whole floor nearly, with windows that look all ways, and air and sunshine galore. It was nursery first and then playroom and gymnasium, I should judge; for the windows are barred for little children, and there are rings and things in the walls.

The paint and paper look as if a boys' school had used it. It is stripped off – the paper – in great patches all around the head of my bed, about as far as I can reach, and in a great place on the other side of the room low down. I never saw a worse paper in my life.

One of those sprawling flamboyant patterns committing every artistic sin.

It is dull enough to confuse the eye in following, pronounced enough to constantly irritate and provoke study, and when you follow the lame uncertain curves for a little distance they suddenly commit suicide – plunge off at outrageous angles, destroy themselves in unheard of contradictions.

The colour is repellent, almost revolting; a smouldering unclean yellow, strangely faded by the slow-turning sunlight.

It is a dull yet lurid orange in some places, a sickly sulphur tint in others.

No wonder the children hated it! I should hate it myself if I had to live in this room long.

There comes John, and I must put this away – he hates to have me write a word.

We have been here two weeks, and I haven't felt like writing before, since that first day.

I am sitting by the window now, up in this atrocious nursery, and there is nothing to hinder my writing as much as I please, save lack of strength.

John is away all day, and even some nights when his cases are serious.

I am glad my case is not serious!

But these nervous troubles are dreadfully depressing.

John does not know how much I really suffer. He knows there is no *reason* to suffer, and that satisfies him.

Of course it is only nervousness. It does weigh on me so not to do my duty in any way!

I meant to be such a help to John, such a real rest and comfort, and here I am a comparative burden already!

Nobody would believe what an effort it is to do what little I am able, – to dress and entertain, and order things.

It is fortunate Mary is so good with the baby. Such a dear baby!

And yet I *cannot* be with him, it makes me so nervous.

I suppose John never was nervous in his life. He laughs at me so about this wallpaper!

At first he meant to repaper the room, but afterwards he said that I was letting it get the better of me, and that nothing was worse for a nervous patient than to give way to such fancies.

He said that after the wallpaper was changed it would be the heavy bedstead, and then the barred windows, and then that gate at the head of the stairs, and so on.

'You know the place is doing you good,' he said, 'and really, dear, I don't care to renovate the house just for a three months' rental.'

'Then do let us go downstairs,' I said, 'there are such pretty rooms there.'

Then he took me in his arms and called me a blessed little goose, and said he would go down cellar, if I wished, and have it whitewashed into the bargain.

But he is right enough about the beds and windows and things.

It is an airy and comfortable room as any one need wish, and, of course, I would not be so silly as to make him uncomfortable just for a whim.

I'm really getting quite fond of the big room, all but that horrid paper.

Out of one window I can see the garden, those mysterious deep-shaded arbours, the riotous old-fashioned flowers, and bushes and gnarly trees.

Out of another I get a lovely view of the bay and a little private wharf belonging to the estate. There is a beautiful shaded lane that runs down there from the house. I always fancy I see people walking in these numerous paths and arbours, but John has cautioned me not to give way to fancy in the least. He says that with my imaginative power and habit of story-making, a nervous weakness like mine is sure to lead to all manner of excited fancies, and that I ought to use my will and good sense to check the tendency. So I try.

I think sometimes that if I were only well enough to write a little it would relieve the press of ideas and rest me.

But I find I get pretty tired when I try.

It is so discouraging not to have any advice and companionship about my work. When I get really well, John says we will ask Cousin Henry and Julia down for a long visit; but he says he would as soon put fireworks in my pillowcase as to let me have those stimulating people about now.

I wish I could get well faster.

But I must not think about that. This paper looks to me as if it *knew* what a vicious influence it had!

There is a recurrent spot where the pattern lolls like a broken neck and two bulbous eyes stare at you upside down.

I get positively angry with the impertinence of it and the everlast-ingness. Up and down and sideways they crawl, and those absurd, unblinking eyes are everywhere. There is one place where two breadths didn't match, and the eyes go all up and down the line, one a little higher than the other.

I never saw so much expression in an inanimate thing before, and we all know how much expression they have! I used to lie awake as a child and get more entertainment and terror out of blank walls and plain furniture than most children could find in a toy-store.

I remember what a kindly wink the knobs of our big, old bureau used to have, and there was one chair that always seemed like a strong friend.

I used to feel that if any of the other things looked too fierce I could always hop into that chair and be safe.

The furniture in this room is no worse than inharmonious, however, for we had to bring it all from downstairs. I suppose when this was used as a playroom they had to take the nursery things out, and no wonder! I never saw such ravages as the children have made here.

The wallpaper, as I said before, is torn off in spots, and it sticketh closer than a brother[1] – they must have had perseverance as well as hatred.

Then the floor is scratched and gouged and splintered, the plaster itself is dug out here and there, and this great heavy bed which is all we found in the room, looks as if it had been through the wars.

But I don't mind it a bit – only the paper.

There comes John's sister. Such a dear girl as she is, and so careful of me! I must not let her find me writing.

She is a perfect and enthusiastic housekeeper, and hopes for no better profession. I verily believe she thinks it is the writing which made me sick!

But I can write when she is out, and see her a long way off from these windows.

There is one that commands the road, a lovely shaded winding road, and one that just looks off over the country. A lovely country, too, full of great elms and velvet meadows.

This wallpaper has a kind of subpattern in a different shade, a particularly irritating one, for you can only see it in certain lights, and not clearly then.

But in the places where it isn't faded and where the sun is just so – I can see a strange, provoking, formless sort of figure, that seems to skulk about behind that silly and conspicuous front design.

There's sister on the stairs!

Well, the Fourth of July is over! The people are all gone and I am tired out. John thought it might do me good to see a little company, so we just had mother and Nellie and the children down for a week.

Of course I didn't do a thing. Jennie sees to everything now.

But it tired me all the same.

John says if I don't pick up faster he shall send me to Weir Mitchell[2] in the fall.

But I don't want to go there at all. I had a friend who was in his hands once, and she says he is just like John and my brother, only more so!

Besides, it is such an undertaking to go so far.

I don't feel as if it was worth while to turn my hand over for anything, and I'm getting dreadfully fretful and querulous.

I cry at nothing, and cry most of the time.

Of course I don't when John is here, or anybody else, but when I am alone.

And I am alone a good deal just now. John is kept in town very often by serious cases, and Jennie is good and lets me alone when I want her to.

So I walk a little in the garden or down that lovely lane, sit on the porch under the roses and lie down up here a good deal.

I'm getting really fond of the room in spite of the wallpaper. Perhaps *because* of the wallpaper.

It dwells in my mind so!

I lie here on this great immovable bed – it is nailed down, I believe – and follow that pattern about by the hour. It is as good as gymnastics, I assure you. I start, we'll say, at the bottom, down in the corner over there where it has not been touched, and I determine for the thousandth time that I *will* follow that pointless pattern to some sort of a conclusion.

I know a little of the principle of design, and I know this thing was not arranged on any laws of radiation, or alternation, or repetition, or symmetry, or anything else that I ever heard of.

It is repeated, of course, by the breadths, but not otherwise.

Looked at in one way each breadth stands alone, the bloated curves and flourishes – a kind of 'debased Romanesque' with *delirium tremens*[3] – go waddling up and down in isolated columns of fatuity.

But, on the other hand, they connect diagonally, and the sprawling outlines run off in great slanting waves of optic horror, like a lot of wallowing seaweeds in full chase.

The whole thing goes horizontally, too, at least it seems so, and I exhaust myself in trying to distinguish the order of its going in that direction.

They have used a horizontal breadth for a frieze, and that adds wonderfully to the confusion.

There is one end of the room where it is almost intact, and there, when the crosslights fade and the low sun shines directly upon it, I can almost fancy radiation after all – the interminable grotesque seem to form around a common centre and rush off in headlong plunges of equal distraction.

It makes me tired to follow it. I will take a nap I guess.

I don't know why I should write this.

I don't want to.

I don't feel able.

And I know John would think it absurd. But I *must* say what I feel and think in some way – it is such a relief!

But the effort is getting to be greater than the relief.

Half the time now I am awfully lazy, and lie down ever so much.

John says I mustn't lose my strength, and has me take cod liver oil and lots of tonics and things, to say nothing of ale and wine and rare meat.

Dear John! He loves me very dearly, and hates to have me sick. I tried to have a real earnest reasonable talk with him the other day, and tell him how I wish he would let me go and make a visit to Cousin Henry and Julia.

But he said I wasn't able to go, nor able to stand it after I got there; and I did not make out a very good case for myself, for I was crying before I had finished.

It is getting to be a great effort for me to think straight. Just this nervous weakness I suppose.

And dear John gathered me up in his arms, and just carried me upstairs and laid me on the bed, and sat by me and read to me till it tired my head.

He said I was his darling and his comfort and all he had, and that I must take care of myself for his sake, and keep well.

He says no one but myself can help me out of it, that I must use my will and self-control and not let any silly fancies run away with me.

There's one comfort, the baby is well and happy, and does not have to occupy this nursery with the horrid wallpaper.

If we had not used it, that blessed child would have! What a fortunate escape! Why, I wouldn't have a child of mine, an impressionable little thing, live in such a room for worlds.

I never thought of it before, but it is lucky that John kept me here after all, I can stand it so much easier than a baby, you see.

Of course I never mention it to them any more – I am too wise, – but I keep watch of it all the same.

There are things in that paper that nobody knows but me, or ever will.

Behind that outside pattern the dim shapes get clearer every day.

It is always the same shape, only very numerous.

And it is like a woman stooping down and creeping about behind that pattern. I don't like it a bit. I wonder – I begin to think – I wish John would take me away from here!

It is so hard to talk with John about my case because he is so wise, and because he loves me so.

But I tried it last night.

It was moonlight. The moon shines in all around just as the sun does.

I hate to see it sometimes, it creeps so slowly, and always comes in by one window or another.

John was asleep and I hated to waken him, so I kept still and watched the moonlight on that undulating wallpaper till I felt creepy.

The faint figure behind seemed to shake the pattern, just as if she wanted to get out.

I got up softly and went to feel and see if the paper *did* move, and when I came back John was awake.

'What is it, little girl?' he said. 'Don't go walking about like that – you'll get cold.'

I thought it was a good time to talk, so I told him that I really was not gaining here, and that I wished he would take me away.

'Why, darling!' said he, 'our lease will be up in three weeks, and I can't see how to leave before.

'The repairs are not done at home, and I cannot possibly leave town just now. Of course if you were in any danger, I could and would, but you really are better, dear, whether you can see it or not. I am a doctor, dear, and I know. You are gaining flesh and colour, your appetite is better, I feel really much easier about you.'

'I don't weigh a bit more,' said I, 'nor as much; and my appetite may be better in the evening when you are here, but it is worse in the morning when you are away!'

'Bless her little heart!' said he with a big hug, 'she shall be as sick as she pleases! But now let's improve the shining hours[4] by going to sleep, and talk about it in the morning!'

'And you won't go away?' I asked gloomily.

'Why, how can I, dear? It is only three weeks more and then we will take a nice little trip of a few days while Jennie is getting the house ready. Really dear you are better!'

'Better in body perhaps –' I began, and stopped short, for he sat up straight and looked at me with such a stern, reproachful look that I could not say another word.

'My darling,' said he, 'I beg of you, for my sake and for our child's sake, as well as for your own, that you will never for one instant let that idea enter your mind! There is nothing so dangerous, so fascinating, to a temperament like yours. It is a false and foolish fancy. Can you not trust me as a physician when I tell you so?'

So of course I said no more on that score, and we went to sleep before long. He thought I was asleep first, but I wasn't, and lay there for hours trying to decide whether that front pattern and the back pattern really did move together or separately.

On a pattern like this, by daylight, there is a lack of sequence, a defiance of law, that is a constant irritant to a normal mind.

The colour is hideous enough, and unreliable enough, and infuriating enough, but the pattern is torturing.

You think you have mastered it, but just as you get well underway in following, it turns a back-somersault and there you are. It slaps you in the face, knocks you down and tramples upon you. It is like a bad dream.

The outside pattern is a florid arabesque, reminding one of a fungus. If you can imagine a toadstool in joints, an interminable string of toadstools, budding and sprouting in endless convolutions – why, that is something like it.

That is, sometimes!

There is one marked peculiarity about this paper, a thing nobody seems to notice but myself, and that is that it changes as the light changes.

When the sun shoots in through the east window – I always watch for that first long, straight ray – it changes so quickly that I never can quite believe it.

That is why I watch it always.

By moonlight – the moon shines in all night when there is a moon – I wouldn't know it was the same paper.

At night in any kind of light, in twilight, candlelight, lamplight, and worst of all by moonlight, it becomes bars! The outside pattern I mean, and the woman behind it is as plain as can be.

I didn't realize for a long time what the thing was that showed behind, that dim sub-pattern, but now I am quite sure it is a woman.

By daylight she is subdued, quiet. I fancy it is the pattern that keeps her so still. It is so puzzling. It keeps me quiet by the hour.

I lie down ever so much now. John says it is good for me, and to sleep all I can.

Indeed he started the habit by making me lie down for an hour after each meal.

It is a very bad habit I am convinced, for you see I don't sleep.

And that cultivates deceit, for I don't tell them I'm awake – O no!

The fact is I am getting a little afraid of John.

He seems very queer sometimes, and even Jennie has an inexplicable look.

It strikes me occasionally, just as a scientific hypothesis, – that perhaps it is the paper!

I have watched John when he did not know I was looking, and come into the room suddenly on the most innocent excuses, and I've caught him several times *looking at the paper!* And Jennie too. I caught Jennie with her hand on it once.

She didn't know I was in the room, and when I asked her in a quiet, a very quiet voice, with the most restrained manner possible, what she was doing with the paper – she turned around as if she had been caught stealing, and looked quite angry – asked me why I should frighten her so!

Then she said that the paper stained everything it touched, that she had found yellow smooches on all my clothes and John's, and she wished we would be more careful!

Did not that sound innocent? But I know she was studying that pattern, and I am determined that nobody shall find it out but myself!

Life is very much more exciting now than it used to be. You see I have something more to expect, to look forward to, to watch. I really do eat better, and am more quiet than I was.

John is so pleased to see me improve! He laughed a little the other day, and said I seemed to be flourishing in spite of my wallpaper.

I turned it off with a laugh. I had no intention of telling him it was *because* of the wallpaper – he would make fun of me. He might even want to take me away.

I don't want to leave now until I have found it out. There is a week more, and I think that will be enough.

I'm feeling ever so much better! I don't sleep much at night, for it is so interesting to watch developments; but I sleep a good deal in the daytime.

In the daytime it is tiresome and perplexing.

There are always new shoots on the fungus, and new shades of yellow all over it. I cannot keep count of them, though I have tried conscientiously.

It is the strangest yellow, that wallpaper! It makes me think of all the yellow things I ever saw – not beautiful ones like buttercups, but old foul, bad yellow things.

But there is something else about that paper – the smell! I noticed it the moment we came into the room, but with so much air and sun it was not bad. Now we have had a week of fog and rain, and whether the windows are open or not, the smell is here.

It creeps all over the house.

I find it hovering in the dining room, skulking in the parlour, hiding in the hall, lying in wait for me on the stairs.

It gets into my hair.

Even when I go to ride, if I turn my head suddenly and surprise it – there is that smell!

Such a peculiar odour, too! I have spent hours in trying to analyse it, to find what it smelled like.

It is not bad – at first, and very gentle, but quite the subtlest, most enduring odour I ever met.

In this damp weather it is awful, I wake up in the night and find it hanging over me.

It used to disturb me at first. I thought seriously of burning the house – to reach the smell.

But now I am used to it. The only thing I can think of that it is like is the *colour* of the paper! A yellow smell.

There is a very funny mark on this wall, low down, near the mopboard. A streak that runs round the room. It goes behind every piece of furniture, except the bed, a long, straight, even *smooch*, as if it had been rubbed over and over.

I wonder how it was done and who did it, and what they did it for. Round and round and round – round and round and round – it makes me dizzy!

I really have discovered something at last.

Through watching so much at night, when it changes so, I have finally found out.

The front pattern *does* move – and no wonder! The woman behind shakes it!

Sometimes I think there are a great many women behind, and sometimes only one, and she crawls around fast, and her crawling shakes it all over.

Then in the very bright spots she keeps still, and in the very shady spots she just takes hold of the bars and shakes them hard.

And she is all the time trying to climb through. But nobody could climb through that pattern – it strangles so; I think that is why it has so many heads.

They get through, and then the pattern strangles them off and turns them upside down, and makes their eyes white!

If those heads were covered or taken off it would not be half so bad.

I think that woman gets out in the daytime!

And I'll tell you why – privately – I've seen her!

I can see her out of every one of my windows!

It is the same woman, I know, for she is always creeping, and most women do not creep by daylight.

I see her in that long shaded lane, creeping up and down. I see her in those dark grape arbours, creeping all around the garden.

I see her on that long road under the trees, creeping along, and when a carriage comes she hides under the blackberry vines.

I don't blame her a bit. It must be very humiliating to be caught creeping by daylight!

I always lock the door when I creep by daylight. I can't do it at night, for I know John would suspect something at once.

And John is so queer now, that I don't want to irritate him. I wish he would take another room! Besides, I don't want anybody to get that woman out at night but myself.

I often wonder if I could see her out of all the windows at once.

But, turn as fast as I can, I can only see out of one at one time.

And though I always see her, she *may* be able to creep faster than I can turn!

I have watched her sometimes away off in the open country, creeping as fast as a cloud shadow in a high wind.

If only that top pattern could be gotten off from the under one! I mean to try it, little by little.

I have found out another funny thing, but I shan't tell it this time! It does not do to trust people too much.

There are only two more days to get this paper off, and I believe John is beginning to notice. I don't like the look in his eyes.

And I heard him ask Jennie a lot of professional questions about me. She had a very good report to give.

She said I slept a good deal in the daytime.

John knows I don't sleep very well at night, for all I'm so quiet!

He asked me all sorts of questions, too, and pretended to be very loving and kind.

As if I couldn't see through him!

Still, I don't wonder he acts so, sleeping under this paper for three months.

It only interests me, but I feel sure John and Jennie are secretly affected by it.

Hurrah! This is the last day, but it is enough. John to stay in town over night, and won't be out until this evening.

Jennie wanted to sleep with me – the sly thing! but I told her I should undoubtedly rest better for a night all alone.

That was clever, for really I wasn't alone a bit! As soon as it was moonlight and that poor thing began to crawl and shake the pattern, I got up and ran to help her.

I pulled and she shook, I shook and she pulled, and before morning we had peeled off yards of that paper.

A strip about as high as my head and half around the room.

And then when the sun came and that awful pattern began to laugh at me, I declared I would finish it today!

We go away tomorrow, and they are moving all my furniture down again to leave things as they were before.

Jennie looked at the wall in amazement, but I told her merrily that I did it out of pure spite at the vicious thing.

She laughed and said she wouldn't mind doing it herself, but I must not get tired.

How she betrayed herself that time!

But I am here, and no person touches this paper but me, – not *alive!*

She tried to get me out of the room – it was too patent! But I said it was so quiet and empty and clean now that I believed I would lie down again and sleep all I could; and not to wake me even for dinner – I would call when I woke.

So now she is gone, and the servants are gone, and the things are gone, and there is nothing left but that great bedstead nailed down, with the canvas mattress we found on it.

We shall sleep downstairs tonight, and take the boat home tomorrow.

I quite enjoy the room, now it is bare again.

How those children did tear about here!

This bedstead is fairly gnawed!

But I must get to work.

I have locked the door and thrown the key down into the front path.

I don't want to go out, and I don't want to have anybody come in, till John comes.

I want to astonish him.

I've got a rope up here that even Jennie did not find. If that woman does get out, and tries to get away, I can tie her!

But I forgot I could not reach far without anything to stand on!

This bed will *not* move!

I tried to lift and push it until I was lame, and then I got so angry I bit off a little piece at one corner – but it hurt my teeth.

Then I peeled off all the paper I could reach standing on the floor. It sticks horribly and the pattern just enjoys it! All those strangled heads and bulbous eyes and waddling fungus growths just shriek with derision!

I am getting angry enough to do something desperate. To jump out of the window would be admirable exercise, but the bars are too strong even to try.

Besides I wouldn't do it. Of course not. I know well enough that a step like that is improper and might be misconstrued.

I don't like to *look* out of the windows even – there are so many of those creeping women, and they creep so fast.

I wonder if they all come out of that wallpaper as I did?

But I am securely fastened now by my well-hidden rope – you don't get *me* out in the road there!

I suppose I shall have to get back behind the pattern when it comes night, and that is hard!

It is so pleasant to be out in this great room and creep around as I please!

I don't want to go outside. I won't, even if Jennie asks me to.

For outside you have to creep on the ground, and everything is green instead of yellow.

But here I can creep smoothly on the floor, and my shoulder just fits in that long smooch around the wall, so I cannot lose my way.

Why there's John at the door!

It is no use, young man, you can't open it!

How he does call and pound!

Now he's crying for an axe.

It would be a shame to break down that beautiful door!

'John dear!' said I in the gentlest voice, 'the key is down by the front steps, under a plantain leaf!'

That silenced him for a few moments.

Then he said – very quietly indeed, 'Open the door, my darling!'

'I can't,' said I. 'The key is down by the front door under a plantain leaf!'

And then I said it again, several times, very gently and slowly, and said it so often that he had to go and see, and he got it of course, and came in. He stopped short by the door.

'What is the matter?' he cried. 'For God's sake, what are you doing!'

I kept on creeping just the same, but I looked at him over my shoulder.

'I've got out at last,' said I, 'in spite of you and Jane! And I've pulled off most of the paper, so you can't put me back!'

Now why should that man have fainted? But he did, and right across my path by the wall, so that I had to creep over him every time!

GEORGE EGERTON

A Cross Line

The rather flat notes of a man's voice float out into the clear air, singing the refrain of a popular music-hall ditty. There is something incongruous between the melody and the surroundings. It seems profane, indelicate, to bring this slangy, vulgar tune, and with it the mental picture of footlight flare and fantastic dance into the lovely freshness of this perfect spring day.

A woman sitting on a felled tree turns her head to meet its coming, and an expression flits across her face in which disgust and humorous appreciation are subtly blended. Her mind is nothing if not pictur-esque; her busy brain, with all its capabilities choked by a thousand vagrant fancies, is always producing pictures and finding associations between the most unlikely objects. She has been reading a little sketch written in the daintiest language of a fountain scene in Tanagra,[1] and her vivid imagination has made it real to her. The slim, graceful maids grouped around it filling their exquisitely-formed earthen jars, the dainty poise of their classic heads, and the flowing folds of their draperies have been actually present with her; and now? – why, it is like the entrance of a half-tipsy vagabond player bedizened in tawdry finery – the picture is blurred. She rests her head against the trunk of a pine tree behind her, and awaits the singer. She is sitting on an incline in the midst of a wilderness of trees; some have blown down, some have been cut down, and the lopped branches lie about; moss and bracken and trailing bramble, fir cones, wild rose bushes and speckled red 'fairy hats'[2] fight for life in wild confusion. A disused quarry to the left is an ideal haunt of pike, and to the right a little river rushes along in haste to join a greater sister that is fighting a troubled way to the sea. A row of stepping stones crosses it, and if you were to

48

stand on one you would see shoals of restless stone loach 'Beardies'[3] darting from side to side. The tails of several ducks can be seen above the water, and the paddle of their balancing feet, and the gurgling suction of their bills as they search for larvae can be heard distinctly between the hum of insect, twitter of bird and rustle of stream and leaf. The singer has changed his lay to a whistle, and presently he comes down the path a cool, neat, grey-clad figure, with a fishing creel slung across his back, and a trout rod held on his shoulder. The air ceases abruptly, and his cold grey eyes scan the seated figure with its gypsy ease of attitude, a scarlet shawl that has fallen from her shoulders forming an accentuative background to the slim roundness of her waist.

Persistent study, coupled with a varied experience of the female animal, has given the owner of the grey eyes some facility in classing her, although it has not supplied him with any definite data as to what any one of the species may do in a given circumstance. To put it in his own words, in answer to a friend who chaffed him on his untiring pursuit of women as an interesting problem :

'If a fellow has had much experience of his fellow man he may divide him into types, and, given a certain number of men and a certain number of circumstances, he is pretty safe on hitting on the line of action each type will strike; 't aint so with woman. You may always look out for the unexpected, she generally upsets a fellow's calculations, and you are never safe in laying odds on her. Tell you what, old chappie, we may talk about superior intellect; but, if a woman wasn't handicapped by her affection, or need of it, the cleverest chap in Christendom would be just a bit of putty in her hands. I find them more fascinating as problems than anything going. Never let an opportunity slip to get new data – never!'

He did not now. He met the frank, unembarrassed gaze of eyes that would have looked with just the same bright enquiry at the advent of a hare, or a toad, or any other object that might cross her path, and raised his hat with respectful courtesy, saying, in the drawling tone habitual with him –

'I hope I am not trespassing?'

'I can't say; you may be, so may I, but no one has ever told me so!'

A pause. His quick glance has noted the thick wedding ring on her slim brown hand, and the flash of a diamond in its keeper. A lady decidedly. Fast? perhaps. Original? undoubtedly. Worth knowing? rather.

'I am looking for a trout stream, but the directions I got were rather vague; might I—'

'It's straight ahead, but you won't catch anything now, at least not here, sun's too glaring and water too low, a mile up you may, in an hour's time.'

'Oh, thanks awfully for the tip. You fish then?'

'Yes, sometimes.'

'Trout run big here?' (What odd eyes the woman has, kind of magnetic.)

'No, seldom over a pound, but they are very game.'

'Rare good sport isn't it, whipping a stream? There is so much besides the mere catching of fish. The river and the trees and the quiet sets a fellow thinking – kind of sermon – makes a chap feel good, don't it?'

She smiles assentingly. And yet what the devil is she amused at he queries mentally. An inspiration. He acts upon it, and says eagerly:

'I wonder – I don't half like to ask – but fishing puts people on a common footing, don't it? You knowing the stream, you know, would you tell me what are the best flies to use?'

'I tie my own, but—'

'Do you? how clever of you! wish I could,' and sitting down on the other end of the tree, he takes out his fly book, 'but I interrupted you, you were going to say?'

'Only,' stretching out her hand (of a perfect shape but decidedly brown) for the book, 'that you might give the local fly-tyer a trial, he'll tell you.

'Later on, end of next month, or perhaps later, you might try the oak-fly, the natural fly you know; a horn is the best thing to hold them in, they get out of anything else – and put two on at a time.'

'By Jove, I must try that dodge!'

He watches her as she handles his book and examines the contents critically, turning aside some with a glance, fingering others almost tenderly, holding them daintily and noting the cock of wings and the hint of tinsel, with her head on one side; a trick of hers he thinks.

'Which do you like most, wet or dry fly?' (She is looking at some dry flies.)

'Oh,' with that rare smile, 'at the time I swear by whichever happens to catch most fish. Perhaps, really, dry fly. I fancy most of these flies are better for Scotland or England. Up to this March-brown has been the most killing thing. But you might try an "orange-grouse", that's always good here; with perhaps a "hare's ear" for a change – and put on a "coachman" for the evenings. My husband (he steals a side look at her) brought home some beauties yesterday evening.'

'Lucky fellow!'

She returns the book. There is a tone in his voice as he says this that jars on her, sensitive as she is to every inflection of a voice, with an intuition that is almost second sight. She gathers up her shawl. She has a cream-coloured woollen gown on, and her skin looks duskily foreign by contrast. She is on her feet before he can regain his, and says, with a cool little bend of her head: 'Good afternoon, I wish you a full basket!'

Before he can raise his cap she is down the slope, gliding with easy steps that have a strange grace, and then springing lightly from stone to stone across the stream. He feels small, snubbed some way, and he sits down on the spot where she sat and, lighting his pipe, says 'check!'

She is walking slowly up the garden path. A man in his shirtsleeves is stooping amongst the tender young peas. A bundle of stakes lies next him, and he whistles softly and all out of tune as he twines the little tendrils round each new support. She looks at his broad shoulders and narrow flanks; his back is too long for great strength, she thinks. He hears her step, and smiles up at her from under the shadow of his broad-leafed hat.

'How do you feel now, old woman?'

'Beastly. I've got that horrid qualmish feeling again. I can't get rid of it.'

He has spread his coat on the side of the path and pats it for her to sit down.

'What is it (anxiously)? if you were a mare I'd know what to do for you. Have a nip of whisky?'

He strides off without waiting for her reply and comes back with it and a biscuit, kneels down and holds the glass to her lips.

'Poor little woman, buck up! You'll see that'll fix you. Then you go by and by and have a shy at the fish.'

She is about to say something when a fresh qualm attacks her and she does not.

He goes back to his tying.

'By Jove!' he says suddenly, 'I forgot. Got something to show you!'

After a few minutes he returns carrying a basket covered with a piece of sacking. A dishevelled-looking hen, with spread wings trailing and her breast bare from sitting on her eggs, screeches after him. He puts it carefully down and uncovers it, disclosing seven little balls of yellow fluff splashed with olive green. They look up sideways with bright round eyes, and their little spoon bills look disproportionately large.

'Aren't they beauties (enthusiastically)? This one is just out,' taking up an egg, 'mustn't let it get chilled.' There is a chip out of it and a piece of hanging skin. 'Isn't it funny?' he asks, showing her how it is curled in the shell, with its paddles flattened and its bill breaking through the chip, and the slimy feathers sticking to its violet skin.

She suppresses an exclamation of disgust, and looks at his fresh-tinted skin instead. He is covering basket, hen, and all –

'How you love young things!' she says.

'Some. I had a filly once, she turned out a lovely mare! I cried when I had to sell her, I wouldn't have let any one in God's world mount her.'

'Yes, you would!'

'Who?' with a quick look of resentment.

'Me!'

'I wouldn't!'

'What! you wouldn't?'

'I wouldn't!'

'I think you would if I wanted to!' with a flash out of the tail of her eye.

'No, I wouldn't!'

'Then you would care more for her than for me. I would give you your choice (passionately), her or me!'

'What nonsense!'

'May be (concentrated), but it's lucky she isn't here to make deadly sense of it.' A humble-bee buzzes close to her ear, and she is roused to a sense of facts, and laughs to think how nearly they have quarrelled over a mare that was sold before she knew him.

Some evenings later, she is stretched motionless in a chair, and yet she conveys an impression of restlessness; a sensitively nervous person would feel it. She is gazing at her husband, her brows are drawn together, and make three little lines. He is reading, reading quietly, without moving his eyes quickly from side to side of the page as she does when she reads, and he pulls away at a big pipe with steady enjoyment. Her eyes turn from him to the window, and follow the course of two clouds, then they close for a few seconds, then open to watch him again. He looks up and smiles.

'Finished your book?'

There is a singular soft monotony in his voice; the organ with which she replies is capable of more varied expression.

'Yes, it is a book makes one think. It would be a greater book if he were not an Englishman. He's afraid of shocking the big middle class. You wouldn't care about it.'

'Finished your smoke?'

'No, it went out, too much fag to light up again! No (protestingly), never you mind, old boy, why do you?'

He has drawn his long length out of his chair, and, kneeling down beside her, guards a lighted match from the incoming evening air. She draws in the smoke contentedly, and her eyes smile back with a general vague tenderness.

'Thank you, dear old man!'

'Going out again?' negative head shake.

'Back aching?' affirmative nod, accompanied by a steadily aimed puff of smoke, that she has been carefully inhaling, into his eyes.

'Scamp! Have your booties off?'

'Oh, don't you bother, Lizzie will do it!'

He has seized a foot from under the rocker, and, sitting on his heels, holds it on his knee, whilst he unlaces the boot; then he loosens the stocking under her toes, and strokes her foot gently.

'Now, the other!' Then he drops both boots outside the door, and fetching a little pair of slippers, past their first smartness, from the bedroom, puts one on. He examines the left foot; it is a little swollen round the ankle, and he presses his broad fingers gently round it as one sees a man do to a horse with windgalls. Then he pulls the rocker nearer to his chair and rests the slipperless foot on his thigh. He relights his pipe, takes up his book and rubs softly from ankle to toes as he reads.

She smokes and watches him, diverting herself by imagining him in the hats of different periods. His is a delicate-skinned face with regular features; the eyes are fine, in colour and shape with the luminous clearness of a child's; his pointed beard is soft and curly. She looks at his hand, – a broad strong hand with capable fingers, – the hand of a craftsman, a contradiction to the face with its distinguished delicacy. She holds her own up with a cigarette poised between the first and second fingers, idly pleased with its beauty of form and delicate nervous slightness. One speculation chases the other in her quick brain; odd questions as to race arise; she dives into theories as to the why and wherefore of their distinctive natures, and holds a mental debate in which she takes both sides of the question impartially. He has finished his pipe, laid down his book, and is gazing dreamily, with his eyes darkened by their long lashes, and a look of tender melancholy in their clear depths, into space.

'What are you thinking of?' There is a look of expectation in her quivering nervous little face.

He turns to her, chafing her ankle again.

'I was wondering if lobworms would do for—'

He stops. A strange look of disappointment flits across her face and is lost in an hysterical peal of laughter.

'You are the best emotional check I ever knew,' she gasps.

He stares at her in utter bewilderment, and then a slow smile creeps to his eyes and curves the thin lips under his moustache, a smile at her.

'You seem amused, Gypsy!'

She springs out of her chair and seizes book and pipe; he follows the latter anxiously with his eyes until he sees it laid safely on the table. Then she perches herself, resting her knees against one of his legs, whilst she hooks her feet back under the other –

'Now I am all up, don't I look small?'

He smiles his slow smile. 'Yes, I believe you are made of gutta percha.'

She is stroking out all the lines in his face with the tip of her finger; then she runs it through his hair. He twists his head half impatiently, she desists.

'I divide all the people in the world,' she says, 'into those who like their hair played with, and those who don't. Having my hair brushed gives me more pleasure than anything else; it's delicious. I'd *purr* if I knew how. I notice (meditatively) I am never in sympathy with those who don't like it; I am with those who do. I always get on with them.'

'You are a queer little devil!'

'Am I? I shouldn't have thought you would have found out I was the latter at all. I wish I were a man! I believe if I were a man, I'd be a disgrace to my family.'

'Why?'

'I'd go on a jolly old spree!'

He laughs: 'Poor little woman, is it so dull?'

There is a gleam of devilry in her eyes, and she whispers solemnly –

'Begin with a D,' and she traces imaginary letters across his forehead, and ending with a flick over his ear, says, 'and that is the tail of the y!'

After a short silence she queries –

'Are you fond of me?' She is rubbing her chin up and down his face.

'Of course I am, don't you know it?'

'Yes, perhaps I do,' impatiently; 'but I want to be told it. A woman doesn't care a fig for a love as deep as the death-sea and as silent, she wants something that tells her it in little waves all the time. It isn't the love, you know, it's the being loved; it isn't really the man, it's his loving!'

'By Jove, you're a rum un!'

'I wish I wasn't then. I wish I was as commonplace as—. You don't tell me anything about myself (a fierce little kiss), you might, even if it were lies. Other men who cared for me told me things about my eyes, my hands, anything. I don't believe you notice.'

'Yes I *do*, little one, only I think it.'

'Yes, but I don't care a bit for your thinking; if I can't see what's in your head what good is it to me?'

'I wish I could understand you, dear!'

'I wish to God you could. Perhaps if you were badder and I were gooder we'd meet halfway. *You* are an awfully good old chap; it's just men like you send women like me to the devil!'

'But you are good (kissing her), a real good chum! You understand a fellow's weak points. You don't blow him up if he gets on a bit. Why (enthusiastically), being married to you is like chumming with a chap! Why (admiringly), do you remember before we were married, when I let that card fall out of my pocket? Why, I couldn't have told another girl about her. She wouldn't have believed that I *was* straight. She'd have thrown me over. And you sent her a quid because she was sick. You are a great little woman!'

'Don't see it! (she is biting his ear). Perhaps I was a man last time, and some hereditary memories are cropping up in this incarnation!'

He looks so utterly at sea that she has to laugh again, and, kneeling up, shuts his eyes with kisses, and bites his chin and shakes it like a terrier in her strong little teeth.

'You imp! was there ever such a woman!'

Catching her wrists, he parts his knees and drops her on to the rug. Then, perhaps the subtle magnetism that is in her affects him, for he stoops and snatches her up and carries her up and down, and then over to the window and lets the fading light with its glimmer of moonshine play on her odd face with its tantalizing changes. His eyes dilate and his colour deepens as he crushes her soft little body to him and carries her off to her room.

Summer is waning and the harvest is ripe for ingathering, and the voice of the reaping machine is loud in the land. She is stretched on her back on the short heather-mixed moss at the side of a bog stream. Rod and creel are flung aside, and the wanton breeze, with the breath of coolness it has gathered in its passage over the murky dykes of black bog water, is playing with the tail fly, tossing it to and fro with a half threat to fasten it to a prickly spine of golden gorse. Bunches of bog-wool nod their fluffy heads, and through the myriad indefinite sounds comes the regular scrape of a strickle on the scythe of a reaper in a neighbouring meadow. Overhead a flotilla of clouds is steering from the south in a north-easterly direction. Her eyes follow them. Old time galleons, she thinks, with their wealth of snowy sail spread, riding breast to breast up a wide blue fjord after victory. The sails of the last are rose flushed, with a silver edge. Somehow she thinks of Cleopatra sailing down to meet Antony,[4] and a great longing fills her soul to sail off somewhere too — away from the daily need of dinner-getting and the recurring Monday with its washing; life with its tame duties and virtuous monotony. She fancies herself in Arabia on the back of a swift steed. Flashing eyes set in dark faces surround her, and she can see the clouds of sand swirl, and feel the swing under her of his rushing stride. Her thoughts shape themselves into a wild song, a song to her steed of flowing mane and satin skin; an uncouth rhythmical jingle with a feverish beat; a song to the untamed spirit that dwells in her. Then she fancies she is on the stage of an ancient theatre out in the open air, with hundreds of faces upturned towards her. She is gauze-clad in a cobweb garment of wondrous tissue. Her arms are clasped by jewelled snakes, and one with quivering diamond fangs coils round her hips. Her hair floats loosely, and her feet are sandal-clad, and the delicate breath of vines and the salt freshness of an incoming sea seems to fill her nostrils. She bounds forward and dances, bends her lissom waist and curves her slender arms, and gives to the soul of each man what he craves, be it good or evil. And she can feel now, lying here in the shade of Irish hills with her head resting on her scarlet shawl and her eyes closed, the grand intoxicating power of swaying all these human souls to wonder and applause. She can see herself with parted lips and panting, rounded breasts, and a dancing devil in each glowing eye, sway voluptuously to the wild music that rises, now slow, now fast, now deliriously wild, seductive, intoxicating, with a human note of passion in its strain. She can feel the answering shiver of feeling that quivers up to her from the dense audience, spellbound by the motion of her glancing feet, and she flies swifter and swifter, and lighter and lighter, till the very serpents seem alive with jewelled scintillations. One quivering, gleaming, daring bound, and she stands with outstretched arms and passion-filled eyes, poised on one slender foot, asking a supreme note to finish her dream of motion. And the men rise to a man and answer her, and cheer, cheer till the echoes shout from the surrounding hills and tumble wildly down the crags. The clouds have sailed away, leaving long feathery streaks in their wake. Her eyes have an inseeing look, and she is tremulous with excitement. She can hear yet that last grand shout, and the strain of that old-time music that she has never heard in this life of hers, save as an inner accompaniment to the memory of hidden things, born with her, not of this time.

And her thoughts go to other women she has known, women good and bad, school friends, casual acquaintances, women workers – joyless machines for grinding daily corn, unwilling maids grown old in the endeavour to get settled, patient wives who bear little ones to indifferent husbands until they wear out – a long array. She busies herself with questioning. Have they, too, this thirst for excitement, for change, this restless craving for sun and love and motion? Stray words, half confidences, glimpses through soul-chinks of suppressed fires, actual outbreaks, domestic catastrophes, how the ghosts dance in the cells of her memory! And she laughs, laughs softly to herself because the denseness of man, his chivalrous conservative devotion to the female idea he has created blinds him, perhaps happily, to the problems of her complex nature. Ay, she mutters musingly, the wisest of them can only say we are enigmas. Each one of them sets about solving the riddle of the *ewig weibliche* – and well it is that the workings of our hearts are closed to them, that we are cunning enough or *great* enough to seem to be what they would have us, rather than be what we are. But few of them have had the insight to find out the key to our seeming contradictions. The why a refined, physically fragile woman will mate with a brute, a mere male animal with primitive passions – and love him – the why strength and beauty appeal more often than the more subtly fine qualities of mind or heart – the why women (and not the innocent ones) will condone sins that men find hard to forgive in their fellows. They have all overlooked the eternal wildness, the untamed primitive savage temperament that lurks in the mildest, best woman. Deep in through ages of convention this primeval trait burns, an untameable quantity that may be concealed but is never eradicated by culture – the keynote of woman's witchcraft and woman's strength. But it is there, sure enough, and each woman is conscious of it in her truth-telling hours of quiet self-scrutiny – and each woman in God's wide world will deny it, and each woman will help another to conceal it – for the woman who tells the truth and is not a liar about these things is untrue to her sex and abhorrent to man, for he has fashioned a model on imaginary lines, and he has said, 'so I would have you,' and every woman is an unconscious liar, for so man loves her. And when a Strindberg or a Nietzsche[5] arises and peers into the recesses of her nature and dissects her ruthlessly, the men shriek out louder than the women, because the truth is at all times unpalatable, and the gods they have set up are dear to them . . .

'Dreaming, or speering into futurity? You have the look of a seer. I believe you are half a witch!'

And he drops his grey-clad figure on the turf. He has dropped his drawl long ago, in midsummer.

'Is not every woman that? Let us hope I'm, for my friends, a white one.'

'A-ah! Have you many friends?'

'That is a query! If you mean many correspondents, many persons who send me Christmas cards, or remember my birthday, or figure in my address-book? No.'

'Well, grant I don't mean that!'

'Well, perhaps, yes. Scattered over the world, if my death were belled out, many women would give me a tear, and some a prayer. And many men would turn back a page in their memory and give me a kind thought, perhaps a regret, and go back to their work with a feeling of having lost something – that they never possessed. I am a creature of moments. Women have told me that I came into their lives just when they needed me. Men had no need to tell me, I felt it. People have needed me more than I them. I have given freely whatever they craved from me in the way of understanding or love. I have touched sore places they showed me and healed them, but they never got at me. I have been for myself, and helped myself, and borne the burden of my own mistakes. Some have chafed at my self-sufficiency and have called me fickle – not understanding that they gave me nothing, and that when I had served them, their moment was ended, and I was to pass on. I read people easily, I am written in black letter to most—'

'To your husband!'

'He (quickly) – we will not speak of him; it is not loyal.'

'Do not I understand you a little?'

'You do not misunderstand me.'

'That is something.'

'It is much!'

'Is it? (searching her face). It is not one grain of sand in the desert that stretches between you and me, and you are as impenetrable as a sphinx at the end of it. This (passionately) is my moment, and what have you given me?'

'Perhaps less than other men I have known; but you want less. You are a little like me, you can stand alone. And yet (her voice is shaking), have I given you nothing?'

He laughs, and she winces – and they sit silent, and they both feel as if the earth between them is laid with infinitesimal electric threads vibrating with a common pain. Her eyes are filled with tears that burn but don't fall, and she can see his somehow through her closed lids, see their cool greyness troubled by sudden fire, and she rolls her handkerchief into a moist cambric ball between her cold palms.

'You have given me something – something to carry away with me – an infernal want. You ought to be satisfied. I am infernally miserable.'

'You (nearer) have the most tantalizing mouth in the world when your lips tremble like that. I . . . What! can you cry? You?'

'Yes, even I can cry!'

'You dear woman! (pause) And I can't help you!'

'You can't help me. No man can. Don't think it is because you are you I cry, but because you probe a little nearer into the real me that I feel so.'

'Was it necessary to say that? (reproachfully). Do you think I don't

know it? I can't for the life of me think how you, with that free gypsy
nature of yours, could bind yourself to a monotonous country life,
with no excitement, no change. I wish I could offer you my yacht. Do
you like the sea?'

'I love it, it answers one's moods.'

'Well, let us play pretending, as the children say. Grant that I could,
I would hang your cabin with your own colours; fill it with books, all
those I have heard you say you care for; make it a nest as rare as the
bird it would shelter. You would reign supreme; when your highness
would deign to honour her servant I would come and humour your
every whim. If you were glad, you could clap your hands and order
music, and we would dance on the white deck, and we would skim
through the sunshine of Southern seas on a spice-scented breeze. You
make me poetical. And if you were angry you could vent your feelings
on me, and I would give in and bow my head to your mood. And we
would drop anchor and stroll through strange cities, go far inland and
glean folklore out of the beaten track of everyday tourists. And at
night when the harbour slept we would sail out through the moonlight
over silver seas. You are smiling, you look so different when you smile;
do you like my picture?'

'Some of it!'

'What not?'

'You!'

'Thank you.'

'You asked me. Can't you understand where the spell lies? It is the
freedom, the freshness, the vague danger, the unknown that has a
witchery for me, ay, for every woman!'

'Are you incapable of affection, then?'

'Of course not, I share (bitterly) that crowning disability of my sex.
But not willingly, I chafe under it. My God, if it were not for that, we
women would master the world. I tell you men would be no match
for us. At heart we care nothing for laws, nothing for systems. All
your elaborately reasoned codes for controlling morals or man do not
weigh a jot with us against an impulse, an instinct. We learn those
things from you, you tamed, amenable animals; they are not natural
to us. It is a wise disposition of providence that this untameableness

of ours is corrected by our affections. We forge our own chains in a moment of softness, and then' (bitterly) 'we may as well wear them with a good grace. Perhaps many of our seeming contradictions are only the outward evidences of inward chafing. Bah! the qualities that go to make a Napoleon[6] – superstition, want of honour, disregard of opinion and the eternal I – are oftener to be found in a woman than a man. Lucky for the world perhaps that all these attributes weigh as nothing in the balance with the need to love if she be a good woman, to be loved if she is of a coarser fibre.'

'I never met any one like you, you are a strange woman!'

'No, I am merely a truthful one. Women talk to me – why, I can't say – but always they come, strip their hearts and souls naked and let me see the hidden folds of their natures. The greatest tragedies I have ever read are child's play to those I have seen acted in the inner life of outwardly commonplace women. A woman must beware of speaking the truth to a man; he loves her the less for it. It is the elusive spirit in her that he divines but cannot seize, that fascinates and keeps him.'

There is a long silence, the sun is waning and the scythes are silent, and overhead the crows are circling, a croaking irregular army, homeward bound from a long day's pillage.

She has made no sign, yet so subtly is the air charged with her that he feels but a few moments remain to him. He goes over and kneels beside her and fixes his eyes on her odd dark face. They both tremble, yet neither speaks. His breath is coming quickly, and the bistre stains about her eyes seem to have deepened, perhaps by contrast as she has paled.

'Look at me!'

She turns her head right round and gazes straight into his face. A few drops of sweat glisten on his forehead.

'You witch woman! what am I to do with myself? Is my moment ended?'

'I think so.'

'Lord, what a mouth!'

'Don't, oh don't!'

'No, I won't. But do you mean it? Am I, who understand your every mood, your restless spirit, to vanish out of your life? You can't mean it. Listen; are you listening to me? I can't see your face; take down your hands. Go back over every chance meeting you and I have had together since I met you first by the river, and judge them fairly. Today is Monday; Wednesday afternoon I shall pass your gate, and if – if my moment is ended, and you mean to send me away, to let me go with this weary aching . . .'

'A-ah!' she stretches out one brown hand appealingly, but he does not touch it.

'*Hang something white on the lilac bush!*'

She gathers up creel and rod, and he takes her shawl, and, wrapping it round her, holds her a moment in it, and looks searchingly into her eyes, then stands back and raises his hat, and she glides away through the reedy grass.

Wednesday morning she lies watching the clouds sail by. A late rose spray nods into the open window, and the petals fall every time. A big bee buzzes in and fills the room with his bass note, and then dances out again. She can hear his footstep on the gravel. Presently he looks in over the half window.

'Get up and come out, 'twill do you good. Have a brisk walk!'

She shakes her head languidly, and he throws a great soft dewy rose with sure aim on her breast.

'Shall I go in and lift you out and put you, "nighty" and all, into your tub?'

'No (impatiently). I'll get up just now.'

The head disappears, and she rises wearily and gets through her dressing slowly, stopped every moment by a feeling of faintness. He finds her presently rocking slowly to and fro with closed eyes, and drops a leaf with three plums in it on to her lap.

'I have been watching four for the last week, but a bird, greedy beggar, got one this morning early – try them. Don't you mind, old girl, I'll pour out my own tea!'

She bites into one and tries to finish it, but cannot.

'You are a good old man!' she says, and the tears come unbidden to her eyes, and trickle down her cheeks, dropping on to the plums, streaking their delicate bloom. He looks uneasily at her, but doesn't know what to do, and when he has finished his breakfast he stoops over her chair and strokes her hair, saying, as he leaves a kiss on the top of her head –

'Come out into the air, little woman; do you a world of good!' And presently she hears the sharp thrust of his spade above the bee's hum, leaf rustle and the myriad late summer sounds that thrill through the air. It irritates her almost to screaming point. There is a practical non-sympathy about it, she can distinguish the regular one, two, three, the thrust, interval, then pat, pat, on the upturned sod. Today she wants some one, and her thoughts wander to the grey-eyed man who never misunderstands her, and she wonders what he would say to her. Oh, she wants some one so badly to soothe her. And she yearns for the little mother who is twenty years under the daisies. The little mother who is a faint memory strengthened by a daguerreotype in which she sits with silk-mittened hands primly crossed on the lap of her moiré gown, a diamond brooch fastening the black velvet ribbon crossed so stiffly over her lace collar, the shining tender eyes looking steadily out and her hair in the fashion of fifty-six. How that spade dominates over every sound! And what a sickening pain she has; an odd pain, she never felt it before. Supposing she were to die, she tries to fancy how she would look. They would be sure to plaster her curls down. He might be digging her grave – no, it is the patch where the early peas grew; the peas that were eaten with the twelve weeks' ducklings; she remembers them, little fluffy golden balls with waxen bills, and such dainty paddles. Remembers holding an egg to her ear and listening to it cheep inside before even there was a chip in the shell. Strange how things come to life. What! she sits bolt upright and holds tightly to the chair, and a questioning, awesome look comes over her face. Then the quick blood creeps up through her olive skin right up to her temples, and she buries her face in her hands and sits so a long time.

The maid comes in and watches her curiously, and moves softly about. The look in her eyes is the look of a faithful dog, and she loves her with the same rare fidelity. She hesitates, then goes into the bedroom and stands thoughtfully, with her hands clasped over her breast.

She is a tall, thin, flat-waisted woman, with misty blue eyes and a receding chin. Her hair is pretty.

She turns as her mistress comes in, with an expectant look on her face. She has taken up a nightgown, but holds it idly.

'Lizzie, had you ever a child?'

The girl's long left hand is ringless, yet she asks it with a quiet insistence as if she knew what the answer would be, and the odd eyes read her face with an almost cruel steadiness. The girl flushes painfully and then whitens, her very eyes seem to pale, and her under lip twitches as she jerks out huskily –

'Yes!'

'What happened it?'

'It died, Ma'm.'

'Poor thing! Poor old Liz!'

She pats the girl's hand softly, and the latter stands dumbly and looks down at both hands, as if fearful to break the wonder of a caress. She whispers hesitatingly –

'Have you, have you any little things left?'

And she laughs such a soft, cooing little laugh, like the churring of a ringdove, and nods shyly back in reply to the tall maid's questioning look. The latter goes out, and comes back with a flat, red-painted deal box and unlocks it. It does not hold very much, and the tiny garments are not of costly material, but the two women pore over them as a gem collector over a rare stone. She has a glimpse of thick crested paper as the girl unties a packet of letters, and looks away until she says tenderly –

'Look, Ma'm!'

A little bit of hair inside a paper heart. It is almost white, so silky, and so fine, that it is more like a thread of bog-wool than a baby's hair. And the mistress, who is a wife, puts her arms round the tall maid, who has never had more than a moral claim to the name, and kisses her in her quick way.

The afternoon is drawing on; she is kneeling before an open trunk with flushed cheeks and sparkling eyes. A heap of unused, dainty lace trimmed ribbon-decked cambric garments is scattered around her. She holds the soft scented web to her cheek and smiles musingly.

Then she rouses herself and sets to work, sorting out the finest, with the narrowest lace and tiniest ribbon, and puckers her swarthy brows, and measures lengths along her middle finger. Then she gets slowly up, as if careful of herself as a precious thing, and half afraid.

'Lizzie!'

'Yes, Ma'm!'

'Wasn't it lucky they were too fine for every day? They will be so pretty. Look at this one with the tiny valenciennes edging. Why, one nightgown will make a dozen little shirts – such elfin-shirts as they are too – and Lizzie!'

'Yes, Ma'm!'

'Just hang it out on the lilac bush; mind, the lilac bush!'

'Yes, Ma'm.'

'Or Lizzie, wait – I'll do it myself!'

KATE CHOPIN

Désirée's Baby

As the day was pleasant, Madame Valmondé drove over to L'Abri to see Désirée and the baby.

It made her laugh to think of Désirée with a baby. Why, it seemed but yesterday that Désirée was little more than a baby herself; when Monsieur in riding through the gateway of Valmondé had found her lying asleep in the shadow of the big stone pillar.

The little one awoke in his arms and began to cry for 'Dada'. That was as much as she could do or say. Some people thought she might have strayed there of her own accord, for she was of the toddling age. The prevailing belief was that she had been purposely left by a party of Texans, whose canvas-covered wagon, late in the day, had crossed the ferry that Coton Maïs kept, just below the plantation. In time Madame Valmondé abandoned every speculation but the one that Désirée had been sent to her by a beneficent Providence to be the child of her affection, seeing that she was without child of the flesh. For the girl grew to be beautiful and gentle, affectionate and sincere, – the idol of Valmondé.

It was no wonder, when she stood one day against the stone pillar in whose shadow she had lain asleep, eighteen years before, that Armand Aubigny riding by and seeing her there, had fallen in love with her. That was the way all the Aubignys fell in love, as if struck by a pistol shot. The wonder was that he had not loved her before; for he had known her since his father brought him home from Paris, a boy of eight, after his mother died there. The passion that awoke in him that day, when he saw her at the gate, swept along like an avalanche, or like a prairie fire, or like anything that drives headlong over all obstacles.

Monsieur Valmondé grew practical and wanted things well considered: that is, the girl's obscure origin. Armand looked into her eyes and did not care. He was reminded that she was nameless. What did it matter about a name when he could give her one of the oldest and proudest in Louisiana? He ordered the *corbeille* from Paris, and contained himself with what patience he could until it arrived; then they were married.

Madame Valmondé had not seen Désirée and the baby for four weeks. When she reached L'Abri she shuddered at the first sight of it, as she always did. It was a sad looking place, which for many years had not known the gentle presence of a mistress, old Monsieur Aubigny having married and buried his wife in France, and she having loved her own land too well ever to leave it. The roof came down steep and black like a cowl, reaching out beyond the wide galleries that encircled the yellow stuccoed house. Big, solemn oaks grew close to it, and their thick-leaved, far-reaching branches shadowed it like a pall. Young Aubigny's rule was a strict one, too, and under it his Negroes had forgotten how to be gay, as they had been during the old master's easy-going and indulgent lifetime.

The young mother was recovering slowly, and lay full length, in her soft white muslins and laces, upon a couch. The baby was beside her, upon her arm, where he had fallen asleep, at her breast. The yellow nurse woman sat beside a window fanning herself.

Madame Valmondé bent her portly figure over Désirée and kissed her, holding her an instant tenderly in her arms. Then she turned to the child.

'This is not the baby!' she exclaimed, in startled tones. French was the language spoken at Valmondé in those days.

'I knew you would be astonished,' laughed Désirée, 'at the way he has grown. The little *cochon de lait!* Look at his legs, mamma, and his hands and fingernails, – real fingernails. Zandrine had to cut them this morning. Isn't it true, Zandrine?'

The woman bowed her turbaned head majestically, 'Mais si, Madame.'

'And the way he cries,' went on Désirée, 'is deafening. Armand heard him the other day as far away as La Blanche's[1] cabin.'

Madame Valmondé had never removed her eyes from the child. She lifted it and walked with it over to the window that was lightest. She scanned the baby narrowly, then looked as searchingly at Zandrine, whose face was turned to gaze across the fields.

'Yes, the child has grown, has changed,' said Madame Valmondé, slowly, as she replaced it beside its mother. 'What does Armand say?'

Désirée's face became suffused with a glow that was happiness itself.

'Oh, Armand is the proudest father in the parish, I believe, chiefly because it is a boy, to bear his name; though he says not, – that he would have loved a girl as well. But I know it isn't true. I know he says that to please me. And mamma,' she added, drawing Madame Valmondé's head down to her, and speaking in a whisper, 'he hasn't punished one of them – not one of them – since baby is born. Even Négrillon, who pretended to have burnt his leg that he might rest from work – he only laughed, and said Négrillon was a great scamp. Oh, mamma, I'm so happy; it frightens me.'

What Désirée said was true. Marriage, and later the birth of his son had softened Armand Aubigny's imperious and exacting nature greatly. This was what made the gentle Désirée so happy, for she loved him desperately. When he frowned she trembled, but loved him. When he smiled, she asked no greater blessing of God. But Armand's dark, handsome face had not often been disfigured by frowns since the day he fell in love with her.

When the baby was about three months old, Désirée awoke one day to the conviction that there was something in the air menacing her peace. It was at first too subtle to grasp. It had only been a disquieting suggestion; an air of mystery among the blacks; unexpected visits from far-off neighbours who could hardly account for their coming. Then a strange, an awful change in her husband's manner, which she dared not ask him to explain. When he spoke to her, it was with averted eyes, from which the old love-light seemed to have gone out. He absented himself from home; and when there, avoided her presence and that of her child, without excuse. And the very spirit of Satan seemed suddenly to take hold of him in his dealings with the slaves. Désirée was miserable enough to die.

She sat in her room, one hot afternoon, in her *peignoir*, listlessly drawing through her fingers the strands of her long, silky brown hair that hung about her shoulders. The baby, half naked, lay asleep upon her own great mahogany bed, that was like a sumptuous throne, with its satin-lined half-canopy. One of La Blanche's little quadroon boys – half naked too – stood fanning the child slowly with a fan of peacock feathers. Désirée's eyes had been fixed absently and sadly upon the baby, while she was striving to penetrate the threatening mist that she felt closing about her. She looked from her child to the boy who stood beside him, and back again; over and over. 'Ah!' It was a cry that she could not help; which she was not conscious of having uttered. The blood turned like ice in her veins, and a clammy moisture gathered upon her face.

She tried to speak to the little quadroon boy; but no sound would come, at first. When he heard his name uttered, he looked up, and his mistress was pointing to the door. He laid aside the great, soft fan, and obediently stole away, over the polished floor, on his bare tiptoes.

She stayed motionless, with gaze riveted upon her child, and her face the picture of fright.

Presently her husband entered the room, and without noticing her, went to a table and began to search among some papers which covered it.

'Armand,' she called to him, in a voice which must have stabbed him, if he was human. But he did not notice. 'Armand,' she said again. Then she rose and tottered towards him. 'Armand,' she panted once more, clutching his arm, 'look at our child. What does it mean? tell me.'

He coldly but gently loosened her fingers from about his arm and thrust the hand away from him. 'Tell me what it means!' she cried despairingly.

'It means,' he answered lightly, 'that the child is not white; it means that you are not white.'

A quick conception of all that this accusation meant for her nerved her with unwonted courage to deny it. 'It is a lie; it is not true, I am white! Look at my hair, it is brown; and my eyes are grey, Armand, you know they are grey. And my skin is fair,' seizing his wrist. 'Look at my hand; whiter than yours, Armand,' she laughed hysterically.

'As white as La Blanche's,' he returned cruelly; and went away leaving her alone with their child.

When she could hold a pen in her hand, she sent a despairing letter to Madame Valmondé.

'My mother, they tell me I am not white. Armand has told me I am not white. For God's sake tell them it is not true. You must know it is not true. I shall die. I must die. I cannot be so unhappy, and live.'

The answer that came was as brief:

'My own Désirée: Come home to Valmondé; back to your mother who loves you. Come with your child.'

When the letter reached Désirée she went with it to her husband's study, and laid it open upon the desk before which he sat. She was like a stone image: silent, white, motionless after she placed it there.

In silence he ran his cold eyes over the written words. He said nothing. 'Shall I go, Armand?' she asked in tones sharp with agonized suspense.

'Yes, go.'

'Do you want me to go?'

'Yes, I want you to go.'

He thought Almighty God had dealt cruelly and unjustly with him; and felt, somehow, that he was paying Him back in kind when he stabbed thus into his wife's soul. Moreover he no longer loved her, because of the unconscious injury she had brought upon his home and his name.

She turned away like one stunned by a blow, and walked slowly towards the door, hoping he would call her back.

'Goodbye, Armand,' she moaned.

He did not answer her. That was his last blow at fate.

Désirée went in search of her child. Zandrine was pacing the sombre gallery with it. She took the little one from the nurse's arms with no word of explanation, and descending the steps, walked away, under the live-oak branches.

It was an October afternoon; the sun was just sinking. Out in the still fields the Negroes were picking cotton.

Désirée had not changed the thin white garment nor the slippers which she wore. Her hair was uncovered and the sun's rays brought a golden gleam from its brown meshes. She did not take the broad, beaten road which led to the far-off plantation of Valmondé. She walked across a deserted field, where the stubble bruised her tender feet, so delicately shod, and tore her thin gown to shreds.

She disappeared among the reeds and willows that grew thick along the banks of the deep, sluggish bayou; and she did not come back again.

Some weeks later there was a curious scene enacted at L'Abri. In the centre of the smoothly swept back yard was a great bonfire. Armand Aubigny sat in the wide hallway that commanded a view of the spectacle; and it was he who dealt out to a half dozen Negroes the material which kept this fire ablaze.

A graceful cradle of willow, with all its dainty furbishings, was laid upon the pyre, which had already been fed with the richness of a priceless *layette*. Then there were silk gowns, and velvet and satin ones added to these; laces, too, and embroideries; bonnets and gloves; for the *corbeille* had been of rare quality.

The last thing to go was a tiny bundle of letters; innocent little scribblings that Désirée had sent to him during the days of their espousal. There was the remnant of one back in the drawer from which he took them. But it was not Désirée's; it was part of an old letter from his mother to his father. He read it. She was thanking God for the blessing of her husband's love: —

'But, above all,' she wrote, 'night and day, I thank the good God for having so arranged our lives that our dear Armand will never know that his mother, who adores him, belongs to the race that is cursed with the brand of slavery.'

She-Notes

'Mr Soozie! My Toozie! My Soozie!'

It is the voice of a man, and he sings. He has grey eyes, and wears a grey Norfolk-broad.[1] They accentuate one another; the pine trees also accentuate his fishing rod. His hum blends with the bleating of the *Bufo vulgaris* and the cooing of *Coleoptera*.

Beside a fallen pine lies a woman (*genus*, in fact, *muliebre*). Where the tree fell there she lies. Her fresh animal instinct sniffs the music-hall refrain; the footlights of the Pavillon Rouge[2] mix rather weirdly with a vision, just rudely interrupted, of terra-cottas from Tanagra. Not every woman thinks of these things in a wood.

The male is a student of the Eternal Femininity. Already, while still out of gunshot, he has noticed her wedding ring and the diamond keeper.

'Talking of keepers,' he begins, with the affected drawl now sufficiently familiar to the reader, 'are we trespassing here?'

She replies in her frank unembarrassed way. 'Better ask a p'leece-man,' she says.

(A lady, obviously! Worth cultivating? Bet your braces!)

'After trout, you know. Any local tips in flies?'

A rare smile comes with her ready answer. ' "Pick-me-ups" after a heavy night; "Henry Clays" after lunch; "spotted cocktails" for the evening. Like a "coachman" myself; sometimes find them quite killing!'

'Happy coachman!'

A chill comes over the sylvan scene with these reckless words. She has gathered her cream-coloured mittens about her wrists; the contrast at once strikes him; in the subdued evening light he can see that her hands are unwashed. She bows coolly, and is off across the stream like a water-snake.

She is lounging nervously on the edge of the parlour-grate. There are two (an acute observer would say three) furrows on her fore-head.

'Off your pipe, old chappie? Feel a bit cheap?' (It is her husband who speaks in this way.)

'Yes, beastly, thanks, old man!'

'Try a nip o' whisky. No soda; soda for boys. There, that's right! Buck up! What's your book?'

'Oh! one of WILDE's little things. I like WILDE; he shocks the middle classes. Only the middle classes are so easily shocked!'

He smiles a gentle, dull smile. There is a long pause; he cannot follow her swift eternally feminine fancy.

'What's it now, old buffer? A brass for your thoughts!'

'I was thinking, little woman, of a filly foal I once had. She grew up to be a mare. I never would have let anyone on God's beautiful earth ride her.'

'I'd have ridden her!'

'No, you wouldn't!'

'Yes, I would!' (passionately and concentratedly).

'Well, I sold her anyway. Lucky the beast isn't here now to spoil our conjugal unity!'

The crisis had past. Another moment and she might have left him for ever lonely and forlorn! But in a twinkling her wild, free instinct doubles at a tangent. With a supple bound she is on his shoulders curling her lithe fishing boots into one of his waistcoat pockets. Surely gypsy blood runs in her veins!

'Oh! I wish I were a devil' (it is the lady speaking); 'yes, a d-e-v-i-l!'

'But you *are*, old woman, you *are!* and such a dear little devil!'

'Say it again, old man!' (kissing him fiercely in the left eye and worrying his ear like a ferret), 'I love to hear you call me that. We women yearn for praise!'

'You're a rare brick, old dear; and you're never jealous. Look at that photo of the other girl! Some women would have cut up rough about it. But *you* – why, you sent her a quid when she was peckish, and she chewed it for a week! Was there ever such a little chip?'

PART 2

She is lying on her back in a bog stream. Strangely enough there are white clouds waltzing along the sky. To her fancy, which is nothing if not picturesque, they are a troop of fairy geese on their way to Michaelmas. No? well then, plainly they are ANTONY and CLEO-PATRA. And oh! the dalliance, the wild free life of Egypt! No dinners to order; very little washing on Mondays.

Presto! In imagination she is on a stage. She is a *Tableau Vivant!* All the fauteuils have their glasses up. She has pink overalls, with a cestus round her neck. Her lissom limbs scintillate; she dances slightly. KILANYI[3] says she must try and keep still. A moment more and there is a lovely cat-call from the gallery; she can still hear it above the orchestra, as the next tableau is being wheeled on. It *was* a supreme keynote!

And the other women? Crushed, joyless, machines – misunderstood! How can the dense brute male read the enigma of the Female Idea? They think us innocent! not we! but we all keep up the deception and lie courageously. They will never know that we are really primitive, untameable, ineradicable animalculae.

'Got the blue devils, little witch?' (It is the grey man. He has dropped his drawl and his fly-book. They have been getting on nicely, thank you, since we saw them last.)

'Yes, we are all witches, we women. We can read men but they can't read us.'

'Can't *I* read you?'

'*Me*, the real ineffable *me*? Yes, perhaps just a little. You have a dash of the Everlasting Female in you.' As she speaks she rolls up her shawl into an infinitesimal pellet.

'Well, look here' (desperately). 'What do you say to a trip in my yacht? Southern seas! Venice! Constantinople! Olympia! And then, when the winds are hushed and the steam is shut off for the night, we would fly with no visible means of locomotion over the silvery deep! You smile? Where is the pain?'

'Oh! if I could only have the yacht without you in it!' (He winces.) 'Yes, I say, give us women freedom and we would all go one better than NAPOLEON. NELSON[4] knew nothing of the eternal I! Bah! and he was blind in the other.'

'You strange creature!'

'No, not strange; only true. Were I more elusive I might be more fascinating.'

A long silence broken only by the chirp of a grasshopper. The air is charged like a battery. It seems that a submarine cable connects these two souls. Nevertheless, she distinctly observes that the grasshopper has strained his Achilles-tendon. Curious that at such a climax the minutest detail should not escape her. Am I right in thinking that no novelist has as yet detected this remarkable phenomenon? He comes nearer (I mean the grey man). His skin beneath his collar blushes a rich cobalt.

'Is my little moment up?' he gasps. (His stop-watch is in his trembling hand.)

'Lord! what a cheek you have!'

'Don't, oh, don't say that!'

'Very well, I withdraw it.'

'But listen!' (she is dropping asleep); 'listen, I say!' (she will be snoring directly); 'if my moment is really ended – and my stop-watch points to the fact – and if you mean to send me away, *hang something white on the gooseberry-bush* (our *gooseberry-bush*) *tomorrow about the ninth hour!*' She rises and is gone like a water-snake.

It is tomorrow about the eighth hour. She is still in bed. There is a nod at the window. It is all right; only a blushing sweet-william. On the mantelpiece is a daguerreotype of her late aunt, in a velvet bodice and other things. But it is not *that* which drives her crazy. It is her husband's cheery pickaxe in the garden. Is he really digging her grave? Why, surely, no; he is simply arranging the onion-bed. Yet what an interesting corpse she would make! The pity is that one can never see one's own corpse in the glass. Stay, is that BETSY?

'Oh! BETSY' (the young cook enters demurely for orders),

'I wonder had you ever a lover?'

'Well, Ma'm, what do *you* think?'

'Say, what happened him, anyway?'

'Why, he left me, Ma'm, left me for Another; and' (regretfully) 'we might have married, and had such *heavenly* twins;[5] and, oh! he *had* such a beautiful crest on his writing paper!'

A moment's tension follows; the next sees the lady feeling for a coin in her dress-pocket. She spins it deftly. 'Heads, he stays! tails, he goes! Tails! by all that is virtuous.'

'BETSY!' (Her voice is firm, like a quickset hedge.) 'BETSY! I cannot spare my "nighty" just now, but your white apron will do as well. You *do* love me, don't you?' (Kisses her.) 'Then for *my* sake go and hang yourself for a little while on the gooseberry-bush. Mind! the *gooseberry*-bush!'

'Yes, Ma'm.'

A rare fidelity! And so few men could have understood or even spelt the why in BETSY!

Two hours later she wakes up and remembers the faithful girl! Perhaps it is even now too late! She hurries through her toilet. The daguerreotype shows no sign. Threads of bog-wool float persistently in the summer air. She is by the gooseberry-bush with a stout pair of scissors. Too late! The girl is gone! Another hand, a hand that held a stopwatch, has cut her down, and BETSY is by this time a free and unfettered woman, on her way to a yacht.

The grey man, after all, had his consolation.

THOMAS HARDY

An Imaginative Woman

When William Marchmill had finished his enquiries for lodgings at the well-known watering place of Solentsea in Upper Wessex,[1] he returned to the hotel to find his wife. She, with the children, had rambled along the shore, and Marchmill followed in the direction indicated by the military-looking hall-porter.

'By Jove, how far you've gone! I am quite out of breath,' Marchmill said, rather impatiently, when he came up with his wife, who was reading as she walked, the three children being considerably further ahead with the nurse.

Mrs Marchmill started out of the reverie into which the book had thrown her. 'Yes,' she said, 'you've been such a long time. I was tired of staying in that dreary hotel. But I am sorry if you have wanted me, Will?'

'Well, I have had trouble to suit myself. When you see the airy and comfortable rooms heard of, you find they are stuffy and uncomfortable. Will you come and see if what I've fixed on will do? There is not much room, I am afraid; but I can light on nothing better. The town is rather full.'

The pair left the children and nurse to continue their ramble, and went back together.

In age well-balanced, in personal appearance fairly matched and in domestic requirements conformable, in temper this couple differed, though even here they did not often clash, he being equable, if not lymphatic, and she decidedly nervous and sanguine.[2] It was to their tastes and fancies, those smallest, greatest particulars, that no common denominator could be applied. Marchmill considered his wife's likes and inclinations somewhat silly; she considered his sordid and

78

material. The husband's business was that of a gunmaker in a thriving city northwards, and his soul was in that business always; the lady was best characterized by that superannuated phrase of elegance 'a votary of the muse'.[3] An impressionable, palpitating creature was Ella, shrinking humanely from detailed knowledge of her husband's trade whenever she reflected that everything he manufactured had for its purpose the destruction of life. She could only recover her equanimity by assuring herself that some, at least, of his weapons were sooner or later used for the extermination of horrid vermin and animals almost as cruel to their inferiors in species as human beings were to theirs.

She had never antecedently regarded this occupation of his as any objection to having him for a husband. Indeed, the necessity of getting life-leased at all cost, a cardinal virtue which all good mothers teach, kept her from thinking of it at all till she had closed with William, had passed the honeymoon, and reached the reflecting stage. Then, like a person who has stumbled upon some object in the dark, she wondered what she had got; mentally walked round it, estimated it; whether it were rare or common; contained gold, silver or lead; were a clog or a pedestal, everything to her or nothing.

She came to some vague conclusions, and since then had kept her heart alive by pitying her proprietor's obtuseness and want of refinement, pitying herself, and letting off her delicate and ethereal emotions in imaginative occupations, daydreams and night-sighs, which perhaps would not much have disturbed William if he had known of them.

Her figure was small, elegant and slight in build, tripping, or rather bounding, in movement. She was dark-eyed, and had that marvellously bright and liquid sparkle in each pupil which characterizes persons of Ella's cast of soul, and is too often a cause of heartache to the possessor's male friends, ultimately sometimes to herself. Her husband was a tall, long-featured man, with a brown beard; he had a pondering regard; and was, it must be added, usually kind and tolerant to her. He spoke in squarely shaped sentences, and was supremely satisfied with a condition of sublunary things which made weapons a necessity.

Husband and wife walked till they had reached the house they were in search of, which stood in a terrace facing the sea, and was fronted by a small garden of wind-proof and salt-proof evergreens, stone steps leading up to the porch. It had its number in the row, but, being rather larger than the rest, was in addition sedulously distinguished as Coburg House by its landlady, though everybody else called it 'Thirteen, New Parade'. The spot was bright and lively now; but in winter it became necessary to place sandbags against the door, and to stuff up the keyhole against the wind and rain, which had worn the paint so thin that the priming and knotting showed through.

The householder, who had been watching for the gentleman's return, met them in the passage, and showed the rooms. She informed them that she was a professional man's widow, left in needy circumstances by the rather sudden death of her husband, and she spoke anxiously of the conveniences of the establishment.

Mrs Marchmill said that she liked the situation and the house; but, it being small, there would not be accommodation enough, unless she could have all the rooms.

The landlady mused with an air of disappointment. She wanted the visitors to be her tenants very badly, she said, with obvious honesty. But unfortunately two of the rooms were occupied permanently by a bachelor gentleman. He did not pay season prices, it was true; but as he kept on his apartments all the year round, and was an extremely nice and interesting young man, who gave no trouble, she did not like to turn him out for a month's 'let', even at a high figure. 'Perhaps, however,' she added, 'he might offer to go for a time.'

They would not hear of this, and went back to the hotel, intending to proceed to the agent's to enquire further. Hardly had they sat down to tea when the landlady called. Her gentleman, she said, had been so obliging as to offer to give up his rooms for three or four weeks rather than drive the newcomers away.

'It is very kind, but we won't inconvenience him in that way,' said the Marchmills.

'O, it won't inconvenience him, I assure you!' said the landlady eloquently. 'You see, he's a different sort of young man from most – dreamy, solitary, rather melancholy – and he cares more to be here when the south-westerly gales are beating against the door, and the sea washes over the Parade, and there's not a soul in the place, than he does now in the season. He'd just as soon be where, in fact, he's going temporarily, to a little cottage on the Island opposite,[4] for a change.' She hoped therefore that they would come.

The Marchmill family accordingly took possession of the house next day, and it seemed to suit them very well. After luncheon Mr Marchmill strolled out towards the pier, and Mrs Marchmill, having despatched the children to their outdoor amusements on the sands, settled herself in more completely, examining this and that article, and testing the reflecting powers of the mirror in the wardrobe door.

In the small back sitting-room, which had been the young bachelor's, she found furniture of a more personal nature than in the rest. Shabby books, of correct rather than rare editions, were piled up in a queerly reserved manner in corners, as if the previous occupant had not conceived the possibility that any incoming person of the season's bringing could care to look inside them. The landlady hovered on the threshold to rectify anything that Mrs Marchmill might not find to her satisfaction.

'I'll make this my own little room,' said the latter, 'because the books are here. By the way, the person who has left seems to have a good many. He won't mind my reading some of them, Mrs Hooper, I hope?'

'O dear no, ma'am. Yes, he has a good many. You see, he is in the literary line himself somewhat. He is a poet – yes, really a poet – and he has a little income of his own, which is enough to write verses on, but not enough for cutting a figure, even if he cared to.'

'A poet! O, I did not know that.'

Mrs Marchmill opened one of the books, and saw the owner's name written on the title-page. 'Dear me!' she continued; 'I know his name very well – Robert Trewe – of course I do; and his writings! And it is *his* rooms we have taken, and *him* we have turned out of his home?'

Ella Marchmill, sitting down alone a few minutes later, thought with interested surprise of Robert Trewe. Her own latter history will best explain that interest. Herself the only daughter of a struggling man of letters, she had during the last year or two taken to writing poems, in an endeavour to find a congenial channel in which to let flow her painfully embayed emotions, whose former limpidity and sparkle seemed departing in the stagnation caused by the routine of a practical household and the gloom of bearing children to a commonplace father. These poems, subscribed with a masculine pseudonym, had appeared in various obscure magazines, and in two cases in rather prominent ones. In the second of the latter the page which bore her effusion at the bottom, in smallish print, bore at the top, in large print, a few verses on the same subject by this very man, Robert Trewe. Both of them had, in fact, been struck by a tragic incident reported in the daily papers, and had used it simultaneously as an inspiration, the editor remarking in a note upon the coincidence, and that the excellence of both poems prompted him to give them together.

After that event Ella, otherwise 'John Ivy', had watched with much attention the appearance anywhere in print of verse bearing the signature of Robert Trewe, who, with a man's unsusceptibility on the question of sex, had never once thought of passing himself off as a woman. To be sure, Mrs Marchmill had satisfied herself with a sort of reason for doing the contrary in her case; since nobody might believe in her inspiration if they found that the sentiments came from a pushing tradesman's wife, from the mother of three children by a matter-of-fact small-arms manufacturer.

Trewe's verse contrasted with that of the rank and file of recent minor poets in being impassioned rather than ingenious, luxuriant rather than finished. Neither *symboliste* nor *décadent*,[5] he was a pessimist in so far as that character applies to a man who looks at the worst contingencies as well as the best in the human condition. Being little attracted by excellences of form and rhythm apart from content, he sometimes, when feeling outran his artistic speed, perpetrated sonnets in the loosely rhymed Elizabethan fashion, which every right-minded reviewer said he ought not to have done.

With sad and hopeless envy Ella Marchmill had often and often scanned the rival poet's work, so much stronger as it always was than her own feeble lines. She had imitated him, and her inability to touch his level would send her into fits of despondency. Months passed away thus, till she observed from the publishers' list that Trewe had collected his fugitive pieces into a volume, which was duly issued, and was much or little praised according to chance, and had a sale quite sufficient to pay for the printing.

This step onward had suggested to John Ivy the idea of collecting her pieces also, or at any rate of making up a book of her rhymes by adding many in manuscript to the few that had seen the light, for she had been able to get no great number into print. A ruinous charge was made for costs of publication; a few reviews noticed her poor little volume; but nobody talked of it, nobody bought it and it fell dead in a fortnight – if it had ever been alive.

The author's thoughts were diverted to another groove just then by the discovery that she was going to have a third child, and the collapse of her poetical venture had perhaps less effect upon her mind than it might have done if she had been domestically unoccupied. Her husband had paid the publisher's bill with the doctor's, and there it all had ended for the time. But, though less than a poet of her century, Ella was more than a mere multiplier of her kind, and latterly she had begun to feel the old afflatus once more. And now by an odd conjunction she found herself in the rooms of Robert Trewe.

She thoughtfully rose from her chair and searched the apartment with the interest of a fellow tradesman. Yes, the volume of his own verse was among the rest. Though quite familiar with its contents, she read it here as if it spoke aloud to her, then called up Mrs Hooper, the landlady, for some trivial service, and enquired again about the young man.

'Well, I'm sure you'd be interested in him, ma'am, if you could see him, only he's so shy that I don't suppose you will.' Mrs Hooper seemed nothing loth to minister to her tenant's curiosity about her predecessor. 'Lived here long? Yes, nearly two years. He keeps on his rooms even when he's not here: the soft air of this place suits his chest, and he likes to be able to come back at any time. He is mostly writing or reading, and doesn't see many people, though, for the matter of that, he is such a good, kind young fellow that folks would only be too glad to be friendly with him if they knew him. You don't meet kind-hearted people every day.'

'Ah, he's kind-hearted . . . and good.'

'Yes; he'll oblige me in anything if I ask him. "Mr Trewe," I say to him sometimes, "you are rather out of spirits." "Well, I am, Mrs Hooper," he'll say, "though I don't know how you should find it out." "Why not take a little change?" I ask. Then in a day or two he'll say that he will take a trip to Paris, or Norway, or somewhere; and I assure you he comes back all the better for it.'

'Ah, indeed! His is a sensitive nature, no doubt.'

'Yes. Still he's odd in some things. Once when he had finished a poem of his composition late at night he walked up and down the room rehearsing it; and the floors being so thin – jerry-built houses, you know, though I say it myself – he kept me awake up above him till I wished him further . . . But we get on very well.'

This was but the beginning of a series of conversations about the rising poet as the days went on. On one of these occasions Mrs Hooper drew Ella's attention to what she had not noticed before: minute scribblings in pencil on the wallpaper behind the curtains at the head of the bed.

'O! let me look,' said Mrs Marchmill, unable to conceal a rush of tender curiosity as she bent her pretty face close to the wall.

'These,' said Mrs Hooper, with the manner of a woman who knew things, 'are the very beginnings and first thoughts of his verses. He has tried to rub most of them out, but you can read them still. My belief is that he wakes up in the night, you know, with some rhyme in his head, and jots it down there on the wall lest he should forget it by the morning. Some of these very lines you see here I have seen afterwards in print in the magazines. Some are newer; indeed, I have not seen that one before. It must have been done only a few days ago.'

'O yes!'

Ella Marchmill flushed without knowing why, and suddenly wished her companion would go away, now that the information was imparted. An indescribable consciousness of personal interest rather than literary made her anxious to read the inscription alone; and she accordingly waited till she could do so, with a sense that a great store of emotion would be enjoyed in the act.

Perhaps because the sea was choppy outside the Island, Ella's husband found it much pleasanter to go sailing and steaming about without his wife, who was a bad sailor, than with her. He did not disdain to go thus alone on board the steamboats of the cheap-trippers, where there was dancing by moonlight, and where the couples would come suddenly down with a lurch into each other's arms; for, as he blandly told her, the company was too mixed for him to take her amid such scenes. Thus, while this thriving manufacturer got a great deal of change and sea air out of his sojourn here, the life, external at least, of Ella was monotonous enough, and mainly consisted in passing a certain number of hours each day in bathing and walking up and down a stretch of shore. But the poetic impulse having again waxed strong, she was possessed by an inner flame which left her hardly conscious of what was proceeding around her.

She had read till she knew by heart Trewe's last little volume of verses, and spent a great deal of time in vainly attempting to rival some of them, till, in her failure, she burst into tears. The personal element in the magnetic attraction exercised by this circumambient, unapproachable master of hers was so much stronger than the intellectual and abstract that she could not understand it. To be sure, she was surrounded noon and night by his customary environment, which literally whispered of him to her at every moment; but he was a man she had never seen, and that all that moved her was the instinct to specialize a waiting emotion on the first fit thing that came to hand did not, of course, suggest itself to Ella.

In the natural way of passion under the too practical conditions which civilization has devised for its fruition, her husband's love for her had not survived, except in the form of fitful friendship, any more than, or even so much as, her own for him; and, being a woman of very living ardours, that required sustenance of some sort, they were beginning to feed on this chancing material, which was, indeed, of a quality far better than chance usually offers.

One day the children had been playing hide-and-seek in a closet, whence, in their excitement, they pulled out some clothing. Mrs Hooper explained that it belonged to Mr Trewe, and hung it up in the closet again. Possessed of her fantasy, Ella went later in the afternoon, when nobody was in that part of the house, opened the closet, unhitched one of the articles, a mackintosh, and put it on, with the waterproof cap belonging to it.

'The mantle of Elijah!'[6] she said. 'Would it might inspire me to rival him, glorious genius that he is!'

Her eyes always grew wet when she thought like that, and she turned to look at herself in the glass. *His* heart had beat inside that coat, and *his* brain had worked under that hat at levels of thought she would never reach. The consciousness of her weakness beside him made her feel quite sick. Before she had got the things off her the door opened, and her husband entered the room.

'What the devil—'

She blushed, and removed them.

'I found them in the closet here,' she said, 'and put them on in a freak. What have I else to do? You are always away!'

'Always away? Well . . .'

That evening she had a further talk with the landlady, who might herself have nourished a half-tender regard for the poet, so ready was she to discourse ardently about him.

'You are interested in Mr Trewe, I know, ma'am,' she said; 'and he has just sent to say that he is going to call tomorrow afternoon to look up some books of his that he wants, if I'll be in, and he may select them from your room?'

'O yes!'

'You could very well meet Mr Trewe then, if you'd like to be in the way!'

She promised with secret delight, and went to bed musing of him.

Next morning her husband observed: 'I've been thinking of what you said, Ell: that I have gone about a good deal and left you without much to amuse you. Perhaps it's true. Today, as there's not much sea, I'll take you with me on board the yacht.'

For the first time in her experience of such an offer Ella was not glad. But she accepted it for the moment. The time for setting out drew near, and she went to get ready. She stood reflecting. The longing to see the poet she was now distinctly in love with overpowered all other considerations.

'I don't want to go,' she said to herself. 'I can't bear to be away! And I won't go.'

She told her husband that she had changed her mind about wishing to sail. He was indifferent, and went his way.

For the rest of the day the house was quiet, the children having gone out upon the sands. The blinds waved in the sunshine to the soft, steady stroke of the sea beyond the wall; and the notes of the Green Silesian band,[7] a troop of foreign gentlemen hired for the season, had drawn almost all the residents and promenaders away from the vicinity of Coburg House. A knock was audible at the door.

Mrs Marchmill did not hear any servant go to answer it, and she became impatient. The books were in the room where she sat; but nobody came up. She rang the bell.

'There is some person waiting at the door,' she said.

'O no, ma'am! He's gone long ago. I answered it,' the servant replied, and Mrs Hooper came in herself.

'So disappointing!' she said. 'Mr Trewe not coming after all!'

'But I heard him knock, I fancy!'

'No; that was somebody enquiring for lodgings who came to the wrong house. I forgot to tell you that Mr Trewe sent a note just before lunch to say I needn't get any tea for him, as he should not require the books, and wouldn't come to select them.'

Ella was miserable, and for a long time could not even reread his mournful ballad on 'Severed Lives',[8] so aching was her erratic little heart, and so tearful her eyes. When the children came in with wet stockings, and ran up to her to tell her of their adventures, she could not feel that she cared about them half as much as usual.

'Mrs Hooper, have you a photograph of – the gentleman who lived here?' She was getting to be curiously shy in mentioning his name.

'Why, yes. It's in the ornamental frame on the mantelpiece in your own bedroom, ma'am.'

'No; the Royal Duke and Duchess are in that.'

'Yes, so they are; but he's behind them. He belongs rightly to that frame, which I bought on purpose; but as he went away he said: "Cover me up from those strangers that are coming, for God's sake. I don't want them staring at me, and I am sure they won't want me staring at them." So I slipped in the Duke and Duchess temporarily in front of him, as they had no frame, and Royalties are more suitable for letting furnished than a private young man. If you take 'em out you'll see him under. Lord, ma'am, he wouldn't mind if he knew it! He didn't think the next tenant would be such an attractive lady as you, or he wouldn't have thought of hiding himself, perhaps.'

'Is he handsome?' she asked timidly.

'*I* call him so. Some, perhaps, wouldn't.'

'Should I?' she asked, with eagerness.

'I think you would, though some would say he's more striking than handsome; a large-eyed thoughtful fellow, you know, with a very electric flash in his eye when he looks round quickly, such as you'd expect a poet to be who doesn't get his living by it.'

'How old is he?'

'Several years older than yourself, ma'am; about thirty-one or two, I think.'

Ella was, as a matter of fact, a few months over thirty herself; but she did not look nearly so much. Though so immature in nature, she was entering on that tract of life in which emotional women begin to suspect that last love may be stronger than first love; and she would soon, alas, enter on the still more melancholy tract when at least the vainer ones of her sex shrink from receiving a male visitor otherwise than with their backs to the window or the blinds half down. She reflected on Mrs Hooper's remark, and said no more about age.

Just then a telegram was brought up. It came from her husband, who had gone down the Channel as far as Budmouth with his friends in the yacht, and would not be able to get back till next day.

After her light dinner Ella idled about the shore with the children till dusk, thinking of the yet uncovered photograph in her room, with a serene sense of something ecstatic to come. For, with the subtle luxuriousness of fancy in which this young woman was an adept, on learning that her husband was to be absent that night she had refrained from incontinently rushing upstairs and opening the picture frame, preferring to reserve the inspection till she could be alone, and a more romantic tinge be imparted to the occasion by silence, candles, solemn sea and stars outside, than was afforded by the garish afternoon sunlight.

The children had been sent to bed, and Ella soon followed, though it was not yet ten o'clock. To gratify her passionate curiosity she now made her preparations, first getting rid of superfluous garments and putting on her dressing gown, then arranging a chair in front of the table and reading several pages of Trewe's tenderest utterances. Next she fetched the portrait frame to the light, opened the back, took out the likeness and set it up before her.

It was a striking countenance to look upon. The poet wore a luxuriant black moustache and imperial, and a slouched hat[9] which shaded the forehead. The large dark eyes described by the landlady showed an unlimited capacity for misery; they looked out from beneath well-shaped brows as if they were reading the universe in the microcosm of the confronter's face, and were not altogether overjoyed at what the spectacle portended.

Ella murmured in her lowest, richest, tenderest tone: 'And it's *you* who've so cruelly eclipsed me these many times!'

As she gazed long at the portrait she fell into thought, till her eyes filled with tears, and she touched the cardboard with her lips. Then she laughed with a nervous lightness, and wiped her eyes.

She thought how wicked she was, a woman having a husband and three children, to let her mind stray to a stranger in this unconscionable manner. No, he was not a stranger! She knew his thoughts and feelings as well as she knew her own; they were, in fact, the self-same thoughts and feelings as hers, which her husband distinctly lacked; perhaps luckily for himself, considering that he had to provide for family expenses.

'He's nearer my real self, he's more intimate with the real me than Will is, after all, even though I've never seen him,' she said.

She laid his book and picture on the table at the bedside, and when she was reclining on the pillow she reread those of Robert Trewe's verses which she had marked from time to time as most touching and true. Putting these aside she set up the photograph on its edge upon the coverlet, and contemplated it as she lay. Then she scanned again by the light of the candle the half-obliterated pencillings on the wallpaper beside her head. There they were – phrases, couplets, bouts-rimés, beginnings and middles of lines, ideas in the rough, like Shelley's scraps, and the least of them so intense, so sweet, so palpitating that it seemed as if his very breath, warm and loving, fanned her cheeks from those walls, walls that had surrounded his head times and times as they surrounded her own now. He must often have put up his hand so – with the pencil in it. Yes, the writing was sideways, as it would be if executed by one who extended his arm thus.

These inscribed shapes of the poet's world,

'Forms more real than living man,
Nurslings of immortality',[10]

were, no doubt, the thoughts and spirit-strivings which had come to him in the dead of night, when he could let himself go and have no fear of the frost of criticism. No doubt they had often been written up hastily by the light of the moon, the rays of the lamp, in the blue-grey dawn, in full daylight perhaps never. And now her hair was dragging where his arm had lain when he secured the fugitive fancies; she was sleeping on a poet's lips,[11] immersed in the very essence of him, permeated by his spirit as by an ether.

While she was dreaming the minutes away thus, a footstep came upon the stairs, and in a moment she heard her husband's heavy step on the landing immediately without.

'Ell, where are you?'

What possessed her she could not have described, but, with an instinctive objection to let her husband know what she had been doing, she slipped the photograph under the pillow just as he flung open the door with the air of a man who had dined not badly.

'O, I beg pardon,' said William Marchmill. 'Have you a headache? I am afraid I have disturbed you.'

'No, I've not got a headache,' said she. 'How is it you've come?'

'Well, we found we could get back in very good time after all, and I didn't want to make another day of it, because of going somewhere else tomorrow.'

'Shall I come down again?'

'O no. I'm as tired as a dog. I've had a good feed, and I shall turn in straight off. I want to get out at six o'clock tomorrow if I can . . . I shan't disturb you by my getting up; it will be long before you are awake.' And he came forward into the room.

While her eyes followed his movements, Ella softly pushed the photograph further out of sight.

'Sure you're not ill?' he asked, bending over her.

'No, only wicked!'

'Never mind that.' And he stooped and kissed her. 'I wanted to be with you tonight.'

Next morning Marchmill was called at six o'clock; and in waking and yawning she heard him muttering to himself: 'What the deuce is this that's been crackling under me so?' Imagining her asleep he searched round him and withdrew something. Through her half-opened eyes she perceived it to be Mr Trewe.

'Well, I'm damned!' her husband exclaimed.

'What, dear?' said she.

'O, you are awake? Ha! ha!'

'What *do* you mean?'

'Some bloke's photograph – a friend of our landlady's, I suppose. I wonder how it came here; whisked off the mantelpiece by accident perhaps when they were making the bed.'

'I was looking at it yesterday, and it must have dropped in then.'

'O, he's a friend of yours? Bless his picturesque heart!'

Ella's loyalty to the object of her admiration could not endure to hear him ridiculed. 'He's a clever man!' she said, with a tremor in her gentle voice which she herself felt to be absurdly uncalled for. 'He is a rising poet – the gentleman who occupied two of these rooms before we came, though I've never seen him.'

'How do you know, if you've never seen him?'

'Mrs Hooper told me when she showed me the photograph.'

'O, well, I must up and be off. I shall be home rather early. Sorry I can't take you today, dear. Mind the children don't go getting drowned.'

That day Mrs Marchmill enquired if Mr Trewe were likely to call at any other time.

'Yes,' said Mrs Hooper. 'He's coming this day week to stay with a friend near here till you leave. He'll be sure to call.'

Marchmill did return quite early in the afternoon; and, opening some letters which had arrived in his absence, declared suddenly that he and his family would have to leave a week earlier than they had expected to do – in short, in three days.

'Surely we can stay a week longer?' she pleaded. 'I like it here.'

'I don't. It is getting rather slow.'

'Then you might leave me and the children!'

'How perverse you are, Ell! What's the use? And have to come to fetch you! No: we'll all return together; and we'll make out our time in North Wales or Brighton a little later on. Besides, you've three days longer yet.'

It seemed to be her doom not to meet the man for whose rival talent she had a despairing admiration, and to whose person she was now absolutely attached. Yet she determined to make a last effort; and having gathered from her landlady that Trewe was living in a lonely spot not far from the fashionable town on the Island opposite, she crossed over in the packet from the neighbouring pier the following afternoon.

What a useless journey it was! Ella knew but vaguely where the house stood, and when she fancied she had found it, and ventured to enquire of a pedestrian if he lived there, the answer returned by the man was that he did not know. And if he did live there, how could she call upon him? Some women might have the assurance to do it, but she had not. How crazy he would think her. She might have asked him to call upon her, perhaps; but she had not the courage for that, either. She lingered mournfully about the picturesque seaside eminence till it was time to return to the town and enter the steamer for recrossing, reaching home for dinner without having been greatly missed.

At the last moment, unexpectedly enough, her husband said that he should have no objection to letting her and the children stay on till the end of the week, since she wished to do so, if she felt herself able to get home without him. She concealed the pleasure this extension of time gave her; and Marchmill went off the next morning alone.

But the week passed, and Trewe did not call.

On Saturday morning the remaining members of the Marchmill family departed from the place which had been productive of so much fervour in her. The dreary, dreary train; the sun shining in moted beams upon the hot cushions; the dusty permanent way; the mean rows of wire – these things were her accompaniment: while out of the window the deep blue sea-levels disappeared from her gaze, and with them her poet's home. Heavy-hearted, she tried to read, and wept instead.

Mr Marchmill was in a thriving way of business, and he and his family lived in a large new house, which stood in rather extensive grounds a few miles outside the midland city wherein he carried on his trade. Ella's life was lonely here, as the suburban life is apt to be, particularly at certain seasons; and she had ample time to indulge her taste for lyric and elegiac composition. She had hardly got back when she encountered a piece by Robert Trewe in the new number of her favourite magazine, which must have been written almost immediately before her visit to Solentsea, for it contained the very couplet she had seen pencilled on the wallpaper by the bed, and Mrs Hooper had declared to be recent. Ella could resist no longer, but seizing a pen impulsively, wrote to him as a brother-poet, using the name of John Ivy, congratulating him in her letter on his triumphant executions in metre and rhythm of thoughts that moved his soul, as compared with her own browbeaten efforts in the same pathetic trade.

To this address there came a response in a few days, little as she had dared to hope for it – a civil and brief note, in which the young poet stated that, though he was not well acquainted with Mr Ivy's verse, he recalled the name as being one he had seen attached to some very promising pieces; that he was glad to gain Mr Ivy's acquaintance by letter, and should certainly look with much interest for his productions in the future.

There must have been something juvenile or timid in her own epistle, as one ostensibly coming from a man, she declared to herself; for Trewe quite adopted the tone of an elder and superior in this reply. But what did it matter? He had replied; he had written to her with his own hand from that very room she knew so well, for he was now back again in his quarters.

The correspondence thus begun was continued for two months or more, Ella Marchmill sending him from time to time some that she considered to be the best of her pieces, which he very kindly accepted, though he did not say he sedulously read them, nor did he send her any of his own in return. Ella would have been more hurt at this than she was if she had not known that Trewe laboured under the impression that she was one of his own sex.

Yet the situation was unsatisfactory. A flattering little voice told her that, were he only to see her, matters would be otherwise. No doubt she would have helped on this by making a frank confession of womanhood, to begin with, if something had not happened, to her delight, to render it unnecessary. A friend of her husband's, the editor of the most important newspaper in their city and county, who was dining with them one day, observed during their conversation about the poet that his (the editor's) brother the landscape-painter was a friend of Mr Trewe's, and that the two men were at that very moment in Wales together.

Ella was slightly acquainted with the editor's brother. The next morning down she sat and wrote, inviting him to stay at her house for a short time on his way back, and requesting him to bring with him, if practicable, his companion Mr Trewe, whose acquaintance she was anxious to make. The answer arrived after some few days. Her correspondent and his friend Trewe would have much satisfaction in accepting her invitation on their way southward, which would be on such and such a day in the following week.

Ella was blithe and buoyant. Her scheme had succeeded; her beloved though as yet unseen one was coming. 'Behold, he standeth behind our wall; he looked forth at the windows, showing himself through the lattice,' she thought ecstatically. 'And, lo, the winter is past, the rain is over and gone, the flowers appear on the earth, the time of the singing of birds is come, and the voice of the turtle is heard in our land.'[12]

But it was necessary to consider the details of lodging and feeding him. This she did most solicitously, and awaited the pregnant day and hour.

It was about five in the afternoon when she heard a ring at the door and the editor's brother's voice in the hall. Poetess as she was, or as she thought herself, she had not been too sublime that day to dress with infinite trouble in a fashionable robe of rich material, having a faint resemblance to the *chiton* of the Greeks, a style just then in vogue among ladies of an artistic and romantic turn, which had been obtained by Ella of her Bond Street dressmaker when she was last in London. Her visitor entered the drawing room. She looked towards his rear; nobody else came through the door. Where, in the name of the God of Love, was Robert Trewe?

'O, I'm sorry,' said the painter, after their introductory words had been spoken. 'Trewe is a curious fellow, you know, Mrs Marchmill. He said he'd come; then he said he couldn't. He's rather dusty. We've been doing a few miles with knapsacks, you know; and he wanted to get on home.'

'He – he's not coming?'

'He's not; and he asked me to make his apologies.'

'When did you p-p-part from him?' she asked, her nether lip starting off quivering so much that it was like a *tremolo*-stop opened in her speech. She longed to run away from this dreadful bore and cry her eyes out.

'Just now, in the turnpike road yonder there.'

'What! he has actually gone past my gates?'

'Yes. When we got to them – handsome gates they are, too, the finest bit of modern wrought-iron work I have seen – when we came to them we stopped, talking there a little while, and then he wished me goodbye and went on. The truth is, he's a little bit depressed just now, and doesn't want to see anybody. He's a very good fellow, and a warm friend, but a little uncertain and gloomy sometimes; he thinks too much of things. His poetry is rather too erotic and passionate, you know, for some tastes; and he has just come in for a terrible slating from the — *Review* that was published yesterday; he saw a copy of it at the station by accident. Perhaps you've read it?'

'No.'

'So much the better. O, it is not worth thinking of; just one of those articles written to order, to please the narrow-minded set of subscribers upon whom the circulation depends. But he's upset by it. He says it is the misrepresentation that hurts him so; that, though he can stand a fair attack, he can't stand lies that he's powerless to refute and stop from spreading. That's just Trewe's weak point. He lives so much by himself that these things affect him much more than they would if he were in the bustle of fashionable or commercial life. So he wouldn't come here, making the excuse that it all looked so new and monied – if you'll pardon —'

'But – he must have known – there was sympathy here! Has he never said anything about getting letters from this address?'

'Yes, yes, he has, from John Ivy – perhaps a relative of yours, he thought, visiting here at the time?'

'Did he – like Ivy, did he say?'

'Well, I don't know that he took any great interest in Ivy.'

'Or in his poems?'

'Or in his poems – so far as I know, that is.'

Robert Trewe took no interest in her house, in her poems or in their writer. As soon as she could get away she went into the nursery and tried to let off her emotion by unnecessarily kissing the children, till she had a sudden sense of disgust at being reminded how plain looking they were, like their father.

The obtuse and single-minded landscape-painter never once perceived from her conversation that it was only Trewe she wanted, and not himself. He made the best of his visit, seeming to enjoy the society of Ella's husband, who also took a great fancy to him, and showed him everywhere about the neighbourhood, neither of them noticing Ella's mood.

The painter had been gone only a day or two when, while sitting upstairs alone one morning, she glanced over the London paper just arrived, and read the following paragraph: –

'SUICIDE OF A POET

'Mr Robert Trewe, who has been favourably known for some years as one of our rising lyrists, committed suicide at his lodgings at Solentsea on Saturday evening last by shooting himself in the right temple with a revolver. Readers hardly need to be reminded that Mr Trewe has recently attracted the attention of a much wider public than had hitherto known him, by his new volume of verse, mostly of an impassioned kind, entitled "Lyrics to a Woman Unknown", which has been already favourably noticed in these pages for the extraordinary gamut of feeling it traverses, and which has been made the subject of a severe, if not ferocious, criticism in the — *Review*. It is supposed, though not certainly known, that the article may have partially conduced to the sad act, as a copy of the review in question was found on his writing table; and he has been observed to be in a somewhat depressed state of mind since the critique appeared.'

Then came the report of the inquest, at which the following letter was read, it having been addressed to a friend at a distance:—

'DEAR —, — Before these lines reach your hands I shall be delivered from the inconveniences of seeing, hearing and knowing more of the things around me. I will not trouble you by giving my reasons for the step I have taken, though I can assure you they were sound and logical. Perhaps had I been blessed with a mother, or a sister, or a female friend of another sort tenderly devoted to me, I might have thought it worthwhile to continue my present existence. I have long dreamt of such an unattainable creature, as you know; and she, this undis-coverable, elusive one, inspired my last volume; the imaginary woman alone, for, in spite of what has been said in some quarters, there is no real woman behind the title. She has continued to the last unrevealed, unmet, unwon. I think it desirable to mention this in order that no blame may attach to any real woman as having been the cause of my decease by cruel or cavalier treatment of me. Tell my landlady that I am sorry to have caused her this unpleasantness; but my occupancy of the rooms will soon be forgotten. There are ample funds in my name at the bank to pay all expenses.

R. TREWE.'

Ella sat for a while as if stunned, then rushed into the adjoining chamber and flung herself upon her face on the bed.

Her grief and distraction shook her to pieces; and she lay in this frenzy of sorrow for more than an hour. Broken words came every now and then from her quivering lips: 'O, if he had only known of me – known of me – me! . . . O, if I had only once met him – only once; and put my hand upon his hot forehead – kissed him – let him know how I loved him – that I would have suffered shame and scorn, would have lived and died, for him! Perhaps it would have saved his dear life! ... But no – it was not allowed! God is a jealous God;[13] and that happiness was not for him and me!'

All possibilities were over; the meeting was stultified. Yet it was almost visible to her in her fantasy even now, though it could never be substantiated –

> 'The hour which might have been, yet might not be,
> Which man's and woman's heart conceived and bore,
> Yet whereof life was barren.'[14]

She wrote to the landlady at Solentsea in the third person, in as subdued a style as she could command, enclosing a postal order for a sovereign, and informing Mrs Hooper that Mrs Marchmill had seen in the papers the sad account of the poet's death, and having been, as Mrs Hooper was aware, much interested in Mr Trewe during her stay at Coburg House, she would be obliged if Mrs Hooper could obtain a small portion of his hair before his coffin was closed down, and send it her as a memorial of him, as also the photograph that was in the frame.

By the return-post a letter arrived containing what had been requested. Ella wept over the portrait and secured it in her private drawer; the lock of hair she tied with white ribbon and put in her bosom, whence she drew it and kissed it every now and then in some unobserved nook.

'What's the matter?' said her husband, looking up from his newspaper on one of these occasions. 'Crying over something? A lock of hair? Whose is it?'

'He's dead!' she murmured.

'Who?'

'I don't want to tell you, Will, just now, unless you insist!' she said, a sob hanging heavy in her voice.

'O, all right.'

'Do you mind my refusing? I will tell you some day.'

'It doesn't matter in the least, of course.'

He walked away whistling a few bars of no tune in particular; and when he had got down to his factory in the city the subject came into Marchmill's head again.

He, too, was aware that a suicide had taken place recently at the house they had occupied at Solentsea. Having seen the volume of poems in his wife's hand of late, and heard fragments of the landlady's conversation about Trewe when they were her tenants, he all at once said to himself, 'Why of course it's he! . . . How the devil did she get to know him ? What sly animals women are!'

Then he placidly dismissed the matter, and went on with his daily affairs. By this time Ella at home had come to a determination. Mrs Hooper, in sending the hair and photograph, had informed her of the day of the funeral; and as the morning and noon wore on an overpowering wish to know where they were laying him took possession of the sympathetic woman. Caring very little now what her husband or any one else might think of her eccentricities, she wrote Marchmill a brief note, stating that she was called away for the afternoon and evening, but would return on the following morning. This she left on his desk, and having given the same information to the servants, went out of the house on foot.

When Mr Marchmill reached home early in the afternoon the servants looked anxious. The nurse took him privately aside, and hinted that her mistress's sadness during the past few days had been such that she feared she had gone out to drown herself. Marchmill reflected. Upon the whole he thought that she had not done that. Without saying whither he was bound he also started off, telling them not to sit up for him. He drove to the railway station, and took a ticket for Solentsea.

It was dark when he reached the place, though he had come by a fast train, and he knew that if his wife had preceded him thither it could only have been by a slower train, arriving not a great while before his own. The season at Solentsea was now past: the parade was gloomy, and the flys were few and cheap. He asked the way to the Cemetery, and soon reached it. The gate was locked, but the keeper let him in, declaring, however, that there was nobody within the precincts. Although it was not late, the autumnal darkness had now become intense; and he found some difficulty in keeping to the serpentine path which led to the quarter where, as the man had told him, the one or two interments for the day had taken place. He stepped upon the grass, and, stumbling over some pegs, stooped now and then to discern if possible a figure against the sky. He could see none; but lighting on a spot where the soil was trodden, beheld a crouching object beside a newly made grave. She heard him, and sprang up.

'Ell, how silly this is!' he said indignantly. 'Running away from home – I never heard such a thing! Of course I am not jealous of this unfortunate man; but it is too ridiculous that you, a married woman with three children and a fourth coming, should go losing your head like this over a dead lover! . . . Do you know you were locked in? You might not have been able to get out all night.'

She did not answer.

'I hope it didn't go far between you and him, for your own sake.'

'Don't insult me, Will.'

'Mind, I won't have any more of this sort of thing; do you hear?'

'Very well,' she said.

He drew her arm within his own, and conducted her out of the Cemetery. It was impossible to get back that night; and not wishing to be recognized in their present sorry condition he took her to a miserable little coffee-house close to the station, whence they departed early in the morning, travelling almost without speaking, under the sense that it was one of those dreary situations occurring in married life which words could not mend, and reaching their own door at noon.

The months passed, and neither of the twain ever ventured to start a conversation upon this episode. Ella seemed to be only too frequently in a sad and listless mood, which might almost have been called pining. The time was approaching when she would have to undergo the stress of childbirth for a fourth time, and that apparently did not tend to raise her spirits.

'I don't think I shall get over it this time!' she said one day.

'Pooh! what childish foreboding! Why shouldn't it be as well now as ever?'

She shook her head. 'I feel almost sure I am going to die; and I should be glad, if it were not for Nelly, and Frank, and Tiny.'

'And me!'

'You'll soon find somebody to fill my place,' she murmured, with a sad smile. 'And you'll have a perfect right to; I assure you of that.'

'Ell, you are not thinking still about that – poetical friend of yours?'

She neither admitted nor denied the charge. 'I am not going to get over my illness this time,' she reiterated. 'Something tells me I shan't.'

This view of things was rather a bad beginning, as it usually is; and, in fact, six weeks later, in the month of May, she was lying in her room, pulseless and bloodless, with hardly strength enough left to follow up one feeble breath with another, the infant for whose unnecessary life she was slowly parting with her own being fat and well. Just before her death she spoke to Marchmill softly: –

'Will, I want to confess to you the entire circumstances of that – about you know what – that time we visited Solentsea. I can't tell what possessed me – how I could forget you so, my husband! But I had got into a morbid state: I thought you had been unkind; that you had neglected me; that you weren't up to my intellectual level, while he was, and far above it. I wanted a fuller appreciator, perhaps, rather than another lover —'

She could get no further then for very exhaustion; and she went off in sudden collapse a few hours later, without having said anything more to her husband on the subject of her love for the poet. William Marchmill, in truth, like most husbands of several years' standing, was little disturbed by retrospective jealousies, and had not shown the least anxiety to press her for confessions concerning a man dead and gone beyond any power of inconveniencing him more.

But when she had been buried a couple of years it chanced one day that, in turning over some forgotten papers that he wished to destroy before his second wife entered the house, he lighted on a lock of hair in an envelope, with the photograph of the deceased poet, a date being written on the back in his late wife's hand. It was that of the time they spent at Solentsea.

Marchmill looked long and musingly at the hair and portrait, for something struck him. Fetching the little boy who had been the death of his mother, now a noisy toddler, he took him on his knee, held the lock of hair against the child's head, and set up the photograph on the table behind, so that he could closely compare the features each countenance presented. By a known but inexplicable trick of Nature there were undoubtedly strong traces of resemblance to the man Ella had never seen; the dreamy and peculiar expression of the poet's face sat, as the transmitted idea, upon the child's, and the hair was of the same hue.

'I'm damned if I didn't think so!' murmured Marchmill. 'Then she *did* play me false with that fellow at the lodgings! Let me see: the dates – the second week in August . . . the third week in May . . . Yes . . . yes . . . Get away, you poor little brat! You are nothing to me!'

GEORGE EGERTON

Virgin Soil

The bridegroom is waiting in the hall; with a trifle of impatience he is tracing the pattern of the linoleum with the point of his umbrella. He curbs it and laughs, showing his strong white teeth at a remark of his best man; then compares the time by his hunter with the clock on the stairs. He is florid, bright-eyed, loose-lipped, inclined to stoutness, but kept in good condition; his hair is crisp, curly, slightly grey; his ears peculiar, pointed at their tops like a faun's. He looks very big and well-dressed, and, when he smiles, affable enough.

Upstairs a young girl, with the suns of seventeen summers on her brown head, is lying with her face hidden on her mother's shoulder; she is sobbing with great childish sobs, regardless of reddened eyes and the tears that have splashed on the silk of her grey, going-away gown.

The mother seems scarcely less disturbed than the girl. She is a fragile-looking woman with delicate fair skin, smoothly parted thin chestnut hair, dove-like eyes and a monotonous piping voice. She is flushing painfully, making a strenuous effort to say something to the girl, something that is opposed to the whole instincts of her life.

She tries to speak, parts her lips only to close them again, and clasp her arms tighter round the girl's shoulders; at length she manages to say with trembling, uncertain pauses:

'You are married now, darling, and you must obey' – she lays a stress upon the word – 'your husband in all things – there are – there are things you should know – but – marriage is a serious thing, a sacred thing' – with desperation – 'you must believe that what your husband tells you is right – let him guide you – tell you—'

There is such acute distress in her usually unemotional voice that the girl looks up and scans her face – her blushing, quivering, faded face. Her eyes are startled, fawn-like eyes as her mother's, her skin too is delicately fair, but her mouth is firmer, her jaw squarer and her piquant, irregular nose is full of character. She is slightly built, scarcely fully developed in her fresh youth.

'What is it that I do not know, mother? What is it?' – with anxious impatience. 'There is something more – I have felt it all these last weeks in your and the others' looks – in his, in the very atmosphere – but why have you not told me before – I —' Her only answer is a gush of helpless tears from the mother, and a sharp rap at the door, and the bridegroom's voice, with an imperative note that it strikes the nervous girl is new to it, that makes her cling to her mother in a close, close embrace, drop her veil and go out to him.

She shakes hands with the best man, kisses the girl friend who has acted as bridesmaid – the wedding has been a very quiet one – and steps into the carriage. The Irish cook throws an old shoe after them from the side door, but it hits the trunk of an elder tree, and falls back on to the path, making that worthy woman cross herself and mutter of ill-omens and bad luck to follow; for did not a magpie cross the path first thing this morning when she went to open the gate, and wasn't a red-haired woman the first creature she clapped eyes on as she looked down the road?

Half an hour later the carriage pulls up at the little station and the girl jumps out first; she is flushed, and her eyes stare helplessly as the eyes of a startled child, and she trembles with quick running shudders from head to foot. She clasps and unclasps her slender, grey-gloved hands so tightly that the stitching on the back of one bursts.

He has called to the stationmaster, and they go into the refreshment room together; the latter appears at the door and, beckoning to a porter, gives him an order.

She takes a long look at the familiar little place. They have lived there three years, and yet she seems to see it now for the first time; the rain drips, drips monotonously off the zinc roof, the smell of the dust is fresh and the white pinks in the borders are beaten into the gravel.

Then the train runs in; a first-class carriage, marked 'engaged', is attached, and he comes for her; his hot breath smells of champagne, and it strikes her that his eyes are fearfully big and bright, and he offers her his arm with such a curious amused proprietary air that the girl shivers as she lays her hand in it.

The bell rings, the guard locks the door, the train steams out and as it passes the signal-box, a large well-kept hand, with a signet ring on the little finger, pulls down the blind on the window of an engaged carriage.

Five years later, one afternoon on an autumn day, when the rain is falling like splashing tears on the rails, and the smell of the dust after rain fills the mild air with freshness, and the white chrysanthemums struggle to raise their heads from the gravel path into which the sharp shower has beaten them, the same woman, for there is no trace of girlhood in her twenty-two years, slips out of a first-class carriage; she has a dressing bag in her hand.

She walks with her head down and a droop in her shoulders; her quickness of step is due rather to nervous haste than elasticity of frame. When she reaches the turn of the road, she pauses and looks at the little villa with the white curtains and gay tiled window-boxes. She can see the window of her old room; distinguish every shade in the changing leaves of the creeper climbing up the south wall; hear the canary's shrill note from where she stands.

Never once has she set foot in the peaceful little house with its air of genteel propriety since that eventful morning when she left it with him; she has always framed an excuse.

Now as she sees it a feeling of remorse fills her heart, and she thinks of the mother living out her quiet years, each day a replica of the one gone before, and her resolve weakens; she feels inclined to go back, but the waning sun flickers over the panes in the window of the room she occupied as a girl. She can recall how she used to run to the open window on summer mornings and lean out and draw in the dewy freshness and welcome the day, how she has stood on moonlight nights and danced with her bare white feet in the strip of moonlight, and let her fancies fly out into the silver night, a young girl's dreams of the beautiful, wonderful world that lay outside.

A hard dry sob rises in her throat at the memory of it, and the fleeting expression of softness on her face changes to a bitter disillusion.

She hurries on, with her eyes down, up the neat gravelled path, through the open door into the familiar sitting room.

The piano is open with a hymn book on the stand; the grate is filled with fresh green ferns, a bowl of late roses perfume the room from the centre of the table. The mother is sitting in her easy chair, her hands folded across a big white Persian cat on her lap; she is fast asleep. Some futile lace work, her thimble and bright scissor are placed on a table near her.

Her face is placid, not a day older than that day five years ago. Her glossy hair is no greyer, her skin is clear, she smiles in her sleep. The smile rouses a sort of sudden fury in the breast of the woman standing in her dusty travelling cloak at the door, noting every detail in the room. She throws back her veil and goes over and looks at herself in the mirror over the polished chiffonnier – scans herself pitilessly. Her skin is sallow with the dull sallowness of a fair skin in ill-health, and the fringe of her brown hair is so lacking in lustre that it affords no contrast. The look of fawn-like shyness has vanished from her eyes, they burn sombrefully and resentfully in their sunken orbits, there is a dragged look about the mouth; and the keynote of her face is a cynical disillusion. She looks from herself to the reflection of the mother, and then turning sharply with a suppressed exclamation goes over, and shaking the sleeping woman not too gently, says:

'Mother, wake up, I want to speak to you!'

The mother starts with frightened eyes, stares at the other woman as if doubting the evidence of her sight, smiles, then cowed by the unresponsive look in the other face, grows grave again, sits still and stares helplessly at her, finally bursting into tears with a

'Flo, my dear, Flo, is it really you?'

The girl jerks her head impatiently and says drily:

'Yes, that is self-evident. I am going on a long journey. I have something to say to you before I start! Why on earth are you crying?'

There is a note of surprised wonder in her voice mixed with impatience.

The older woman has had time to scan her face and the dormant motherhood in her is roused by its weary anguish. She is ill, she thinks, in trouble. She rises to her feet; it is characteristic of the habits of her life, with its studied regard for the observance of small proprieties, and distrust of servants as a class, that she goes over and closes the room door carefully.

This hollow-eyed, sullen woman is so unlike the fresh girl who left her five years ago that she feels afraid. With the quiet selfishness that has characterized her life she has accepted the excuses her daughter has made to avoid coming home, as she has accepted the presents her son-in-law has sent her from time to time. She has found her a husband well-off in the world's goods, and there her responsibility ended. She approaches her hesitatingly; she feels she ought to kiss her, there is something unusual in such a meeting after so long an absence; it shocks her, it is so unlike the one she has pictured; she has often looked forward to it, often; to seeing Flo's new frocks, to hearing of her town life.

'Won't you take off your things? You will like to go to your room?'

She can hear how her own voice shakes; it is really inconsiderate of Flo to treat her in this strange way.

'We will have some tea,' she adds.

Her colour is coming and going, the lace at her wrist is fluttering. The daughter observes it with a kind of dull satisfaction, she is taking out her hatpins carefully. She notices a portrait in a velvet case upon the mantelpiece; she walks over and looks at it intently. It is her father, the father who was killed in India in a hill skirmish when she was a little lint-locked[1] maid barely up to his knee. She studies it with new eyes, trying to read what man he was, what soul he had, what part of him is in her, tries to find herself by reading him. Something in his face touches her, strikes some underlying chord in her, and she grinds her teeth at a thought it rouses.

'She must be ill, she must be very ill,' says the mother, watching her, 'to think I daren't offer to kiss my own child!' She checks the tears that keep welling up, feeling that they may offend this woman who is so strangely unlike the girl who left her. The latter has turned from her scrutiny of the likeness and sweeps her with a cold criticizing look as she turns towards the door, saying:

'I *should* like some tea. I will go upstairs and wash off the dust.'

Half an hour later the two women sit opposite one another in the pretty room. The younger one is leaning back in her chair watching the mother pour out the tea, following the graceful movements of the white, blue-veined hands amongst the tea things – she lets her wait on her; they have not spoken beyond a commonplace remark about the heat, the dust, the journey.

'How is Philip, is he well?' The mother ventures to ask with a feeling of trepidation, but it seems to her that she ought to ask about him.

'He is quite well, men of his type usually are; I may say he is particularly well just now, he has gone to Paris with a girl from the Alhambra!'[2]

The older woman flushes painfully, and pauses with her cup halfway to her lips and lets the tea run over unheeded on to her dainty silk apron.

'You are spilling your tea,' the girl adds with malicious enjoyment.

The woman gasps: 'Flo, but Flo, my dear, it is dreadful! What would your poor father have said! *no wonder* you look ill, dear, how shocking! Shall I – ask the vicar to – to remonstrate with him? —'

'My dear mother, what an extraordinary idea! These little trips have been my one solace. I assure you, I have always hailed them as lovely oases in the desert of matrimony, resting-places on the journey. My sole regret was their infrequency. That is very good tea, I suppose it is the cream.'

The older woman puts her cup on the tray and stares at her with frightened eyes and paled cheeks.

'I am afraid I don't understand you, Florence. I am old-fashioned' – with a little air of frigid propriety – 'I have always looked upon matrimony as a sacred thing. It is dreadful to hear you speak this way; you should have tried to save Philip – from – from such a shocking sin.'

The girl laughs, and the woman shivers as she hears her. She cries –

'I would never have thought it of Philip. My poor dear, I am afraid you must be very unhappy.'

'Very,' with a grim smile, 'but it is over now, I have done with it. I am not going back.'

If a bomb had exploded in the quiet, pretty room the effect could hardly have been more startling than her almost cheerful statement. A big bee buzzes in and bangs against the lace of the older woman's cap and she never heeds it, then she almost screams:

'Florence, Florence, my dear, you can't mean to desert your husband! Oh, think of the disgrace, the scandal, what people will say, the' – with an uncertain quaver – 'the sin. You took a solemn vow, you know, and you are going to break it —'

'My dear mother, the ceremony had no meaning for me, I simply did not know what I was signing my name to, or what I was vowing to do. I might as well have signed my name to a document drawn up in Choctaw. I have no remorse, no prick of conscience at the step I am taking; my life must be my own. They say sorrow chastens, I don't believe it; it hardens, embitters; joy is like the sun, it coaxes all that is loveliest and sweetest in human nature. No, I am not going back.'

The older woman cries, wringing her hands helplessly:

'I can't understand it. You must be very miserable to dream of taking such a serious step.'

'As I told you, I am. It is a defect of my temperament. How many women really take the man nearest to them as seriously as I did! I think few. They finesse and flatter and wheedle and coax, but truth there is none. I couldn't do that, you see, and so I went to the wall. I don't blame them; it must be so, as long as marriage is based on such unequal terms, as long as man demands from a wife as a right, what he must sue from a mistress as a favour; until marriage becomes for many women a legal prostitution, a nightly degradation, a hateful yoke under which they age, mere bearers of children conceived in a sense of duty, not love. They bear them, birth them, nurse them and begin again without choice in the matter, growing old, unlovely, with all joy of living swallowed in a senseless burden of reckless maternity, until their love, granted they started with that, the mystery, the crowning glory of their lives, is turned into a duty they submit to with distaste instead of a favour granted to a husband who must become a new lover to obtain it.'

'But men are different, Florence; you can't refuse a husband, you might cause him to commit sin.'

'Bosh, mother, he is responsible for his own sins, we are not bound to dry-nurse his morality. Man is what we have made him, his very faults are of our making. No wife is bound to set aside the demands of her individual soul for the sake of imbecile obedience. I am going to have some more tea.'

The mother can only whimper:

'It is dreadful! I thought he made you such an excellent husband, his position too is so good, and he is so highly connected.'

'Yes, and it is as well to put the blame in the right quarter. Philip is as God made him, he is an animal with strong passions, and he avails himself of the latitude permitted him by the laws of society. Whatever of blame, whatever of sin, whatever of misery is in the whole matter rests *solely* and *entirely* with you, mother' – the woman sits bolt upright '– and with no one else – that is why I came here – to tell you that – I have promised myself over and over again that I would tell you. It is with you, and you alone the fault lies.'

There is so much of cold dislike in her voice that the other woman recoils and whimpers piteously:

'You must be ill, Florence, to say such wicked things. What have I done? I am sure I devoted myself to you from the time you were little; I refused' – dabbing her eyes with her cambric handkerchief – 'ever so many good offers. There was young Fortescue in the artillery, such a good-looking man, and such an elegant horseman, he was quite infatuated about me; and Jones, to be sure he was in business, but he was most attentive. Every one said I was a devoted mother; I can't think what you mean, I —'

A smile of cynical amusement checks her.

'Perhaps not. Sit down, and I'll tell you.'

She shakes off the trembling hand, for the mother has risen and is standing next to her, and pushes her into a chair, and paces up and down the room. She is painfully thin, and drags her limbs as she walks.

'I say it is your fault, because you reared me a fool, an idiot, ignorant of everything I ought to have known, everything that concerned me and the life I was bound to lead as a wife; my physical needs, my coming passion, the very meaning of my sex, my wifehood and motherhood to follow. You gave me not one weapon in my hand to defend myself against the possible attacks of man at his worst. You sent me out to fight the biggest battle of a woman's life, the one in which she ought to know every turn of the game, with a white gauze' – she laughs derisively – 'of maiden purity as a shield.'

Her eyes blaze, and the woman in the chair watches her as one sees a frog watch a snake when it is put into its case.

'I was fourteen when I gave up the gooseberry-bush theory as the origin of humanity; and I cried myself ill with shame when I learnt what maternity meant, instead of waking with a sense of delicious wonder at the great mystery of it. You gave me to a man, nay more, you told me to obey him, to believe that whatever he said would be right, would be my duty; knowing that the meaning of marriage was a sealed book to me, that I had no real idea of what union with a man meant. You delivered me body and soul into his hands without preparing me in any way for the ordeal I was to go through. You sold me for a home, for clothes, for food; you played upon my ignorance, I won't say innocence, that is different. You told me, you and your sister, and your friend the vicar's wife, that it would be an anxiety off your mind if I were comfortably settled —'

'It is wicked of you to say such dreadful things!' the mother cries, 'and besides' – with a touch of asperity – 'you married him willingly, you seemed to like his attentions —'

'How like a woman! What a thorough woman you are, mother! The good old-fashioned kitten with a claw in her paw! Yes, I married him willingly; I was not eighteen, I had known no men; was pleased that you were pleased – and, as you say, I liked his attentions. He had tact enough not to frighten me, and I had not the faintest conception of what marriage with him meant. I had an idea' – with a laugh – 'that the words of the minister settled the matter. Do you think that if I had realized how fearfully close the intimacy with him would have been that my whole soul would not have stood up in revolt, the whole woman in me cried out against such a degradation of myself?' Her words tremble with passion, and the woman who bore her feels as if she is being lashed by a whip. 'Would I not have shuddered at the thought of *him* in such a relationship? – and waited, waited until I found the man who would satisfy me, body and soul – to whom I would have gone without any false shame, of whom I would think with gladness as the father of a little child to come, for whom the white fire of love or passion, call it what you will, in my heart would have burned clearly and saved me from the feeling of loathing horror that has made my married life a nightmare to me – ay, made me a murderess in heart over and over again. This is not exaggeration. It has killed the sweetness in me, the pure thoughts of womanhood – has made me hate myself and *hate you*. Cry, mother, if you will; you don't know how much you have to cry for – I have cried myself barren of tears. Cry over the girl you killed' – with a gust of passion – 'why didn't you strangle me as a baby? It would have been kinder; my life has been a hell, mother – I felt it vaguely as I stood on the platform waiting, I remember the mad impulse I had to jump down under the engine as it came in, to escape from the dread that was chilling my soul. What have these years been? One long crucifixion, one long submittal to the desires of a man I bound myself to in ignorance of what it meant; every caress' – with a cry – 'has only been the first note of that. Look at me' – stretching out her arms – 'look at this wreck of my physical self; I wouldn't dare to show you the heart or the soul underneath. He has stood on his rights; but do you think, if I had known, that I would have given such insane obedience, from a mistaken sense of duty, as would lead to this? I have my rights too, and my duty to myself; if I had only recognized them in time.

'Sob away, mother; I don't even feel for you – I have been burnt too badly to feel sorry for what will only be a tiny scar to you; I have all the long future to face with all the world against me. Nothing will induce me to go back. Better anything than that; food and clothes are poor equivalents for what I have had to suffer – I can get them at a cheaper rate. When he comes to look for me, give him that letter. He will tell you he has only been an uxorious husband, and that you reared me a fool. You can tell him too, if you like, that I loathe him, shiver at the touch of his lips, his breath, his hands; that my whole body revolts at his touch; that when he has turned and gone to sleep, I have watched him with such growing hatred that at times the temptation to kill him has been so strong that I have crept out of bed and walked the cold passage in my bare feet until I was too benumbed to feel anything; that I have counted the hours to his going away, and cried out with delight at the sight of the retreating carriage!'

'You are very hard, Flo; the Lord soften your heart! Perhaps' – with trepidation – 'if you had had a child —'

'Of his – that indeed would have been the last straw – no, mother.'

There is such a peculiar expression of satisfaction over something – of some inner understanding, as a man has when he dwells on the successful accomplishment of a secret purpose – that the mother sobs quietly, wringing her hands.

'I did not know, Flo, I acted for the best; you are very hard on me!'

Later, when the bats are flitting across the moon, and the girl is asleep – she has thrown herself half-dressed on the narrow white bed of her girlhood, with her arms folded across her breast and her hands clenched – the mother steals into the room. She has been turning over the contents of an old desk; her marriage certificate, faded letters on foreign paper and a bit of Flo's hair cut off each birthday, and a sprig of orange-blossom she wore in her hair. She looks faded and grey in the silver light, and she stands and gazes at the haggard face in its weary sleep. The placid current of her life is disturbed, her heart is roused, something of her child's soul-agony has touched the sleeping depths of her nature. She feels as if scales have dropped from her eyes, as if the instincts and conventions of her life are toppling over, as if all the needs of protesting women of whom she has read with a vague displeasure have come home to her. She covers the girl tenderly, kisses her hair and slips a little roll of notes into the dressing bag on the table and steals out, with the tears running down her cheeks.

When the girl looks into her room as she steals by, when the morning light is slanting in, she sees her kneeling, her head, with its straggling grey hair, bowed in tired sleep. It touches her. Life is too short, she thinks, to make any one's hours bitter; she goes down and writes a few kind words in pencil and leaves them near her hand, and goes quickly out into the road.

The morning is grey and misty, with faint yellow stains in the east, and the west wind blows with a melancholy sough in it – the first whisper of the fall, the fall that turns the world of nature into a patient suffering from phthisis – delicate season of decadence, when the loveliest scenes have a note of decay in their beauty; when a poisoned arrow pierces the marrow of insect and plant, and the leaves have a hectic flush and fall, fall and shrivel and curl in the night's cool; and the chrysanthemums, the 'goodbye summers' of the Irish peasants, have a sickly tinge in their white. It affects her, and she finds herself saying: 'Wither and die, wither and die, make compost for the loves of the spring, as the old drop out and make place for the new, who forget them, to be in their turn forgotten.' She hurries on, feeling that her autumn has come to her in her spring, and a little later she stands once more on the platform where she stood in the flush of her girlhood, and takes the train in the opposite direction.

The Undefinable

A Fantasia

That certain Something.

RUSKIN

It was a hot summer evening, and I had gone into the studio after dinner to sit opposite my last-accomplished work, and smoke a cigarette to add to my joy in the contemplation thereof. It is a great moment even for a great artist when he can sit and sigh in solitary satisfaction before a finished picture. I had looked at it while I was waiting for dinner, and even in that empty hour it had seemed most masterly; so that now, when I may perhaps – if I apologize in advance for the unacademical vulgarism of the idea – be allowed to say that I was comfortably replete, I expected to feel in it that which surpasses the merely masterly of talent (to which degree of excellence ordinary painters, undowered by the divine afflatus, may attain by eminent industry) and approaches the superb – ecstatic. Well, in a word, if I may venture – with all becoming diffidence, and only, it will be understood, for the good-natured purpose of making myself intelligible to the general reader – if I may venture to quote a remarkable critic of mine, a most far-seeing fellow, who, in recognizing the early promise of my work, in the early days when I was still struggling to scale those heights to which I afterwards so successfully attained, aptly described whatever of merit I had then displayed as 'the undefinable of genius' – this was what I had come to recognize on the great canvas before me, to feel, to revel in, to *know* in the utmost significance of the term as something all-comprehensive enough to be evident to the meanest man's capacity in its power to make him feel, while yet remaining beyond the range of language to convey. I had sat some time, however; my cigarette was half finished; the enjoyable sensation of having dined was uninterrupted by any feeling of regret on the subject of what I had eaten. I had, in fact, forgotten what I had eaten, which, when the doctor has put us under stoppages, as the military phrase is, and we have, nevertheless, ventured upon forbidden fruit, I take to be a proof that we have done so with impunity. The balmy summer air blew in upon me freshly from the garden through the south lattice of the studio; blackbird and thrush no longer lilted their love-songs – it was late; but a nightingale from the top of a tall tree, unseen, filled the innermost recesses of audition with inimitable sound. The hour, the scene – and the man, I may say – were all that is best calculated to induce the proper appreciation of a noble work of art; and the pale grey shades of evening had been dispelled by the radiant intensity of the electric light; but, although I had reclined in a deep easy chair long enough to finish a cigarette, not a single fibre of feeling had responded to the call of the canvas upon it. I felt the freshness, the nightingale's note in the stillness; that luxurious something of kinship which comes from the near neighbourhood of a great city with companionable effect when one is well disposed. But the work of art before me moved me no more than a fresh canvas standing ready stretched upon the easel, with paints and palette lying ready for use beside it would have done – not so much, in fact, for such preparations were only made when a new idea was burning in my being to be expressed; I should have been feeling it then; but now I was conscious of nothing more entrancing than the cold ashes of an old one. Yes! cold ashes, quite extinct, they were, and I found myself forced to acknowledge it, although, of course, I assured myself at the same time that the fault was in my mood of the moment, not in the picture. If I went out into the streets and brought in a varied multitude to gaze, I never doubted but that I should hear them shout again those paeans of praise to which I had long become accustomed – accustomed, too, as we are to the daily bread which we eat without much thought or appetite, but cannot do without. But certainly on this particular evening, while I gazed, persistent thoughts obtruded themselves instead of refined sensations. As I rounded that exquisite arm I remembered now that I had had in my mind the pleasurable certainty that the smiles of the Lady Catherine Claridge, her little invitations to 'come when you have nothing better to do – but not on my regular day, you know. *You* will always find me at home,' and her careless-seeming hint of a convenient hour, meant as much as I cared to claim. There had been in her blush, I knew, the material for my little romance of that season. And then, as I flecked in those floating clouds, I had been calculating the cost of these little romances, and deciding the sum it would be necessary to set upon this picture, in order to cover the more than usually extravagant outlay which would be entailed by her gentle ladyship's idea of my princely habits. When I was engaged upon those love-limpid eyes, it had occurred to me to calculate how much a year I should lose by spending the price of this picture, instead of reserving it as capital to be invested; and here I had asked myself, was it wise to lavish so much on one caprice? Then suddenly my mind had glanced off to the last Levée. I had certainly been slighted on that occasion – obviously neglected – allowed to pass with the kind of nod of recognition which does for a faithful lackey. At the recollection of it my forehead contracted with anger, the pride of performance forsook me, my effect had not come to those eyes, and I threw down my brush in disgust. I had gone over all that ground afterwards, for it is well known that I am nothing if not painstaking, and, indeed, my work is everywhere quoted in proof of the assertion that genius obviously *is* an infinite capacity for taking pains. But now again, as I gazed, the effect that I had tried for was absent; the whole work answered no more to my expectation than if it had been altogether stale, flat and unprofitable; and there gradually took possession of me a great amazement, not to say alarm, as I forced myself to acknowledge that there must be some blunting of my faculties to account for the powerlessness of the picture to move me as it ought. What could be the matter with me? Loss of nerve-power? Visions of delicate artistic susceptibilities injured when not actually wiped out by the coarse influences of indigestion, horrid possibilities, had begun to assail me rudely, when the ringing of the studio bell suddenly startled me back to my normal state of mind. It rang once sharply, and, although it is not my habit to answer bells for myself, I arose on some unaccountable impulse, and, going to the outer door of the studio, which opened on to a flight of steps leading down into the road, did so on this occasion.

A young woman was waiting without. The electric light from behind me fell full upon her face. I did not think her particularly attractive in appearance, and the direct look of her eyes into mine was positively distasteful. It was the kind of glance which either fascinates or creates a feeling of repulsion. Coming from a creature whose exterior does not please, such a glance inevitably repels, especially if there is anything commanding in it, and more particularly the command of a strong nature in an inferior position, when it is likely to cause a degree of irritation which would, amongst unrefined people, result in an outburst of rough hostility; but with us, of course, only expresses itself in a courtly coldness.

'Do you want a model?' the young woman asked, speaking without a particle of respect or apology, as if to an equal.

I would have answered in the negative shortly, and shut the door, but for – I had it just now, but for the moment it has escaped me. However, I shall remember it by and by, and for the present it is only necessary to state that I did not say 'No', and shut the door. I hesitated.

'You can't tell, of course, until you see me,' the applicant pursued in a confident tone. 'I had better come in and show myself.'

And involuntarily I stood aside to let her pass, conscious at the same time that I was bending my body from the waist, although I certainly never meant to bow to a model. My position necessitates so many bows, however, that it has really become more natural for me to acknowledge the approach of a fellow creature so, than in any other posture.

Ah! now I recall what it was that had made me hesitate – her voice. It was not the voice of a common model. And as she passed into the studio before me now, she struck me as not being a common person of any kind. Someone in distress, I thought, driven to earn an honest penny. All sorts of people come in this way to us artists, and we do what we can for them without asking questions. Sometimes we get an invaluable model with distinct marks of superior breeding, in this way; a king's daughter, displaying in every lineament the glory of race, which inspires. Oftener it is a pretty 'young lady' out of a situation. The latter appears in every academy by the name of some classical celebrity. But then, again, we have applicants like the present, not attractive, whom it would be folly to engage to sit, however willing we may be to oblige them by employing them. In such cases a sovereign or so is gratefully accepted, as a rule, and there the matter ends; and I had put my hand in my pocket now as I followed my visitor in, thinking for a moment that I could satisfy her with such substantial proof of sympathy, and get rid of her; but directly she stopped and turned to me, I felt an unaccountable delicacy about doing so. 'This is no beggar, no ordinary object of charity,' I thought; 'it would be an insult to offer her anything that she has not earned.'

She had placed herself full in the light for my inspection, with her back to my picture, and I looked at her attentively, gauging the possibility of making anything out of such a face, and the rather tall bundle of loose, light wraps which was the figure she presented. 'Hopeless!' was my first impression; 'I'm not sure', the second; and the third, 'Skin delicate, features regular, eyes' – but there the fault was, I discovered, not in the shape or colour, but in the expression of them. They were the mocking eyes of that creature most abhorrent to the soul of man, a woman who claims to rule and does not care to please; eyes out of which an imperious spirit shone independently, not looking up, but meeting mine on the same level. Now, a really attractive, womanly woman looks up, clings, depends, so that a man can never forget his own superiority in her presence.

'Well?' she broke in upon my reflections, prolonging the word melodiously.

And instantly it occurred to me that as I had not yet begun another serious work, I might as well do a good deed, and keep my hand in at the same time, by making a study of her. Certainly, the type was uncommon.

'Yes,' I replied, speaking, to my own surprise, in a satisfied tone, as if I were receiving instead of conferring a favour, although I cannot understand why I should have done so. 'You may come tomorrow and give me some sittings. Be here at ten.'

She was turning away without a word, and she had not ventured to look at the picture; but this I thought was natural diffidence, so I called her back, feeling that a man in my position might, without loss of dignity, give the poor creature a treat.

'You may look at the picture if you like,' I said, speaking involuntarily very much as I should have done to – well, to the Lady Catherine Claridge herself!

She glanced at the picture over her shoulder. 'Pooh!' she said. 'Do you call that a picture?' And then she looked up in my face and laughed.

When next I found myself thinking coherently, it was about her teeth. 'What wonderful white ones she has!' I was saying to myself. But the studio door was shut, and all echo of her departing footsteps had died away long before I arrived at that reflection.

The next morning I was in the studio before ten o'clock, and the first thing I did was to cover my new work with a curtain, and then I set my palette. But a quarter past ten arrived and no model. Half-past – this was hardly respectful. Eleven, twelve, luncheon, light literature, a drive, the whole day – what could the woman mean? I had intended to take tea with Lady Catherine, but just as I approached the house, I was suddenly seized with a curious dislike of the visit, an unaccountable distaste for herself and everything about her, which impelled me to drive on past the place without casting a glance in that direction. I wondered afterwards if she had seen me, but I did not care in the least whether she had or not.

After dinner, as on the previous evening, I retired to the studio to enjoy a cigarette; but this time I sat with my back to the picture, before which the curtain still remained drawn, and looked out of the lattice at the lights which leaves take when fluttering in the moonlight; and listened to the nightingale – until there stole upon my senses something – that something which did not come to me out of my picture the night before. I found myself in a moment drinking in the beauty of the night with long, deep sighs, and thinking thoughts – thoughts like the thoughts of youth, which are 'long, long thoughts'.[1] I had even felt the first thrill of a great aspiration, when I was disturbed again by the ringing of the studio bell. Again, involuntarily, I hastened to open the door, and there she stood in exactly the same position at the foot of the steps, looking up at me with her eyes that repelled – but no! I was mistaken. How could I have thought her eyes repellent? They were merrily dancing, mischievous eyes, that made you smile in spite of yourself.

'Well, I didn't come, you see,' she said in a casual way. 'I knew you wouldn't be ready for me.'

'Not ready for you?' I exclaimed, without thinking whether I ought to condescend to parley with a model. 'Why, I waited for you the whole morning.'

'Oh, that is nothing,' she answered cheerfully – 'nothing, at least, if nothing comes of it. You must wait, you know, to recover yourself. You've lost such a lot. What is the use of having paint on your palette if the rage to apply it is not *here*?' She looked up at me with big, bright, earnest eyes as she spoke, and clasped her hands over her chest. Then she stooped and peeped unceremoniously under my arm into the studio. 'Ah!' she said, 'you have covered that thing up' – meaning my picture! 'That's right. And you've been sitting by the lattice – there's your chair. Last night it was in front of the easel. Well! I will look in tomorrow, just to see how you are getting on. No trouble, I assure you. There! you can shut the door. If you stand there when I am gone, staring at the spot where I stood as you did last night, you'll be in a draught and catch cold, which is risky for a middle-aged man, just now especially, with so much influenza about. Goodnight!'

She turned to walk away as she spoke, and her gait was like music in motion, she moved so rhythmically.

'What an extraordinary person!' I exclaimed, when she was out of sight. While she was with me, however, she did not seem extraordinary, and it was only after she had gone that I even recognized the utter incongruity of my own attitude towards her when under the immediate influence of her singular personality.

But what was it that set me thinking of Martha troubled about many things[2] when she mentioned the draught and the influenza? And also reminded me that to be a great artist one must be a great man in the sense of being a good one?

Now, somehow, next morning I knew better than to expect her at ten o'clock. I noticed that the paint had dried on my palette, and ordered my man to clean it, but I did not set it afresh, for what, I asked myself, is the use of paint on a palette if one has nothing to express?

The day was devoted to social duties. I went in and out several times, asking always on my return if anyone had been, to which my man, an old and faithful servant, invariably replied as if he understood me, 'Not even a model, sir.'

I had had to attend a Levée in the afternoon, and when it was over, one of the dukes, a noted connoisseur, asked me if I would 'be so good' as to show him my new picture – the exact expression was: 'Your last great work.' Other gentlemen came up while he was speaking to me, and it ended in several of them returning with me forthwith to view the picture.

I had not looked at it myself since I had covered it up, and now that I was forced to draw the curtain from before it, I felt it to be a distasteful duty.

'Well, that *is* a picture!' the duke exclaimed, and all the other gentlemen praised the work in a choice variety of elegantly selected phrases. They even looked as if they liked it, a fact which clearly proved to me they had not one of them got further than I had myself before dinner on the eventful evening when *she* first appeared.

I was to have dined out that day, but just as I was about to step into my carriage, I saw a figure in loose, light draperies, charmingly disposed, approaching. (What was it made me think of Lot's wife?)[3] I turned back into the house on the instant, and retired to the studio, the outer door of which I opened at once for her convenience.

She walked straight in without ceremony.

'You were going to some feeding function tonight, I suppose,' she observed. Then she looked round, chose a chair and sat herself down deliberately.

I remained standing myself with my hands folded, regarding her with an expression in which I hoped she would see good-natured tolerance of one of the whimsical sex struggling with a certain amount of impatience carefully controlled. And she did study my face and attitude critically for some seconds; then she shook her head.

'Don't like it!' she exclaimed. 'No native dignity in it, because anybody could see that you are posing.'

Involuntarily I altered my position, planting myself more firmly on my feet.

'That's better,' she said, and then she looked at me again, frowning intently, and once more shook her head. 'You live too well, you know,' she admonished me. 'There is a certain largeness in your very utterance which bespeaks high feeding, and an oleosaccharine quality in the courtly urbanity even of your everyday manner which comes of constant repletion. One is obliged to fall into it oneself to express it properly,' she added apologetically. 'But you are a prince now, you know; you're not an artist. You've eaten all that out of yourself.'

'I am not a great eater,' I protested, in a tone which should have shown her that I was gravely offended by the liberty of language she allowed herself.

'Well, don't be huffy,' she said. 'It is not so much in the matter of meat and drink that your appetite is gross, I allow; it was the Tree of Life[4] to which I alluded. You cannot pretend that you only nibble at that! You know you deny yourself none of it, so long as what you can reach is sufficiently refined to please you. You have fed your senses to such a monstrous girth that they have crowded the soul out of you. What you put into your pictures now is knowledge, not inspiration. But that is the way with all of you artist-princes at present. Inspiration is extinct at Hampstead and in St John's Wood, and even here, on Melbury Hill, there is scarcely a flicker.' She slowly removed her outer wrap, and as she put the long pin with a black glass head which had held it together carefully back in it, she added emphatically: 'People may look at your pictures to their heads' content, but their hearts you never touch.'

She sat still, looking gravely at the ground, for a few seconds after this last utterance; then she rose in her deliberate, languid way, and went, with her long wrap depending from her left arm and gracefully trailing after her, up to the picture, and drew aside the curtain that concealed it.

'Now, look at that!' she exclaimed. 'Your flesh is flesh, and your form is form; likewise your colour is colour, and your draperies are drapery – although too luxuriant, as a rule; you riot in fulness and folds with an effect that is wormy – but there isn't a scrap of human interest in the whole composition, and the consequence is a notable flatness and insipidity, as of soup without salt.' She looked close into the picture, then drew back and contemplated it from a little distance, with her head on one side, and then she carefully covered it up with the curtain, remarking as she did so contemptuously, 'There is not a scrap of "that certain something" in it, you know; it is merely a clever contrivance of paint upon canvas.'

'But there is pleasure in the contemplation of a coat of colour laid on with a master's hand,' I modestly observed, changing my balance from one leg to the other, and crisping the fingers of my left hand as they lay upon the right.

'For some people,' she replied; 'there is an order of mind, mind in its infancy, which can be so diverted. We have a pet frame-maker at home [*Who can she be?*], and one day when he brought back a new picture we thought we would give him a treat, so we took him into the picture gallery [*A picture gallery argues a mansion*], and invited him to look at the pictures, and then we watched him walking down the long length of it slowly, passing in review a whole sequence of art, ancient and modern. [*She must belong to considerable people, there are not many such private collections.*] But not a muscle of his face moved until he came to an exquisite little modern gem – it was not one of yours,' she hastened to assure me. I made a deprecating gesture to show her I had not the egotism to suppose it might be. 'Gems by you are exceedingly difficult to procure,' she proceeded, in a tone which suggested something sarcastical, but I failed to comprehend. 'Well,' she pursued, 'our good frame-maker stopped opposite to that gem. His countenance, which had been sombre as that of one who patiently accomplishes a task, now cleared, his eyes brightened intelligently, his cheeks flushed, his lips parted to exclaim, and I thought to myself, "Now for a genuine glimpse of the soul of a working man!" He looked again, as if to make sure before he committed himself, then, turning to me, he exclaimed triumphantly, "*I* made that frame!"'

'Ah – yes,' I was conscious of murmuring politely. 'Extremely good! But we were talking about paint.'

'Oh, well, of course, if you can't see the point —' She shrugged her shoulders and turned the palms of her hands outwards. Then she sat down again and looked at my feet. I shifted them uneasily.

'I was going out to dinner,' I ventured at last, breaking in upon her meditations tentatively.

'I know,' she responded, with a sigh, as if she were wearied in mind. 'It would be just as well to send the carriage back. There is no use keeping the coachman and horses at the door. I daresay the cook has some cutlets that will do for us.'

'I am sure I shall be delighted if you will do me the honour—' I was beginning, when again she laughed in my face, showing much of her magnificent set of strong white teeth. Why did I never dream of opposing her?

'Oh, come now!' she exclaimed, apparently much amused; 'you are not at Court, you know. Here in the studio you should be artistic, not artificial; and what you don't feel you shouldn't pretend to feel. Shall we dine here? Put that thing back,' – pointing to the picture – 'pull out the throne – it will make a capital low table – and order in two easy chairs for us to recline upon opposite to each other. You are nothing if not classical in appearance. Fancy you in a frock-coat, with spats upon your boots! and you in modern evening dress! It is absurd! You should wear a toga.'

I was going to say something about the incongruity of such a costume, but she would not let me speak. 'Just wait a moment,' she said; 'it is my innings.[5] And nobody knows better than I do that High Street, Kensington, would be more amazed than edified by the apparition of yourself in a toga, or, better still – for I take you to be more Greek than Roman – clad in the majestic folds of the *himation*, and without a cravat – admirably as either would set off your attractive personal appearance. Here on the hill, however, it is different. I tell you, you are nothing if not classical, both in your person and your work; but a modern man must add of the enlightenment of today that which was wanting to the glory of the Greeks. Your work at present is purely Greek – form without character, passionless perfection, imperfectly perfect, wanting the spirit part,[6] which was not in Greece, but is, or ought to be, in you; without which the choicest masterpiece of old was merely "icily regular, splendidly null",[7] with which the veriest street arab put upon canvas is "equal to the god"! I tell you, you are a true Greek, but you must be something more, for this is not

Athens in Greece, but Melbury Hill, Kensington, London, W.[8] –
coming whence we will accept nothing but positive perfection, which
is form *and* character, flesh and blood, body and soul, the divine in
the human— But there!' she broke off. 'That is as much as you must
have at present. And I am fatigued. Do get the room arranged and
order in dinner, while I retire to refresh myself by indulging in the
comfort of a bath. I suppose I shall find one somewhere, with hot and
cold water laid on.'

She walked with easy grace out of the studio into the house when
she had spoken, leaving me gravely perplexed. And again I wonder
why, at the time, it never occurred to me to oppose her; but certainly
it never did.

My difficulty now was how to make the arrangements she required
without taking the whole establishment into my confidence; but while
I still stood in the attitude in which she had left me – an attitude, I
believe, of considerable dignity, the right foot being a little in advance,
at right angles to the left, and the left elbow supported on the back of
the right hand, so that the fingers caressed the left cheek – my faithful
old confidential servant entered.

'Beg pardon, sir,' he began – and I could see that he was perturbed
and anxious, like one in dread lest he shall not perform the duty
exacted of him satisfactorily – 'but the lady said you wanted me to
arrange the scene for the new picture.'

Instantly I understood her delicate manner of getting me out of my
difficulty, and having given my man full directions, I stood looking
on while the necessary arrangements were being completed, making
a suggestion now and then as to the disposition of table decorations,
and myself choosing the draperies that were to decorate the lounges
upon which we were to recline. While so engaged, I, as it were – if I
may venture to use such an expression – warmed to the work. At first
I had looked on as a grown-up person might do when viewing with
pleased toleration the preparations for some childish frolic; but as the
arrangements neared completion, and I gradually beheld one end of
my studio transformed with the help of rare ancient vessels, statues
and furniture of the most antique design, which I had collected for
the purposes of my art, into such a scene as Apelles[9] himself might

have countenanced, I felt an unwonted glow of enthusiasm, and fell to adjusting hangings and dragging lounges about myself. It was a close evening, and the extraordinary exertion made me so hot, that, without a thought of my dignity, I dashed my coat and vest on the floor, and worked in my shirtsleeves.

'That's right!' said a tuneful voice at last, and upon looking round, I saw my model – or guest of the evening, shall I say? She was standing between two heavy curtains which screened off one side of the studio from an outer apartment. Her right hand was raised high in the act of holding one of the curtains back, and her bare, round arm shone ivory-white against the dark folds of the curtains. It was a striking attitude, instinct with a singular grace and charm, both of which, on looking back, I now recognize as having been eminently characteristic; and their immediate effect upon me was to make me entreat her not to move for a moment until I had caught the pose in a rapid sketch. She signified her consent by standing quiescent as a statue, while I hastily got out my materials, choosing charcoal for my medium, and set to work. And so great was my eagerness that I actually remained in my shirtsleeves without being aware of the fact – a statement which will, I know, astonish my friends, and appear to them to be incredible, even upon my own authority. But there must have been something powerfully – what shall I say? – demoralizing? – about this extraordinary woman. And yet it was not at all that, but elevating rather; even my model manservant, to judge by his countenance, felt her effect. Her mere presence seemed to be making him, 'the reptile equal' – for the moment in his own estimation – 'to the god',[10] that is to say, to me. Under the strange, benign influence of her appearance as she stood there, I could see that he had suddenly ceased to be an impassive serving-machine, and had become an emotional human being. There was interest in his eyes, and admiration, besides an all-devouring anxiety to be equal to the occasion – a disinterested trepidation on my account, as well as on his own. He was fearful that I should not answer to expectation, as was evident from the way that he, hitherto the most respectful of fellows, forgot himself, and ventured upon the liberty of looking on, first at the model and then at my sketch as it progressed. He came and peeped over my shoulder, went up to the model for a nearer view, then stepped off again to see her from another point, as we do when studying a fascinating object; and so inevitable did it seem even for a manservant to think and feel in her presence, that I allowed his demonstrations to pass unreproved, as though it were part of the natural order of things for a lackey so to comport himself.

But in the meantime the attention to my subject which the making of the sketch necessitated brought about a revelation. As I rapidly read each lineament for the purpose of fixing it on my paper, I asked myself involuntarily how I could possibly have supposed for a moment that this magnificent creature was unattractive? Why, from the crown of her head to the sole of her foot – what expression! There was a volume of verse in her glance – Oh, Sappho! – a bounteous vitality in her whole person – Oh, Ceres! – an atmosphere of life, of love, surrounded her – Oh, Venus! – a modest reserve of womanhood – Diana![11] – a—

'Get on, do!' she broke in upon my fervid analysis.

An *aplomb*, I concluded, a confidence of intellect; decision, intelligence and force of fine feeling combined in her which brought her up to date.

'Yes,' she observed, dropping the curtain, and coming forward when I had finished my sketch – in which, by the way, she took not the slightest interest, for she did not cast so much as a glance upon it. 'Yes,' she repeated, as if in answer to my thoughts – I wonder if perchance I had uttered them aloud? 'Yes, you are right. I commend you. I *am* a woman with all the latest improvements. The creature the world wants. Nothing can now be done without me.' She silently surveyed me after this with critical eyes. 'But hop out of that ridiculous dress, *do*', she said at last, 'and get into something suitable for summer, for a man of your type, and for the occasion.'

I instantly unbuttoned a brace.

'Hold on a moment,' she said rather hastily. 'Where is your classical wardrobe?'

My man, who had been waiting on her words, as it were, ran to a large carved chest at the further end of the studio, and threw up the lid for answer.

'Johnson,[12] as he appears in St Paul's Cathedral, may be all very well for people at church to contemplate; but that isn't my idea of a dinner dress,' she proceeded.

She was walking towards the chest as she spoke, and I noticed that her own dress, which had struck me at first as purely classical, was not really of any form with which I was acquainted, ancient or modern; but was of a design which I believe to be perfectly new, or, at all events, a most original variation upon already known designs. It was made of several exquisitely harmonized tints of soft silk.

When she reached the great chest, she stood a moment looking into it, and then began to pull the things out and throw them on the floor behind her, diving down deeper and deeper into the chest, till she had to stand on tiptoe to reach in at all, and the upper part of her body disappeared at every plunge. Near the bottom she found what she wanted. This proved to be a short-sleeved tunic, reaching to the knees, with a handsome Greek border embroidered upon it; some massive gold bracelets; a pair of sandals; and a small harp, such as we associate with Homer.[13]

She gathered all these things up in her arms, brought them to me, and threw them down at my feet. 'There!' she exclaimed; 'be quick! I want my dinner.'

With which she delicately withdrew until my toilette was complete.

When she returned, she held in her hand a laurel wreath, tied at the back with a bow of ribbon, and with the leaves lying symmetrically towards the front, where they met in a point. It was the form which appears in ancient portraits crowning the heads of distinguished men.

I had placed myself near a pedestal, with the harp in my hand, and, as she approached, felt conscious of nothing but my bare legs. My man, who had helped to attire me, also stood by, with deprecating glances entreatingly bespeaking her approval.

Having crowned me, she stepped back to consider the effect, and instantly she became convulsed with laughter. My servant assumed a dejected attitude upon this, and silently slunk away.

'Oh, dear! Oh, dear!' she exclaimed. 'If Society could only see you now! It isn't that you don't look well,' she hastened to reassure me – 'and I trust you will kindly excuse my inopportune mirth. It is a disease of the mind which I inherit from an ancestor of mine, who was a funny man. He worked for a comic paper, and was expected to make new jokes every week on the three same subjects: somebody drunk, somebody's mother-in-law, something unhappy – or low for prefer- ence – in married life; a consequence of which strain upon his mind was the setting up of the deplorable disease of inopportune mirth, which has unfortunately been transmitted to me. But I am altogether an outcome of the age, you will perceive, an impossible mixture of incongruous qualities, which are all in a ferment at present, but will eventually resolve themselves, as chemical combinations do, into an altogether unexpected, and, seeing that already the good is out- weighing the bad and indifferent ingredients, admirable composition, we will hope. But, as I was going to say, those ambrosial locks and that classic jowl of yours, not to mention your manly arms embraceleted, and—' But here she hesitated, apparently not liking to mention my legs, although she looked at them. 'Well,' she hurriedly summed up, 'I always said you would look lovely in a toga, and the short tunic is also artistic in its own way. But now let us dine; I am mortal hungry.'

I was about to hasten, harp in hand, across the studio to ring for dinner, but the moment I moved she went off again into convulsions of laughter.

'Excuse me,' she implored, drying her eyes, 'but it *is* so classical! I can't help it, really! Just to see you go gives me little electric shocks all over! But don't be huffy. You never looked nicer, I declare. And you can put on a toga, you know, if the tunic isn't enough. It *is* somewhat skimpy, I confess, for a man of your girth.'

When she had spoken, she went to the chest and obligingly looked me out some yards of stuff, which she said, when properly draped, would do for a toga; and having arranged it upon my shoulders to please herself, she conducted me to one of the couches, remarking that dinner would be sure to come all in good time, and recommending me to employ the interval in cultivating a cheerful frame of mind, 1, 2, 3, 4, 5, 6, 7 – a copybook precept, good for the digestion when practised, she insisted, as she thoughtfully adjusted my harp; after which she begged me to assume a classical attitude, and then proceeded to dispose herself in like manner on the other couch opposite.

'This is delicious,' she said, sighing luxuriously as she sank upon it. 'I guess the Greeks and Romans never really knew what comfort was. Imagine an age without springs!'

Dinner was now served by my man, who was, I could see, still shaking in his shoes with anxiety lest everything should not be to her mind. He had donned a red gown, similar to that worn by attendants at the Royal Academy on state occasions, and was suffering a good deal from the heat in consequence. But the dinner was all that could be desired, as my guest herself observed. And she should have known, too, for she ate with a will. 'I must tell you,' she explained, 'Aesculapius[14] prescribed a tonic for me on one occasion, and I have been taking it, off and on, ever since, so that I am almost all appetite.'

What was it that made me think at that moment of Venus's visit to Aesculapius?

We were now at dessert, nibbling fruit and sipping wine, and my face was suffused with smiles, but my companion looked grave, and I thought that her mood was resolving itself into something serious by the sober way she studied my face.

'Excuse me, but your wreath is all on one side,' she remarked at last – quite by the way, however.

I rose hastily to readjust the wreath at a mirror, and then returned and leisurely resumed my seat. I had been about to speak, but something new in the demeanour of the lady opposite caused me to forget my intention. There was an indescribable grace in her attitude, a perfect *abandon* to the repose of the moment which was in itself an evidence of strength in reserve, and fascinating to a degree. But the curious thing about the impression that she was now making upon me is that she had not moved. She had been reclining in an easy manner since the servant left the room, with her arm resting on the back of her couch, twirling a flower in her fingers, and hadn't swerved from the pose a fraction; only a certain quietude had settled upon her, and was emanating from her forcibly, as I felt. And with this quietude there came to me quite suddenly a new and solemn sense of responsibility, something grave and glad which I cannot explain, something which caused me an exquisite sense of pleasurable emotion, and made me feel the richer for the experience. My first thought was of England

and America, of the glorious womanhood of this age of enlightenment, compared with the creature as she existed merely for man's use and pleasure of old; the toy-woman, drudge, degraded domestic animal, beast of intolerable burdens. How could the sons of slaves ever be anything but slaves themselves? slaves of various vices, the most execrable form of bondage. To paint – to paint this woman as she is! – in her youth, in her strength, in her beauty – in her insolence, even! in the fearless candour of her perfect virtue; the trifler of an idle hour, the strong, true spirit of an arduous day – to paint her so that man may feel her divinity and worship that!

I had covered my eyes with my hands, so as the better to control my emotions and collect my thoughts; but now a current of cold air playing upon my limbs, and the faint sith[15] of silk, aroused me. I looked up. The couch was empty.

The next morning she arrived by ten o'clock in a very ugly old grey cloak. I was engaged at the moment in reading the report in a morning paper of the dinner at which I ought to have appeared on the previous evening, and the letter of apology for my unavoidable absence which I forgot to mention that my guest had induced me to send. She came and read the report over my shoulder.

'That is graceful,' was her comment upon my letter. 'You are a charming phrase-maker. Such neatness of expression is not common. But,' she added severely, 'it is also disgraceful, because you didn't mean a word of it. And an artist should be an honest, earnest man, incapable of petty subterfuge; otherwise, however great he may be, he falls short of the glory, just as you do. But there!' she added plaintively, 'you know all that – or, at all events, you used to know it.'

' "He is the greatest artist who has the greatest number" '[16] – I was beginning, when she interrupted me abruptly.

'Oh, I know! You have it all off by heart so pat!' she exclaimed. 'But what good do precepts do you? Why, if maxims could make an artist, I should be one myself, for I know them all; and I am no artist!'

'I don't know that,' slipped from me unawares.

'That is because you have become a mere appraiser of words,' she declared. 'You, as an artist, would have divined that if I could paint myself I should not be here. I should be doing what I want for myself, instead of using my peculiar power to raise you to the necessary altitude.'

'Oh, of course!' I hastened to agree, apologetically, feeling myself on familiar ground at last. 'The delicate, subtly inspiring presence is the woman's part; the rough work is for man, the interpreter. No woman has ever truly distinguished herself except in her own sphere.'

'Now, no cant, *please*,' she exclaimed. 'You are not a pauper priest, afraid that the offertory will fall off if he doesn't keep the upper hand of all the women in the parish.'

'But,' I protested, 'few women have ever —'

'Now just reflect,' she interrupted, 'and you will remember that in the days of our slavery there were more great women than there have ever been great men who were also slaves; so that now that our full emancipation is imminent, why, you shall see what you shall see.'

'Then why don't you paint?' I asked her blandly.

'All in good time,' she answered suavely. 'But I have not come to bandy words with you, nor to be irritated by hearing nonsensical questions asked by a man of your age and standing. I am here to be painted. Just set your palette while I see to my attire. You seem to have forgotten lately that a woman is a creature of clothes in these days – and there never were more delightful days, by the way, since the world began.'

When she returned, she ascended the throne, but before falling into a set attitude, she addressed me: 'The great stories of the world are deathless and ageless, because of the human nature that is in them, and you know that in your head, but your heart does not feel it a bit. Your sentiments are irreproachable, but they have survived the vivifying flush of feeling, parent of sympathetic insight, upon which you formed them, and the mere dry knowledge that remains is no use for creative purposes. All through Nature strong emotion is the motive of creation, and in art, also, the power to create is invariably the outcome of an ardent impulse. But there you stand, in full conceit beside your canvas, with your palette and brushes in your hand, a mere cool, calculating workman, without an atom of love or reverence, not

SARAH GRAND

to mention inspiration, to warm your higher faculties into life and action; and in that mood you have the assurance to believe that you have only to choose to paint me as I am, and you will be able to do so – able to paint, not merely a creature of a certain shape, but a creature of boundless possibilities, instinct with soul – no, though, I wrong you,' she broke off scornfully. 'The soul of me, the part that an artist should specially crave to render through the medium of this outer shell, which of itself alone is hardly worth the trouble of copying on to the canvas, has never cost you a thought. Rounded form, healthy flesh and lively glances are all that appeal to you now.'

I bent my head, considering if this were true; but even while I asked myself the question I was conscious of a curious shock – a shock of awakening, as it were, a thrill that traversed my body in warm, swift currents, making me tingle. I knew what it was in a moment – her enthusiasm. She had communicated it to me occultly, a mere spark of it at first, but even that was animating to a degree that was delicious.

'Don't put anything on canvas that you cannot glorify,' she resumed. 'The mere outer husk of me is nothing, I repeat; you must interpret – you must reveal the beyond of that – the grace, I mean, all resplendent within.' She clasped her hands upon her breast, and looked into my eyes. 'You remember your first impression when I offered myself as a model?' she pursued. I felt ashamed of my own lack of thought, and hung my head. 'Compare your present idea of my attractions with that, and see for yourself how far you have lapsed. You have descended from art to artificiality, I tell you. You have ceased to see and render like a sentient being; you are nothing now but a painting machine. *Now!*' she exclaimed, clapping her hands together, 'stand straight and look at me!'

Like one electrified, I obeyed.

'I am the woman who stood at the outer door of your studio and summoned you to judge me; the same whom, in your spiritual obscurity, you then found wanting. Rend now that veil of flesh, and look! Who was at fault?'

'I was,' burst from me involuntarily.

When I had spoken, I clasped my palette, and hastily selected a brush. Her exaltation had rapidly gained upon me. I was consumed

134

with the rage to paint her – or, rather, to paint that in her which I suddenly saw and could reproduce upon canvas, but could not otherwise express.

Slowly, without another word, she lapsed into an easy attitude, fixing her wonderful eyes upon mine. For a moment my vision was clouded; I saw nothing but mist. As that cleared, however, there penetrated to the inner recesses of my being – there was revealed to me— But the tone-poets must find the audible expression of it. My limit is to make it visible.

But never again, I said to myself as I painted, shall mortal stand before a work of mine unmoved; never again shall it be said: 'Well, it may be my ignorance, which it would be bad taste for me to display in the presence of a picture by so great a man; but, all the same, I must say I can't see anything in it.' No, never again! if I have to sacrifice every delight of the body to keep my spiritual vision unobscured; for there is no joy like this joy, nothing else which is human which so nearly approaches the divine as the exercise of this power.

'For heaven's sake don't move!' I implored.

She had not moved, but the whole expression of her face had changed with an even more disastrous effect. The glorious light which had illuminated such enthusiasm in me had passed out of her eyes, giving place to that cold, critical expression which repelled, and she smiled enigmatically.

'I can't stand here all day,' she said, stepping down from the throne. 'You know now what you want.'

She was at the outer door as she pronounced those words, and the instant after she had uttered them she was gone, absolutely gone, before I could remonstrate.

I had thrown myself on my knees to beg for another hour, and now, when I realized the cruelty of her callous desertion of me at such a juncture, I sank beside the easel utterly overcome, and remained for I cannot tell how long in a kind of stupor, from which, however, I was at length aroused by a deep-drawn sigh.

I looked up, and then I rose to my feet.

It was my faithful servant who had sighed. He was standing at gaze before the all-unfinished work. I looked at it myself.

'It is wonderful, sir,' he said, speaking in an undertone, as if in the presence of something sacred.

Yes, it was wonderful, even then, and what would it be when it was finished? Finished! How could I finish it without a model – without that model in particular? I recognized her now – a free woman, a new creature, a source of inspiration the like of which no man hitherto has even imagined in art or literature. Why had she deserted me? – for she had, and I knew it at once. I felt she would not return, and she never did; nor have I ever been able to find her, although I have been searching for her ever since. You may see me frequently in the corner of an open carriage, with my man seated on the box beside the coachman; and as we drive through the streets, we gaze up at the windows, and into the faces of the people we pass, in the hope that some day we shall see her; but never a glimpse, as yet, have we obtained.

My man says that such capricious conduct is just what you might expect of a woman, old-fashioned or new; but I cannot help thinking myself that both in her coming and her going, her insolence and her ideality, her gravity and her levity, there was a kind of allegory. 'With all my faults, nothing uncommonly great can be done without my countenance,' this was what she seemed to have said to me; 'but my countenance you shall not have to perfection until the conceit of you is conquered, and you acknowledge all you owe me. Give me my due; and when *you* help *me*, I will help *you!*'

KATE CHOPIN

The Story of an Hour

Knowing that Mrs Mallard was afflicted with a heart trouble, great care was taken to break to her as gently as possible the news of her husband's death.

It was her sister Josephine who told her, in broken sentences; veiled hints that revealed in half concealing. Her husband's friend Richards was there, too, near her. It was he who had been in the newspaper office when intelligence of the railroad disaster was received, with Brently Mallard's name leading the list of 'killed'. He had only taken the time to assure himself of its truth by a second telegram, and had hastened to forestall any less careful, less tender friend in bearing the sad message.

She did not hear the story as many women have heard the same, with a paralysed inability to accept its significance. She wept at once, with sudden, wild abandonment, in her sister's arms. When the storm of grief had spent itself she went away to her room alone. She would have no one follow her.

There stood, facing the open window, a comfortable, roomy arm-chair. Into this she sank, pressed down by a physical exhaustion that haunted her body and seemed to reach into her soul.

She could see in the open square before her house the tops of trees that were all aquiver with the new spring life. The delicious breath of rain was in the air. In the street below a pedlar was crying his wares. The notes of a distant song which some one was singing reached her faintly, and countless sparrows were twittering in the eaves.

There were patches of blue sky showing here and there through the clouds that had met and piled one above the other in the west facing her window.

She sat with her head thrown back upon the cushion of the chair, quite motionless, except when a sob came up into her throat and shook her, as a child who has cried itself to sleep continues to sob in its dreams.

She was young, with a fair, calm face, whose lines bespoke repression and even a certain strength. But now there was a dull stare in her eyes, whose gaze was fixed away off yonder on one of those patches of blue sky. It was not a glance of reflection, but rather indicated a suspension of intelligent thought.

There was something coming to her and she was waiting for it, fearfully. What was it? She did not know; it was too subtle and elusive to name. But she felt it, creeping out of the sky, reaching toward her through the sounds, the scents, the colour that filled the air.

Now her bosom rose and fell tumultuously. She was beginning to recognize this thing that was approaching to possess her, and she was striving to beat it back with her will – as powerless as her two white slender hands would have been.

When she abandoned herself a little whispered word escaped her slightly parted lips. She said it over and over under her breath: 'free, free, free!' The vacant stare and the look of terror that had followed it went from her eyes. They stayed keen and bright. Her pulses beat fast, and the coursing blood warmed and relaxed every inch of her body.

She did not stop to ask if it were or were not a monstrous joy that held her. A clear and exalted perception enabled her to dismiss the suggestion as trivial.

She knew that she would weep again when she saw the kind, tender hands folded in death; the face that had never looked save with love upon her, fixed and grey and dead. But she saw beyond that bitter moment a long procession of years to come that would belong to her absolutely. And she opened and spread her arms out to them in welcome.

There would be no one to live for her during those coming years; she would live for herself. There would be no powerful will bending hers in that blind persistence with which men and women believe they have a right to impose a private will upon a fellow creature. A kind intention or a cruel intention made the act seem no less a crime as she looked upon it in that brief moment of illumination.

And yet she had loved him – sometimes. Often she had not. What did it matter! What could love, the unsolved mystery, count for in face of this possession of self-assertion which she suddenly recognized as the strongest impulse of her being!

'Free! Body and soul free!' she kept whispering.

Josephine was kneeling before the closed door with her lips to the keyhole, imploring for admission. 'Louise, open the door! I beg; open the door – you will make yourself ill. What are you doing, Louise? For heaven's sake open the door.'

'Go away. I am not making myself ill.' No; she was drinking in a very elixir of life through that open window.

Her fancy was running riot along those days ahead of her. Spring days, and summer days, and all sorts of days that would be her own. She breathed a quick prayer that life might be long. It was only yesterday she had thought with a shudder that life might be long.

She arose at length and opened the door to her sister's importunities. There was a feverish triumph in her eyes, and she carried herself unwittingly like a goddess of Victory. She clasped her sister's waist, and together they descended the stairs. Richards stood waiting for them at the bottom.

Some one was opening the front door with a latchkey. It was Brently Mallard who entered, a little travel-stained, composedly carrying his grip-sack and umbrella. He had been far from the scene of accident, and did not even know there had been one. He stood amazed at Josephine's piercing cry; at Richards' quick motion to screen him from the view of his wife.

But Richards was too late.

When the doctors came they said she had died of heart disease – of joy that kills.

ELLA D'ARCY

The Pleasure-Pilgrim

I

Campbell was on his way to Schloss Altenau, for a second quiet season
with his work. He had spent three profitable months there a year ago,
and he was hoping now for a repetition of that good fortune. His
thoughts outran the train; and long before his arrival at the Hamelin
railway station, he was enjoying his welcome by the Ritterhausens,
was revelling in the ease and comfort of the old Castle, and was
contrasting the pleasures of his homecoming – for he looked upon
Schloss Altenau as a sort of temporary home – with his recent cheerless
experiences of lodging houses in London, hotels in Berlin and strange
indifferent faces everywhere. He thought with especial satisfaction of
the Maynes, and of the good talks Mayne and he would have together,
late at night, before the great fire in the hall, after the rest of the
household had gone to bed. He blessed the adverse circumstances
which had turned Schloss Altenau into a boarding house, and had
reduced the Freiherr Ritterhausen to eke out his shrunken revenues
by the reception, as paying guests, of English and American pleasure-
pilgrims.

He rubbed the blurred window pane with the fringed end of the
strap hanging from it, and, in the snow-covered landscape reeling
towards him, began to recognize objects that were familiar. Hamelin
could not be far off . . . In another ten minutes the train came to a
standstill.

He stepped down with a sense of relief from the overheated atmosphere of his compartment into the cold, bright February afternoon,
and saw through the open station doors one of the Ritterhausen

140

carriages awaiting him, with Gottlieb in his second-best livery on the box. Gottlieb showed every reasonable consideration for the Baron's boarders, but had various methods of marking his sense of the immense abyss separating them from the family. The use of his second-best livery was one of these methods. Nevertheless, he turned a friendly German eye up to Campbell, and in response to his cordial 'Guten Tag, Gottlieb. Wie geht's? Und die Herrschaften?'[1] expressed his pleasure at seeing the young man back again.

While Campbell stood at the top of the steps that led down to the carriage and the Platz, looking after the collection of his luggage and its bestowal by Gottlieb's side, he became aware of two persons, ladies, advancing towards him from the direction of the Wartsaal. It was surprising to see any one at any time in Hamelin Station. It was still more surprising when one of these ladies addressed him by name.

'You are Mr Campbell, are you not?' she said. 'We have been waiting for you to go back in the carriage together. When we found this morning that there was only half an hour between your train and ours, I told the Baroness it would be perfectly absurd to send to the station twice. I hope you won't mind our company?'

The first impression Campbell received was of the magnificent apparel of the lady before him; it would have been noticeable in Paris or Vienna – it was extravagant here. Next, he perceived that the face beneath the upstanding feathers and the curving hat-brim was that of so very young a girl, as to make the furs and velvets seem more incongruous still. But the sense of incongruity vanished with the intonation of her first phrase, which told him she was an American. He had no standards for American conduct. It was clear that the speaker and her companion were inmates of the Schloss.

He bowed, and murmured the pleasure he did not feel. A true Briton, he was intolerably shy; and his heart sank at the prospect of a three-mile drive with two strangers who evidently had the advantage of knowing all about him, while he was in ignorance of their very names. As he took his place opposite to them in the carriage, he unconsciously assumed a cold, blank stare, pulling nervously at his moustache, as was his habit in moments of discomposure. Had his companions been British also, the ordeal of the drive must have been a terrible one; but these young American ladies showed no sense of embarrassment whatever.

'We've just come back from Hanover,' said the girl who had already spoken to him. 'I go over once a week for a singing lesson, and my little sister comes along to take care of me.'

She turned a narrow, smiling glance from Campbell to her little sister, and then back to Campbell again. She had red hair; freckles on her nose, and the most singular eyes he had ever seen; slit-like eyes, set obliquely in her head, Chinese fashion.

'Yes, Lulie requires a great deal of taking care of,' assented the little sister sedately, though the way in which she said this seemed to imply something less simple than the words themselves. The speaker bore no resemblance to Lulie. She was smaller, thinner, paler. Her features were straight, a trifle peaked; her skin sallow; her hair of a nondescript brown. She was much less gorgeously dressed. There was even a suggestion of shabbiness in her attire, though sundry isolated details of it were handsome too. She was also much less young; or so, at any rate, Campbell began by pronouncing her. Yet presently he wavered. She had a face that defied you to fix her age. Campbell never fixed it to his own satisfaction, but veered in the course of that drive (as he was destined to do during the next few weeks) from point to point up and down the scale from eighteen to thirty-five. She wore a spotted veil, and beneath it a pince-nez, the lenses of which did something to temper the immense amount of humorous meaning which lurked in her gaze. When her pale prominent eyes met Campbell's, it seemed to the young man that they were full of eagerness to add something at his expense to the stores of information they had already garnered up. They chilled him with misgivings; there was more comfort to be found in her sister's shifting, red-brown glances.

'Hanover is a long way to go for lessons,' he observed, forcing himself to be conversational. 'I used to go there myself about once a week, when I first came to Schloss Altenau, for tobacco, or notepaper, or to get my hair cut. But later on I did without, or contented myself with what Hamelin, or even the village, could offer me.'

'Nannie and I,' said the young girl, 'meant to stay only a week at Altenau, on our way to Hanover, where we were going to pass the winter; but the Castle is just too lovely for anything.' She raised her eyelids the least little bit as she looked at him, and such a warm and friendly gaze shot out, that Campbell was suddenly thrilled. Was she pretty, after all? He glanced at Nannie; she, at least, was indubitably plain. 'It's the very first time we've ever stayed in a castle,' Lulie went on; 'and we're going to remain right along now, until we go home in the spring. Just imagine living in a house with a real moat, and a drawbridge, and a Rittersaal, and suits of armour that have been actually worn in battle! And oh, that delightful iron collar and chain! You remember it, Mr Campbell? It hangs right close to the gateway on the courtyard side. And you know, in old days the Ritterhausens used it for the punishment of their serfs. There are horrible stories connected with it. Mr Mayne can tell you them. But just think of being chained up there like a dog! So wonderfully picturesque.'

'For the spectator perhaps,' said Campbell, smiling. 'I doubt if the victim appreciated the picturesque aspect of the case.'

With this Lulie disagreed. 'Oh, I think he must have been interested,' she said. 'It must have made him feel so absolutely part and parcel of the Middle Ages. I persuaded Mr Mayne to fix the collar round my neck the other day; and though it was very uncomfortable, and I had to stand on tiptoe, it seemed to me that all at once the courtyard was filled with knights in armour, and crusaders, and palmers, and things; and there were flags flying and trumpets sounding; and all the dead and gone Ritterhausens had come down from their picture-frames, and were walking about in brocaded gowns and lace ruffles.'

'It seemed to require a good deal of persuasion to get Mr Mayne to unfix the collar again,' said the little sister. 'How at last did you manage it?'

But Lulie replied irrelevantly: 'And the Ritterhausens are such perfectly lovely people, aren't they, Mr Campbell? The old Baron is a perfect dear. He has such a grand manner. When he kisses my hand I feel nothing less than a princess. And the Baroness is such a funny, busy, delicious little round ball of a thing. And she's always playing bagatelle, isn't she? Or else cutting up skeins of wool for carpet-making.' She meditated a moment. 'Some people always *are* cutting things up in order to join them together again,' she announced, in her fresh drawling young voice.

'And some people cut things up, and leave other people to do the reparation,' commented the little sister enigmatically.

And meantime the carriage had been rattling over the cobble-paved streets of the quaint mediaeval town, where the houses stand so near together that you may shake hands with your opposite neighbour; where allegorical figures, strange birds and beasts, are carved and painted over the windows and doors; and where to every distant sound you lean your ear to catch the fairy music of the Pied Piper, and at every street corner you look to see his tatterdemalion form with the frolicking children at his heels.

Then the Weser bridge was crossed, beneath which the ice floes jostled and ground themselves together, as they forced their way down the river; and the carriage was rolling smoothly along country roads, between vacant snow-decked fields.

Campbell's embarrassment began to wear off. Now that he was getting accustomed to the girls, he found neither of them awe-inspiring. The red-haired one had a simple childlike manner that was charming. Her strange little face, with its piquant irregularity of line, its warmth of colour, began to please him. What though her hair was red, the uncurled wisp which strayed across her white forehead was soft and alluring; he could see soft masses of it tucked up beneath her hat-brim as she turned her head. When she suddenly lifted her red-brown lashes, those queer eyes of hers had a velvety softness too. Decidedly, she struck him as being pretty – in a peculiar way. He felt an immense accession of interest in her. It seemed to him that he was the discoverer of her possibilities. He did not doubt that the rest of the world called her plain; or at least odd-looking. He, at first, had only seen the freckles on her nose, her oblique-set eyes. He wondered now what she thought of herself, how she appeared to Nannie. Probably as a very ordinary little girl; sisters stand too close to see each other's qualities. She was too young to have had much opportunity of hearing flattering truths from strangers; and besides, the average stranger would see nothing in her to call for flattering truths. Her charm was something subtle, out-of-the-common, in defiance of all known rules of beauty. Campbell saw superiority in himself for recognizing it, for formulating it; and he was not displeased to be aware that it would always remain caviare to the multitude.

The carriage had driven through the squalid village of Dürrendorf, had passed the great Ritterhausen barns and farm-buildings, on the tie-beams of which are carved Bible texts in old German; had turned in at the wide open gates of Schloss Altenau, where Gottlieb always whipped up his horses to a fast trot. Full of feeling both for the pocket and the dignity of the Ritterhausens, he would not use up his beasts in unnecessary fast driving. But it was to the credit of the family that he should reach the Castle in fine style. And so he thundered across the drawbridge, and through the great archway pierced in the north wing, and over the stones of the cobbled courtyard, to pull up before the door of the hall, with much clattering of hoofs and a final elaborate whip-flourish.

2

'I'm jolly glad to have you back,' Mayne said, that same evening, when, the rest of the boarders having retired to their rooms, he and Campbell were lingering over the hall fire for a talk and smoke. 'I've missed you awfully, old chap, and the good times we used to have here. I've often meant to write to you, but you know how one shoves off letter-writing day after day, till at last one is too ashamed of one's indolence to write at all. But tell me – you had a pleasant drive from Hamelin? What do you think of our young ladies?'

'Those American girls? But they're charming,' said Campbell, with enthusiasm. 'The red-haired one is particularly charming.'

At this Mayne laughed so strangely that Campbell questioned him in surprise. 'Isn't she charming?'

'My dear chap,' Mayne told him, 'the red-haired one, as you call her, is the most remarkably charming young person I've ever met or read of. We've had a good many American girls here before now – you remember the good old Choate family, of course – they were here in your time, I think? – but we've never had anything like this Miss Lulie Thayer. She is something altogether unique.'

Campbell was struck with the name. 'Lulie – Lulie Thayer,' he repeated. 'How pretty it is!' And, full of his great discovery, he felt he must confide it to Mayne, at least. 'Do you know,' he went on, '*she* is really very pretty too? I didn't think so at first, but after a bit I discovered that she is positively quite pretty – in an odd sort of way.'

Mayne laughed again. 'Pretty, pretty!' he echoed in derision. 'Why, *lieber Gott im Himmel*, where are your eyes? Pretty! The girl is beautiful, gorgeously beautiful; every trait, every tint, is in complete, in absolute harmony with the whole. But the truth is, of course, we've all grown accustomed to the obvious, the commonplace; to violent contrasts; blue eyes, black eyebrows, yellow hair; the things that shout for recognition. You speak of Miss Thayer's hair as red. What other colour would you have, with that warm, creamy skin? And then, what a red it is! It looks as though it had been steeped in red wine.'

'Ah, what a good description,' said Campbell, appreciatively. 'That's just it – steeped in red wine.'

'Though it's not so much her beauty,' Mayne continued. 'After all, one has met beautiful women before now. It's her wonderful generosity, her complaisance. She doesn't keep her good things to herself. She doesn't condemn you to admire from a distance.'

'How do you mean?' Campbell asked, surprised again.

'Why, she's the most egregious little flirt I've ever met. And yet, she's not exactly a flirt, either. I mean she doesn't flirt in the ordinary way. She doesn't talk much, or laugh, or apparently make the least claims on masculine attention. And so all the women like her. I don't believe there's one, except my wife, who has an inkling as to her true character. The Baroness, as you know, never observes anything. *Seigneur Dieu!* if she knew the things I could tell her about Miss Lulie! For I've had opportunities of studying her. You see, I'm a married man, and not in my first youth, and the looker-on generally gets the best view of the game. But you, who are young and charming and already famous – we've had your book here, by the by, and there's good stuff in it – you're going to have no end of pleasant experiences. I can see she means to add you to her ninety-and-nine other spoils; I saw it from the way she looked at you at dinner. She always begins with those velvety red-brown glances. She began that way with March and Prendergast and Willie Anson, and all the men we've had here since her arrival. The next thing she'll do will be to press your hand under the tablecloth.'

'Oh come, Mayne, you're joking,' cried Campbell a little brusquely. He thought such jokes in bad taste. He had a high ideal of Woman, an immense respect for her; he could not endure to hear her belittled, even in jest. 'Miss Thayer is refined and charming. No girl of her class would do such things.'

'But what is her class? Who knows anything about her? All we know is that she and her uncanny little friend – her little sister, as she calls her, though they're no more sisters than you and I are – they're not even related – all we know is, that she and Miss Dodge (that's the little sister's name) arrived here one memorable day last October from the Kronprinz Hotel at Waldeck-Pyrmont. By the by, it was the Choates, I believe, who told her of the Castle – hotel acquaintants – you know how travelling Americans always cotton to each other. And we've picked up a few little auto and biographical notes from her and Miss Dodge since. *Zum Beispiel*, she's got a rich father somewhere away back in Michigan, who supplies her with all the money she wants. And she's been travelling about since last May: Paris, Vienna, the Rhine, Düsseldorf, and so on here. She must have had some rich experiences, by Jove, for she's done everything. Cycled in Paris; you should see her in her cycling costume, she wears it when the Baron takes her out shooting – she's an admirable shot by the way, an accomplishment learned, I suppose, from some American cowboy – then in Berlin she did a month's hospital nursing; and now she's studying the higher branches of the Terpsichorean art. You know she was in Hanover today. Did she tell you what she went for?'

'To take a singing lesson,' said Campbell, remembering the reason she had given.

'A singing lesson! Do you sing with your legs? A dancing lesson, *mein lieber*. A dancing lesson from the ballet master of the Hof Theatre. She could deposit a kiss on your forehead with her foot, I don't doubt. I must ask her if she can do the *grand écart* yet.' And when Campbell, in astonishment, wondered why on earth she should wish to learn such things, 'Oh, to extend her opportunities,' Mayne explained, 'and to acquire fresh sensations. She's an adventuress. Yes, an adventuress, but an end-of-the-century one. She doesn't travel for profit, but for pleasure. She has no desire to swindle her neighbour, but to amuse herself. And she's clever; she's read a good deal; she knows how to apply her reading to practical life. Thus, she's learned from Herrick not to be coy;[2] and from Shakespeare that sweet-and-twenty is the time for kissing and being kissed.[3] She honours her masters in the observance. She was not in the least abashed when, one day, I suddenly came upon her teaching that damned idiot, young Anson, two new ways of kissing.'

Campbell's impressions of the girl were readjusting themselves completely, but for the moment he was unconscious of the change. He only knew that he was partly angry, partly incredulous, and inclined to believe that Mayne was chaffing him.

'But, Miss Dodge,' he objected, 'the little sister, she is older; old enough to look after her friend. Surely she could not allow a young girl placed in her charge to behave in such a way—'

'Oh, that little Dodge girl,' said Mayne contemptuously; 'Miss Thayer pays the whole shot, I understand, and Miss Dodge plays gooseberry, sheepdog, jackal, what you will. She finds her reward in the other's cast-off finery. The silk blouse she was wearing tonight, I've good reason for remembering, belonged to Miss Lulie. For, during a brief season, I must tell you, my young lady had the caprice to show attentions to your humble servant. I suppose my being a married man lent me a factitious fascination. But I didn't see it. That kind of girl doesn't appeal to me. So she employed Miss Dodge to do a little active canvassing. It was really too funny; I was coming in one day after a walk in the woods; my wife was trimming bonnets, or had neuralgia, or something. Anyhow, I was alone, and Miss Dodge contrived to waylay me in the middle of the courtyard. "Don't you find it vurry dull walking all by yourself?" she asked me; and then blinking up in her strange little short-sighted way—she's really the weirdest little creature —"Why don't you make love to Lulie?" she said; "you'd find her vurry charming." It took me a minute or two to recover presence of mind enough to ask her whether Miss Thayer had commissioned her to tell me so. She looked at me with that cryptic smile of hers; "She'd like you to do so, I'm sure," she finally remarked, and pirouetted away. Though it didn't come off, owing to my bashfulness, it was then that Miss Dodge appropriated the silk "waist"; and Providence, taking pity on Miss Thayer's forced inactivity, sent along March, a young fellow reading for the army, with whom she had great doings. She fooled him to the top of his bent; sat on his knee; gave him a lock of her hair, which, having no scissors handy, she burned off with a cigarette taken from his mouth; and got him to offer her marriage. Then she turned round and laughed in his face, and took up with a Dr Weber, a cousin of the Baron's, under the other man's very eyes. You never saw anything like the unblushing coolness with which she would permit March to catch her in Weber's arms.'

'Come,' Campbell protested again, 'aren't you drawing it rather strong?'

'On the contrary, I'm drawing it mild, as you'll discover presently for yourself; and then you'll thank me for forewarning you. For she makes love – desperate love, mind you – to every man she meets. And goodness knows how many she hasn't met in the course of her career, which began presumably at the age of ten, in some "Amur'can" hotel or watering place. Look at this.' Mayne fetched an alpenstock from a corner of the hall; it was decorated with a long succession of names, which, ribbon-like, were twisted round and round it, carved in the wood. 'Read them,' insisted Mayne, putting the stick in Campbell's hands. 'You'll see they're not the names of the peaks she has climbed, or the towns she has passed through; they're the names of the men she has fooled. And there's room for more; there's still a good deal of space, as you see. There's room for yours.'

Campbell glanced down the alpenstock – reading here a name, there an initial, or just a date – and jerked it impatiently from him on to a couch. He wished with all his heart that Mayne would stop, would talk of something else, would let him get away. The young girl had interested him so much; he had felt himself so drawn towards her; he had thought her so fresh, so innocent. But Mayne, on the contrary, was warming to his subject, was enchanted to have some one to listen to his stories, to discuss his theories, to share his cynical amusement.

'I don't think, mind you,' he said, 'that she is a bit interested herself in the men she flirts with. I don't think she gets any of the usual sensations from it, you know. My theory is, she does it for mere devilry, for a laugh. Or, and this is another theory, she is actuated by some idea of retribution. Perhaps some woman she was fond of – her mother even – who knows? – was badly treated at the hands of a man. Perhaps this girl has constituted herself the Nemesis[4] for her sex, and goes about seeing how many masculine hearts she can break, by way of revenge. Or can it be that she is simply the newest development of the New Woman – she who in England preaches and bores you, and in America practises and pleases? Yes, I believe she's the American edition, and so new that she hasn't yet found her way into fiction. She's the pioneer of the army coming out of the West, that's going to destroy the existing scheme of things, and rebuild it nearer to the heart's desire.'

'Oh, damn it all, Mayne,' cried Campbell, rising abruptly, 'why not say at once that she's a wanton, and have done with it? Who wants to hear your rotten theories?' And he lighted his candle without another word, and went off to bed.

3

It was four o'clock, and the Baron's boarders were drinking their afternoon coffee, drawn up in a semicircle round the hall fire. All but Campbell, who had carried his cup away to a side table, and, with a book open beside him, appeared to be reading assiduously. In reality he could not follow a line of what he read; he could not keep his thoughts from Miss Thayer. What Mayne had told him was germinating in his mind. Knowing his friend as he did, he could not on reflection doubt his word. In spite of much superficial cynicism, Mayne was incapable of speaking lightly of any young girl without good cause. It now seemed to Campbell that, instead of exaggerating the case, Mayne had probably understated it. He asked himself with horror, what had this girl not already known, seen, permitted? When now and again his eyes travelled over, perforce, to where she sat, her red head leaning against Miss Dodge's knee, and seeming to attract to, and concentrate upon itself all the glow of the fire, his forehead set itself in frowns, and he returned to his book with an increased sense of irritation.

'I'm just sizzling up, Nannie,' Miss Thayer presently complained, in her childlike, drawling little way; 'this fire is too hot for anything.' She rose and shook straight her loose tea-gown, a marvellous plush and lace garment created in Paris, which would have accused a duchess of wilful extravagance. She stood smiling round a moment, pulling on and off with her right hand a big diamond ring which decorated the left. At the sound of her voice Campbell had looked up, and his cold, unfriendly eyes encountered hers. He glanced rapidly past her, then back to his book. But she, undeterred, with a charming sinuous movement and a frou-frou of trailing silks, crossed over towards him. She slipped into an empty chair next his.

'I'm going to do you the honour of sitting beside you, Mr Campbell,' she said sweetly.

'It's an honour I've done nothing whatever to merit,' he answered, without looking at her, and turned a page.

'The right retort,' she approved; 'but you might have said it a little more cordially.'

'I don't feel cordial.'

'But why not? What has happened? Yesterday you were so nice.'

'Ah, a good deal of water has run under the bridge since yesterday.'

'But still the river remains as full,' she told him, smiling, 'and still the sky is as blue. The thermometer has even risen six degrees.'

'What did you go into Hanover for yesterday?' Campbell suddenly asked her.

She flashed him a comprehending glance from half-shut eyes. 'I think men gossip a great deal more than women,' she observed, 'and they don't understand things either. They try to make all life suit their own preconceived theories. And why, after all, should I not wish to learn dancing thoroughly? There's no harm in that.'

'Only, why call it singing?' Campbell enquired.

Miss Thayer smiled. 'Truth is so uninteresting!' she said, and paused. 'Except in books. One likes it there. And I wanted to tell you,

I think your books perfectly lovely. I know them, most all. I've read them away home. They're very much thought of in America. Only last night I was saying to Nannie how glad I am to have met you, for I think we're going to be great friends, aren't we, Mr Campbell? At least, I hope so, for you can do me so much good, if you will. Your books always make me feel real good; but you yourself can help me much more.'

She looked up at him with one of her warm, narrow, red-brown glances, which yesterday would have thrilled his blood, and today merely stirred it to anger.

'You overestimate my abilities,' he said coldly; 'and, on the whole, I fear you will find writers a very disappointing race. You see, they put their best into their books. So not to disillusion you too rapidly' – he rose – 'will you excuse me? I have some work to do.' And he left her sitting there alone.

But he did no work when he got to his room. Whether Lulie Thayer was actually present or not, it seemed that her influence was equally disturbing to him. His mind was full of her: of her singular eyes, her quaint intonation, her sweet, seductive praise. Twenty-four hours ago such praise would have been delightful to him: what young author is proof against appreciation of his books? Now, Campbell simply told himself that she laid the butter on too thick; that it was in some analogous manner she had flattered up March, Anson, and all the rest of the men that Mayne had spoken of. He supposed it was the first step in the process by which he was to be fooled, twisted round her finger, added to the list of victims who strewed her conquering path. He had a special fear of being fooled. For beneath a somewhat supercilious exterior, the dominant note of his character was timidity, distrust of his own merits; and he knew he was single-minded – one-idea'd almost – if he were to let himself go, to get to care very much for a woman, for such a girl as this girl, for instance, he would lose himself completely, be at her mercy absolutely. Fortunately, Mayne had let him know her character. He could feel nothing but dislike for her – disgust, even; and yet he was conscious how pleasant it would be to believe in her innocence, in her candour. For she was so adorably pretty; her flower-like beauty grew upon him; her head, drooping a little on one side when she looked up, was so like a flower bent by its own weight. The texture of her cheeks, her lips, was delicious as the petals of a flower. He found he could recall with perfect accuracy every detail of her appearance: the manner in which the red hair grew round her temples; the way in which it was loosely and gracefully fastened up behind with just a single tortoiseshell pin. He recollected the suspicion of a dimple that shadowed itself in her cheek when she spoke, and deepened into a delicious reality every time she smiled. He remembered her throat; her hands, of a beautiful whiteness, with pink palms and pointed fingers. It was impossible to write. He speculated long on the ring she wore on her engaged finger. He mentioned this ring to Mayne the next time he saw him.

'Engaged? very much so, I should say. Has got a *fiancé* in every capital of Europe probably. But the ring-man is the *fiancé en titre*. He writes to her by every mail, and is tremendously in love with her. She shows me his letters. When she's had her fling, I suppose she'll go back and marry him. That's what these little American girls do, I'm told; sow their wild oats here with us, and settle down into *bonnes ménagères* over yonder. Meanwhile, are you having any fun with her? Aha, she presses your hand? The "gesegnete Mahlzeit" business after dinner is an excellent institution, isn't it? She'll tell you how much she loves you soon; that's the next move in the game.'

But so far she had done neither of these things, for Campbell gave her no opportunities. He was guarded in the extreme, ungenial; avoiding her even at the cost of civility. Sometimes he was downright rude. That especially occurred when he felt himself inclined to yield to her advances. For she made him all sorts of silent advances, speaking with her eyes, her sad little mouth, her beseeching attitude. And then one evening she went further still. It occurred after dinner in the little green drawing room. The rest of the company were gathered together in the big drawing room beyond. The small room has deep embrasures to the windows. Each embrasure holds two old faded green velvet sofas in black oaken frames, and an oaken oblong table stands between them. Campbell had flung himself down on one of these sofas in the corner nearest the window. Miss Thayer, passing through the room, saw him, and sat down opposite. She leaned her elbows on the table, the laces of her sleeves falling away from her round white arms, and clasped her hands.

'Mr Campbell, tell me, what have I done? How have I vexed you? You have hardly spoken two words to me all day. You always try to avoid me.' And when he began to utter evasive banalities, she stopped him with an imploring 'Ah, don't! I love you. You know I love you. I love you so much I can't bear you to put me off with mere phrases.'

Campbell admired the well-simulated passion in her voice, remembered Mayne's prediction and laughed aloud.

'Oh, you may laugh,' she said, 'but I'm serious. I love you, I love you with my whole soul.' She slipped round the end of the table, and came close beside him. His first impulse was to rise; then he resigned himself to stay. But it was not so much resignation that was required, as self-mastery, cool-headedness. Her close proximity, her fragrance, those wonderful eyes raised so beseechingly to his, made his heart beat.

'Why are you so cold?' she said. 'I love you so, can't you love me a little too?'

'My dear young lady,' said Campbell, gently repelling her, 'what do you take me for? A foolish boy like your friends Anson and March? What you are saying is monstrous, preposterous. Ten days ago you'd never even seen me.'

'What has length of time to do with it?' she said. 'I loved you at first sight.'

'I wonder,' he observed judicially, and again gently removed her hand from his, 'to how many men you have not already said the same thing?'

'I've never meant it before,' she said quite earnestly, and nestled closer to him, and kissed the breast of his coat, and held her mouth up towards his. But he kept his chin resolutely high, and looked over her head.

'How many men have you not already kissed, even since you've been here?'

'But there've not been many here to kiss!' she exclaimed naïvely.

'Well, there was March; you kissed him?'

'No, I'm quite sure I didn't.'

'And young Anson; what about him? Ah, you don't answer! And then the other fellow – what's his name – Prendergast – you've kissed him?'

'But, after all, what is there in a kiss?' she cried ingenuously. 'It means nothing, absolutely nothing. Why, one has to kiss all sorts of people one doesn't care about.'

Campbell remembered how Mayne had said she had probably known strange kisses since the age of ten; and a wave of anger with her, of righteous indignation, rose within him.

'To me,' said he, 'to all right-thinking people, a young girl's kisses are something pure, something sacred, not to be offered indiscriminately to every fellow she meets. Ah, you don't know what you have lost! You have seen a fruit that has been handled, that has lost its bloom? You have seen primroses, spring flowers gathered and thrown away in the dust? And who enjoys the one, or picks up the others? And this is what you remind me of – only you have deliberately, of your own perverse will, tarnished your beauty, and thrown away all the modesty, the reticence, the delicacy, which make a young girl so infinitely dear. You revolt me, you disgust me. I want nothing from you but to be let alone. Kindly take your hands away, and let me go.'

He shook her roughly off and got up, then felt a moment's curiosity to see how she would take the repulse.

Miss Thayer never blushed: had never, he imagined, in her life done so. No faintest trace of colour now stained the warm pallor of her rose-leaf skin; but her eyes filled up with tears, two drops gathered on the under lashes, grew large, trembled an instant and then rolled unchecked down her cheeks. Those tears somehow put him in the wrong, and he felt he had behaved brutally to her, for the rest of the night.

He began to seek excuses for her: after all, she meant no harm: it was her upbringing, her *genre*: it was a *genre* he loathed; but perhaps he need not have spoken so harshly. He thought he would find a more friendly word for her next morning; and he loitered about the Mahlsaal, where the boarders come in to breakfast as in an hotel just when it suits them, till past eleven; but she did not come. Then, when he was almost tired of waiting, Miss Dodge put in an appearance, in a flannel wrapper, and her front hair twisted up in steel pins.

Campbell judged Miss Dodge with even more severity than he did Miss Thayer; there was nothing in this weird little creature's appearance to temper justice with mercy. It was with difficulty that he brought himself to enquire after her friend.

'Lulie is sick this morning,' she told him. 'I've come down to order her some broth. She couldn't sleep any last night, because of your unkindness to her. She's vurry, vurry unhappy about it.'

'Yes, I'm sorry for what I said. I had no right to speak so strongly, I suppose. But I spoke strongly because I feel strongly. However, there's no reason why my bad manners should make her unhappy.'

'Oh, yes, there's vurry good reason,' said Miss Dodge. 'She's vurry much in love with you.'

Campbell looked at the speaker long and earnestly to try and read her mind; but the prominent blinking eyes, the cryptic physiognomy, told him nothing.

'Look here,' he said brusquely, 'what's your object in trying to fool me like this? I know all about your friend. Mayne has told me. She has cried "Wolf" too often before to expect to be believed now.'

'But, after all,' argued Miss Dodge, blinking more than ever behind her glasses, 'the wolf did really come at last, you know; didn't he? Lulie is really in love this time. We've all made mistakes in our lives, haven't we? But that's no reason for not being right at last. And Lulie has cried herself sick.'

Campbell was a little shaken. He went and repeated the conversation to Mayne, who laughed derisively.

'Capital, capital!' he cried; 'excellently contrived. It quite supports my latest theory about our young friend. She's an actress, a born comédienne. She acts always, and to every one: to you, to me, to the Ritterhausens, to the Dodge girl – even to herself when she is quite alone. And she has a great respect for her art; she'll carry out her role, *coûte que coûte*, to the bitter end. She chooses to pose as in love with you; you don't respond; the part now requires that she should sicken and pine. Consequently, she takes to her bed, and sends her confidante to tell you so. Oh, it's colossal, it's *famos!*'

4

'If you can't really love me,' said Lulie Thayer – 'and I know I've been a bad girl and don't deserve that you should – at least, will you allow me to go on loving you?'

She walked by Campbell's side, through the solitary, uncared-for park of Schloss Altenau. It was three weeks later in the year, and the spring feeling in the air stirred the blood. All round were signs and tokens of spring; in the busy gaiety of bird and insect life; in the purple flower-tufts which thickened the boughs of the ash trees; in the young green things pushing up pointed heads from amidst last season's dead leaves and grasses. The snow-wreaths, that had for so long decorated the distant hills, were shrinking perceptibly away beneath the strong March sunshine.

There was every invitation to spend one's time out of doors, and Campbell passed long mornings in the park, or wandering through the woods and the surrounding villages. Miss Thayer often accompanied him. He never invited her to do so, but when she offered him her company, he could not, or at least did not, refuse it.

'May I love you? Say,' she entreated.

'"Wenn ich Dich liebe, was geht's Dich an?"[5] he quoted lightly. 'Oh, no, it's nothing to me, of course. Only don't expect me to believe you – that's all.'

This disbelief of his was the recurring decimal of their conversation. No matter on what subject they began, they always ended thus. And the more sceptical he showed himself, the more eager she became. She exhausted herself in endeavours to convince him.

They had reached the corner in the park where the road to the Castle turns off at right angles from the road to Dürrendorf. The ground rises gently on the park-side to within three feet of the top of the boundary wall, although on the other side there is a drop of at least twenty feet. The broad wall-top makes a convenient seat. Campbell and the girl sat down on it. At his last words she wrung her hands together in her lap.

'But how can you disbelieve me?' she cried, 'when I tell you I love you, I adore you? when I swear it to you? And can't you see for yourself? Why, every one at the Castle sees it.'

'Yes, you afford the Castle a good deal of unnecessary amusement; and that shows you don't understand what love really is. Real love is full of delicacy, of reticences, and would feel itself profaned if it became the jest of the servants' hall.'

'It's not so much my love for you, as your rejection of it, which has made me talked about.'

'Isn't it rather on account of the favours you've lavished on all my predecessors?'

She sprang to her feet, and walked up and down in agitation.

'But, after all, surely, mistakes of that sort are not to be counted against us? I did really think I was in love with Mr March. Willie Anson doesn't count. He's an American too, and he understands things. Besides, he is only a boy. And how could I know I should love you before I had met you? And how can I help loving you now I have? You're so different from other men. You're good, you're honourable, you treat women with respect. Oh, I do love you so, I do love you! Ask Nannie if I don't.'

The way in which Campbell shrugged his shoulders clearly expressed the amount of reliance he would place on any testimony from Miss Dodge. He could not forget her 'Why don't you make love to Lulie?' addressed to a married man. Such a want of principle argued an equal want of truth.

Lulie seemed on the brink of weeping.

'I wish I were dead,' she struggled to say; 'life's impossible if you won't believe me. I don't ask you any longer to love me. I know I've been a bad girl, and I don't deserve that you should; but if you won't believe that I love you, I don't want to live any longer.'

Campbell confessed to himself that she acted admirably, but that the damnable iteration of the one idea became monotonous. He sought a change of subject. 'Look there,' he said, 'close by the wall, what's that jolly little blue flower? It's the first I've seen this year.'

He showed her where, at the base of the wall, a solitary blossom rose above a creeping stem and glossy dark green leaves.

Lulie, all smiles again, picked it with childlike pleasure. 'Oh, if that's the first you've seen,' she cried, 'you can take a wish. Only you mustn't speak until someone asks you a question.'

She began to fasten it in his coat. 'It's just as blue as your eyes,' she said. 'You have such blue and boyish eyes, you know. Stop, stop, that's not a question,' and seeing that he was about to speak, she laid her finger across his mouth. 'You'll spoil the charm.'

She stepped back, folded her arms and seemed to dedicate herself to eternal silence; then relenting suddenly:

'Do you believe me?' she entreated.

'What's become of your ring?' Campbell answered beside the mark. He had noticed its absence from her finger while she had been fixing in the flower.

'Oh, my engagement's broken.'

Campbell asked how the fiancé would like that.

'Oh, he won't mind. He knows I only got engaged because he worried so. And it was always understood between us that I was to be free if I ever met any one I liked better.'

Campbell asked her what sort of fellow this accommodating fiancé was.

'Oh, he's all right. And he's very good too. But he's not a bit clever, and don't let us talk about him. He makes me tired.'

'But you're wrong,' Campbell told her, 'to throw away a good, a sincere affection. If you really want to reform and turn over a new leaf, as you are always telling me you do, I should advise you to go home and marry him.'

'What, when I'm in love with you?' she cried reproachfully. 'Would that be right?'

'It's going to rain,' said Campbell. 'Didn't you feel a drop just then? And it's getting near lunchtime. Shall we go in?'

Their shortest way led through the little cemetery in which the departed Ritterhausens lay at peace, in the shadow of their sometime home.

'When I die the Baron has promised I shall be buried here,' said Lulie pensively; 'just here, next to his first wife. Don't you think it would be lovely to be buried in a beautiful, peaceful, baronial graveyard instead of in some horrid, crowded city cemetery?'

Mayne met them as they entered the hall. He noticed the flower in his friend's coat. 'Ah, my dear chap, been treading the – periwinkle path of dalliance, I see? How many desirable young men have I not witnessed, led down the same broad way by the same seductive lady! Always the same thing; nothing changes but the flower according to the season.'

When Campbell reached his room he took the poor periwinkle out of his coat, and threw it away into the stove.

And yet, had it not been for Mayne, Miss Thayer might have triumphed after all; might have convinced Campbell of her passion, or have added another victim to her long list. But Mayne had set himself as determinedly to spoil her game, as she was bent on winning it. He had always the cynical word, the apt reminiscence ready, whenever he saw signs on Campbell's part of surrender. He was very fond of Campbell. He did not wish him to fall a prey to the wiles of this little American siren. He had watched her conduct in the past with a dozen different men; he genuinely believed she was only acting in the present.

Campbell, for his part, began to experience an ever-increasing exasperation in the girl's presence. Yet he did not avoid it; he could not well avoid it, she followed him about so persistently: but his speech would overflow with bitterness towards her. He would say the cruellest things; then remembering them when alone, be ashamed of his brutalities. But nothing he said ever altered her sweetness of temper or weakened the tenacity of her purpose. His rebuffs made her beautiful eyes run over with tears, but the harshest of them never elicited the least sign of resentment. There would have been something touching as well as comic in this dog-like humility, which accepted everything as welcome at his hands, had he not been imbued with Mayne's conviction that it was all an admirable piece of acting. Or when for a moment he forgot the histrionic theory, then invariably there would come a chance word in her conversation which would fill him with cold rage. They would be talking of books, travels, sport, what not, and she would drop a reference to this man or to that. So-and-so had taken her to Bullier's,[6] she had learned skating with this other; Duroy, the *prix de Rome* man, had painted her as Hebe,[7] Franz Weber had tried to teach her German by means of Heine's poems.[8] And he got glimpses of long vistas of amourettes played in every state in America, in every country of Europe, since the very beginning, when, as a mere child, elderly men, friends of her father's, had held her on their knee and fed her on sweetmeats and kisses. It was sickening to think of; it was pitiable. So much youth and beauty tarnished; the possibility for so much good thrown away. For if one could only blot out her record, forget it, accept her for what she chose to appear, a more endearing companion no man could desire.

5

It was a wet afternoon; the rain had set in at midday, with a grey determination, which gave no hopes of clearing. Nevertheless, Mayne had accompanied his wife and the Baroness into Hamelin. 'To take up a servant's character, and expostulate with a recalcitrant dress-maker,' he explained to Campbell, and wondered what women would do to fill up their days were it not for the perennial crimes of dress-makers and domestic servants. He himself was going to look in at the English Club; wouldn't Campbell come too? There was a fourth seat in the carriage. But Campbell was in no social mood; he felt his temper going all to pieces; a quarter of an hour of Mrs Mayne's society would have brought on an explosion. He thought he must be alone; and yet when he had read for half an hour in his room he wondered vaguely what Lulie was doing; he had not seen her since luncheon. She always gave him her society when he could very well dispense with it, but on a wet day like this, when a little conversation would be tolerable, of course she stayed away. Then there came down the long Rittersaal the tapping of high heels, and a well-known knock at his door.

He went over and opened it. Miss Thayer, in the plush and lace tea-gown, fronted him serenely.

'Am I disturbing you?' she asked; and his mood was so capricious that, now she was standing there on his threshold, he thought he was annoyed at it. 'It's so dull,' she said persuasively: 'Nannie's got a sick headache, and I daren't go downstairs, or the Baron will annex me to play Halma.⁹ He always wants to play Halma on wet days.'

'And what do you want to do?' said Campbell, leaning against the doorpost, and letting his eyes rest on the strange piquant face in its setting of red hair.

'To be with you, of course.'

'Well,' said he, coming out and closing the door, 'I'm at your service. What next?'

They strolled together through the room and listened to the falling rain. The Rittersaal occupies all the space on the first floor that the hall and four drawing rooms do below. Wooden pillars support the ceiling, dividing the apartment lengthwise into a nave and two aisles. Down the middle are long tables, used for ceremonial banquets. Six windows look into the courtyard, and six out over the open country. The centre pane of each window is emblazoned with a Ritterhausen shield. Between the windows hang family portraits, and the sills are broad and low and cushioned in faded velvet.

'How it rains!' said Lulie, stopping before one of the south windows; 'why, you can't see anything for the rain, and there's no sound at all but the rain either. I like it. It makes me feel as though we had the whole world to ourselves.'

Then, 'Say, what would you like to do?' she asked him. 'Shall I fetch over my pistols, and we'll practise with them? You've no notion how well I can shoot. We couldn't hurt anything here, could we?'

Campbell thought they might practise there without inconvenience, and Lulie, bundling up the duchess tea-gown over one arm, danced off in very unduchess-like fashion to fetch the case. It was a charming little box of cedar-wood and mother-o'-pearl, lined with violet velvet; and two tiny revolvers lay inside, hardly more than six inches long, with silver engraved handles.

'I won them in a bet,' she observed complacently, 'with the Hon. Billie Thornton. He's an Englishman, you know, the son of Lord Thornton. I knew him in Washington two years ago last fall. He bet I couldn't hit a three-cent piece at twenty yards and I did. Aren't they perfectly sweet? Now, can't you contrive a target?'

Campbell went back to his room, drew out a rough diagram, and pasted it down on to a piece of cardboard. Then this was fixed up by means of a penknife driven into the wood of one of the pillars, and Campbell, with his walking stick laid down six successive times, measured off the distance required, and set a chalk mark across the floor. Lulie took the first shot. She held the little weapon up at arm's length above her head, the first finger stretched out along the barrel; then dropping her hand sharply so that the finger pointed straight at the butt, she pulled the trigger with the third. There was the sharp report, the tiny smoke film – and when Campbell went up to examine results, he found she had only missed the very centre by a quarter of an inch.

Lulie was exultant. 'I don't seem to have got out of practice any,' she remarked. 'I'm so glad, for I used to be a very good shot. It was Hiram P. Ladd who taught me. He's the crack shot of Montana. What! you don't know Hiram P.? Why, I should have supposed everyone must have heard of him. He had the next ranch to my Uncle Samuel's, where I used to go summers, and he made me do an hour's pistol practice every morning after bathing. It was he who taught me swimming too – in the river.'

'Damnation,' said Campbell under his breath, then shot in his turn, and shot wide. Lulie made another bull's-eye, and after that a white. She urged Campbell to continue, which he sullenly did, and again missed.

'You see I don't come up to your Hiram P. Ladd,' he remarked savagely, and put the pistol down, and walked over to the window. He stood with one foot on the cushioned seat, staring out at the rain, and pulling moodily at his moustache.

Lulie followed him, nestled up to him, lifted the hand that hung passive by his side, put it round her waist and held it there. Campbell, lost in thought, let it remain so for a second; then remembered how she had doubtless done this very same thing with other men in this very room. All her apparently spontaneous movements, he told himself, were but the oft-used pieces in the game she played so skilfully.

'Let go,' he said, and flung himself down on the window seat, looking up at her with darkening eyes.

She sitting meekly in the other corner folded her offending hands in her lap.

'Do you know, your eyes are not a bit nice when you're cross?' she said; 'they seem to become quite black.'

He maintained a discouraging silence.

She looked over at him meditatively.

'I never cared a bit for Hiram P., if that's what you mean,' she remarked presently.

'Do you suppose I care a button if you did?'

'Then why did you leave off shooting, and why won't you talk to me?'

He vouchsafed no reply.

Lulie spent some moments immersed in thought. Then she sighed deeply, and recommenced on a note of pensive regret.

'Ah, if I'd only met you sooner in life, I should be a very different girl.'

The freshness which her quaint, drawling enunciation lent to this time-dishonoured formula, made Campbell smile, till, remembering all its implications, his forehead set in frowns again.

Lulie continued her discourse. 'You see,' said she, 'I never had any one to teach me what was right. My mother died when I was quite a child, and my father has always let me do exactly as I pleased, so long as I didn't bother him. Then I've never had a home, but have always lived around in hotels and places: all winter in New York or Washington, and summers out at Longbranch or Saratoga. It's true we own a house in Detroit, on Lafayette Avenue, that we reckon as home, but we don't ever go there. It's a bad sort of life for a girl, isn't it?' she pleaded.

'Horrible,' he said mechanically. His mind was at work. The loose threads of his angers, his irritations, his desires, were knitting themselves together, weaving themselves into something over-mastering and definite.

The young girl meanwhile was moving up towards him along the seat, for the effect which his sharpest rebuke produced on her never lasted more than four minutes. She now again possessed herself of his hand, and holding it between her own, began to caress it in childlike fashion, pulling the fingers apart and closing them again, spreading it palm downwards on her lap, and laying her own little hand over it, to exemplify the differences between them. He let her be; he seemed unconscious of her proceedings.

'And then,' she continued, 'I've always known a lot of young fellows who've liked to take me round; and no one ever objected to my going with them, and so I went. And I enjoyed it, and there wasn't any harm in it, just kissing and making believe, and nonsense. But I never really cared for one of them – I can see that now, when I compare them with you; when I compare what I felt for them with what I feel for you. Oh, I do love you so much,' she murmured; 'don't you believe me?' She lifted his hand to her lips and covered it with kisses.

He pulled it roughly from her. 'I wish you'd give over such fool's play,' he told her, got up, walked to the table, came back again, stood looking at her with sombre eyes and dilating pupils.

'But I do love you,' she repeated, rising and advancing towards him.

'For God's sake, drop that damned rot,' he cried out with sudden fury. 'It wearies me, do you hear? it sickens me. Love, love – my God, what do you know about it? Why, if you really loved me, really loved any man – if you had any conception of what the passion of love is, how beautiful, how fine, how sacred – the mere idea that you could not come to your lover fresh, pure, untouched, as a young girl should – that you had been handled, fondled, and God knows what besides, by this man and the other – would fill you with such horror for yourself, with such supreme disgust – you would feel yourself so unworthy, so polluted . . . that . . . that . . . by God! you would take up that pistol there, and blow your brains out!'

Lulie seemed to find the idea quite entertaining. She picked the pistol up from where it lay in the window, examined it critically, with her pretty head drooping on one side, and then sent one of her long red-brown caressing glances up towards him.

'And suppose I were to,' she asked lightly, 'would you believe me then?'

'Oh, . . . well . . . then, perhaps! If you showed sufficient decency to kill yourself, perhaps I might,' said he, with ironical laughter. His ebullition had relieved him; his nerves were calmed again. 'But nothing short of that would ever make me.'

ELLA D'ARCY

With her little tragic air, which seemed to him so like a smile disguised, she raised the weapon to the bosom of her gown. There came a sudden, sharp crack, a tiny smoke film. She stood an instant swaying slightly, smiling certainly, distinctly outlined against the background of rain-washed window, of grey falling rain, the top of her head cutting in two the Ritterhausen escutcheon. Then all at once there was nothing at all between him and the window – he saw the coat of arms entire – but a motionless, inert heap of plush and lace, and fallen wine-red hair, lay at his feet upon the floor.

'Child, child, what have you done?' he cried with anguish, and kneeling beside her, lifted her up, and looked into her face.

When from a distance of time and place Campbell was at last able to look back with some degree of calmness on the catastrophe, the element in it which stung him most keenly was this: he could never convince himself that Lulie had really loved him after all. And the only two persons who had known them both, and the circumstances of the case, sufficiently well to have resolved his doubts one way or the other, held diametrically opposite views.

'Well, listen, then, and I'll tell you how it was,' Miss Nannie Dodge had said to him impressively, the day before he left Schloss Altenau for ever. 'Lulie was tremendously, terribly in love with you. And when she found that you wouldn't care about her, she didn't want to live any more. As to the way in which it happened, you don't need to reproach yourself for that. She'd have done it, anyhow. If not then, why later. But it's all the rest of your conduct to her that was so mean. Your cold, cruel, complacent British unresponsiveness. I guess you'll never find another woman to love you as Lulie did. She was just the darlingest, the sweetest, the most loving girl in the world.'

Mayne, on the other hand, summed it up in this way. 'Of course, old chap, it's horrible to think of: horrible, horrible, horrible! I can't tell you how badly I feel about it. For she was a gorgeously beautiful creature. That red hair of hers! Good Lord! You won't come across such hair as that again in a lifetime. But, believe me, she was only fooling with you. Once she had you in her hunting noose, once her buccaneering instincts satisfied, and she'd have chucked you as she did all the rest. As to her death, I've got three theories – no, two – for the first being that she compassed it in a moment of genuine emotion, we may dismiss, I think, as quite untenable. The second is, that it arose from pure misadventure. You had both been shooting, hadn't you? Well, she took up the pistol and pulled the trigger from mere mischief, to frighten you, and quite forgetting one barrel was still loaded. And the third is, it was just her histrionic sense of the fitness of things. The role she had played so long and so well now demanded a sensational finale in the centre of the stage. And it's the third theory I give the preference to. She was the most consummate little actress I ever met.'

Tommy, the Unsentimental

'Your father says he has no business tact at all, and of course that's dreadfully unfortunate.'

'Business,' replied Tommy, 'he's a baby in business; he's good for nothing on earth but to keep his hair parted straight and wear that white carnation in his buttonhole. He has 'em sent down from Hastings twice a week as regularly as the mail comes, but the drafts he cashes lie in his safe until they are lost, or somebody finds them. I go up occasionally and send a package away for him myself. He'll answer your notes promptly enough, but his business letters – I believe he destroys them unopened to shake the responsibility of answering them.'

'I am at a loss to see how you can have such patience with him, Tommy, in so many ways he is thoroughly reprehensible.'

'Well, a man's likeableness don't depend at all on his virtues or acquirements, nor a woman's either, unfortunately. You like them or you don't like them, and that's all there is to it. For the why of it you must appeal to a higher oracle than I. Jay is a likeable fellow, and that's his only and sole acquirement, but after all it's a rather happy one.'

'Yes, he certainly is that,' replied Miss Jessica, as she deliberately turned off the gas jet and proceeded to arrange her toilet articles. Tommy watched her closely and then turned away with a baffled expression.

Needless to say, Tommy was not a boy, although her keen grey eyes and wide forehead were scarcely girlish, and she had the lank figure of an active half grown lad. Her real name was Theodosia, but during Thomas Shirley's frequent absences from the bank she had attended to his business and correspondence signing herself 'T. Shirley', until everyone in Southdown called her 'Tommy'. That blunt sort of familiarity is not unfrequent in the West, and is meant well enough. People rather expect some business ability in a girl there, and they respect it immensely. That Tommy undoubtedly had, and if she had not, things would have gone at sixes and sevens in the Southdown National. For Thomas Shirley had big land interests in Wyoming that called him constantly away from home, and his cashier, little Jay Ellington Harper, was, in the local phrase, a weak brother in the bank. He was the son of a friend of old Shirley's, whose papa had sent him West, because he had made a sad mess of his college career, and had spent too much money and gone at too giddy a pace down East. Conditions changed the young gentleman's life, for it was simply impossible to live either prodigally or rapidly in Southdown, but they could not materially affect his mental habits or inclinations. He was made cashier of Shirley's bank because his father bought in half the stock, but Tommy did his work for him.

The relation between these two young people was peculiar; Harper was, in his way, very grateful to her for keeping him out of disgrace with her father and showed it by a hundred little attentions which were new to her and much more agreeable than the work she did for him was irksome. Tommy knew that she was immensely fond of him, and she knew at the same time that she was thoroughly foolish for being so. As she expressed it, she was not of his sort, and never would be. She did not often take pains to think, but when she did she saw matters pretty clearly, and she was of a peculiarly unfeminine mind that could not escape meeting and acknowledging a logical conclusion. But she went on liking Jay Ellington Harper, just the same. Now Harper was the only foolish man of Tommy's acquaintance. She knew plenty of active young businessmen and sturdy ranchers, such as one meets about live Western towns, and took no particular interest in them, probably just because they were practical and sensible and thoroughly of her own kind. She knew almost no women, because in those days there were few women in Southdown who were in any sense interesting, or interested in anything but babies and salads. Her best friends were her father's old business friends, elderly men who had seen a good deal of the world, and who were very proud and fond of Tommy. They recognized a sort of squareness and honesty of spirit in the girl that Jay Ellington Harper never discovered, or, if he did, knew too little of its rareness to value highly. Those old speculators and men of business had always felt a sort of responsibility for Tom Shirley's little girl, and had rather taken her mother's place, and been her advisers on many points upon which men seldom feel at liberty to address a girl. She was just one of them; she played whist and billiards with them, and made their cocktails for them, not scorning to take one herself occasionally. Indeed, Tommy's cocktails were things of fame in Southdown, and the professional compounders of drinks always bowed respectfully to her as though acknowledging a powerful rival.

Now all these things displeased and puzzled Jay Ellington Harper, and Tommy knew it full well, but clung to her old manner of living with a stubborn pertinacity, feeling somehow that to change would be both foolish and disloyal to the Old Boys. And as things went on, the seven Old Boys made greater demands upon her time than ever, for they were shrewd men, most of them, and had not lived fifty years in this world without learning a few things and unlearning many more. And while Tommy lived on in the blissful delusion that her role of indifference was perfectly played and without a flaw, they suspected how things were going and were perplexed as to the outcome. Still, their confidence was by no means shaken, and as Joe Elsworth said to Joe Sawyer one evening at billiards, 'I think we can pretty nearly depend on Tommy's good sense.'

They were too wise to say anything to Tommy, but they said just a word or two to Thomas Shirley, Sr, and combined to make things very unpleasant for Mr Jay Ellington Harper.

At length their relations with Harper became so strained that the young man felt it would be better for him to leave town, so his father started him in a little bank of his own up in Red Willow. Red Willow, however, was scarcely a safe distance, being only some twenty-five miles north, upon the Divide,[1] and Tommy occasionally found excuse to run upon her wheel to straighten out the young man's business for him. So when she suddenly decided to go East to school for a year, Thomas, Sr, drew a sigh of great relief. But the seven Old Boys shook their heads; they did not like to see her gravitating toward the East; it was a sign of weakening, they said, and showed an inclination to experiment with another kind of life, Jay Ellington Harper's kind.

But to school Tommy went, and from all reports conducted herself in a most seemly manner; made no more cocktails, played no more billiards. She took rather her own way with the curriculum, but she distinguished herself in athletics, which in Southdown counted for vastly more than erudition.

Her evident joy on getting back to Southdown was appreciated by everyone. She went about shaking hands with everybody, her shrewd face, that was so like a clever wholesome boy's, held high with happiness. As she said to old Joe Elsworth one morning, when they were driving behind his stud through a little thicket of cottonwood scattered along the sun-parched bluffs,

'It's all very fine down East there, and the hills are great, but one gets mighty homesick for this sky, the old intense blue of it, you know. Down there the skies are all pale and smoky. And this wind, this hateful, dear, old everlasting wind that comes down like the sweep of cavalry and is never tamed or broken, O Joe, I used to get hungry for this wind! I couldn't sleep in that lifeless stillness down there.'

'How about the people, Tom?'

'O, they are fine enough folk, but we're not their sort, Joe, and never can be.'

'You realize that, do you, fully?'

'Quite fully enough, thank you, Joe.' She laughed rather dismally, and Joe cut his horse with the whip.

The only unsatisfactory thing about Tommy's return was that she brought with her a girl she had grown fond of at school, a dainty, white, languid bit of a thing, who used violet perfumes and carried a sunshade. The Old Boys said it was a bad sign when a rebellious girl like Tommy took to being sweet and gentle to one of her own sex, the worst sign in the world.

The new girl was no sooner in town than a new complication came about. There was no doubt of the impression she made on Jay Ellington Harper. She indisputably had all those little evidences of good breeding that were about the only things which could touch the timid, harassed young man who was so much out of his element. It was a very plain case on his part, and the souls of the seven were troubled within them. Said Joe Elsworth to the other Joe,

'The heart of the cad is gone out to the little muff, as is right and proper and in accordance with the eternal fitness of things. But there's the other girl who has the blindness that may not be cured, and she gets all the rub of it. It's no use, I can't help her, and I am going to run down to Kansas City for awhile. I can't stay here and see the abominable suffering of it.' He didn't go, however.

There was just one other person who understood the hopelessness of the situation quite as well as Joe, and that was Tommy. That is, she understood Harper's attitude. As to Miss Jessica's she was not quite so certain, for Miss Jessica, though pale and languid and addicted to sunshades, was a maiden most discreet. Conversations on the subject usually ended without any further information as to Miss Jessica's feelings, and Tommy sometimes wondered if she were capable of having any at all.

At last the calamity which Tommy had long foretold descended upon Jay Ellington Harper. One morning she received a telegram from him begging her to intercede with her father; there was a run on his bank and he must have help before noon. It was then ten thirty, and the one sleepy little train that ran up to Red Willow daily had crawled out of the station an hour before. Thomas Shirley, Sr, was not at home.

'And it's a good thing for Jay Ellington he's not, he might be more stony hearted than I,' remarked Tommy, as she closed the ledger and turned to the terrified Miss Jessica. 'Of course we're his only chance, no one else would turn their hand over to help him. The train went an hour ago and he says it must be there by noon. It's the only bank in the town, so nothing can be done by telegraph. There is nothing left but to wheel for it. I may make it, and I may not. Jess, you scamper up to the house and get my wheel out, the tyre may need a little attention. I will be along in a minute.'

'O, Theodosia, can't I go with you? I must go!'

'You go! O, yes, of course, if you want to. You know what you are getting into, though, it's twenty-five miles uppish grade and hilly, and only an hour and a quarter to do it in.'

'O, Theodosia, I can do anything now!' cried Miss Jessica, as she put up her sunshade and fled precipitately. Tommy smiled as she began cramming banknotes into a canvas bag, 'Maybe you can, my dear, and maybe you can't.'

The road from Southdown to Red Willow is not by any means a favourite bicycle road; it is rough, hilly and climbs from the river bottoms up to the big Divide by a steady up grade, running white and hot through the scorched cornfields and grazing lands where the long-horned Texan cattle browse about in the old buffalo wallows. Miss Jessica soon found that with the pedalling that had to be done there was little time left for emotion of any sort, or little sensibility for anything but the throbbing, dazzling heat that had to be endured. Down there in the valley the distant bluffs were vibrating and dancing with the heat, the cattle, completely overcome by it, had hidden under the shelving banks of the 'draws', and the prairie dogs had fled to the bottom of their holes that are said to reach to water. The whirr of the seventeen-year locust was the only thing that spoke of animation, and that ground on as if only animated and enlivened by the sickening, destroying heat. The sun was like hot brass, and the wind that blew up from the south was hotter still. But Tommy knew that wind was their only chance. Miss Jessica began to feel that unless she could stop and get some water she was not much longer for this vale of tears. She suggested this possibility to Tommy, but Tommy only shook her head, 'Take too much time', and bent over her handle bars, never lifting her eyes from the road in front of her. It flashed upon Miss Jessica that Tommy was not only very unkind, but that she sat very badly on her wheel and looked aggressively masculine and professional when she bent her shoulders and pumped like that. But just then Miss Jessica found it harder than ever to breathe, and the bluffs across the river began doing serpentines and skirt dances, and more important and personal considerations occupied the young lady.

When they were fairly over the first half of the road, Tommy took out her watch. 'Have to hurry up, Jess, I can't wait for you.'

'O, Tommy, I can't,' panted Miss Jessica, dismounting and sitting down in a little heap by the roadside. 'You go on, Tommy, and tell him, – tell him I hope it won't fail, and I'd do anything to save him.'

By this time the discreet Miss Jessica was reduced to tears, and Tommy nodded as she disappeared over the hill laughing to herself. 'Poor Jess, anything but the one thing he needs. Well, your kind have the best of it generally, but in little affairs of this sort my kind come out rather strongly. We're rather better at them than at dancing. It's only fair, one side shouldn't have all.'

Just at twelve o'clock, when Jay Ellington Harper, his collar crushed and wet about his throat, his eyeglass dimmed with perspiration, his hair hanging damp over his forehead, and even the ends of his moustache dripping with moisture, was attempting to reason with a score of angry Bohemians,[2] Tommy came quietly through the door, grip in hand. She went straight behind the grating, and standing screened by the bookkeeper's desk, handed the bag to Harper and turned to the spokesman of the Bohemians,

'What's all this business mean, Anton? Do you all come to bank at once nowadays?'

'We want 'a money, want 'a our money, he no got it, no give it,' bawled the big beery Bohemian.

'O, don't chaff 'em any longer, give 'em their money and get rid of 'em, I want to see you,' said Tommy carelessly, as she went into the consulting room.

When Harper entered half an hour later, after the rush was over, all that was left of his usual immaculate appearance was his eyeglass and the white flower in his buttonhole.

'This has been terrible!' he gasped. 'Miss Theodosia, I can never thank you.'

'No,' interrupted Tommy. 'You never can, and I don't want any thanks. It was rather a tight place, though, wasn't it? You looked like a ghost when I came in. What started them?'

'How should I know? They just came down like the wolf on the fold. It sounded like the approach of a ghost dance.'

'And of course you had no reserve? O, I always told you this would come, it was inevitable with your charming methods. By the way, Jess sends her regrets and says she would do anything to save you. She started out with me, but she has fallen by the wayside. O, don't be alarmed, she is not hurt, just winded. I left her all bunched up by the road like a little white rabbit. I think the lack of romance in the escapade did her up about as much as anything; she is essentially romantic. If we had been on fiery steeds bespattered with foam I think she would have made it, but a wheel hurt her dignity. I'll tend bank; you'd better get your wheel and go and look her up and comfort her. And as soon as it is convenient, Jay, I wish you'd marry her and be done with it, I want to get this thing off my mind.'

Jay Ellington Harper dropped into a chair and turned a shade whiter.

'Theodosia, what do you mean? Don't you remember what I said to you last fall, the night before you went to school? Don't you remember what I wrote you – '

Tommy sat down on the table beside him and looked seriously and frankly into his eyes.

'Now, see here, Jay Ellington, we have been playing a nice little game, and now it's time to quit. One must grow up sometime. You are horribly wrought up over Jess, and why deny it? She's your kind: and clean daft about you, so there is only one thing to do. That's all.'

Jay Ellington wiped his brow, and felt unequal to the situation. Perhaps he really came nearer to being moved down to his stolid little depths than he ever had before. His voice shook a good deal and was very low as he answered her.

'You have been very good to me. I didn't believe any woman could be at once so kind and clever. You almost made a man of even me.'

'Well, I certainly didn't succeed. As to being good to you, that's rather a break, you know; I am amiable, but I am only flesh and blood after all. Since I have known you I have not been at all good, in any sense of the word, and I suspect I have been anything but clever. Now take mercy upon Jess – and me – and go. Go on, that ride is beginning to tell on me. Such things strain one's nerve. Thank Heaven he's gone at last and had sense enough not to say anything more. It was growing rather critical. As I told him I am not at all super-human.'

After Jay Ellington Harper had bowed himself out, when Tommy sat alone in the darkened office, watching the flapping blinds, with the bank books before her, she noticed a white flower on the floor. It was the one Jay Ellington Harper had worn in his coat and had dropped in his nervous agitation. She picked it up and stood holding it a moment, biting her lip. Then she dropped it into the grate and turned away, shrugging her thin shoulders.

'They are awful idiots, half of them, and never think of anything beyond their dinner. But O, how we do like 'em!'

ALICE MEYNELL

A Woman in Grey

The mothers of Professors were indulged in the practice of jumping at conclusions, and were praised for their impatience of the slow process of reason.

Professors have written of the mental habits of women as though they accumulated generation by generation upon women, and passed over their sons. Professors take it for granted, obviously by some process other than the slow process of reason, that women derive from their mothers and grandmothers, and men from their fathers and grandfathers. This, for instance, was written lately: 'This power [it matters not what] would be about equal in the two sexes but for the influence of heredity, which turns the scale in favour of the woman, as for long generations the surroundings and conditions of life of the female sex have developed in her a greater degree of the power in question than circumstances have required from men.' 'Long generations' of subjection are, strangely enough, held to excuse the timorousness and the shifts of women today. But the world, unknowing, tampers with the courage of its sons by such a slovenly indulgence. It tampers with their intelligence by fostering the ignorance of women.

And yet Shakespeare confessed the participation of man and woman in their common heritage. It is Cassius who speaks:

> 'Have you not love enough to bear with me
> When that rash humour which my mother gave me
> Makes me forgetful?'

And Brutus who replies:

> 'Yes, Cassius, and from henceforth
> When you are over-earnest with your Brutus
> He'll think your mother chides, and leave you so.'[1]

Dryden confessed it also in his praises of Anne Killigrew:

> 'If by traduction came thy mind,
>   Our wonder is the less to find
> A soul so charming from a stock so good.
> Thy father was transfused into thy blood.'[2]

The winning of Waterloo upon the Eton playgrounds[3] is very well; but there have been some other, and happily minor, fields that were not won – that were more or less lost. Where did this loss take place, if the gains were secured at football? This enquiry is not quite so cheerful as the other. But while the victories were once going forward in the playground, the defeats or disasters were once going forward in some other place, presumably. And this was surely the place that was not a playground, the place where the future wives of the football players were sitting still while their future husbands were playing football.

This is the train of thought that followed the grey figure of a woman on a bicycle in Oxford Street. She had an enormous and top-heavy omnibus at her back. All the things on the near side of the street – the things going her way – were going at different paces, in two streams, overtaking and being overtaken. The tributary streets shot omnibuses and carriages, cabs and carts – some to go her own way, some with an impetus that carried them curving into the other current, and other some making a straight line right across Oxford Street into the street opposite. Besides all the unequal movement, there were the stoppings. It was a delicate tangle to keep from knotting. The nerves of the mouths of horses bore the whole charge and answered it, as they do every day.

The woman in grey, quite alone, was immediately dependent on no nerves but her own, which almost made her machine sensitive. But this alertness was joined to such perfect composure as no flutter of a moment disturbed. There was the steadiness of sleep, and a vigilance more than that of an ordinary waking.

At the same time, the woman was doing what nothing in her youth could well have prepared her for. She must have passed a childhood unlike the ordinary girl's childhood, if her steadiness or her alertness had ever been educated, if she had been rebuked for cowardice, for the egoistic distrust of general rules or for claims of exceptional chances. Yet here she was, trusting not only herself but a multitude of other people; taking her equal risk; giving a watchful confidence to averages – that last, perhaps, her strangest and greatest success.

No exceptions were hers, no appeals, and no forewarnings. She evidently had not in her mind a single phrase, familiar to women, made to express no confidence except in accidents, and to proclaim a prudent foresight of the less probable event. No woman could ride a bicycle along Oxford Street with any such baggage as that about her.

The woman in grey had a watchful confidence not only in a multitude of men but in a multitude of things. And it is very hard for any untrained human being to practise confidence in things in motion – things full of force, and, what is worse, of forces. Moreover, there is a supreme difficulty for a mind accustomed to search timorously for some little place of insignificant rest on any accessible point of stable equilibrium; and that is the difficulty of holding itself nimbly secure in an equilibrium that is unstable. Who can deny that women are generally used to look about for the little stationary repose just described ? Whether in intellectual or in spiritual things, they do not often live without it.

She, nonetheless, fled upon unstable equilibrium, escaped upon it, depended upon it, trusted it, was 'ware of it, was on guard against it, as she sped amid her crowd: her own unstable equilibrium, her machine's, that of the judgement, the temper, the skill, the perception, the strength of men and horses.

She had learnt the difficult peace of suspense. She had learnt also the lowly and self-denying faith in common chances. She had learnt to be content with her share – no more – in common security, and to be pleased with her part in common hope. For all this, it may be repeated, she could have had but small preparation. Yet no anxiety was hers, no uneasy distrust and disbelief of that human thing – an average of life and death.

To this courage the woman in grey had attained with a spring, and she had seated herself suddenly upon a place of detachment between earth and air, freed from the principal detentions, weights and embarrassments of the usual life of fear. She had made herself, as it were, light, so as not to dwell either in security or danger, but to pass between them. She confessed difficulty and peril by her delicate evasions, and consented to rest in neither. She would not owe safety to the mere motionlessness of a seat on the solid earth, but she used gravitation to balance the slight burdens of her wariness and her confidence. She put aside all the pride and vanity of terror, and leapt into an unsure condition of liberty and content.

She leapt, too, into a life of moments. No pause was possible to her as she went, except the vibrating pause of a perpetual change and of an unflagging flight. A woman, long educated to sit still, does not suddenly learn to live a momentary[4] life without strong momentary resolution. She has no light achievement in limiting not only her foresight, which must become brief, but her memory, which must do more; for it must rather cease than become brief. Idle memory wastes time and other things. The moments of the woman in grey as they dropped by must needs disappear, and be simply forgotten, as a child forgets. Idle memory, by the way, shortens life, or shortens the sense of time, by linking the immediate past clingingly to the present. Here may possibly be found one of the reasons for the length of a child's time, and for the brevity of the time that succeeds. The child lets his moments pass by and quickly become remote through a thousand little successive oblivions. He has not yet the languid habit of recall.

'Thou art my warrior,' said Volumnia. 'I holp to frame thee.'[5]

Shall a man inherit his mother's trick of speaking, or her habit and attitude, and not suffer something, against his will, from her bequest of weakness, and something, against his heart, from her bequest of folly? From the legacies of an unlessoned mind, a woman's heirs-male are not cut off in the Common Law of the generations of mankind. Brutus knew that the valour of Portia was settled upon his sons.

RUDOLPH DIRCKS

Ellen

She had now been a waitress at the little café off Cheapside for something over two years; her circumstances had not changed during that time; she herself had scarcely changed; her features had, perhaps, developed a little and become more defined, her manner less hesitating – and that was all. That was all, at least, that was noticeable. A great change, however, had occurred in her between then and now that was not noticeable; that silent, miraculous change, so imperceptible, so profound, which works in a woman between the ages of eighteen and twenty.

She had come during those two years to have an exaggerated, almost a morbid idea of her own want of good looks; she had observed that regular frequenters of the café – young city clerks, journalists and the rest – avoided the series of marble-topped tables at which she served for those which were attended by other girls smarter and prettier; she rarely received the little attentions which the other girls among themselves proclaimed. It was the stray customer, the bird of passage, who kept her busy. But, as a matter of fact, it was not her want of good looks that kept the younger men aloof; it was something in her manner, an absence, perhaps, of that fictitious spirit of gaiety, of that alert responsiveness, which men find so arresting in women. Really, she was not at all bad-looking.

Still, this neglect ate into her heart a little. She regretted her want of adaptability, of the faculty of being able to assume all those charming (as they seemed to her) little airs and graces, partly natural, partly cultivated, which so became the other girls; she, it is true, rather despised these coquetries of her companions, but her own deficiencies of the sort made her feel at times particularly dull and stupid and angry with herself. One or two of the girls at the café had, during her time, married one or two of the young men who came there, and would afterwards pay an occasional visit to the place, certainly in pretty frocks, and, to all appearance, radiant and happy. But these girls were fortunate. Others, again, had suddenly disappeared, and none knew whither; but as their disappearance happened to be simultaneous with a break in the regular attendance of certain customers, dark stories were whispered to which the non-appearance of the missing ones seemed to lend colour.

After a while, Ellen did not mind so much being neglected; the smart of the sting became less and less painful, till finally, she rather, if anything, preferred escaping the attentions which fell to the share of the other girls. This may have been partly owing to the view which she came to take of men; her position had provided her with opportunities for arriving at a generalization, and she came to think of men as either silly or wicked – silly, when they were attracted by the trivial insincerities of the girls in the café; wicked, when they took advantage of their rarer simplicity. She did not conceive now, that she would ever fall in love, that anyone would ever fall in love with her.

All the same, as the two years advanced, Ellen began to feel a curious isolation of the heart, an emptiness which she never attributed to the absence of a lover. Besides, she had an intuitive suspicion that she possessed qualities which would be fatal to her retaining the affections of a husband, that there would be little joy for her in the companionship which would place her in the position of a wife. Not that she thought anything very clearly about these things; the vague emotions and sensations which moved her, the detached things which floated in her mind, had not yet found the relief which comes with realization; her impulses were not remotely guided by self-consciousness. A sense of loneliness oppressed her, which was not diminished by the companionship of her fellow servants at the café, and she wanted companionship of some sort. It was dreadful for her at times to feel so much alone, to feel that there was nothing in the world, in this great London, which she really cared for; that there was no one, since the death of her father and mother, who really cared for her.

She had this sense of loneliness even in the busiest time of the day, when an enormous wave of traffic swept by outside the café, and, inside, all was stir and movement. Even amid all this stir and din, when she was occupied in flitting from one table to another, in taking orders and attending to them, even at such moments her thoughts would be playing to another tune, her soul would be filled with unrest and impatience. Life, indeed, became a great struggle for her. Sometimes she said to herself that she would run away – from she knew not what, where she knew not to; and sometimes she wished very sincerely that she were dead.

She had seen many strange faces during those two years; at last it began to dawn upon her that one of these faces which had been strange was becoming familiar; a face with a fair, pointed beard and blue eyes. Beyond, however, merely ordering what he wanted, he had not spoken to her; it was improbable that he had noticed her; but his regular attendance at the tables at which she served began to attract the attention of the other girls, who derived some entertainment from hinting to Ellen that she was carrying on a flirtation, a suggestion which happened to be sufficiently inappropriate to appeal to their sense of humour. It was in keeping with Ellen's temperament that no romantic ideas entered her head at this point, where, possibly, the least susceptible of her companions would – as women will – have woven a complete fabric of foolish sentiment. Still, as he continued to come regularly, she began involuntarily to feel a certain liking for him; the fact of his never attempting to enter into any sort of conversation with her had its not unpleasant side for her. So, by and by, they both seemed to begin to know each other in this silent way. And yet there came moments when Ellen felt somehow that she would like to talk to him, to tell him all about herself, and what she felt. His presence accentuated a dimly realized need for self-expression, of pouring into some ear the flood of vague sentiments which possessed her. She could not talk to the other girls; they would not understand, or they would laugh at her; but she could, she felt, talk to this fair-bearded man with the blue eyes. But not at the café; she would rather remain silent for ever than do that. Then, how?

This idea of speaking to him, of sharing with him her whole confidence, seized upon her, and developed with an intensity which caused her ceaseless perturbation and pain.

After a little time, indeed, they drifted, naturally enough, into a conventional intercourse, almost monosyllabic, uninteresting, which seemed to her hopelessly trivial – but how to advance beyond it! Once or twice she thought she observed a look of interrogation in the blue eyes, a look which invited her confidence, and, at the same time, occasioned her a poignant feeling of self-consciousness – there, at the café, while meeting the significant glances, the partly ironical, partly suggestive, glances of her companions. No! she could not speak to him there; she had nothing to say to him there. Yet it was hard to resist the appeal of his eyes.

'You are looking pale. Do you go out much?' he said to her one day.

'No; only home and back.'

'Ah! you should.'

'We don't close till seven,' she said. Then, their eyes meeting, she continued irresistibly: 'Will you meet me tonight?'

It was not till an hour or so later that she realized that she was to meet him that evening at the principal entrance to St Paul's; that she realized that she herself had made the appointment. She had leapt the barrier, and was shocked at the extent of her daring, a little humiliated even; yet, above everything, singularly elated and careless. She had never breathed so freely.

But when they met, the need for self-expression was no longer apparent; she only felt stupid and shy. He suggested that they should go to a theatre or to an exhibition at Earl's Court, but she would not go to either place. Then they walked along the Embankment, between Blackfriars Bridge and Charing Cross. He talked a good deal, but she hardly caught or understood what he said, and was quietly irresponsive. There was in his manner an air of familiarity which slightly repelled her; she began to wish that she had not, after all, asked him to meet her; to think of abruptly leaving him. Once he put his arm through hers, and was surprised at the startled expression which sprang to her face as she quickly drew apart from him. After this his manner changed, and she felt more at ease. The incident had defined her attitude.

Reaching the gardens on the Embankment, near Charing Cross, they entered a gate and sat on one of the seats. There were some children playing about on the path whose antics amused her, and led her to talk about her own childhood, to tell him of those dear, half-forgotten things which everyone remembers so well, of that dim world of curious fancies which all of us at one time inhabited. He was sympathetic, and they talked on so in the fading light until it was time for the gates of the garden to be closed. As they passed through them, their intimacy had become as natural and easy as she could have dared to hope.

They crossed the Strand and penetrated the maze of streets which lead in the direction of King's Cross, where she had her lodging. And now all the things that had lain in her mind, all the incoherent emotions that had possessed her, became coherent and simple, derived shape and form in the attempt to express them. She told him all about her present life, about the other girls in the café and their sentimental episodes. She told him of the feeling of loneliness, of abstraction, of the vague itching at her heart which never ceased.

At last they reached a house in one of the outlying streets of Regent Square.

'I don't know why I asked you to meet me tonight,' she said, stopping at the door of this house; 'I don't know what is the matter with me. But I wanted to speak to someone. And I couldn't speak to the other girls; they would have only made fun of me, I think. I feel happier now that I have had a nice long talk with someone – still – there is – something – something –' She paused a moment, and then proceeded, rather abruptly: 'I don't want to be married, the same as most girls do; I don't like men, as a rule – at least, not in that way . . . besides, I think I should always be happier remaining as I am at present, working for myself, independent.'

She gave a little shriek of delight at a thought which suddenly occurred to her, a flash of mental illumination, which enabled her to divine the source of all her perplexities, which instantly enabled her to solve the problem of her happiness; a thought which filled her poor, empty heart. 'I think,' she said, softly, 'if I had a baby, my very own, I should want nothing – nothing in this world more than that!'

Her lips quivered and tears came into her eyes, exquisitely tender tears.

She then turned to the door and opened it with a latchkey.

'Are you living alone?' he asked.

'Yes, quite alone,' she said, retreating into the passage without turning.

He followed her a couple of paces, and then stood with one foot on the doorstep. He looked into the passage, but could not make out whether she were standing there in the dark or not. He wondered if she were standing there. Then taking the handle of the door he drew it gently to, and went down the street.

GEORGE EGERTON

A Nocturne

I have rather nice diggings. I got them last year, just after you went on that Egyptian racket. They are on the embankment, within sight of Cleopatra's Needle.[1] I like that anachronism of a monument; it has a certain fascination for me. I can see it at night, if I lean out of my window, outlined above the light-flecked river sacred to our sewer goddess that runs so sullenly under its canopy of foggy blue.

To me the embankment has beauties unsurpassed in any city in Europe. I never tire of it at night. The opaque blotches of the plane-trees' foliage, the glistening water, the dotted lines of golden light, the great blocks of buildings rearing to the clouds like shadow monuments, the benches laden with human flotsam and jetsam.

I was leaning out of my window one night in November, in a lull in the rainfall; big Ben had just boomed out one, when I noticed a woman rise from a seat below. She had been sitting there an hour, for I had seen the light shine on her hair, yellow hair like a child's, when I went down to the pillar box at midnight.

Her carriage was that of a gentlewoman. Curious how gait tells. She walked a little way, stumbled, stood with her hand pressed to her heart, – a drunken woman would have lurched again. Then she went to the parapet, and leant against it, staring into the water.

A good many women I have known could not gaze steadily into running water, or look down from a height without feeling more than an impulse to throw themselves over – something impelled them to it, so they have assured me. I don't know the reason for it any more than I know why a man always buttons from left to right; a woman from right to left. It's a fact, though. The buttonholes on a woman's garments are always made on the right side, never on the left; and it is just as awkward for her to button our way, as for us to try hers. – Hang it, man, I know it's so. I got a poor woman to make me some pyjamas, and she put the darned buttonholes wrong side. I had to get the beastly things changed. – Well, to come back to the story, I didn't like the way that lady looked into the river; it had rained all day, the streets glistened with water, and a north-east wind scooped round the corners. I went down to have a look at her. Just as I crossed over she dropped her head in an odd sort of way, took a step out, then fell back against the wall. The measured beat of a policeman's step struck the pavement a little farther down. I steadied her, and asked:

'Are you ill, madam; can I help you?'

She lifted the strangest face I ever saw to mine. It was like some curious mask – more than a flesh and blood phiz. Her eyes were beautifully set and burned sombrely; they looked as live eyes might through the sockets of a mask. Her yellow hair seemed like a wig against her forehead and temples. She started and shrank as I touched her; her teeth chattered.

'Yes, I *am* ill; I feel faint, strangely faint . . .'

She evidently suffered from some heart trouble. There was a bluish tinge around her mouth. She rocked on her feet, her lids drooped. I put my arm through hers; the steps came nearer; she roused and moaned mutteringly:

'Yes, I'm only resting; I'll move on in a few minutes.'

'Come with me,' I said; 'you can't stay here; try and walk.'

She came all right, in a dazed sort of way, though. All the under floors of the building in which I have my rooms are offices, so we met no one. She panted a bit as she mounted the stairs. I kept close behind, in case of a fall. Her boots must have been broken, for she left little wet splotches on each step. I showed her into the room. The electric light roused her; she hesitated and coloured up, – it was the most curious thing I ever saw, the way her face thawed and quickened. She turned round, and looked straight at me; I braced myself to meet her eyes, miserable, honest eyes they were too, that probed me like steel; she would have detected the least sign of bad faith, like a shot.

I pushed an armchair nearer the fire; she sat down, leant back her head against the cushion, and before she could say whatever she intended to, fainted dead away. Faith, it gave me an uncomfortable sensation. I forced some brandy between her teeth and tried to pull her round. I like doing things for women, – any kind of woman almost, – they all interest me tremendously. I don't think I do them. Women seem at fault some way in their choice of men, they so often give themselves to brutes or sneaks – it may be these types don't scruple to seize the opportune moment with them.

I took off her hat, a quiet, little black felt affair, positively soaked with rain. She had lovely hair, glossy yellow, not 'brown at the roots' kind, you know; it had a crinkle in it, and the line down the middle of her head was white as an almond. I hate the type of blonde that has a pink skin to her scalp. I concluded she couldn't have been long in the streets, for the bit of white at her neck and the handkerchief in her lap were clean, – a day's soil at most. She wore woollen gloves; I pulled them off; she opened her eyes, closed them again. She wore an old-fashioned thin wedding ring on her right hand, perhaps her mother's; she had pretty, long hands; but hands don't attract me like feet or ears. I belong to the race of men to whom temptation comes in the guise of little feet. An instep or ankle appeals irresistibly to my senses; I acknowledge it frankly; it's damned odd, but I can't help it – the appeal, I mean. My friend Foote says, delicately perfumed *lingerie* is his weak spot; his fall is sure at a flutter of lace and ribbon. To be virtuous, he would have to live in a land where the drying of women's frillikins on a clothes-line would be prohibited by law. Her feet were not pretty, although her boots were decently cut. What an odd face she had; I can see it in white relief on the red of the leather. A bit like Christine Nilsson[2] about the forehead, big clever nose, tremendous jaw, – a devil or a saint, or I'm no judge. She opened her eyes at last. I held out the glass; she shuddered, pushed it away almost roughly and said:

'No, please not that, I am afraid of it; I daren't touch it, it would be so easy to get to want it – when one is miserable.'

'Quite right; suppose you have some tea instead.'

She flushed and smiled; the saint was certainly uppermost just then.

'You are *very* good; yes, I should like some.'

I am rather a dab at making tea. Lloyd gets me the best in the market; never get good tea in a woman's house, – afraid of the price or something.

'You had better take off that wet jacket.'

Odd woman that; she stood up at once – she was still shaking – and took it off, hanging it over an oak stool. She was a well set up woman, of the thoroughbred flat, spare English type; getting on for the age the lady novelists find interesting, – thirty, perhaps. They may say what they like though, there is nothing like milk-fresh youth. By the Lord Harry, it's a beauty in itself! The plainest fresh-skinned wench with the dew of life in her eyes is worth ten of any beauty of thirty-five. Her dress was literally soaked, it hung heavily about her ankles; there were two wet patches too, where her feet had rested. I dug the poker into the fire, and said, without looking round:

'You'll be laid up tomorrow if you keep that skirt on; go into the other room and take it off; don't mind me, I've seen petticoats before now. Hang it to dry before the fire and put your boots in the fender. You'll see a collection of Eastern footwear – it's rather a fad of mine – on the wall, find a pair to fit and slip them on . . .'

Didn't see her face, busy with the kettle. A moment's silence, then I heard the door shut softly. Admirable woman that! when I come to think of it, the only woman I ever met who could do a thing without arguing about it; never wanted a reason, never gave any. It's curious, the inclination women have to gab about everything; they spoil a caress by asking you if you liked it. The weather had not improved; I felt quite glad I had kept on my diggings. The adventure was one after my own heart. I would honour my unknown lady with my best china. I took down an old Worcester cup and saucer, tipped the sugar into my prettiest lacquer bowl, put out some sandwiches and biscuits, and was surveying my arrangements when the door behind me opened. By Jove, how rarely that woman changed when she smiled! it reminded me of the first spray of almond bloom one sees in spring in some dingy, sordid London street. It youthened her, melted the stark, hungry grip about her mouth. I suppose the petticoat was too short or something – women are so devilishly illogical. I have seen halfway down a woman's back and bosom, and she didn't mind in the least;

yet she'd have fainted at the idea of showing the calf of her decently stockinged leg.

She had taken down an old Jap kimono, once a gorgeous affair, but time had faded the flowery broidery on the plum-blue ground to mellow half-tones.

Her embarrassment was pretty to see; what a fetching thing a woman is when she is perfectly natural. I pointed to the chair, and uncovered the teapot.

She sat down and poured out the tea rather awkwardly, I don't fancy it lay much in her line. She drank it eagerly, but paled a bit when I offered her a sandwich. I know that sensation, I had it during the last days of the Siege of Paris;[3] ask me to tell you about that some other time – the poor thing was faint with hunger, the very sight of food made her feel sick, she put her handkerchief to her mouth; I took the sandwiches away and got out some dry biscuits.

'Have some more tea?' I said, 'and try these dry biscuits by and by, when you feel better.'

She leant back; she had the prettiest line of throat I ever saw, quite white and soft, under that jaw, too. I poured out some more tea for her.

'You have been fasting too long; when did you eat last? . . .'

'Not since yesterday morning!'

Good God! She forgot that the hour made it over two days.

She put the tea down and said simply:

'May I ask you for a cigarette? I think I should feel better if I were to smoke one or two. I don't feel as if I could eat just now.'

'Of course,' I said; 'how jolly that you smoke! You must have some of my special baccy.' She was smoking tranquilly when a gust of wind howled and shook the window sash viciously, and the rain rattled like gravel thrown against the panes. She started and looked at the clock, the hands pointed to 1–45; the colour rushed to her face; I took the bull by the horns.

'My dear lady, don't bother about the hour, time is an entirely artificial arrangement. You can't go out in that rain, it's not to be thought of. You wouldn't be out on that seat, if you had any shelter to go to. I don't want to know anything you don't volunteer to tell me. You do me proud in accepting my hospitality, such as it is; indeed you do, it's a charity; I hate going to bed. When you have had a good rest you'll think of some way out of the snarl, whatever it is. Good baccy, ain't it?'

She held out her hand and gave mine an honest grip, as a nice lad might have done. Those big, grey eyes of hers got black when the tears filled them.

She was a vexatious sort of contradictory person; there was a tantalizing lack of finality about her – just as you had made up your mind that she was really deuced ugly, she flushed and bloomed and sparkled into downright charm, and before you had time to drink it in she was plain again. Her voice too was twin to her face. It was deep, and at times harsh with sudden soft rushing inflections and tender lilts in it.

'You have Irish blood in you?' I ventured.

'Yes, on the distaff side; how did you know?'

'Oh, voice, and I suppose it's the kin feeling of race.'

We talked of a good many things during the next hour. I noticed that her eyes wandered wistfully to my books. I rather pride myself on some of my specimens of rare binding – two little shelves represent a good many years' income.

'Do you like books?' I asked. She caught what I meant at once, and her face lit up. I gave her my only heirloom, an, from me at least, unpurchasable, Aldine classic.[4] She positively handled it lovingly. The more I think of that woman, the more I am persuaded of her rarity; one is almost afraid to give one of one's book pets into most women's hands. She knew it at once – didn't say anything banal or gushing, only, 'I love the peculiar olive colour of the leather.'

'Have you ever seen any of Le Gaston's work? Look how well the lines of gold dot-work tell upon the scarlet of the morocco. How it has kept its colour. Machinery and cloth have played the deuce with the art of it.'

'If I were a rich woman I'd have any book I cared to keep especially bound for myself.'

Funny situation! Well, I suppose it was, rather. But if you come to think of it, the rummiest situations and most unlikely incidents in life are just those that don't get treated in fiction. Most poor devils have to write with one eye fixed on the mental limitations of their publisher or the index expurgatorius[5] of the booksellers; that is, if they want to pay income tax.

She dropped off to sleep with a book in her lap. I covered her knees with a rug, turned out the light; the glow of the fire surrounded her with a magic circle. I went and lay down; I can sleep or wake at will. I decided to sleep till five. She had never stirred. I made up the fire; it was jolly to think of her there in the warmth instead of being out in that awful night, perhaps bobbing under a barge or knocking against the arches in the swirl of that filthy water.

I went back and slept till seven, tubbed, and took a peep at her. Her face looked good as a child's in her sleep, but a child that had suffered under bad treatment and grown prematurely old. It was dreadfully haggard; that woman had been slowly starving to death.

It was one of those beastly mornings, fine under protest, with a sun that looked as if he had been making a night of it. I hate the mornings, except out in wild nature; someway in civilization they are always a sort of ill-natured comment on the night before. Like some excellent women, there is a brutal lack of semi-tone about them. I slipped the bolt on the door; Bates never came up unless I rang for him, but sometimes fellows drop in for a pick me up or a devil, – by the way, a red herring done in whisky isn't half bad.

She woke in a fright with a fearsome sort of half cry. I expect she thought she had been asleep on that seat. I knew the beastly morning would unsettle her, she was right as a trivet the night before. She flushed horribly when she realized where she was, and the time, and stammered:

'I'm so sorry, oh, I *am* so sorry! I was so tired, I really couldn't help myself. I haven't slept for many nights, you know, and one gets so stupid –'

'That's all right. I've been asleep, slept like a top; always do. Suppose you freshen up a bit in my dressing room; your frock is dry. You will find hot water and things if you look about, – help yourself. I am going to lock you in if you don't mind: I want my man to fix things up a bit . . .'

She flushed again. I'll stake my oath that kind of blush hurts a woman.

My usual hour is eleven, but Bates cleared up and laid breakfast without an atom of expression in his face or voice. Odd man, Bates! He brought enough for two; makes a good living, that fellow, by an expedient regulation of the organs of sight and hearing. He finished at last, never knew him take so long; he asked:

'Shall you want me again, sir?'

'No, I'll shove the tray outside, I am going out later on, not in to anyone.'

'All right, sir.'

I knocked at the door as I unlocked it. She came out, self-possessed, straight and somewhat stiffly slim in her black frock. I bet she could ride.

'You look better already,' I cried; 'would you like tea better than coffee? No! come, then.'

She took her seat, outwardly unembarrassed, anyhow. I opened the papers and glanced at the headings. The 'Globe'[6] was lying on a chair; I don't know why I got it; she asked me might she see it. She glanced at the first page, and whatever she saw pleased her. I dawdled through my meal, for I did not know how to get any further with her. She was not the sort, you see, one could give a kiss and a quid and say, 'Now, run along Polly, and don't get into any more trouble than you can help.' However, she gave me a lead herself, for when we had finished she came over, put out her hand and – well what she said don't matter, anyway, it made me feel a bally idiot. I put her into the armchair without any ceremony and pushed over the cigarettes, saying:

'Can't talk unless I smoke. Now, my dear lady, granted you consider you owe me something, suppose you take it out in as much confidence as you care to give away. How did you come to be without a bed last night?'

'Simply enough; to explain, I must go back a bit. Some years ago a younger brother and I were left almost penniless. Neither of us had been brought up to do anything except to get rid of money in the most happy-go-lucky way. That makes it difficult to get a living when even the trained people are crowded out. We got it as best we could. I've played the piano at bean feasts, "devilled" at 6d. an hour, done whatever offered itself, don't you know,' she had a trick of ending her statement that way. 'We kept together, were saving to emigrate. Then he was ill for months; he died at Christmas. That broke me up, don't you know; I was very fond of him; and left me without a penny. I went as nurse companion to a Christian gentlewoman in Bath at £12 a year; pay for my own washing. I broke down under it in six months. Came to town ill, and went into the fever hospital three days after, stayed there six weeks; had to go to a convalescent home for a month. It was very cheap, but it took all I had left. I couldn't get anything to do. I tried for a place as domestic; I didn't look it, so they said. Things have been going steadily from bad to worse, don't you know? I used to work at the British Museum. A fortnight ago my landlady gave me notice; she wasn't a bad sort, but she had the brokers in herself, and there was a sale. I had to leave; she let me take my box to her sister's for a few days. I sat in St James' Park the night before last, and sent a description of it to a paper –' She hesitated. 'I have been trying journalism, paragraphs, and articles,' and with the most abject tone of apology, 'verse, rubbish, you know; but sometimes it gets taken. Only one has to wait such a time before one knows. I have had a turnover[7] in the "Globe"; it's a guinea, and there was another last night . . .'

(I had skimmed it, not half a bad one on 'Adder lore in the Fens,' . . .) 'I'll get along all right now; it was rather bad last night; I was overtired or . . .'

I interrupted her.

'My dear woman, you can't go far on a guinea with arrears of rent, however small, to pay out of it.'

To cut it all short, I proposed to give her a note to an editress I know, a jolly, good little woman, who would stretch more than a point to serve me. I hinted as delicately as I could that she had better not let her feelings rush her ever, and give away the genesis of our acquaintance; sort of thing, you know, might be annotated badly. She gave me her word of honour that she would let me know the result, and see me next day if nothing came of the interview. She took my pasteboard. I got Bates out of the way with an empty gladstone bag and a note to Paddy Foote, to take it in and say nothing. She put on her things whilst I wrote the note; I watched her put on her hat; she looked better without it.

'I am going to speak of you as "bearer",' I said. 'I won't ask your name now; I'd like to learn it just when you like – or leave it to chance – I've an idea you'd rather . . .'

She nodded gravely; we shook hands – she has lovely eyes, as I said before – and went, leaving one the poorer by herself.

I haven't a thing belonging to her except the ashes of her cigarette. I tipped it into my match-box; I suppose I am a damned fool; most Irishmen are, in one way or another.

It's curious how things have a knack of running twos; I had never met her before that night, and yet, that same evening, as I came out of the Charing Cross post office, I felt a touch on my arm, turned round, and, by Jove, there she was. The little woman had fixed her up all right, and things were going to hum, so she said.

Sometimes, when the rain beats, and that beastly old river yawns like a grave, I stand up at the window and look down. I never felt a want in my old digs before. It was jolly to have a woman – a woman of that kind, you know – taking an interest in one's first editions.

KATE CHOPIN

Miss McEnders

I

When Miss Georgie McEnders had finished an elaborately simple toilet of grey and black, she divested herself completely of rings, bangles, brooches – everything to suggest that she stood in friendly relations with fortune. For Georgie was going to read a paper upon 'The Dignity of Labour' before the Woman's Reform Club; and if she was blessed with an abundance of wealth, she possessed a no less amount of good taste.

Before entering the neat victoria that stood at her father's too-sumptuous door – and that was her special property – she turned to give certain directions to the coachman. First upon the list from which she read was inscribed: 'Look up Mademoiselle Salambre.'

'James,' said Georgie, flushing a pretty pink, as she always did with the slightest effort of speech, 'we want to look up a person named Mademoiselle Salambre, in the southern part of town, on Arsenal street,' indicating a certain number and locality. Then she seated herself in the carriage, and as it drove away proceeded to study her engagement list further and to knit her pretty brows in deep and complex thought.

'Two o'clock – look up M. Salambre,' said the list. 'Three-thirty – read paper before Woman's Ref. Club. Four-thirty –' and here followed cabalistic abbreviations which meant: 'Join committee of ladies to investigate moral condition of St Louis factory-girls. Six o'clock – dine with papa. Eight o'clock – hear Henry George's lecture on Single Tax.'

So far, Mademoiselle Salambre was only a name to Georgie

McEnders, one of several submitted to her at her own request by her furnishers, Push and Prodem, an enterprising firm charged with the construction of Miss McEnders' very elaborate trousseau. Georgie liked to know the people who worked for her, as far as she could.

She was a charming young woman of twenty-five, though almost too white-souled for a creature of flesh and blood. She possessed ample wealth and time to squander, and a burning desire to do good – to elevate the human race, and start the world over again on a comfortable footing for everybody.

When Georgie had pushed open the very high gate of a very small yard she stood confronting a robust German woman, who, with dress tucked carefully between her knees, was in the act of noisily 'redding' the bricks.

'Does M'selle Salambre live here?' Georgie's tall, slim figure was very erect. Her face suggested a sweet peach blossom, and she held a severely simple lorgnon up to her short-sighted blue eyes.

'Ya! ya! aber oop stairs!' cried the woman brusquely and impatiently. But Georgie did not mind. She was used to greetings that lacked the ring of cordiality.

When she had ascended the stairs that led to an upper porch she knocked at the first door that presented itself, and was told to enter by Mlle Salambre herself.

The woman sat at an opposite window, bending over a bundle of misty white goods that lay in a fluffy heap in her lap. She was not young. She might have been thirty, or she might have been forty. There were lines about her round, piquante face that denoted close acquaintance with struggles, hardships and all manner of unkind experiences.

Georgie had heard a whisper here and there touching the private character of Mlle Salambre which had determined her to go in person and make the acquaintance of the woman and her surroundings; which latter were poor and simple enough, and not too neat. There was a little child at play upon the floor.

Mlle Salambre had not expected so unlooked-for an apparition as Miss McEnders, and seeing the girl standing there in the door she removed the eyeglasses that had assisted her in the delicate work, and stood up also.

'Mlle Salambre, I suppose?' said Georgie, with a courteous inclination.

'Ah! Mees McEndairs! What an agree'ble surprise! Will you be so kind to take a chair.' Mademoiselle had lived many years in the city, in various capacities, which brought her in touch with the fashionable set. There were few people in polite society whom Mademoiselle did not know – by sight, at least; and their private histories were as familiar to her as her own.

'You 'ave come to see your – the work?' the woman went on with a smile that quite brightened her face. 'It is a pleasure to handle such fine, such delicate quality of goods, Mees,' and she went and laid several pieces of her handiwork upon the table beside Georgie, at the same time indicating such details as she hoped would call forth her visitor's approval.

There was something about the woman and her surroundings, and the atmosphere of the place, that affected the girl unpleasantly. She shrank instinctively, drawing her invisible mantle of chastity closely about her. Mademoiselle saw that her visitor's attention was divided between the lingerie and the child upon the floor, who was engaged in battering a doll's unyielding head against the unyielding floor.

'The child of my neighbour downstairs,' said Mademoiselle, with a wave of the hand which expressed volumes of unutterable ennui. But at that instant the little one, with instinctive mistrust, and in seeming defiance of the repudiation, climbed to her feet and went rolling and toddling towards her mother, clasping the woman about the knees, and calling her by the endearing title which was her own small right.

A spasm of annoyance passed over Mademoiselle's face, but still she called the child '*Chene*,' as she grasped its arm to keep it from falling. Miss McEnders turned every shade of carmine.

'Why did you tell me an untruth?' she asked, looking indignantly into the woman's lowered face. 'Why do you call yourself "Mademoiselle" if this child is yours?'

'For the reason that it is more easy to obtain employment. For reasons that you would not understand,' she continued, with a shrug of the shoulders that expressed some defiance and a sudden disregard for consequences. 'Life is not all *couleur de rose*, Mees McEndairs; you do not know what life is, you!' And drawing a handkerchief from an apron pocket she mopped an imaginary tear from the corner of her eye, and blew her nose till it glowed again.

Georgie could hardly recall the words or actions with which she quitted Mademoiselle's presence. As much as she wanted to, it had been impossible to stand and read the woman a moral lecture. She had simply thrown what disapproval she could into her hasty leave-taking, and that was all for the moment. But as she drove away, a more practical form of rebuke suggested itself to her not too nimble intelligence – one that she promised herself to act upon as soon as her home was reached.

When she was alone in her room, during an interval between her many engagements, she then attended to the affair of Mlle Salambre.

Georgie believed in discipline. She hated unrighteousness. When it pleased God to place the lash in her hand she did not hesitate to apply it. Here was this Mlle Salambre living in her sin. Not as one who is young and blinded by the glamour of pleasure, but with cool and deliberate intention. Since she chose to transgress, she ought to suffer, and be made to feel that her ways were iniquitous and invited rebuke. It lay in Georgie's power to mete out a small dose of that chastisement which the woman deserved, and she was glad that the opportunity was hers.

She seated herself forthwith at her writing table, and penned the following note to her furnishers:

'MESSRS. PUSH & PRODEM.
Gentlemen – Please withdraw from Mademoiselle Salambre all work of mine, and return same to me at once – finished or unfinished.

Yours truly,
GEORGIE MCENDERS.'

2

On the second day following this summary proceeding, Georgie sat at her writing table, looking prettier and pinker than ever, in a luxurious and soft-toned robe de chambre that suited her own delicate colouring, and fitted the pale amber tints of her room decorations.

There were books, pamphlets and writing material set neatly upon the table before her. In the midst of them were two framed photographs, which she polished one after another with a silken scarf that was near.

One of these was a picture of her father, who looked like an Englishman, with his clean-shaved mouth and chin, and closely-cropped side whiskers, just turning grey. A good-humoured shrewdness shone in his eyes. From the set of his thin, firm lips one might guess that he was in the foremost rank in the interesting game of 'push' that occupies mankind. One might further guess that his cleverness in using opportunities had brought him there, and that a dexterous management of elbows had served him no less. The other picture was that of Georgie's fiancé, Mr Meredith Holt, approaching more closely than he liked to his forty-fifth year and an unbecoming corpulence. Only one who knew beforehand that he was a *viveur* could have detected evidence of such in his face, which told little more than that he was a good-looking and amiable man of the world, who might be counted on to do the gentlemanly thing always. Georgie was going to marry him because his personality pleased her; because his easy knowledge of life – such as she apprehended it – commended itself to her approval; because he was likely to interfere in no way with her 'work'. Yet she might not have given any of these reasons if asked for one. Mr Meredith Holt was simply an eligible man, whom almost any girl in her set would have accepted for a husband.

Georgie had just discovered that she had yet an hour to spare before starting out with the committee of four to further investigate the moral condition of the factory-girl, when a maid appeared with the announcement that a person was below who wished to see her.

'A person? Surely not a visitor at this hour?'

KATE CHOPIN

'I left her in the hall, miss, and she says her name is Mademoiselle Sal-Sal –'

'Oh, yes! Ask her to kindly walk up to my room, and show her the way, please, Hannah.'

Mademoiselle Salambre came in with a sweep of skirts that bristled defiance, and a poise of the head that was aggressive in its backward tilt. She seated herself, and with an air of challenge waited to be questioned or addressed.

Georgie felt at ease amid her own familiar surroundings. While she made some idle tracings with a pencil upon a discarded envelope, she half turned to say:

'This visit of yours is very surprising, madam, and wholly useless. I suppose you guess my motive in recalling my work, as I have done.'

'Maybe I do, and maybe I do not, Mees McEndairs,' replied the woman, with an impertinent uplifting of the eyebrows.

Georgie felt the same shrinking which had overtaken her before in the woman's presence. But she knew her duty, and from that there was no shrinking.

'You must be made to understand, madam, that there is a right way to live, and that there is a wrong way,' said Georgie with more condescension than she knew. 'We cannot defy God's laws with impunity, and without incurring His displeasure. But in His infinite justice and mercy He offers forgiveness, love and protection to those who turn away from evil and repent. It is for each of us to follow the divine way as well as may be. And I am only humbly striving to do His will.'

'A most charming sermon, Mees McEndairs!' mademoiselle interrupted with a nervous laugh; 'it seems a great pity to waste it upon so small an audience. And it grieves me, I cannot express, that I have not the time to remain and listen to its close.'

She arose and began to talk volubly, swiftly, in a jumble of French and English, and with a wealth of expression and gesture which Georgie could hardly believe was natural, and not something acquired and rehearsed.

She had come to inform Miss McEnders that she did not want her work; that she would not touch it with the tips of her fingers. And her little, gloved hands recoiled from an imaginary pile of lingerie with unspeakable disgust. Her eyes had travelled nimbly over the room, and had been arrested by the two photographs on the table. Very small, indeed, were her worldly possessions, she informed the young lady; but as Heaven was her witness – not a mouthful of bread that she had not earned. And her parents over yonder in France! As honest as the sunlight! Poor, ah! for that – poor as rats. God only knew how poor; and God only knew how honest. Her eyes remained fixed upon the picture of Horace McEnders. Some people might like fine houses, and servants, and horses, and all the luxury which dishonest wealth brings. Some people might enjoy such surroundings. As for her! – and she drew up her skirts ever so carefully and daintily, as though she feared contamination to her petticoats from the touch of the rich rug upon which she stood.

Georgie's blue eyes were filled with astonishment as they followed the woman's gestures. Her face showed aversion and perplexity.

'Please let this interview come to an end at once,' spoke the girl. She would not deign to ask an explanation of the mysterious allusions to ill-gotten wealth. But mademoiselle had not yet said all that she had come there to say.

'If it was only me to say so,' she went on, still looking at the likeness, 'but, *cher maître!* Go, yourself, Mees McEndairs, and stand for a while on the street and ask the people passing by how your dear papa has made his money, and see what they will say.'

Then shifting her glance to the photograph of Meredith Holt, she stood in an attitude of amused contemplation, with a smile of commiseration playing about her lips.

'Mr Meredith Holt!' she pronounced with quiet, supressed emphasis – 'ah! *c'est un propre, celui la!*[1] You know him very well, no doubt, Mees McEndairs. You would not care to have my opinion of Mr Meredith Holt. It would make no difference to you, Mees McEndairs, to know that he is not fit to be the husband of a self-respecting barmaid. Oh! you know a good deal, my dear young lady. You can preach sermons in *merveille!*'

When Georgie was finally alone, there came to her, through all her disgust and indignation, an indefinable uneasiness. There was no misunderstanding the intention of the woman's utterances in regard to the girl's fiancé and her father. A sudden, wild, defiant desire came to her to test the suggestion which Mademoiselle Salambre had let fall.

Yes, she would go stand there on the corner and ask the passers-by how Horace McEnders made his money. She could not yet collect her thoughts for calm reflection; and the house stifled her. It was fully time for her to join her committee of four, but she would meddle no further with morals till her own were adjusted, she thought. Then she quitted the house, very pale, even to her lips that were tightly set.

Georgie stationed herself on the opposite side of the street, on the corner, and waited there as though she had appointed to meet some one.

The first to approach her was a kind-looking old gentleman, very much muffled for the pleasant spring day. Georgie did not hesitate an instant to accost him:

'I beg pardon, sir. Will you kindly tell me whose house that is?' pointing to her own domicile across the way.

'That is Mr Horace McEnders' residence, Madame,' replied the old gentleman, lifting his hat politely.

'Could you tell me how he made the money with which to build so magnificent a home?'

'You should not ask indiscreet questions, my dear young lady,' answered the mystified old gentleman, as he bowed and walked away.

The girl let one or two persons pass her. Then she stopped a plumber, who was going cheerily along with his bag of tools on his shoulder.

'I beg pardon,' began Georgie again; 'but may I ask whose residence that is across the street?'

'Yes'um. That's the McEnderses.'

'Thank you; and can you tell me how Mr McEnders made such an immense fortune?'

'Oh, that ain't my business; but they say he made the biggest pile of it in the Whisky Ring.'[2]

So the truth would come to her somehow! These were the people from whom to seek it – who had not learned to veil their thoughts and opinions in polite subterfuge.

When a careless little newsboy came strolling along, she stopped him with the apparent intention of buying a paper from him.

'Do you know whose house that is?' she asked him, handing him a piece of money and nodding over the way.

'W'y, dats ole MicAndrus' house.'

'I wonder where he got the money to build such a fine house.'

'He stole it; dats w'ere he got it. Thank you,' pocketing the change which Georgie declined to take, and he whistled a popular air as he disappeared around the corner.

Georgie had heard enough. Her heart was beating violently now, and her cheeks were flaming. So everybody knew it; even to the street gamins! The men and women who visited her and broke bread at her father's table, knew it. Her co-workers, who strove with her in Christian endeavour, knew. The very servants who waited upon her doubtless knew this, and had their jests about it.

She shrank within herself as she climbed the stairway to her room.

Upon the table there she found a box of exquisite white spring blossoms that a messenger had brought from Meredith Holt, during her absence. Without an instant's hesitation, Georgie cast the spotless things into the wide, sooty fireplace. Then she sank into a chair and wept bitterly.

KATE CHOPIN

A Pair of Silk Stockings

Little Mrs Sommers one day found herself the unexpected possessor of fifteen dollars. It seemed to her a very large amount of money, and the way in which it stuffed and bulged her worn old *porte-monnaie* gave her a feeling of importance such as she had not enjoyed for years.

The question of investment was one that occupied her greatly. For a day or two she walked about apparently in a dreamy state, but really absorbed in speculation and calculation. She did not wish to act hastily, to do anything she might afterward regret. But it was during the still hours of the night when she lay awake revolving plans in her mind that she seemed to see her way clearly toward a proper and judicious use of the money.

A dollar or two should be added to the price usually paid for Janie's shoes, which would insure their lasting an appreciable time longer than they usually did. She would buy so and so many yards of percale for new shirtwaists for the boys and Janie and Mag. She had intended to make the old ones do by skilful patching. Mag should have another gown. She had seen some beautiful patterns, veritable bargains in the shop windows. And still there would be left enough for new stockings – two pairs apiece – and what darning that would save for a while! She would get caps for the boys and sailor-hats for the girls. The vision of her little brood looking fresh and dainty and new for once in their lives excited her and made her restless and wakeful with anticipation.

The neighbours sometimes talked of certain 'better days' that little Mrs Sommers had known before she had ever thought of being Mrs Sommers. She herself indulged in no such morbid retrospection. She had no time – no second of time to devote to the past. The needs of the present absorbed her every faculty. A vision of the future like some dim, gaunt monster sometimes appalled her, but luckily tomorrow never comes.

Mrs Sommers was one who knew the value of bargains; who could stand for hours making her way inch by inch toward the desired object that was selling below cost. She could elbow her way if need be; she had learned to clutch a piece of goods and hold it and stick to it with persistence and determination till her turn came to be served, no matter when it came.

But that day she was a little faint and tired. She had swallowed a light luncheon – no! when she came to think of it, between getting the children fed and the place righted, and preparing herself for the shopping bout, she had actually forgotten to eat any luncheon at all!

She sat herself upon a revolving stool before a counter that was comparatively deserted, trying to gather strength and courage to charge through an eager multitude that was besieging breast-works of shirting and figured lawn. An all-gone limp feeling had come over her and she rested her hand aimlessly upon the counter. She wore no gloves. By degrees she grew aware that her hand had encountered something very soothing, very pleasant to touch. She looked down to see that her hand lay upon a pile of silk stockings. A placard near by announced that they had been reduced in price from two dollars and fifty cents to one dollar and ninety-eight cents; and a young girl who stood behind the counter asked her if she wished to examine their line of silk hosiery. She smiled, just as if she had been asked to inspect a tiara of diamonds with the ultimate view of purchasing it. But she went on feeling the soft, sheeny luxurious things – with both hands now, holding them up to see them glisten, and to feel them glide serpent-like through her fingers.

Two hectic blotches came suddenly into her pale cheeks. She looked up at the girl.

'Do you think there are any eights-and-a-half among these?'

There were any number of eights-and-a-half. In fact, there were more of that size than any other. Here was a light-blue pair; there were some lavender, some all black and various shades of tan and grey. Mrs Sommers selected a black pair and looked at them very long and closely. She pretended to be examining their texture, which the clerk assured her was excellent.

'A dollar and ninety-eight cents,' she mused aloud. 'Well, I'll take this pair.' She handed the girl a five-dollar bill and waited for her change and for her parcel. What a very small parcel it was! It seemed lost in the depths of her shabby old shopping-bag.

Mrs Sommers after that did not move in the direction of the bargain counter. She took the elevator, which carried her to an upper floor into the region of the ladies' waiting rooms. Here, in a retired corner, she exchanged her cotton stockings for the new silk ones which she had just bought. She was not going through any acute mental process or reasoning with herself, nor was she striving to explain to her satisfaction the motive of her action. She was not thinking at all. She seemed for the time to be taking a rest from that laborious and fatiguing function and to have abandoned herself to some mechanical impulse that directed her actions and freed her of responsibility.

How good was the touch of the raw silk to her flesh! She felt like lying back in the cushioned chair and revelling for a while in the luxury of it. She did for a little while. Then she replaced her shoes, rolled the cotton stockings together and thrust them into her bag. After doing this she crossed straight over to the shoe department and took her seat to be fitted.

She was fastidious. The clerk could not make her out; he could not reconcile her shoes with her stockings, and she was not too easily pleased. She held back her skirts and turned her feet one way and her head another way as she glanced down at the polished, pointed-tipped boots. Her foot and ankle looked very pretty. She could not realize that they belonged to her and were a part of herself. She wanted an excellent and stylish fit, she told the young fellow who served her, and she did not mind the difference of a dollar or two more in the price so long as she got what she desired.

It was a long time since Mrs Sommers had been fitted with gloves. On rare occasions when she had bought a pair they were always 'bargains', so cheap that it would have been preposterous and unreasonable to have expected them to be fitted to the hand.

Now she rested her elbow on the cushion of the glove counter, and a pretty, pleasant young creature, delicate and deft of touch, drew a long-wristed 'kid' over Mrs Sommers' hand. She smoothed it down over the wrist and buttoned it neatly, and both lost themselves for a second or two in admiring contemplation of the little symmetrical gloved hand. But there were other places where money might be spent.

There were books and magazines piled up in the window of a stall a few paces down the street. Mrs Sommers bought two high-priced magazines such as she had been accustomed to read in the days when she had been accustomed to other pleasant things. She carried them without wrapping. As well as she could she lifted her skirts at the crossings. Her stockings and boots and well-fitting gloves had worked marvels in her bearing – had given her a feeling of assurance, a sense of belonging to the well-dressed multitude.

She was very hungry. Another time she would have stilled the cravings for food until reaching her own home, where she would have brewed herself a cup of tea and taken a snack of anything that was available. But the impulse that was guiding her would not suffer her to entertain any such thought.

There was a restaurant at the corner. She had never entered its doors; from the outside she had sometimes caught glimpses of spotless damask and shining crystal, and soft-stepping waiters serving people of fashion.

When she entered her appearance created no surprise, no consternation, as she had half feared it might. She seated herself at a small table alone, and an attentive waiter at once approached to take her order. She did not want a profusion; she craved a nice and tasty bite – a half dozen blue-points, a plump chop with cress, a something sweet – a crème-frappée, for instance; a glass of Rhine wine, and after all a small cup of black coffee.

While waiting to be served she removed her gloves very leisurely and laid them beside her. Then she picked up a magazine and glanced through it, cutting the pages[1] with a blunt edge of her knife. It was all very agreeable. The damask was even more spotless than it had seemed through the window, and the crystal more sparkling. There were quiet ladies and gentlemen, who did not notice her, lunching at the small tables like her own. A soft, pleasing strain of music could be heard, and a gentle breeze was blowing through the window. She tasted a bite, and she read a word or two, and she sipped the amber wine and wiggled her toes in the silk stockings. The price of it made no difference. She counted the money out to the waiter and left an extra coin on his tray, whereupon he bowed before her as before a princess of royal blood.

There was still money in her purse, and her next temptation presented itself in the shape of a matinée poster.

It was a little later when she entered the theatre, the play had begun and the house seemed to her to be packed. But there were vacant seats here and there, and into one of them she was ushered, between brilliantly dressed women who had gone there to kill time and eat candy and display their gaudy attire. There were many others who were there solely for the play and acting. It is safe to say there was no one present who bore quite the attitude which Mrs Sommers did to her surroundings. She gathered in the whole – stage and players and people in one wide impression, and absorbed it and enjoyed it. She laughed at the comedy and wept – she and the gaudy woman next to her wept over the tragedy. And they talked a little together over it. And the gaudy woman wiped her eyes and sniffled on a tiny square of filmy, perfumed lace and passed little Mrs Sommers her box of candy.

The play was over, the music ceased, the crowd filed out. It was like a dream ended. People scattered in all directions. Mrs Sommers went to the corner and waited for the cable car.

A man with keen eyes, who sat opposite to her, seemed to like the study of her small, pale face. It puzzled him to decipher what he saw there. In truth, he saw nothing – unless he were wizard enough to detect a poignant wish, a powerful longing that the cable car would never stop anywhere, but go on and on with her for ever.

The Stir Outside The Café Royal

A Story of Miss Van Snoop,
Detective

Colonel Mathurin was one of the aristocrats of crime; at least Mathurin was the name under which he had accomplished a daring bank robbery in Detroit which had involved the violent death of the manager, though it was generally believed by the police that the Rossiter who was at the bottom of some long firm frauds[1] in Melbourne was none other than Mathurin under another name, and that the designer and chief gainer in a sensational murder case in the Midlands was the same mysterious and ubiquitous personage.

But Mathurin had for some years successfully eluded pursuit; indeed, it was generally known that he was the most desperate among criminals, and was determined never to be taken alive. Moreover, as he invariably worked through subordinates who knew nothing of his whereabouts and were scarcely acquainted with his appearance, the police had but a slender clue to his identity.

As a matter of fact, only two people beyond his immediate associates in crime could have sworn to Mathurin if they had met him face to face. One of them was the Detroit bank manager whom he had shot with his own hand before the eyes of his fiancée. It was through the other that Mathurin was arrested, extradited to the States and finally made to atone for his life of crime. It all happened in a distressingly commonplace way, so far as the average spectator was concerned. But the story, which I have pieced together from the details supplied – firstly, by a certain detective sergeant whom I met in a tavern hard by Westminster; and secondly, by a certain young woman named Miss Van Snoop – has an element of romance, if you look below the surface.

It was about half past one o'clock, on a bright and pleasant day, that a young lady was driving down Regent Street in a hansom which she had picked up outside her boarding-house near Portland Road Station. She had told the cabman to drive slowly, as she was nervous behind a horse; and so she had leisure to scan, with the curiosity of a stranger, the strolling crowd that at nearly all hours of the day throngs Regent Street. It was a sunny morning, and everybody looked cheerful. Ladies were shopping, or looking in at the shop windows. Men about town were collecting an appetite for lunch; flower girls were selling 'nice vi'lets, sweet vi'lets, penny a bunch'; and the girl in the cab leaned one arm on the apron and regarded the scene with alert attention. She was not exactly pretty, for the symmetry of her features was discounted by a certain hardness in the set of the mouth. But her hair, so dark as to be almost black, and her eyes of greyish blue set her beyond comparison with the commonplace.

Just outside the Café Royal[2] there was a slight stir, and a temporary block in the foot traffic. A brougham was setting down, behind it was a victoria, and behind that a hansom; and as the girl glanced round the heads of the pair in the brougham, she saw several men standing on the steps. Leaning back suddenly, she opened the trapdoor in the roof.

'Stop here,' she said, 'I've changed my mind.'

The driver drew up by the kerb, and the girl skipped out.

'You shan't lose by the change,' she said, handing him half-a-crown.

There was a tinge of American accent in the voice; and the cabman, pocketing the half-crown with thanks, smiled.

'They may talk about that McKinley tariff,'[3] he soliloquized as he crawled along the kerb towards Piccadilly Circus, 'but it's better 'n free trade – lumps!'

Meanwhile the girl walked slowly back towards the Café Royal, and, with a quick glance at the men who were standing there, entered. One or two of the men raised their eyebrows; but the girl was quite unconscious, and went on her way to the luncheon room.

'American, you bet,' said one of the loungers. 'They'll go anywhere and do anything.'

Just in front of her as she entered was a tall, clean-shaven man, faultlessly dressed in glossy silk hat and frock coat, with a flower in his buttonhole. He looked around for a moment in search of a convenient table. As he hesitated, the girl hesitated; but when the waiter waved him to a small table laid for two, the girl immediately sat down behind him at the next table.

'Excuse me, madam,' said the waiter, 'this table is set for four; would you mind—'

'I guess,' said the girl, 'I'll stay where I am.' And the look in her eyes, as well as a certain sensation in the waiter's palm, ensured her against further disturbance.

The restaurant was full of people lunching, singly or in twos, in threes and even larger parties; and many curious glances were directed to the girl who sat at a table alone and pursued her way calmly through the menu. But the girl appeared to notice no one. When her eyes were off her plate they were fixed straight ahead – on the back of the man who had entered in front of her. The man, who had drunk a half-bottle of champagne with his lunch, ordered a liqueur to accompany his coffee. The girl, who had drunk an aerated water, leaned back in her chair and wrinkled her brows. They were very straight brows, that seemed to meet over her nose when she wrinkled them in perplexity. Then she called a waiter.

'Bring me a sheet of notepaper, please,' she said, 'and my bill.'

The waiter laid the sheet of paper before her, and the girl proceeded, after a few moments' thought, to write a few lines in pencil upon it. When this was done, she folded the sheet carefully, and laid it in her purse. Then, having paid her bill, she returned her purse to her dress pocket, and waited patiently.

In a few minutes the clean-shaven man at the next table settled his bill and made preparations for departure. The girl at the same time drew on her gloves, keeping her eyes immovably upon her neighbour's back. As the man rose to depart, and passed the table at which the girl had been sitting, the girl was looking into the mirror upon the wall, and patting her hair. Then she turned and followed the man out of the restaurant, while a pair at an adjacent table remarked to one another that it was a rather curious coincidence for a man and woman to enter and leave at the same moment when they had no apparent connection.

But what happened outside was even more curious.

The man halted for a moment upon the steps at the entrance. The porter, who was in conversation with a policeman, turned, whistle in hand.

'Hansom, sir?' he asked.

'Yes,' said the clean-shaven man.

The porter was raising his whistle to his lips when he noticed the girl behind.

'Do you wish for a cab, madam?' he asked, and blew upon his whistle.

As he turned again for an answer, he plainly saw the girl, who was standing close behind the clean-shaven man, slip her hand under his coat, and snatch from his hip pocket something which she quickly transferred to her own.

'Well, I'm —' began the clean-shaven man, swinging round and feeling in his pocket.

'Have you missed anything, sir?' said the porter, standing full in front of the girl to bar her exit.

'My cigarette-case is gone,' said the man, looking from one side to another.

'What's this?' said the policeman, stepping forward.

'I saw the woman's hand in the gentleman's pocket, plain as a pikestaff,' said the porter.

'Oh, that's it, is it?' said the policeman, coming close to the girl. 'I thought as much.'

'Come now,' said the clean-shaven man, 'I don't want to make a fuss. Just hand back that cigarette-case, and we'll say no more about it.'

'I haven't got it,' said the girl. 'How dare you? I never touched your pocket.'

The man's face darkened.

'Oh, come now!' said the porter.

'Look here, that won't do,' said the policeman, 'you'll have to come along of me. Better take a four-wheeler, eh, sir?'

For a knot of loafers, seeing something interesting in the wind, had collected round the entrance.

A four-wheeler was called, and the girl entered, closely followed by the policeman and the clean-shaven man.

'I was never so insulted in my life,' said the girl.

Nevertheless, she sat back quite calmly in the cab, as though she was perfectly ready to face this or any other situation, while the policeman watched her closely to make sure that she did not dispose in any surreptitious way of the stolen article.

At the police station hard by, the usual formalities were gone through, and the clean-shaven man was constituted prosecutor. But the girl stoutly denied having been guilty of any offence.

The inspector in charge looked doubtful.

'Better search her,' he said.

And the girl was led off to a room for an interview with the female searcher.

The moment the door closed the girl put her hand into her pocket, pulled out the cigarette-case and laid it upon the table.

'There you are,' she said. 'That will fix matters so far.'

The woman looked rather surprised.

'Now,' said the girl, holding out her arms, 'feel in this other pocket, and find my purse.'

The woman picked out the purse.

'Open it and read the note on the bit of paper inside.'

On the sheet of paper which the waiter had given her, the girl had written these words, which the searcher read in a muttered undertone –

'I am going to pick this man's pocket as the best way of getting him into a police station without violence. He is Colonel Mathurin, alias Rossiter, alias Connell, and he is wanted in Detroit, New York, Melbourne, Colombo and London. Get four men to pin him unawares, for he is armed and desperate. I an a member of the New York detective force – Nora Van Snoop.'

'It's all right,' said Miss Van Snoop, quickly, as the searcher looked up at her after reading the note. 'Show that to the boss – right away.'

The searcher opened the door. After whispered consultation the inspector appeared, holding the note in his hand.

'Now then, be spry,' said Miss Van Snoop. 'Oh, you needn't worry!

I've got my credentials right here,' and she dived into another pocket.

'But do you know – can you be sure,' said the inspector, 'that this is the man who shot the Detroit bank manager?'

'Great heavens! Didn't I see him shoot Will Stevens with my own eyes! And didn't I take service with the police to hunt him out?'

The girl stamped her foot, and the inspector left. For two, three, four minutes, she stood listening intently. Then a muffled shout reached her ears. Two minutes later the inspector returned.

'I think you're right,' he said. 'We have found enough evidence on him to identify him. But why didn't you give him in charge before to the police?'

'I wanted to arrest him myself,' said Miss Van Snoop, 'and I have. Oh, Will! Will!'

Miss Van Snoop sank into a cane-bottomed chair, laid her head upon the table, and cried. She had earned the luxury of hysterics. In half an hour she left the station, and, proceeding to a post office, cabled her resignation to the head of the detective force in New York.

SARAH GRAND

When the Door Opened—

What curious glimpses of life one catches sometimes unawares, scenes that flash forth distinctly from the tangled mass of movement, the crowded details, the inextricable confusion of human affairs as they appear to the looker-on in a great city. Seen amidst all the turmoil, from a hansom cab, from the top of an omnibus, from the platform of an underground station in a train that stops for a minute, from the pavement in a carriage blocked in the stream of traffic, by day and night, from out of the routine, the commonplace doings of people in the commonplace moods and phrases which weave themselves into the length of wholesome lives, they stand out to view, these intervals of intensity, the beginnings of episodes – tragic, heroic, amorous, abject; or the conclusions, which make the turning point the crisis of a life. If it be the beginning, how one aches to know what the end will be; and if it be the end, what would not one give for the first part!

For instance: I was coming home alone late one night by train from a distant suburb, and happened to get into a carriage with three other people. One of them was a man of about forty, with dark hair going grey, and a pleasant, clean-cut, well-disciplined face. The other two were husband and wife, the husband being a good deal older than the wife. There seemed to have been some disagreement between the pair before I got into the carriage, for the lady looked sulky and dejected, while the gentleman was a good deal ruffled. He spoke a word or two to the other passenger, however, in a way which showed that they were acquainted, and also, as it seemed to me, for the purpose of keeping up appearances. The lady, on the contrary, made no attempt to disguise her feelings, but sat silent and rigid, staring into the darkness, until the train stopped, when her husband grimly handed her out, and I was left alone with the third passenger.

We watched the pair walk off together, and it was obvious that the quarrel recommenced before they had taken many steps. My solitary fellow passenger sat opposite to me, and when the two had passed out of sight, our eyes met with an involuntary glance of intelligence, and he shrugged his shoulders slightly.

'I should like to give that pair a piece of advice,' slipped from me unawares.

'Ah!' he said, 'so should I; but it is an impossible thing to do in such cases.'

'I suppose you are thinking that people know their own business best,' I rejoined.

'No, I am not,' he answered. 'The lookers-on see most of the game, you know. But, nevertheless, it is worse than useless to offer advice to a married pair – especially when they are both wrong-headed,' he added. 'But even right-headed people, with the best intentions, make terrible mistakes; and in their own cases too, when they might be expected to know what they are about. Now, that man who was here just now watches his wife, and keeps her shut up, or only allows her out under escort, as if he thought that she would certainly misconduct herself if ever she had an opportunity. The consequence is that she is growing to dislike and despise him, and he may drive her in the end to do the very thing he is guarding against. I cannot understand how a man can care to have a bond-slave, always under orders, for a wife. Personally, I prefer a free woman; and I should be sorry to think that liberty means licence in any but exceptional cases.'

'But there, it seems to me, a difficulty arises,' I observed. 'How is a man to tell which will prove an exceptional case?'

'Oh, I should think there is no difficulty about that,' he answered. 'Girls give indications of character early enough; and at any rate, if they are not trustworthy, dogging them about won't make them so. I don't say, however, that a young and thoughtless girl should be cast entirely upon her own resources; only, what she wants is a companion, not a keeper. However, as I said just now, the right ordering of married lives is a matter in which even the best-intentioned people may make mistakes. I married a girl somewhat younger than myself – about ten years – not that I think that makes a difference if people agree in their tastes. It so happened, however, that we did not agree. I am fond of a quiet life, with full leisure for art and literature, and dislike nothing so much as killing time in idle chatter at entertainments where one is not entertained. My wife, on the contrary, as I found out very soon after we were married, is positively bored by books and pictures, and is never so happy as when she is in the full whirl of the social maëlstrom. Well, I thought the matter out, and the justice of the case seemed to me to demand that she should not require me to go into society, and that I should not require her to stay at home. We were fond of each other, but I could not see why on that account either of us should have our life spoilt by being made to conform to the uncongenial tastes and habits of the other. Marriage must be a perfect institution when there is entire similarity of interests; but if there is not, I cannot see why people should be miserable. So I let my wife go her way and I went mine, and the plan seemed to be answering capitally. There were times when she would have liked me to go out with her, and there were times when I should have been glad if she had stayed at home with me; and occasionally we conformed to one another's secret wishes in these respects, but I cannot say that the self-sacrifice was much of a success. There was one fancy-dress ball – a public affair – that she particularly wanted to go to, and I thought she half hinted that I should accompany her; if so, I did not take the hint; I knew I should be so bored.

'She went to that ball rather conspicuously well-dressed in silver-grey domino, lined with pink silk and trimmed with white lace. Her fan was white ostrich feathers, and her mask was trimmed with lace, which concealed her mouth. She had been quite excited about going, but when it came to the point she did not seem so very eager after all. She was to meet some friends there, and I said I would sit up for her, and she promised not to be late.

'After she had gone, I felt depressed somehow. I got a book and cigar, but did not find either of them absorbing. My mind wandered when I tried to read, and I had to give up at last, and just settle myself to smoke and think things out.

'I began to wonder what my wife was doing at the ball, and if she had found her friends all right. Then it occurred to me that it would be very awkward if, by some mistake, they did not meet. All kinds of people go to these public balls, and manners are apt to be free-and-easy when masks are worn. My wife, even in her domino, gave the impression of youth and good looks. She might be subjected to some annoyance from the bounders who haunt such places. At that moment she might be dancing with some very undesirable partner. Had I done right to let her go alone? I threw my cigar into the fireplace and got up, but without any distinct idea; in fact, I stood for a little, as one does sometimes in a difficulty, with all thought suspended. Then I recollected a fancy dress I had had for a ball I went to before I met my wife. It was the black velvet costume of a Spanish Don of the period of Philip IV – the Velasquez period[1] – a handsome dress copied from a picture, and well made. I went to my studio and there I found it in an old chest, and the mask I had worn along with it.

'It was still early in the night – why not dress and go to the ball also? My wife had taken the carriage, but there were some livery stables near, and I could easily get a brougham. I rang for my man and sent him to fetch me one.

'The ball was in full swing when I arrived, but by great good luck almost the first person I saw was my wife. The silver-grey, pale pink, white lace and white ostrich-feather fan made an easily distinguishable costume, and I recognized her at once, and made my way through the crowd towards her. But as I approached I realized that she could not possibly recognize me. She had never seen me in that dress – she probably did not even know that I had it; yet, although I was walking straight up to her, and she saw that I was, she made no sign of objection. Was it possible that she would let a strange man speak to her, and even encourage him to do so by her attitude? The horrible doubt shot such a pang through my heart that I determined to set it at rest for ever by making the experiment. Without waiting to ask myself whether it was a fair or an unfair thing to do, I addressed her in a feigned voice familiarly.

'"I fancy that you are waiting for me," I said. "Please say that you are."

'"Well, I am waiting for something exciting to happen," she answered, also disguising her voice, and speaking with the easy assurance of one who is accustomed to such encounters; "for standing here alone is not lively."

'For a moment the tawdry splendour of the scene was blotted out. I could neither see nor hear. I recovered myself, however, just as the band struck up, and asked her mechanically if I might have the pleasure of a dance.

'"I shall be delighted," she replied, taking my arm at once, and leading me, rather than waiting to be led, through the motley crew about us to the ballroom, in a free-and-easy way that filled me with consternation. In her right mind, she had always seemed to be reserved with strangers, and I should never have imagined that a mask would have made such a difference.

'She danced with the abandonment of a ballet girl, and when the music ceased, she asked me for ice and liqueur, and showed me the way to the refreshment room. When she had had all she wanted, and it was a good deal, she took my arm again, and we began to walk about. She seemed to know all the ins-and-outs of the place, which surprised me, for I did not suppose that she had ever been there before. I asked her, however.

'"Have I ever been here before!" she ejaculated, "I should just think so! I come whenever I can."

'"Do you tell your husband?" I ventured.

'"Oh, my husband!" she exclaimed. "But who told you that I had a husband, by the way?"

'"I feel sure that a lady of your personal attractions and charms of manner cannot fail to have a husband," I answered.

'"Ah, courtier," she said, "heigho! What a difference between husbands and lovers. Aren't women fools to marry if they can make love for a livelihood?"

'She clasped her hands round my arm as she spoke, and looked up into my face alluringly. Was this the true woman, I wondered, and was that other to whom I was accustomed, only an actress earning her living? No, I could not believe it. I argued with myself that the manner and sentiments were assumed with the dress, that they were part of the masquerade; but she could not have done it so well without much experience, and she confessed that she came here often, which argued deceit, for I had never had a hint of it. Indeed, the reason she gave me for going that night was, that she had never been to a mask-ball. O thrice accursed fool that I was to let her come alone! Yet perhaps it was just as well. I knew that she was frivolous, but had never suspected that she was fast. Indeed, I would have wagered my soul that she was to be trusted anywhere, so she had taken me in finely, and it was just as well that I should know it. Doubtless my friends had known it all along, and pitied me for a blind, weak fool. But it was a shock, I can tell you, and I was in two minds the whole time. In the one I condemned her utterly, in the other I was trying to excuse her. Appearances were all against her certainly; but the habit of love and respect is not to be changed in a moment. And, after all, what had she done that could not be excused? She had talked in a vulgar way certainly, but I had not presumed upon it. If I had taken the slightest liberty, doubtless she would have resented it promptly. Would she?

'Her hand was resting on my arm. I hesitated a moment, then I took it and pressed it. To my horror, she laughed, and returned the pressure.

'"You are waking up, Don Sombre," she said. "I was beginning to fear that you were one of the doomed-to-dumps, you were so cold and dull. But the dumps don't last long when I'm about. I'll soon cheer you up and put some life in you."

'I felt a horrid emotion at these words, and it was some moments before I could master my voice. I was a broken man, and longed to sit down and cry like a child. It was sorrow that had come upon me, not anger. One is not angry where there is no hope; one is crushed. And yet, although I knew there was no hope, I was like a gambler who must stake again. I determined to go a little further, just to give her a last chance.

'"You have cheered me to such good purpose that I do not feel inclined to part with you," I said; "but this crowd is distracting. Let us get out of it. I have a carriage waiting: will you come home with me?"

'"Why, he's quite nervous," she said, laughing. "Now, that *is* nice;

for I could swear, Don Sombre, that you're not accustomed to 'No' from a lady."

'"Why is it nice?" I asked.

'"Well, you wouldn't be nervous if you were indifferent, you know," she said archly. "I can't stand your cold-blooded creatures who don't care a button either way."

'"Then I ought to please you," I answered grimly, "for, as you rightly perceive, I do care greatly. Will you come?"

'She laughed again. Good heavens! Was that acquiescence? I drew her towards the main entrance with the impetuosity of a young lover, and she did not demur. She remarked that I seemed to be impatient, and impatient I was. Every moment was an hour of pain now until the ghastly farce was over. But I could not end it there and then. It was too serious. I must get her home. I went down the street myself to fetch my hired brougham, so that my name might not be called out, and I told the man to go back before I returned to hand her in. I was afraid of a scene in that public place if she suddenly discovered who I was, and it seemed an interminable time until we started. We were clear of the crowd, and off at last, however; but for the first few minutes I sat beside her unable to utter a word, and she began to rally me again on the subject of my gloom. Then she fell up against me, but whether because the carriage lurched, or out of mere wantonness, I could not tell. However, I put my arm round her, and she did not object.

'"Where do you live?" she asked, as we neared the house. "These streets are all alike, and I cannot tell where I am."

'"Well, we are there, at any rate," I answered, as the carriage stopped. I handed her out, and opened the door with my latchkey. The light was so low in the hall I had to take her hand to lead her up to the drawing room. There all was darkness, but I had matches in my pocket, and lit the gas.

'Then I turned to her. She was giggling at something, but did not seem to see where she was.

'"Now, madam," I said sternly, "we will unmask."

'In a moment she had taken hers off, and slipped out of her domino.

'I gazed, I gasped, I fell into a chair! The woman before me was a perfect stranger – a creature with dyed hair, blackened eyelids, and painted cheeks – not the sort of person to be seen with anywhere if one valued one's reputation, and yet I could have gone down on my knees and kissed the hem of her garment, so great was my relief. I shall never forget it! For the first few minutes I could think of nothing, do nothing, but just sit there gazing at her, and smiling idiotically. She was flattered by my attitude, which she mistook for speechless admiration, and she stood still, posing in a theatrical manner, with an affectation of coyness, until I recovered myself.

'My first clear idea was that I must get rid of her; but how to do it without offering her any indignity? I was casting about in my mind for a plausible excuse; but before anything occurred to me, a carriage stopped at the door below, I heard a key turned in the lock, then the rustle of silk, and a light step on the staircase. My wife had returned early as she had promised, and was coming straight up to the drawing room.

'Her hand was already on the handle of the door—'

He broke off at this point and looked out of the window. The train had stopped, but we had not noticed it at the moment.

'Hello!' he exclaimed, 'this is my station!' and out he jumped just as we were moving off again.

I have never seen him since; I do not suppose that I ever shall. So I expect that all my life long I shall be tormented with conjectures as to what happened when that door opened.

KATE CHOPIN

The Storm

A Sequel to 'At the 'Cadian Ball'

I

The leaves were so still that even Bibi thought it was going to rain. Bobinôt, who was accustomed to converse on terms of perfect equality with his little son, called the child's attention to certain sombre clouds that were rolling with sinister intention from the west, accompanied by a sullen, threatening roar. They were at Friedheimer's store and decided to remain there till the storm had passed. They sat within the door on two empty kegs. Bibi was four years old and looked very wise.

'Mama'll be 'fraid, yes,' he suggested with blinking eyes.

'She'll shut the house. Maybe she got Sylvie helpin' her this evenin',' Bobinôt responded reassuringly.

'No; she ent got Sylvie. Sylvie was helpin' her yistiday,' piped Bibi.

Bobinôt arose and going across to the counter purchased a can of shrimps, of which Calixta was very fond. Then he returned to his perch on the keg and sat stolidly holding the can of shrimps while the storm burst. It shook the wooden store and seemed to be ripping great furrows in the distant field. Bibi laid his little hand on his father's knee and was not afraid.

2

Calixta, at home, felt no uneasiness for their safety. She sat at a side window sewing furiously on a sewing machine. She was greatly occupied and did not notice the approaching storm. But she felt very warm and often stopped to mop her face on which the perspiration gathered in beads. She unfastened her white sacque at the throat. It began to grow dark, and suddenly realizing the situation she got up hurriedly and went about closing windows and doors.

Out on the small front gallery she had hung Bobinôt's Sunday clothes to air and she hastened out to gather them before the rain fell. As she stepped outside, Alcée Laballière rode in at the gate. She had not seen him very often since her marriage, and never alone. She stood there with Bobinôt's coat in her hands, and the big raindrops began to fall. Alcée rode his horse under the shelter of a side projection where the chickens had huddled and there were ploughs and a harrow piled up in the corner.

'May I come and wait on your gallery till the storm is over, Calixta?' he asked.

'Come 'long in, M'sieur Alcée.'

His voice and her own startled her as if from a trance, and she seized Bobinôt's vest. Alcée, mounting to the porch, grabbed the trousers and snatched Bibi's braided jacket that was about to be carried away by a sudden gust of wind. He expressed an intention to remain outside, but it was soon apparent that he might as well have been out in the open: the water beat in upon the boards in driving sheets, and he went inside, closing the door after him. It was even necessary to put something beneath the door to keep the water out.

'My! what a rain! It's good two years sence it rain' like that,' exclaimed Calixta as she rolled up a piece of bagging and Alcée helped her to thrust it beneath the crack.

She was a little fuller of figure than five years before when she married; but she had lost nothing of her vivacity. Her blue eyes still retained their melting quality; and her yellow hair, dishevelled by the wind and rain, kinked more stubbornly than ever about her ears and temples.

The rain beat upon the low, shingled roof with a force and clatter that threatened to break an entrance and deluge them there. They were in the dining room – the sitting room – the general utility room. Adjoining was her bedroom, with Bibi's couch alongside her own. The door stood open, and the room with its white, monumental bed, its closed shutters, looked dim and mysterious.

Alcée flung himself into a rocker and Calixta nervously began to gather up from the floor the lengths of a cotton sheet which she had been sewing.

'If this keeps up, *Dieu sait* if the levees goin' to stan' it!' she exclaimed.

'What have you got to do with the levees?'

'I got enough to do! An' there's Bobinôt with Bibi out in that storm – if he only didn' left Friedheimer's!'

'Let us hope, Calixta, that Bobinôt's got sense enough to come in out of a cyclone.'

She went and stood at the window with a greatly disturbed look on her face. She wiped the frame that was clouded with moisture. It was stiflingly hot. Alcé got up and joined her at the window, looking over her shoulder. The rain was coming down in sheets obscuring the view of far-off cabins and enveloping the distant wood in a grey mist. The playing of the lightning was incessant. A bolt struck a tall chinaberry tree at the edge of the field. It filled all visible space with a blinding glare and the crash seemed to invade the very boards they stood upon.

Calixta put her hands to her eyes, and with a cry, staggered backward. Alcée's arm encircled her, and for an instant he drew her close and spasmodically to him.

'*Bonté!*' she cried, releasing herself from his encircling arm and retreating from the window, 'the house'll go next! If I only knew w'ere Bibi was!' She would not compose herself; she would not be seated. Alcée clasped her shoulders and looked into her face. The contact of her warm, palpitating body when he had unthinkingly drawn her into his arms, had aroused all the old-time infatuation and desire for her flesh.

'Calixta,' he said, 'don't be frightened. Nothing can happen. The house is too low to be struck, with so many tall trees standing about. There! aren't you going to be quiet? say, aren't you?' He pushed her hair back from her face that was warm and steaming. Her lips were as red and moist as pomegranate seed. Her white neck and a glimpse of her full, firm bosom disturbed him powerfully. As she glanced up at him the fear in her liquid blue eyes had given place to a drowsy gleam that unconsciously betrayed a sensuous desire. He looked down into her eyes and there was nothing for him to do but to gather her lips in a kiss. It reminded him of Assumption.[1]

'Do you remember – in Assumption, Calixta?' he asked in a low voice broken by passion. Oh! she remembered; for in Assumption he had kissed her and kissed and kissed her; until his senses would well nigh fail, and to save her he would resort to a desperate flight. If she was not an immaculate dove in those days, she was still inviolate; a passionate creature whose very defencelessness had made her defence, against which his honour forbade him to prevail. Now – well, now – her lips seemed in a manner free to be tasted, as well as her round, white throat and her whiter breasts.

They did not heed the crashing torrents, and the roar of the elements made her laugh as she lay in his arms. She was a revelation in that dim, mysterious chamber; as white as the couch she lay upon. Her firm, elastic flesh that was knowing for the first time its birthright, was like a creamy lily that the sun invites to contribute its breath and perfume to the undying life of the world.

The generous abundance of her passion, without guile or trickery, was like a white flame which penetrated and found response in depths of his own sensuous nature that had never yet been reached.

When he touched her breasts they gave themselves up in quivering ecstasy, inviting his lips. Her mouth was a fountain of delight. And when he possessed her, they seemed to swoon together at the very borderland of life's mystery.

He stayed cushioned upon her, breathless, dazed, enervated, with his heart beating like a hammer upon her. With one hand she clasped his head, her lips lightly touching his forehead. The other hand stroked with a soothing rhythm his muscular shoulders.

The growl of the thunder was distant and passing away. The rain beat softly upon the shingles, inviting them to drowsiness and sleep. But they dared not yield.

The rain was over; and the sun was turning the glistening green world into a palace of gems. Calixta, on the gallery, watched Alcée ride away. He turned and smiled at her with a beaming face; and she lifted her pretty chin in the air and laughed aloud.

3

Bobinôt and Bibi, trudging home, stopped without at the cistern to make themselves presentable.

'My! Bibi, w'at will yo' mama say! You ought to be ashame'. You oughtn' put on those good pants. Look at 'em! An' that mud on yo' collar! How you got that mud on yo' collar, Bibi? I never saw such a boy!' Bibi was the picture of pathetic resignation. Bobinôt was the embodiment of serious solicitude as he strove to remove from his own person and his son's the signs of their tramp over heavy roads and through wet fields. He scraped the mud off Bibi's bare legs and feet with a stick and carefully removed all traces from his heavy brogans. Then, prepared for the worst – the meeting with an over-scrupulous housewife, they entered cautiously at the back door.

Calixta was preparing supper. She had set the table and was dripping coffee at the hearth. She sprang up as they came in.

'Oh, Bobinôt! You back! My! but I was uneasy. W'ere you been during the rain? An' Bibi? he ain't wet? he ain't hurt?' She had clasped Bibi and was kissing him effusively. Bobinôt's explanations and apologies which he had been composing all along the way, died on his lips as Calixta felt him to see if he were dry, and seemed to express nothing but satisfaction at their safe return.

'I brought you some shrimps, Calixta,' offered Bobinôt, hauling the can from his ample side pocket and laying it on the table.

'Shrimps! Oh, Bobinôt! you too good fo' anything!' and she gave him a smacking kiss on the cheek that resounded. *J'vous réponds*, we'll have a feas' tonight! umph-umph!'

Bobinôt and Bibi began to relax and enjoy themselves, and when the three seated themselves at table they laughed much and so loud that anyone might have heard them as far away as Laballière's.

4

Alcée Laballière wrote to his wife, Clarisse, that night. It was a loving letter, full of tender solicitude. He told her not to hurry back, but if she and the babies liked it at Biloxi,[2] to stay a month longer. He was getting on nicely; and though he missed them, he was willing to bear the separation a while longer – realizing that their health and pleasure were the first things to be considered.

5

As for Clarisse, she was charmed upon receiving her husband's letter. She and the babies were doing well. The society was agreeable; many of her old friends and acquaintances were at the bay. And the first free breath since her marriage seemed to restore the pleasant liberty of her maiden days. Devoted as she was to her husband, their intimate conjugal life was something which she was more than willing to forgo for a while.

So the storm passed and everyone was happy.

SARAH GRAND

A New Sensation

It was the night of one of her famous little dinners, and she was sitting at the head of her own table, contemplating her guests. The moment was one of those, before the ice cream comes to promote thought by checking digestion, when the conversation is merriest and most intimate; and she knew that she should be satisfied, if not amused and pleased, yet there was no feeling of satisfaction in her heart. It was all so accustomed to her, so stale – foods, fruits, flowers, lights, harmonious colours, luxurious appointments, conventional people – all that goes to secure social success. How well she knew it! and how weary she was of the monotony – the monotony of wealth, than which nothing is more stultifying!

Mere social distinction had been her ambition. To shine in society – that had been her one aim in life – to rival women, to conquer men; and everything – money, position, personal appearance – had been in her favour. Her idea had been to perk about in new clothes and trifle with men; and the idea of the men with whom she trifled had also been to perk about in new clothes and trifle with women. She counted her conquests, boasting of them to her rivals, in satin boudoirs, while her conquests counted her in to their intimates at their clubs just in the same way. Kiss and tell was the practice of men and women alike in that set. With rare exceptions they all lived lives of treachery and intrigue, breaking the sacred laws of hospitality and otherwise betraying their friends, and there was neither love, loyalty nor satisfaction in any of them. For fifteen years she had pursued her pitiful purpose, and had had her triumphs; but now, at thirty-three, sitting there surveying her guests, she was suddenly seized upon by a great distaste for the present, a terrible dread of the future. What had it profited her? So many rivals humiliated, so many men at her feet, and her costumes described in the ladies' papers! The men in her set were too easy of conquest; the women – mere butterflies of fashion and frivolity – were not worth wasting her energies upon, and it is not history they make in the ladies' papers. Yes, certainly; she had shone in her set; but she knew well enough that her set was but a small clique, quite provincial in its narrowness, and altogether discredited by honourable people at home and abroad. So what was the use of it all? And what would be the end of it all? She had done no good in her time, she had made no name for herself. Old age would be upon her by and by; she would have to outlive youth and beauty, which were her stock-in-trade; she would have to descend into joyless oblivion, courted to the last for her money, no doubt, but ending unhonoured, unloved and unregretted.

There was a pause in the chatter. She felt she had been remiss. She should have borne her part in the conversation as hostess, and not snatched that moment for reflection.

'I've been thinking,' she remarked to the man on her right, 'I've been thinking that I need a new sensation.'

'And how do you propose to procure such a thing?' he asked, raising his eyebrows and languidly perusing her face, on which her life had written some tell-tale lines that he perfectly understood.

'You think it not possible?' she said, in the gentle, well-bred way that made her manner so charming.

'I think it would be difficult,' he answered without emphasis, his manner, in its easy indifference, being very much the counterpart of her own.

She turned to the man on the left.

'What do you think?' she said. 'Have I exhausted all the pleasures of all the spheres?'

'The pleasure of being yourself can never be exhausted,' he answered gallantly.

'Fatuous ass!' she thought. 'I knew he would say something to that effect. Why do men expect a woman to be pleased with empty insincerities which are an insult to her intellect?' She caught the eye of a lady opposite, who asked if she had any idea in her mind; but the question was so evidently put for the sake of saying something that she merely smiled archly in response, and the smile carried her easily over the necessity of answering.

When her guests had gone she strolled through the empty rooms. They were decorated to excess and reeked of luxury of the stifling kind reflected from France. Everywhere were hangings, everywhere was silk or satin, even on the ceilings. The house was lined like a bonbon box, and it suddenly seemed to her ridiculous. She felt the artificiality, the stuffiness of it, and her impulse was to tear down the hangings and fling the windows wide open. It would have done her good to use her idle arms, to rouse herself to action, to rise to a burst of energetic enthusiasm, even if only for a moment, and expend it on wrecking the place. But there were servants about. One of them in the hall was rearranging a curtain which had fallen away from the pillar it should have been draping. He looked at the lady as she strolled past him, but saw no sign on her placid face of the turmoil of discontent that was raging within.

She went to her own room and caught her maid yawning.

'I suppose you would be glad to go to bed?' she said, with unwonted consideration.

The woman made an ineffectual attempt to deny her weariness.

'Well, go,' said the lady. 'I don't want you tonight – or, stay – give me the "ABC".'

The maid brought it from an adjoining room.

Her mistress turned over the pages hurriedly, then glanced at the clock. It was too late for a train that night.

'Never mind,' she said. 'I'm dying for a breath of fresh air. Pack up and we'll go into the country the first thing tomorrow morning.'

The next evening saw her settled at a little country inn, looking out over an old, wild common into a lovely lonely land. She had been there before with a picnic party in the height of summer; but she knew that the place had not been at its best then, because summer was like her own set – full-blown, that is to say, as to all its possibilities. Now early spring with its infinite promise was upon the land, and she had come expecting to find that delicious spot at its freshest and fairest, and had not been disappointed.

The evening was heavenly still. She had the long low lattice-window of her rustic parlour wide open, and was lounging on the broad window seat, with her elbow resting on the sill, and her head on her hand, looking out. The pure air held the delicate faint perfume of primroses. It fanned her cheek in gentle gusts intermittently, and when it subsided it was as if it had withdrawn to renew its freshness between each gust.

The tender saffron of the sunset, shading to green, lingered low down in the west. Below, to the left, was a clump of tall trees, whence there came at intervals the first sweet, soft, tentative notes of a nightingale, newly arrived, and not yet in full song. Above at the zenith, out of the clear dark indigo of the sky, a few white stars shone resplendent.

The nightingale! the nightingale!

As the lady sat there it seemed as if something evil and oppressive slipped like a cloud of cobwebs from her jaded soul, releasing it from contamination, and making way for her to come into possession of her better self.

The next morning the sun shone on the white wonder of cherry and pear trees all in full flower. She strolled out early. Dewdrops hung on every blade and branch; birds were building; sweetbriar scented the breeze. She took her way across the common slowly, inhaling deep breaths of the delicious air; looking; listening. Everywhere was colour, freshness, beauty; every little healthy creature was active and occupied; and the birds sang, full-throated, their morning songs. She picked the fragrant flowers from the yellow gorse, handfuls of them, all wet with dew, and felt that her youth was renewed.

At the further side of the common there was a ploughed field, surrounded by a quickset hedge which was all aflush with green where the young buds were bursting – the children's 'bread and cheese'.[1] She picked some of the buds and ate them in memory of the time when she was a little child.

On the other side of the hedge, in the ploughed field, the rooks were busy. Three of them rose and flew away. She saw their bright, dark, glossy wings shine iridescent against the cloud-flecked blue as they passed.

'Three for a wedding!' she said to herself blithely.

Then she turned and found herself face to face with a tall young man in a light tweed suit, and, being surprised, she flushed and dropped her parasol from under her arm where she was carrying it to have her hands free.

'I beg your pardon,' he said, raising his hat; 'I'm afraid I startled you.' He stooped and picked up her parasol for her.

Then he stared into her face with sudden intentness, as if he were taken aback or astonished by something he saw there; and, although she was accustomed to admiring glances, she flushed again, and smiled, and looked young.

Some little hard thing hit her face, then fell on the bosom of her dress. She looked down. It was a scarlet ladybird, speckled with black.

'That's for good luck,' she said.

'It's for fine weather, I should think,' he remarked prosaically.

And she was thankful for his sober prose. One of her own men would have turned the occasion to the usual kind of account with one of the usual fatuous compliments. But he was moving off with another salute.

'Stay,' she exclaimed – 'stay a moment, please! Can you tell me —'

He paused two paces from her and looked at her again with an odd expression.

'Can you tell me where I am?' she pursued. 'For I did not mark my road as I came, and now I don't see mine hostelry; and I doubt if I can find my way back.'

'Ah!' he answered, 'you must pay attention when you wander among the heights and hollows of the common.'

'Heights and hollows?' she exclaimed. 'I see none! Surely it is all one long level, with only shallow undulations?'

'Not shallow,' he said, 'but deep and difficult to find your way among if you are not observant. I've lost myself more than once. But I'm going to the inn now. If you will follow me, I'll show you the shortest cut.'

He strode on as he spoke, leaving her to follow him or not as she chose. She did choose. And as they pursued their way in silence she wondered mightily what manner of man this was, in well-cut clothes – she was apt to measure a man's worth by the cut of his clothes – who spoke with the accent of a gentleman, and lived not so very far from town, yet was so – unexpected. That was the word. But how refreshing it was to meet one such after the sophisticated club men whose every move and mood she could foresee accurately, whatever happened!

'I am staying here. Will you come in and rest?' she said, when they reached the inn, acting thoughtlessly on a hospitable impulse.

'I *am* coming in,' he answered in his slow way. 'I have some business here.'

'Thank you for guiding me,' she jerked out, taken aback and flushing hotly; and she hurried upstairs, leaving him on the doorstep. She entered her little parlour, panting, and threw herself into a chair, feeling horribly humiliated.

Presently there came a knock at the door.

'Come in!' she exclaimed irritably.

'I beg your pardon' – she looked round in surprise – 'you asked me in?'

'Yes,' she said shortly; 'and I thought you took the invitation – oddly.'

'You had gone before I could thank you,' he answered. 'You seem to be a very – sudden – lady. Or is it that I am clownishly slow?'

She looked into his honest, serious face and broke into a smile herself involuntarily, to which he instantly responded. 'What nice teeth he has!' she thought. The physical aspect of the man pleased her immensely. He was such a splendid young animal, so strong and healthy! But beyond that – the mere external man – if there were anything beyond, she was unaware of it.

'If you are clownishly slow, then I am shrewishly quick,' she said. 'Come in now and sit down. Do you live in this neighbourhood?'

He crossed the room in his deliberate way and settled himself in the window seat.

'Yes,' he answered. 'You pass my house on your way from the station.'

'On the way from the station? There is only one house – at least, I only saw one – a great castle sort of place on the other side of a hill, with beautiful gardens all about it.'

'That *is* my house,' he said absently.

He was looking at her with grim intentness. Then, as if with an effort, recollecting himself, he turned his head and looked out over the lovely landscape.

Her respect for him, which had been hovering down about zero, flew up to a hundred when she heard he was the master of a house like that. The man himself she could hardly appreciate, except in the outward aspect of him; but his commercial value, his position and house and acres – those things appealed to her. There is no more commercial-minded person in the world than your fashionable lady of good birth. She would barter her own soul if she could. This one had sold herself in marriage. Her husband, now dead, was an honest old City man, whom she had in her heart despised; but of the two, though his manner lacked the grace and charm of hers, he had been the pleasanter person to live with.

There was a silence after that last remark, but it was one of those silences which are strangely full of meaning; and she felt that there was that in it which was of deeper significance than anything which she had ever heard expressed in words. When those to whom she had hitherto been accustomed were silent, she knew they were searching their shallow pates for more material to make up into idle chatter. They were all effervescence, and cheap at that; but this was still wine of the rarer sort. What was he thinking of? What was he feeling? How strangely still it was! A bird called softly, 'Sip-sip-sip'. Her companion roused himself.

'That's the lesser white-throat,' he remarked. 'I expect he has his nest down there.'

'You must show it to me,' she answered dreamily.

A small copper butterfly and a little blue argus came fluttering into the room, fighting. The copper butterfly was buffeting the argus and spoiling its beauty.

'They fight wherever they meet, those two,' he said, watching the combat. 'They have fought since the beginning of time, and will fight on to the end, I should think. Would you believe that two such pretty creatures could be so pugnacious?'

She only smiled. But she was thinking cynically that she knew some pretty creatures of another species who were quite as bad. The butterflies, still buffeting each other, fluttered once more out into the open.

He rose. 'I must go,' he said.

'You will come again, I hope,' she answered, looking up at him without rising from her chair. The oval of her face showed to advantage in that attitude, and in the contemplation of it he forgot for a moment to answer her.

Then he said in his slow way, 'Yes. Yes. I will come again, thank you. For whom shall I ask?'

'My name is De Vigne,' she answered. 'Lady Flora de Vigne. Do you think it a pretty name?'

He considered a little, and then said 'Humph!' expressively. After which he drew a card-case from his pocket, took out a card, and laid it on the table. Then he bowed and left her.

She sat still for some time after he had gone, with her eyes shut, curiously conscious of everything – the sunshine, the sweet air, the scent of flowers, the 'sip-sip-sip' of the white-throat in the hazel bushes below; but above all of the little white card on the table. Who was he, this young knight of the open countenance, lord of that castle on the hill, and those fair grounds all dappled with spring flowers?

'They are his and he is – mine,' she ventured – reasoning by induction.

A little longer she rested with her eyes shut, giving way to ecstatic feeling. Then she rose, sighed, took up the card and read, 'Adam Woven Poleson, Market Gardener'.

Lady Flora laughed. Every time she looked at the card she laughed. But not mirthfully, for she was all ruffled. It was too absurd! And such a liberty into the bargain! Really things socially were coming to a pretty pass when a market gardener lived in a castle, looked lordly in Scotch tweed and spoke like a gentleman! More than anything she resented the cut of those clothes; any gentleman might have worn them. There was no telling now what sort of person one was speaking to. It was fatuous of her to have asked him to call again – and call again he certainly would. That sort of person is always pushing. Well, there were two ways out of it. Let him come, and then order some vegetables from him, or pack up and go.

She rang for her maid and ordered her to pack. They would catch the evening train after dinner.

Then she strolled out into the old inn garden and threw herself into a chair. Above, the sky was radiant blue, with great masses of snow-white cloud that drifted across it slowly, casting their shadows on the earth, and changing their shape continually.

Behind her the hill rose abruptly, covered with trees. About her were bushes budding and beds bright with spring flowers. In front was the long low house, and high above it, on the other side, appeared some grand old elms. There were bronze buds on the beeches. The horse chestnuts were well out in leaf. Tufts of purple anthers hung from the slender branches of the ash. The thick, rugged boles of the Scotch firs reflected warm, ruddy lights, and their canopies of deep blue-green showed dark against the tenderer foliage of the spring. Little flycatchers flitted in and out among the shrubs, a shy bullfinch piped unseen in an undertone, while a bold thrush on the topmost twig of an elm sang out at intervals divinely. The lady looked and listened without rendering an account of anything to herself; but by degrees the heavenly peace possessed her. What does anything matter so that we are at ease, sitting alone, untroubled, silent and satisfied? This was the first stage. But as the day declined there came a second, when thought was suspended, replaced by an exquisite sensation of well-being, a glow as of warmth and light and colour, and at intervals little shivers of delicate delight when the bird sang – the thrush, the thrush!

'Unpack again, please. I shan't go till tomorrow.' So she announced when she went in to dinner. But for two days after that she wandered about alone with a set countenance, restlessly, in a state of indecision. She wanted to go, and she wanted to stay – she didn't know what she wanted. Only, when she wanted to go, the birds and the butterflies, the trees and flowers, and fresh air, the outlook over the lovely lonely land, and the blue vaulted sky above, held her enchanted; but when she wanted to stay, the sight of that little white card, which she left lying on the table for an object lesson, moved her to joyless mirth, and impelled her forth. Had it but been 'My knight'! But 'My market gardener'! Impossible! She must go. Yet, why should she go? – driven away by the market gardener. Absurd! No! she would stay. She owed it to herself to put the market gardener in his place – that clown, indeed!

'I shall stay. Unpack, please.'

That was her final decision, and her weary maid, accustomed to her senseless caprices, for the third time patiently unpacked.

The next morning Lady Flora awoke in the grey dawn – awoke expectant, though she knew not of what. The spring was rapidly advancing. Cherry and pear tree whitened the ground with their snowflake flowers, and the apple trees in the orchard were tinged with a delicate pink. The little birds were trying their voices softly before they burst out into the full chorus with which they saluted the sunrise. She rose from her bed and leant out of the open window. There was new life in the air, and her pulses throbbed in response to the sweetness and joy of it.

Late in the afternoon she went out and found a bank all blue with angel's eyes; and there she sat, sunk in sensuous delight. She took an unwonted interest now in the world about her, the exquisite world of Nature, the healthy, happy world of tree and flower and bird and beast. It was as if her eyes had been opened to behold a new heaven and a new earth.[2] She had never seen such a spring before, never heard such songbirds. Every day brought its change of scene; they might have been numbered each by its own beauty. Only yesterday the buds of the beeches blushed red against the old grey boles; today their branches shone in the sunshine, all on a sudden bright-tinted with the tenderest green. And there were more butterflies, large white and orange-tip—

She had heard no footfall, but her daylight was darkened, and she looked up – looked up and flushed, and forgot the vegetables.

'I saw your red parasol,' he said. 'At first I thought it was a flower.'

He sat down beside her, very much at his ease, yet not more so than seemed natural. Now that she saw him again, well-dressed, if carelessly, and noted the intonation of his voice and the grace of his manner, she could not think of the incongruous market garden – at least, she did not find it weigh with her in her estimation of the man.

He held a book in his hand.

'What are you reading?' she asked.

He answered dreamily, gazing into the blue distance as if the words were there—

> 'Far flickers the flight of the swallows,
>   Far flutters the weft of the grass,
> Spun dense over desolate hollows,
>   More pale than the clouds as they pass:
> Thick-woven as the web of a witch is
>   Round the heart of a thrall that hath sinned,
> Whose youth and the wreck of its riches
>   Are waifs on the wind.'

There was a little pause, then she laughed her silent, mirthless laugh. 'I scent something ominous,' she said. 'What *is* that thing?'

'Swinburne – By the North Sea.'[3]

She had never even heard of the poem. 'Ah! it is beautiful!' he said, and then he broke out, and half-read, half-recited, one wonderful passage after another; and as she listened she glowed gradually with something like his own enthusiasm. He made little pauses between the passages – silences full of significance.

'It is strange,' he said at last, 'how this poem gets hold of one and sets up a sudden sea-hunger. Out here on the common sometimes I am so seized upon by it that I rush on and on, I don't know why, I don't know where – a sort of reindeer-rush to the sea.'

'You make me feel it, too,' she said.

But she deceived herself. The great yearning she had at her heart was not for the sea.

Alone in the garden late that night, listening to the nightingale now in full song, she said to herself tentatively, 'Adam! And why not – Adam? What was Adam the First but a gardener?'

The grand old gardener and his wife
Smile at the claims of long descent.[4]

And so would she – for the time being, at all events. She would stay and play the idyll out to the end. Exactly what the end would be she forbore to enquire of her inner self. But before it came, all the trees were out of flower, and the young green of the early summer was over the land. And there was no reason why it should have come to an end even then. It might have gone on for ever had she not become impatient of the pastime. It lingered too long in the early stage, however. An idyll to be interesting must swell up into a climax, and the climax must not be too long delayed else the interest flags.

She saw him – saw him continually – meeting him always in the same accidental way, walking and talking with him on terms of easy intimacy; satisfied with his companionship, and yet not satisfied – always expectant of a word that was never pronounced, of the climax that did not come. When would he speak? Naturally he was diffident (my market gardener!), she must encourage him delicately. And she tried, but she did not succeed. Her little, fashionable artifices, which never failed of their effect in her own set, all passed unheeded here. When her shoe came off he put it on again for her stolidly. When her ring stuck on her finger he prosaically suggested soap. If she appeared in a new costume he took not the slightest notice of it, never paid her a compliment, never alluded to her personal appearance at all. Yet she often caught him looking at her with curious intentness, just as all the others had done. What was he waiting for? Why didn't he speak? At last it occurred to her that she might startle him out of his bucolic apathy by announcing suddenly that she was going away. In the restful country people seemed indifferent to change; they were content to let themselves get into a groove and to stay there for ever if only the groove were easy. He must be roused.

The next time he came to the inn she waylaid him. It was towards evening and they strolled into the garden together and sat there side by side, not talking or thinking, just feeling the tranquil, happy beauty of the hour.

'How exquisite it is!' she sighed suddenly. 'And to think that tomorrow at this time I shall be in the whirl of the great wicked city once more! I shall think – I shall long – for – all this.'

'Are you going away?' he exclaimed.

Then there was a pause – that she had expected.

When he did speak it was very slowly. 'I am sorry,' he said simply. 'It has been a great pleasure to me – to come and see you – to talk to you. No lady – like you – had ever come into my life before.'

She rose nervously and they began to pace the garden path together. The nightingales answered each other in the trees above, the darkness deepened and the stars shone out.

He spoke again. 'Before you go I should like to tell you—' he began, then paused, greatly embarrassed. 'You will not think it a liberty?'

'I shall not think anything you may have to say to me a liberty,' she answered in a low voice, plucking at the laurel leaves as she spoke.

'You must have noticed how I stare at you sometimes?'

Noticed it? Her heart leaped. *My* market gardener!

'I feel,' he pursued in his deliberate way, 'I feel, now that you are going away, that I ought to apologize – I ought to explain. That first day that I saw you on the common it struck me – the likeness – an astonishing likeness – which made it a delight to look at you. You are exactly like the girl I am going to marry – older, of course, and with a different expression, but still wonderfully like.'

She stopped short, gasping – the clown!

'What's the matter?' he asked with concern.

'Nothing – nothing,' she answered.

'But you don't seem well?'

'It was nothing, really. It has passed – a sudden pang – unexpected, indescribable – a new sensation, in fact. So you are going to be married? Well, I hope you will be very happy. You must introduce the lady to me. And write to me sometimes, won't you? Now I must go back. Goodbye! Goodbye!'

She waved her hand to him gaily and was gone.

KATE CHOPIN

An Egyptian Cigarette

My friend, the Architect, who is something of a traveller, was showing us various curios which he had gathered during a visit to the Orient.

'Here is something for you,' he said, picking up a small box and turning it over in his hand. 'You are a cigarette-smoker; take this home with you. It was given to me in Cairo by a species of fakir, who fancied I had done him a good turn.'

The box was covered with glazed, yellow paper, so skilfully gummed as to appear to be all one piece. It bore no label, no stamp – nothing to indicate its contents.

'How do you know they are cigarettes?' I asked, taking the box and turning it stupidly around as one turns a sealed letter and speculates before opening it.

'I only know what he told me,' replied the Architect, 'but it is easy enough to determine the question of his integrity.' He handed me a sharp, pointed paper-cutter, and with it I opened the lid as carefully as possible.

The box contained six cigarettes, evidently handmade. The wrappers were of pale-yellow paper, and the tobacco was almost the same colour. It was of finer cut than the Turkish or ordinary Egyptian, and threads of it stuck out at either end.

'Will you try one now, Madam?' asked the Architect, offering to strike a match.

'Not now and not here,' I replied, 'after the coffee, if you will permit me to slip into your smoking den. Some of the women here detest the odour of cigarettes.'

The smoking room lay at the end of a short, curved passage. Its appointments were exclusively Oriental. A broad, low window opened out upon a balcony that overhung the garden. From the divan upon which I reclined, only the swaying tree-tops could be seen. The maple leaves glistened in the afternoon sun. Beside the divan was a low stand which contained the complete paraphernalia of a smoker. I was feeling quite comfortable, and congratulated myself upon having escaped for a while the incessant chatter of the women that reached me faintly.

I took a cigarette and lit it, placing the box upon the stand just as the tiny clock, which was there, chimed in silvery strokes the hour of five.

I took one long inspiration of the Egyptian cigarette. The grey-green smoke arose in a small puffy column that spread and broadened, that seemed to fill the room. I could see the maple leaves dimly, as if they were veiled in a shimmer of moonlight. A subtle, disturbing current passed through my whole body and went to my head like the fumes of disturbing wine. I took another deep inhalation of the cigarette.

'Ah! the sand has blistered my cheek! I have lain here all day with my face in the sand. Tonight, when the everlasting stars are burning, I shall drag myself to the river.'

He will never come back.

Thus far I followed him; with flying feet; with stumbling feet; with hands and knees, crawling; and outstretched arms, and here I have fallen in the sand.

The sand has blistered my cheek; it has blistered all my body, and the sun is crushing me with hot torture. There is shade beneath yonder cluster of palms.

I shall stay here in the sand till the hour and the night comes.

I laughed at the oracles and scoffed at the stars when they told that after the rapture of life I would open my arms inviting death, and the waters would envelop me.

Oh! how the sand blisters my cheek! and I have no tears to quench the fire. The river is cool and the night is not far distant.

I turned from the gods and said: 'There is but one; Bardja is my god.' That was when I decked myself with lilies and wove flowers into a garland and held him close in the frail, sweet fetters.

He will never come back. He turned upon his camel as he rode away. He turned and looked at me crouching here and laughed, showing his gleaming white teeth.

Whenever he kissed me and went away he always came back again. Whenever he flamed with fierce anger and left me with stinging words, he always came back. But today he neither kissed me nor was he angry. He only said:

'Oh! I am tired of fetters, and kisses, and you. I am going away. You will never see me again. I am going to the great city where men swarm like bees. I am going beyond, where the monster stones are rising heavenward in a monument for the unborn ages. Oh! I am tired. You will see me no more.'

And he rode away on his camel. He smiled and showed his cruel white teeth as he turned to look at me crouching here.

How slow the hours drag! It seems to me that I have lain here for days in the sand, feeding upon despair. Despair is bitter and it nourishes resolve.

I hear the wings of a bird flapping above my head, flying low, in circles.

The sun is gone.

The sand has crept between my lips and teeth and under my parched tongue.

If I raise my head, perhaps I shall see the evening star.

Oh! the pain in my arms and legs! My body is sore and bruised as if broken. Why can I not rise and run as I did this morning? Why must I drag myself thus like a wounded serpent, twisting and writhing?

The river is near at hand. I hear it – I see it – Oh! the sand! Oh! the shine! How cool! how cold!

The water! the water! In my eyes, my ears, my throat! It strangles me! Help! will the gods not help me?

Oh! the sweet rapture of rest! There is music in the Temple. And here is fruit to taste. Bardja came with the music – The moon shines and the breeze is soft – A garland of flowers – let us go into the King's garden and look at the blue lily, Bardja.

*

The maple leaves looked as if a silvery shimmer enveloped them. The grey-green smoke no longer filled the room. I could hardly lift the lids of my eyes. The weight of centuries seemed to suffocate my soul that struggled to escape, to free itself and breathe.

I had tasted the depths of human despair.

The little clock upon the stand pointed to a quarter past five. The cigarettes still reposed in the yellow box. Only the stub of the one I had smoked remained. I had laid it in the ashtray.

As I looked at the cigarettes in their pale wrappers, I wondered what other visions they might hold for me; what might I not find in their mystic fumes? Perhaps a vision of celestial peace; a dream of hopes fulfilled; a taste of rapture, such as had not entered into my mind to conceive.

I took the cigarettes and crumpled them between my hands. I walked to the window and spread my palms wide. The light breeze caught up the golden threads and bore them writhing and dancing far out among the maple leaves.

My friend, the Architect, lifted the curtain and entered, bringing me a second cup of coffee.

'How pale you are!' he exclaimed, solicitously. 'Are you not feeling well?'

'A little the worse for a dream,' I told him.

Talma Gordon

The Canterbury Club of Boston was holding its regular monthly meeting at the palatial Beacon Street residence of Dr William Thornton, expert medical practitioner and specialist. All the members were present, because some rare opinions were to be aired by men of profound thought on a question of vital importance to the life of the Republic, and because the club celebrated its anniversary in a home usually closed to society. The Doctor's winters, since his marriage, were passed at his summer home near his celebrated sanatorium. This winter found him in town with his wife and two boys. We had heard much of the beauty of the former, who was entirely unknown to social life, and about whose life and marriage we felt sure a romantic interest attached. The Doctor himself was too bright a luminary of the professional world to remain long hidden without creating comment. We had accepted the invitation to dine with alacrity, knowing that we should be welcomed to a banquet that would feast both eye and palate; but we had not been favoured by even a glimpse of the hostess. The subject for discussion was: 'Expansion; Its Effect upon the Future Development of the Anglo-Saxon throughout the World'.

Dinner was over, but we still sat about the social board discussing the question of the hour. The Hon. Herbert Clapp, eminent jurist and politician, had painted in glowing colours the advantages to be gained by the increase of wealth and the exalted position which expansion would give the United States in the councils of the great governments of the world. In smoothly flowing sentences marshalled in rhetorical order, with compact ideas, and incisive argument, he drew an effective picture with all the persuasive eloquence of the trained orator.

Joseph Whitman, the theologian of worldwide fame, accepted the arguments of Mr Clapp, but subordinated all to the great opportunity which expansion would give to the religious enthusiast. None could doubt the sincerity of this man, who looked once into the idealized face on which heaven had set the seal of consecration.

Various opinions were advanced by the twenty-five men present, but the host said nothing; he glanced from one to another with a look of amusement in his shrewd grey-blue eyes. 'Wonderful eyes,' said his patients who came under their magic spell. 'A wonderful man and a wonderful mind,' agreed his contemporaries, as they heard in amazement of some great cure of chronic or malignant disease which approached the supernatural.

'What do you think of this question, Doctor?' finally asked the president, turning to the silent host.

'Your arguments are good; they would convince almost anyone.'

'But not Doctor Thornton,' laughed the theologian.

'I acquiesce whichever way the result turns. Still, I like to view both sides of a question. We have considered but one tonight. Did you ever think that in spite of our prejudices against amalgamation, some of our descendants, indeed many of them, will inevitably intermarry among those far-off tribes of dark-skinned peoples, if they become a part of this great Union?'

'Among the lower classes that may occur, but not to any great extent,' remarked a college president.

'My experience teaches me that it will occur among all classes, and to an appalling extent,' replied the Doctor.

'You don't believe in intermarriage with other races?'

'Yes, most emphatically, when they possess decent moral development and physical perfection, for then we develop a superior being in the progeny born of the intermarriage. But if we are not ready to receive and assimilate the new material which will be brought to mingle with our pure Anglo-Saxon stream, we should call a halt in our expansion policy.'

'I must confess, Doctor, that in the idea of amalgamation you present a new thought to my mind. Will you not favour us with a few of your main points?' asked the president of the club, breaking the silence which followed the Doctor's remarks.

'Yes, Doctor, give us your theories on the subject. We may not agree with you, but we are all open to conviction.'

The Doctor removed the half-consumed cigar from his lips, drank what remained in his glass of the choice burgundy, and leaning back in his chair contemplated the earnest faces before him.

We may make laws, but laws are but straws in the hands of Omnipotence.

> 'There's a divinity that shapes our ends,
> Rough-hew them how we will.'[1]

And no man may combat fate. Given a man, propinquity, opportunity, fascinating femininity, and there you are. Black, white, green, yellow – nothing will prevent intermarriage. Position, wealth, family, friends – all sink into insignificance before the God-implanted instinct that made Adam, awakening from a deep sleep and finding the woman beside him, accept Eve as bone of his bone; he cared not nor questioned whence she came. So it is with the sons of Adam ever since, through the law of heredity which makes us all one common family. And so it will be with us in our re-formation of this old Republic. Perhaps I can make my meaning clearer by illustration, and with your permission I will tell you a story which came under my observation as a practitioner.

Doubtless all of you heard of the terrible tragedy which occurred at Gordonville, Mass., some years ago, when Capt. Jonathan Gordon, his wife and little son were murdered. I suppose that I am the only man on this side the Atlantic, outside of the police, who can tell you the true story of that crime.

I knew Captain Gordon well; it was through his persuasions that I bought a place in Gordonville and settled down to spending my summers in that charming rural neighbourhood. I had rendered the Captain what he was pleased to call valuable medical help, and I became his family physician. Captain Gordon was a retired sea captain, formerly engaged in the East India[2] trade. All his ancestors had been such; but when the bottom fell out of that business he established the Gordonville Mills with his first wife's money, and settled down as a money-making manufacturer of cotton cloth. The Gordons were old

New England Puritans who had come over in the 'Mayflower';[3] they had owned Gordon Hall for more than a hundred years. It was a baronial-like pile of granite with towers, standing on a hill which commanded a superb view of Massachusetts Bay and the surrounding country. I imagine the Gordon star was under a cloud about the time Captain Jonathan married his first wife, Miss Isabel Franklin of Boston, who brought to him the money which mended the broken fortunes of the Gordon house, and restored this old Puritan stock to its rightful position. In the person of Captain Gordon the austerity of manner and indomitable will-power that he had inherited were combined with a temper that brooked no contradiction.

The first wife died at the birth of her third child, leaving him two daughters, Jeannette and Talma. Very soon after her death the Captain married again. I have heard it rumoured that the Gordon girls did not get on very well with their stepmother. She was a woman with no fortune of her own, and envied the large portion left by the first Mrs Gordon to her daughters.

Jeannette was tall, dark and stern like her father; Talma was like her dead mother, and possessed of great talent, so great that her father sent her to the American Academy at Rome,[4] to develop the gift. It was the hottest of July days when her friends were bidden to an afternoon party on the lawn and a dance in the evening, to welcome Talma Gordon among them again. I watched her as she moved about among her guests, a fairylike blonde in floating white draperies, her face a study in delicate changing tints, like the heart of a flower, sparkling in smiles about the mouth to end in merry laughter in the clear blue eyes. There were all the subtle allurements of birth, wealth and culture about the exquisite creature:

> 'Smiling, frowning evermore,
> Thou art perfect in love-lore,
> Ever varying Madeline,'[5]

quoted a celebrated writer as he stood apart with me, gazing upon the scene before us. He sighed as he looked at the girl.

'Doctor, there is genius and passion in her face. Sometime our little friend will do wonderful things. But is it desirable to be singled out for special blessings by the gods? Genius always carries with it intense capacity for suffering: "Whom the gods love die young."'[6]

'Ah,' I replied, 'do not name death and Talma Gordon together. Cease your dismal croakings; such talk is rank heresy.'

The dazzling daylight dropped slowly into summer twilight. The merriment continued; more guests arrived; the great dancing pagoda built for the occasion was lighted by myriads of Japanese lanterns. The strains from the band grew sweeter and sweeter, and 'all went merry as a marriage bell'.[7] It was a rare treat to have this party at Gordon Hall, for Captain Jonathan was not given to hospitality. We broke up shortly before midnight, with expressions of delight from all the guests.

I was a bachelor then, without ties. Captain Gordon insisted upon my having a bed at the Hall. I did not fall asleep readily; there seemed to be something in the air that forbade it. I was still awake when a distant clock struck the second hour of the morning. Suddenly the heavens were lighted by a sheet of ghastly light; a terrific midsummer thunderstorm was breaking over the sleeping town. A lurid flash lit up all the landscape, painting the trees in grotesque shapes against the murky sky, and defining clearly the sullen blackness of the waters of the bay breaking in grandeur against the rocky coast. I had arisen and put back the draperies from the windows, to have an unobstructed view of the grand scene. A low muttering coming nearer and nearer, a terrific roar, and then a tremendous downpour. The storm had burst.

Now the uncanny howling of a dog mingled with the rattling volleys of thunder. I heard the opening and closing of doors; the servants were about looking after things. It was impossible to sleep. The lightning was more vivid. There was a blinding flash of a greenish-white tinge mingled with the crash of falling timbers. Then before my startled gaze arose columns of red flames reflected against the sky. 'Heaven help us!' I cried; 'it is the left tower; it has been struck and is on fire!'

I hurried on my clothes and stepped into the corridor; the girls were there before me. Jeannette came up to me instantly with anxious face. 'Oh, Doctor Thornton, what shall we do? papa and mamma and little

Johnny are in the old left tower. It is on fire. I have knocked and knocked, but get no answer.'

'Don't be alarmed,' said I soothingly. 'Jenkins, ring the alarm bell,' I continued, turning to the butler who was standing near; 'the rest follow me. We will force the entrance to the Captain's room.'

Instantly, it seemed to me, the bell boomed out upon the now silent air, for the storm had died down as quickly as it arose; and as our little procession paused before the entrance to the old left tower, we could distinguish the sound of the fire engines already on their way from the village.

The door resisted all our efforts; there seemed to be a barrier against it which nothing could move. The flames were gaining headway. Still the same deathly silence within the rooms.

'Oh, will they never get here?' cried Talma, wringing her hands in terror. Jeannette said nothing, but her face was ashen. The servants were huddled together in a panic-stricken group. I can never tell you what a relief it was when we heard the first sound of the firemen's voices, saw their quick movements and heard the ringing of the axes with which they cut away every obstacle to our entrance to the rooms. The neighbours who had just enjoyed the hospitality of the house were now gathered around offering all the assistance in their power. In less than fifteen minutes the fire was out, and the men began to bear the unconscious inmates from the ruins. They carried them to the pagoda so lately the scene of mirth and pleasure, and I took up my station there, ready to assume my professional duties. The Captain was nearest me; and as I stooped to make the necessary examination I reeled away from the ghastly sight which confronted me – *gentlemen, across the Captain's throat was a deep gash that severed the jugular vein!*

The Doctor paused, and the hand with which he refilled his glass trembled violently.

'What is it, Doctor?' cried the men, gathering about me.

'Take the women away; this is murder!'

'Murder!' cried Jeannette, as she fell against the side of the pagoda.

'Murder!' screamed Talma, staring at me as if unable to grasp my meaning.

I continued my examination of the bodies, and found that the same thing had happened to Mrs Gordon and to little Johnny.

The police were notified; and when the sun rose over the dripping town we found them in charge of Gordon Hall, the servants standing in excited knots talking over the crime, the friends of the family confounded, and the two girls trying to comfort each other and realize the terrible misfortune that had overtaken them.

Nothing in the rooms of the left tower seemed to have been disturbed. The door of communication between the rooms of the husband and wife was open, as they had arranged it for the night. Little Johnny's crib was placed beside his mother's bed. In it he was found as though never awakened by the storm. It was quite evident that the assassin was no common ruffian. The chief gave strict orders for a watch to be kept on all strangers or suspicious characters who were seen in the neighbourhood. He made enquiries among the servants, seeing each one separately, but there was nothing gained from them. No one had heard anything suspicious; all had been awakened by the storm. The chief was puzzled. Here was a triple crime for which no motive could be assigned.

'What do you think of it?' I asked him, as we stood together on the lawn.

'It is my opinion that the deed was committed by one of the higher classes, which makes the mystery more difficult to solve. I tell you, Doctor, there are mysteries that never come to light, and this, I think, is one of them.'

While we were talking Jenkins, the butler, an old and trusted servant, came up to the chief and saluted respectfully. 'Want to speak with me, Jenkins?' he asked. The man nodded, and they walked away together.

The story of the inquest was short, but appalling. It was shown that Talma had been allowed to go abroad to study because she and Mrs Gordon did not get on well together. From the testimony of Jenkins it seemed that Talma and her father had quarrelled bitterly about her lover, a young artist whom she had met at Rome, who was unknown to fame, and very poor. There had been terrible things said by each, and threats even had passed, all of which now rose up in judgement against the unhappy girl. The examination of the family solicitor revealed the fact that Captain Gordon intended to leave his daughters only a small annuity, the bulk of the fortune going to his son Jonathan, junior. This was a monstrous injustice, as everyone felt. In vain Talma protested her innocence. Someone must have done it. No one would be benefited so much by these deaths as she and her sister. Moreover, the will, together with other papers, was nowhere to be found. Not the slightest clue bearing upon the disturbing elements in this family, if any there were, was to be found. As the only surviving relatives, Jeannette and Talma became joint heirs to an immense fortune, which only for the bloody tragedy just enacted would, in all probability, have passed them by. Here was the motive. The case was very black against Talma. The foreman stood up. The silence was intense: We 'find that Capt. Jonathan Gordon, Mary E. Gordon and Jonathan Gordon, junior, all deceased, came to their deaths by means of a knife or other sharp instrument in the hands of Talma Gordon.' The girl was like one stricken with death. The flower-like mouth was drawn and pinched; the great sapphire-blue eyes were black with passionate anguish, terror and despair. She was placed in jail to await her trial at the fall session of the criminal court. The excitement in the hitherto quiet town rose to fever heat. Many points in the evidence seemed incomplete to thinking men. The weapon could not be found, nor could it be divined what had become of it. No reason could be given for the murder except the quarrel between Talma and her father and the ill will which existed between the girl and her stepmother.

When the trial was called Jeannette sat beside Talma in the prisoner's dock; both were arrayed in deepest mourning. Talma was pale and careworn, but seemed uplifted, spiritualized, as it were. Upon Jeannette the full realization of her sister's peril seemed to weigh heavily. She had changed much too: hollow cheeks, tottering steps, eyes blazing with fever, all suggestive of rapid and premature decay. From far-off Italy Edward Turner, growing famous in the art world, came to stand beside his girl-love in this hour of anguish.

The trial was a memorable one. No additional evidence had been collected to strengthen the prosecution; when the attorney general rose to open the case against Talma he knew, as everyone else did, that he could not convict solely on the evidence adduced. What was given did not always bear upon the case, and brought out strange stories of Captain Jonathan's methods. Tales were told of sailors who had sworn to take his life, in revenge for injuries inflicted upon them by his hand. One or two clues were followed, but without avail. The judge summed up the evidence impartially, giving the prisoner the benefit of the doubt. The points in hand furnished valuable collateral evidence, but were not direct proof. Although the moral presumption was against the prisoner, legal evidence was lacking to actually convict. The jury found the prisoner 'Not Guilty', owing to the fact that the evidence was entirely circumstantial. The verdict was received in painful silence; then a murmur of discontent ran through the great crowd.

'She must have done it,' said one; 'who else has been benefited by the horrible deed?'

'A poor woman would not have fared so well at the hands of the jury, nor a homely one either, for that matter,' said another.

The great Gordon trial was ended; innocent or guilty, Talma Gordon could not be tried again. She was free; but her liberty, with blasted prospects and fair fame gone for ever, was valueless to her. She seemed to have but one object in her mind: to find the murderer or murderers of her parents and half-brother. By her direction the shrewdest of detectives were employed and money flowed like water, but to no purpose; the Gordon tragedy remained a mystery. I had consented to act as one of the trustees of the immense Gordon estates and business interests, and by my advice the Misses Gordon went abroad. A year later I received a letter from Edward Turner, saying that Jeannette Gordon had died suddenly at Rome, and that Talma, after refusing all his entreaties for an early marriage, had disappeared, leaving no clue as to her whereabouts. I could give the poor fellow no comfort, although I had been duly notified of the death of Jeannette by Talma, in a letter telling me where to forward her remittances, and at the same time requesting me to keep her present residence secret, especially from Edward.

I had established a sanatorium for the cure of chronic diseases at

Gordonville, and absorbed in the cares of my profession I gave little thought to the Gordons. I seemed fated to be involved in mysteries.

A man claiming to be an Englishman, and fresh from the California gold fields, engaged board and professional service at my retreat. I found him suffering in the grasp of the tubercle-fiend – the last stages. He called himself Simon Cameron. Seldom have I seen so fascinating and wicked a face. The lines of the mouth were cruel, the eyes cold and sharp, the smile mocking and evil. He had money in plenty but seemed to have no friends, for he had received no letters and had had no visitors in the time he had been with us. He was an enigma to me; and his nationality puzzled me, for of course I did not believe his story of being English. The peaceful influence of the house seemed to soothe him in a measure, and make his last steps to the mysterious valley as easy as possible. For a time he improved, and would sit or walk about the grounds and sing sweet songs for the pleasure of the other inmates. Strange to say, his malady only affected his voice at times. He sang quaint songs in a silvery tenor of great purity and sweetness that was delicious to the listening ear:

> 'A wet sheet and a flowing sea,
> A wind that follows fast,
> And fills the white and rustling sail
> And bends the gallant mast;
> And bends the gallant mast, my boys;
> While like the eagle free,
> Away the good ship flies, and leaves
> Old England on the lea.'[8]

There are few singers on the lyric stage who could surpass Simon Cameron.

One night, a few weeks after Cameron's arrival, I sat in my office making up my accounts when the door opened and closed; I glanced up, expecting to see a servant. A lady advanced toward me. She threw back her veil, and then I saw that Talma Gordon, or her ghost, stood before me. After the first excitement of our meeting was over, she told me she had come direct from Paris, to place herself in my care. I had studied her attentively during the first moments of our meeting, and

I felt that she was right; unless something unforeseen happened to arouse her from the stupor into which she seemed to have fallen, the last Gordon was doomed to an early death. The next day I told her I had cabled Edward Turner to come to her.

'It will do no good; I cannot marry him,' was her only comment.

'Have you no feeling of pity for that faithful fellow?' I asked her sternly, provoked by her seeming indifference. I shall never forget the varied emotions depicted on her speaking face. Fully revealed to my gaze was the sight of a human soul tortured beyond the point of endurance; suffering all things, enduring all things,[9] in the silent agony of despair.

In a few days Edward arrived, and Talma consented to see him and explain her refusal to keep her promise to him. 'You must be present, Doctor; it is due your long, tried friendship to know that I have not been fickle, but have acted from the best and strongest motives.'

I shall never forget that day. It was directly after lunch that we met in the library. I was greatly excited, expecting I knew not what. Edward was agitated, too. Talma was the only calm one. She handed me what seemed to be a letter, with the request that I would read it. Even now I think I can repeat every word of the document, so indelibly are the words engraved upon my mind:

My Darling Sister Talma: When you read these lines I shall be no more, for I shall not live to see your life blasted by the same knowledge that has blighted mine.

One evening, about a year before your expected return from Rome, I climbed into a hammock in one corner of the veranda outside the breakfast-room windows, intending to spend the twilight hours in lazy comfort, for it was very hot, enervating August weather. I fell asleep. I was awakened by voices. Because of the heat the rooms had been left in semi-darkness. As I lay there, lazily enjoying the beauty of the perfect summer night, my wandering thoughts were arrested by words spoken by our father to Mrs Gordon, for they were the occupants of the breakfast room.

'Never fear, Mary; Johnny shall have it all – money, houses, land and business.'

'But if you do go first, Jonathan, what will happen if the girls contest the will? People will think that they ought to have the money as it appears to be theirs by law. I never could survive the terrible disgrace of the story.'

'Don't borrow trouble; all you would need to do would be to show them papers I have drawn up, and they would be glad to take their annuity and say nothing. After all, I do not think it is so bad. Jeannette can teach; Talma can paint; six hundred dollars a year is quite enough for them.'

I had been somewhat mystified by the conversation until now. This last remark solved the riddle. What could he mean? teach, paint, six hundred a year! With my usual impetuosity I sprang from my resting place, and in a moment stood in the room confronting my father, and asking what he meant. I could see plainly that both were disconcerted by my unexpected appearance.

'Ah, wretched girl! you have been listening. But what could I expect of your mother's daughter?'

At these words I felt the indignant blood rush to my head in a torrent. So it had been all my life. Before you could remember, Talma, I had felt my little heart swell with anger at the disparaging hints and slurs concerning our mother. Now was my time. I determined that tonight I would know why she was looked upon as an outcast, and her children subjected to every humiliation. So I replied to my father in bitter anger:

'I was not listening; I fell asleep in the hammock. What do you mean by a paltry six hundred a year each to Talma and to me? "My mother's daughter" demands an explanation from you, sir, of the meaning of the monstrous injustice that you have always practised toward my sister and me.'

'Speak more respectfully to your father, Jeannette,' broke in Mrs Gordon.

'How is it, madam, that you look for respect from one whom you have delighted to torment ever since you came into this most unhappy family?'

'Hush, both of you,' said Captain Gordon, who seemed to have recovered from the dismay into which my sudden appearance and passionate words had plunged him. 'I think I may as well tell you as to wait. Since you know so much, you may as well know the whole miserable story.' He motioned me to a seat. I could see that he was deeply agitated. I seated myself in a chair he pointed out, in wonder and expectation, – expectation of I knew not what. I trembled. This was a supreme moment in my life; I felt it. The air was heavy with the intense stillness that had settled over us as the common sounds of day gave place to the early quiet of the rural evening. I could see Mrs Gordon's face as she sat within the radius of the lighted hallway. There was a smile of triumph upon it. I clinched my hands and bit my lips until the blood came, in the effort to keep from screaming. What was I about to hear? At last he spoke:

'I was disappointed at your birth, and also at the birth of Talma. I wanted a male heir. When I knew that I should again be a father I was torn by hope and fear, but I comforted myself with the thought that luck would be with me in the birth of the third child. When the doctor brought me word that a son was born to the house of Gordon, I was wild with delight, and did not notice his disturbed countenance. In the midst of my joy he said to me:

'"Captain Gordon, there is something strange about this birth. I want you to see this child."

'Quelling my exultation I followed him to the nursery, and there, lying in the cradle, I saw a child dark as a mulatto, with the characteristic features of the Negro! I was stunned. Gradually it dawned upon me that there was something radically wrong. I turned to the doctor for an explanation.

'"There is but one explanation, Captain Gordon; there is Negro blood in this child."

'"There is no Negro blood in my veins," I said proudly. Then I paused – *the mother!* – I glanced at the doctor. He was watching me intently. The same thought was in his mind. I must have lived a thousand years in that cursed five seconds that I stood there confronting the physician and trying to think. "Come," said I to him, "let us end this suspense." Without thinking of consequences, I hurried away to your mother and accused her of infidelity to her marriage vows. I raved like a madman. Your mother fell into convulsions; her life was despaired of. I sent for Mr and Mrs Franklin, and then I learned the truth. They were childless. One year while on a Southern tour, they befriended an octoroon girl who had been abandoned by her white lover. Her child was a beautiful girl baby. They, being Northern born, thought little of caste distinction because the child showed no trace of Negro blood. They determined to adopt it. They went abroad, secretly sending back word to their friends at a proper time, of the birth of a little daughter. No one doubted the truth of the statement. They made Isabel their heiress, and all went well until the birth of your brother. Your mother and the unfortunate babe died. This is the story which, if known, would bring dire disgrace upon the Gordon family.

'To appease my righteous wrath, Mr Franklin left a codicil to his will by which all the property is left at my disposal save a small annuity to you and your sister.'

I sat there after he had finished his story, stunned by what I had heard. I understood, now, Mrs Gordon's half contemptuous toleration and lack of consideration for us both. As I rose from my seat to leave the room I said to Captain Gordon:

'Still, in spite of all, sir, I am a Gordon, legally born. I will not tamely give up my birthright.'

I left that room a broken-hearted girl, filled with a desire for revenge upon this man, my father, who by his manner disowned us without a regret. Not once in that remarkable interview did he speak of our mother as his wife; he quietly repudiated her and us with all the cold cruelty of relentless caste prejudice. I heard the treatment of your lover's proposal: I knew why Captain Gordon's consent to your marriage was withheld.

The night of the reception and dance was the chance for which I had waited, planned and watched. I crept from my window into the ivy vines, and so down, down, until I stood upon the window sill of Captain Gordon's room in the old left tower. How did I do it, you ask? I do not know. The house was silent after the revel; the darkness of the gathering storm favoured me, too. The lawyer was there that day. The will was signed and put safely away among my father's papers. I was determined to have the will and the other documents bearing upon the case, and I would have revenge, too, for the cruelties we had suffered. With the old East Indian dagger firmly grasped I entered the room and found – that my revenge had been forestalled! The horror of the discovery I made that night restored me to reason and a realization of the crime I meditated. Scarce knowing what I did, I sought and found the papers, and crept back to my room as I had come. Do you wonder that my disease is past medical aid?

I looked at Edward as I finished. He sat, his face covered with his hands. Finally he looked up with a glance of haggard despair: 'God! Doctor, but this is too much. I could stand the stigma of murder, but add to that the pollution of Negro blood! No man is brave enough to face such a situation.'

'It is as I thought it would be,' said Talma sadly, while the tears poured over her white face. 'I do not blame you, Edward.'

He rose from his chair, wrung my hand in a convulsive clasp, turned to Talma and bowed profoundly, with his eyes fixed upon the floor, hesitated, turned, paused, bowed again and abruptly left the room. So those two who had been lovers, parted. I turned to Talma, expecting her to give way. She smiled a pitiful smile, and said: 'You see, Doctor, I knew best.'

From that on she failed rapidly. I was restless. If only I could rouse her to an interest in life, she might live to old age. So rich, so young, so beautiful, so talented, so pure; I grew savage thinking of the injustice of the world. I had not reckoned on the power that never sleeps. Something was about to happen.

On visiting Cameron next morning I found him approaching the end. He had been sinking for a week very rapidly. As I sat by the bedside holding his emaciated hand, he fixed his bright, wicked eyes on me, and asked: 'How long have I got to live?'

'Candidly, but a few hours.'

'Thank you; well, I want death; I am not afraid to die. Doctor, Cameron is not my name.'

'I never supposed it was.'

'No? You are sharper than I thought. I heard all your talk yesterday with Talma Gordon. Curse the whole race!'

He clasped his bony fingers around my arm and gasped: *I murdered the Gordons!*

Had I the pen of a Dumas[10] I could not paint Cameron as he told his story. It is a question with me whether this wheeling planet, home of the suffering, doubting, dying, may not hold worse agonies on its smiling surface than those of the conventional hell. I sent for Talma and a lawyer. We gave him stimulants, and then with broken intervals of coughing and prostration we got the story of the Gordon murder. I give it to you in a few words:

'I am an East Indian, but my name does not matter, Cameron is as good as any. There is many a soul crying in heaven and hell for vengeance on Jonathan Gordon. Gold was his idol; and many a good man walked the plank, and many a gallant ship was stripped of her treasure, to satisfy his lust for gold. His blackest crime was the murder of my father, who was his friend, and had sailed with him for many a year as mate. One night these two went ashore together to bury their treasure. My father never returned from that expedition. His body was afterward found with a bullet through the heart on the shore where the vessel stopped that night. It was the custom then among pirates for the captain to kill the men who helped bury their treasure. Captain Gordon was no better than a pirate. An East Indian never forgets, and I swore by my mother's deathbed to hunt Captain Gordon down until I had avenged my father's murder. I had the plans of the Gordon estate, and fixed on the night of the reception in honour of Talma as the time for my vengeance. There is a secret entrance from the shore to the chambers where Captain Gordon slept; no one knew of it save the Captain and trusted members of his crew. My mother gave me the plans, and entrance and escape were easy.'

So the great mystery was solved. In a few hours Cameron was no more. We placed the confession in the hands of the police, and there the matter ended.

'But what became of Talma Gordon?' questioned the president. 'Did she die?'

'Gentlemen,' said the Doctor, rising to his feet and sweeping the faces of the company with his eagle gaze, 'gentlemen, if you will follow me to the drawing room, I shall have much pleasure in introducing you to my wife – *née* Talma Gordon.'

GEORGE GISSING

A Daughter of the Lodge

For a score of years the Rocketts had kept the lodge of Brent Hall. In the beginning Rockett was head gardener; his wife, the daughter of a shopkeeper, had never known domestic service, and performed her duties at the Hall gates with a certain modest dignity not displeasing to the stately persons upon whom she depended. During the lifetime of Sir Henry the best possible understanding existed between Hall and lodge. Though Rockett's health broke down, and at length he could work hardly at all, their pleasant home was assured to the family; and at Sir Henry's death the nephew who succeeded him left the Rocketts undisturbed. But, under this new lordship, things were not quite as they had been. Sir Edwin Shale, a middle-aged man, had in his youth made a foolish marriage; his lady ruled him, not with the gentlest of tongues, nor always to the kindest purpose, and their daughter, Hilda, asserted her rights as only child with a force of character which Sir Edwin would perhaps have more sincerely admired had it reminded him less of Lady Shale.

While the Hall, in Sir Henry's time, remained childless,[1] the lodge prided itself on a boy and two girls. Young Rockett, something of a scapegrace, was by the baronet's advice sent to sea, and thenceforth gave his parents no trouble. The second daughter, Betsy, grew up to be her mother's help. But Betsy's elder sister showed from early years that the life of the lodge would afford no adequate scope for *her* ambitions. May Rockett had good looks; what was more, she had an intellect which sharpened itself on everything with which it came in contact. The village school could never have been held responsible for May Rockett's acquirements and views at the age of ten; nor could the High School in the neighbouring town altogether account for her mental development at seventeen. Not without misgivings had the health-broken gardener and his wife consented to May's pursuit of the higher learning; but Sir Henry and the kind old Lady Shale seemed to think it the safer course, and evidently there was little chance of the girl's accepting any humble kind of employment: in one way or another she must depend for a livelihood upon her brains. At the time of Sir Edwin's succession Miss Rockett had already obtained a place as governess, giving her parents to understand that this was only, of course, a temporary expedient – a paving of the way to something vaguely, but superbly, independent. Nor was promotion long in coming. At two-and-twenty May accepted a secretaryship to a lady with a mission – concerning the rights of womanhood. In letters to her father and mother she spoke much of the importance of her work, but did not confess how very modest was her salary. A couple of years went by without her visiting the old home; then, of a sudden, she made known her intention of coming to stay at the lodge 'for a week or ten days'. She explained that her purpose was rest; intellectual strain had begun rather to tell upon her, and a few days of absolute tranquillity, such as she might expect under the elms of Brent Hall, would do her all the good in the world. 'Of course,' she added, 'it's unnecessary to say anything about me to the Shale people. They and I have nothing in common, and it will be better for us to ignore each other's existence.'

These characteristic phrases troubled Mr and Mrs Rockett. That the family at the Hall should, if it seemed good to them, ignore the existence of May was, in the Rocketts' view, reasonable enough; but for May to ignore Sir Edwin and Lady Shale, who were just now in residence after six months spent abroad, struck them as a very grave impropriety. Natural respect demanded that, at some fitting moment, and in a suitable manner, their daughter should present herself to her feudal superiors, to whom she was assuredly indebted, though indirectly, for 'the blessings she enjoyed'. This was Mrs Rockett's phrase, and the rheumatic, wheezy old gardener uttered the same opinion in less conventional language. They had no affection for Sir Edwin or his lady, and Miss Hilda they decidedly disliked; their treatment at the hands of these new people contrasted unpleasantly enough with the memory of old times; but a spirit of loyal subordination ruled their blood, and, to Sir Edwin at all events, they felt gratitude for their retention at the lodge. Mrs Rockett was a healthy and capable woman of not more than fifty, but no less than her invalid husband would she have dreaded the thought of turning her back on Brent Hall. Rockett had often consoled himself with the thought that here he should die, here amid the fine old trees that he loved, in the ivy-covered house which was his only idea of home. And was it not a reasonable hope that Betsy, good steady girl, should some day marry the promising young gardener whom Sir Edwin had recently taken into his service, and so re-establish the old order of things at the lodge?

'I half wish May wasn't coming,' said Mrs Rockett, after long and anxious thought. 'Last time she was here she quite upset me with her strange talk.'

'She's a funny girl, and that's the truth,' muttered Rockett from his old leather chair, full in the sunshine of the kitchen window. They had a nice little sitting room; but this, of course, was only used on Sunday, and no particular idea of comfort attached to it. May, to be sure, had always used the sitting room. It was one of the habits which emphasized most strongly the moral distance between her and her parents.

The subject being full of perplexity, they put it aside, and with very mixed feelings awaited their elder daughter's arrival. Two days later a cab deposited at the lodge Miss May, and her dress-basket, and her travelling-bag, and her holdall, together with certain loose periodicals and a volume or two bearing the yellow label of Mudie.[2] The young lady was well dressed in a severely practical way; nothing unduly feminine marked her appearance, and in the matter of collar and necktie she inclined to the example of the other sex; for all that, her soft complexion and bright eyes, her well-turned figure and light, quick movements, had a picturesque value which Miss May certainly did not ignore. She manifested no excess of feeling when her mother and sister came forth to welcome her; a nod, a smile, an offer of her cheek and the pleasant exclamation, 'Well, good people!' carried her through this little scene with becoming dignity.

'You will bring these things inside, please,' she said to the driver, in her agreeable head-voice, with the tone and gesture of one who habitually gives orders.

Her father, bent with rheumatism, stood awaiting her just within. She grasped his hand cordially, and cried on a cheery note, 'Well, father, how are you getting on? No worse than usual, I hope?' Then she added, regarding him with her head slightly aside, 'We must have a talk about your case. I've been going in a little for medicine lately. No doubt your country medico is a duffer. Sit down, sit down, and make yourself comfortable. I don't want to disturb any one. About teatime, isn't it, mother? Tea very weak for me, please, and a slice of lemon with it, if you have such a thing, and just a mouthful of dry toast.'

So unwilling was May to disturb the habits of the family that, half an hour after her arrival, the homely three had fallen into a state of nervous agitation, and could neither say nor do anything natural to them. Of a sudden there sounded a sharp rapping at the window. Mrs Rockett and Betsy started up, and Betsy ran to the door. In a moment or two she came back with glowing cheeks.

'I'm sure I never heard the bell!' she exclaimed with compunction. 'Miss Shale had to get off her bicycle!'

'Was it she who hammered at the window?' asked May coldly.

'Yes – and she was that annoyed.'

'It will do her good. A little anger now and then is excellent for the health.' And Miss Rockett sipped her lemon-tinctured tea with a smile of ineffable contempt.

The others went to bed at ten o'clock, but May, having made herself at ease in the sitting room, sat there reading until after twelve. Nevertheless, she was up very early next morning, and, before going out for a sharp little walk (in a heavy shower), she gave precise directions about her breakfast. She wanted only the simplest things, prepared in the simplest way, but the tone of her instructions vexed and perturbed Mrs Rockett sorely. After breakfast the young lady made a searching enquiry into the state of her father's health, and diagnosed his ailments in such learned words that the old gardener began to feel worse than he had done for many a year. May then occupied herself with correspondence, and before midday sent her sister out to post nine letters.

'But I thought you were going to rest yourself?' said her mother, in an irritable voice quite unusual with her.

'Why, so I am resting!' May exclaimed. 'If you saw my ordinary morning's work! I suppose you have a London newspaper? No? How *do* you live without it? I must run into the town for one this afternoon.'

The town was three miles away, but could be reached by train from the village station. On reflection, Miss Rockett announced that she would use this opportunity for calling on a lady whose acquaintance she desired to make, one Mrs Lindley, who in social position stood on an equality with the family at the Hall, and was often seen there. On her mother's expressing surprise, May smiled indulgently.

'Why shouldn't I know Mrs Lindley? I have heard she's interested in a movement which occupies me a good deal just now. I know she will be delighted to see me. I can give her a good deal of first-hand information, for which she will be grateful. You *do* amuse me, mother,' she added in her blandest tone. 'When will you come to understand what my position is?'

The Rocketts had put aside all thoughts of what they esteemed May's duty towards the Hall; they earnestly hoped that her stay with them might pass unobserved by Lady and Miss Shale, whom, they felt sure, it would be positively dangerous for the girl to meet. Mrs Rockett had not slept for anxiety on this score. The father was also a good deal troubled; but his wonder at May's bearing and talk had, on the whole, an agreeable preponderance over the uneasy feeling. He and Betsy shared a secret admiration for the brilliant qualities which were flashed before their eyes; they privately agreed that May was more of a real lady than either the baronet's hard-tongued wife or the disdainful Hilda Shale.

So Miss Rockett took the early afternoon train, and found her way to Mrs Lindley's, where she sent in her card. At once admitted to the drawing room, she gave a rapid account of herself, naming persons whose acquaintance sufficiently recommended her. Mrs Lindley was a good-humoured, chatty woman, who had a lively interest in everything 'progressive'; a new religion or a new cycling-costume stirred her to just the same kind of happy excitement; she had no prejudices, but a decided preference for the society of healthy, high-spirited, well-to-do people. Miss Rockett's talk was exactly what she liked, for it glanced at innumerable topics of the 'advanced' sort, was much concerned with personalities and avoided all tiresome precision of argument.

'Are you making a stay here?' asked the hostess.

'Oh! I am with my people in the country – not far off,' May answered in an offhand way. 'Only for a day or two.'

Other callers were admitted, but Miss Rockett kept the lead in talk; she glowed with self-satisfaction, feeling that she was really showing to great advantage, and that everybody admired her. When the door again opened the name announced was 'Miss Shale'. Stopping in the middle of a swift sentence, May looked at the newcomer, and saw that it was indeed Hilda Shale, of Brent Hall; but this did not disconcert her. Without lowering her voice she finished what she was saying, and ended in a mirthful key. The baronet's daughter had come into town on her bicycle, as was declared by the short skirt, easy jacket and brown shoes, which well displayed her athletic person. She was a tall, strongly built girl of six-and-twenty, with a face of hard comeliness and magnificent tawny hair. All her movements suggested vigour; she shook hands with a downward jerk, moved about the room with something of a stride and, in sitting down, crossed her legs abruptly.

From the first her look had turned with surprise to Miss Rockett. When, after a minute or two, the hostess presented that young lady to her, Miss Shale raised her eyebrows a little, smiled in another direction and gave a just perceptible nod. May's behaviour was as nearly as possible the same.

'Do you cycle, Miss Rockett?' asked Mrs Lindley.

'No, I don't. The fact is, I have never found time to learn.'

A lady remarked that nowadays there was a certain distinction in not cycling; whereupon Miss Shale's abrupt and rather metallic voice sounded what was meant for gentle irony.

'It's a pity the machines can't be sold cheaper. A great many people who would like to cycle don't feel able to afford it, you know. One often hears of such cases out in the country, and it seems awfully hard lines, doesn't it?'

Miss Rockett felt a warmth ascending to her ears, and made a violent effort to look unconcerned. She wished to say something, but could not find the right words, and did not feel altogether sure of her voice. The hostess, who made no personal application of Miss Shale's remark, began to discuss the prices of bicycles, and others chimed in. May fretted under this turn of the conversation. Seeing that it was not likely to revert to subjects in which she could shine, she rose and offered to take leave.

'Must you really go?' fell with conventional regret from the hostess's lips.

'I'm afraid I must,' Miss Rockett replied, bracing herself under the converging eyes and feeling not quite equal to the occasion. 'My time is so short, and there are so many people I wish to see.'

As she left the house, anger burned in her. It was certain that Hilda Shale would make known her circumstances. She had fancied this revelation a matter of indifference; but, after all, the thought stung her intolerably. The insolence of the creature, with her hint about the prohibitive cost of bicycles! All the harder to bear because hitting the truth. May would have long ago bought a bicycle had she been able to afford it. Straying about the main streets of the town, she looked flushed and wrathful, and could think of nothing but her humiliation.

To make things worse, she lost count of time, and presently found that she had missed the only train by which she could return home. A cab would be too much of an expense; she had no choice but to walk the three or four miles. The evening was close; walking rapidly, and with the accompaniment of vexatious thoughts, she reached the gates of the Hall tired, perspiring, irritated. Just as her hand was on the gate a bicycle-bell trilled vigorously behind her, and, from a distance of twenty yards, a voice cried imperatively –

'Open the gate, please!'

Miss Rockett looked round, and saw Hilda Shale slowly wheeling forward, in expectation that way would be made for her. Deliberately May passed through the side entrance, and let the little gate fall to.

Miss Shale dismounted, admitted herself and spoke to May (now at the lodge door) with angry emphasis.

'Didn't you hear me ask you to open?'

'I couldn't imagine you were speaking to *me*,' answered Miss Rockett, with brisk dignity. 'I supposed some servant of yours was in sight.'

A peculiar smile distorted Miss Shale's full red lips. Without another word she mounted her machine and rode away up the elm avenue.

Now Mrs Rockett had seen this encounter, and heard the words exchanged: she was lost in consternation.

'What *do* you mean by behaving like that, May? Why, I was running out myself to open, and then I saw you were there, and, of course, I thought you'd do it. There's the second time in two days Miss Shale has had to complain about us. How *could* you forget yourself, to behave and speak like that! Why, you must be crazy, my girl!'

'I don't seem to get on very well here, mother,' was May's reply. 'The fact is, I'm in a false position. I shall go tomorrow morning, and there won't be any more trouble.'

Thus spoke Miss Rockett, as one who shakes off a petty annoyance – she knew not that the serious trouble was just beginning. A few minutes later Mrs Rockett went up to the Hall, bent on humbly apologizing for her daughter's impertinence. After being kept waiting for a quarter of an hour she was admitted to the presence of the housekeeper, who had a rather grave announcement to make.

'Mrs Rockett, I'm sorry to tell you that you will have to leave the lodge. My lady allows you two months, though, as your wages have always been paid monthly, only a month's notice is really called for. I believe some allowance will be made you, but you will hear about that. The lodge must be ready for its new occupants on the last day of October.'

The poor woman all but sank. She had no voice for protest or entreaty – a sob choked her; and blindly she made her way to the door of the room, then to the exit from the Hall.

'What in the world is the matter?' cried May, hearing from the sitting room, whither she had retired, a clamour of distressful tongues.

She came into the kitchen, and learnt what had happened.

'And now I hope you're satisfied!' exclaimed her mother, with tearful wrath. 'You've got us turned out of our home – you've lost us the best place a family ever had – and I hope it's a satisfaction to your conceited, overbearing mind! If you'd *tried* for it you couldn't have gone to work better. And much *you* care! We're below you, we are; we're like dirt under your feet! And your father'll go and end his life who knows where, miserable as miserable can be; and your sister'll have to go into service; and as for me —'

'Listen, mother!' shouted the girl, her eyes flashing and every nerve of her body strung. 'If the Shales are such contemptible wretches as to turn you out just because they're offended with *me*, I should have thought you'd have spirit enough to tell them what you think of such behaviour, and be glad never more to serve such brutes! Father, what do *you* say? I'll tell you how it was.'

She narrated the events of the afternoon, amid sobs and ejaculations from her mother and Betsy. Rockett, who was just now in anguish of lumbago, tried to straighten himself in his chair before replying, but sank helplessly together with a groan.

'You can't help yourself, May,' he said at length. 'It's your nature, my girl. Don't worry. I'll see Sir Edwin, and perhaps he'll listen to me. It's the women who make all the mischief. I must try to see Sir Edwin —'

A pang across the loins made him end abruptly, groaning, moaning, muttering. Before the renewed attack of her mother May retreated into the sitting room, and there passed an hour wretchedly enough. A knock at the door without words called her to supper, but she had no appetite, and would not join the family circle. Presently the door opened, and her father looked in.

'Don't worry, my girl,' he whispered. 'I'll see Sir Edwin in the morning.'

May uttered no reply. Vaguely repenting what she had done, she at the same time rejoiced in the recollection of her passage of arms with Miss Shale, and was inclined to despise her family for their pusillanimous attitude. It seemed to her very improbable that the expulsion would really be carried out. Lady Shale and Hilda meant, no doubt, to give the Rocketts a good fright, and then contemptuously pardon them. She, in any case, would return to London without delay, and make no more trouble. A pity she had come to the lodge at all; it was no place for one of her spirit and her attainments.

In the morning she packed. The train which was to take her back to town left at half-past ten, and after breakfast she walked into the village to order a cab. Her mother would scarcely speak to her; Betsy was continually in reproachful tears. On coming back to the lodge she saw her father hobbling down the avenue, and walked towards him to ask the result of his supplication. Rockett had seen Sir Edwin, but only to hear his sentence of exile confirmed. The baronet said he was sorry, but could not interfere; the matter lay in Lady Shale's hands, and Lady Shale absolutely refused to hear any excuses or apologies for the insult which had been offered her daughter.

'It's all up with us,' said the old gardener, who was pale and trembling after his great effort. 'We must go. But don't worry, my girl, don't worry.'

Then fright took hold upon May Rockett. She felt for the first time what she had done. Her heart fluttered in an anguish of self-reproach, and her eyes strayed as if seeking help. A minute's hesitation, then, with all the speed she could make, she set off up the avenue towards the Hall.

Presenting herself at the servants' entrance, she begged to be allowed to see the housekeeper. Of course her story was known to all the domestics, half a dozen of whom quickly collected to stare at her, with more or less malicious smiles. It was a bitter moment for Miss Rockett, but she subdued herself, and at length obtained the interview she sought. With a cold air of superiority and of disapproval the housekeeper listened to her quick, broken sentences. Would it be possible, May asked, for her to see Lady Shale? She desired to – to apologize for – for rudeness of which she had been guilty, rudeness in which her family had no part, which they utterly deplored, but for which they were to suffer severely.

'If you could help me, ma'am, I should be very grateful – indeed I should—'

Her voice all but broke into a sob. That 'ma'am' cost her a terrible effort; the sound of it seemed to smack her on the ears.

'If you will go into the servants' hall and wait,' the housekeeper deigned to say, after reflecting, 'I'll see what can be done.'

And Miss Rockett submitted. In the servants' hall she sat for a long,

long time, observed, but never addressed. The hour of her train went by. More than once she was on the point of rising and fleeing; more than once her smouldering wrath all but broke into flame. But she thought of her father's pale, pain-stricken face, and sat on.

At something past eleven o'clock a footman approached her, and said curtly, 'You are to go up to my lady; follow me.' May followed, shaking with weakness and apprehension, burning at the same time with pride all but in revolt. Conscious of nothing on the way, she found herself in a large room, where sat the two ladies, who for some moments spoke together about a topic of the day placidly. Then the elder seemed to become aware of the girl who stood before her.

'You are Rockett's elder daughter?'

Oh, the metallic voice of Lady Shale! How gratified she would have been could she have known how it bruised the girl's pride!

'Yes, my lady—'

'And why do you want to see me?'

'I wish to apologize – most sincerely – to your ladyship – for my behaviour of last evening—'

'Oh, indeed!' the listener interrupted contemptuously. 'I am glad you have come to your senses. But your apology must be offered to Miss Shale – if my daughter cares to listen to it.'

May had foreseen this. It was the bitterest moment of her ordeal. Flushing scarlet, she turned towards the younger woman.

'Miss Shale, I beg your pardon for what I said yesterday – I beg you to forgive my rudeness – my impertinence—'

Her voice would go no further; there came a choking sound. Miss Shale allowed her eyes to rest triumphantly for an instant on the troubled face and figure, then remarked to her mother –

'It's really nothing to me, as I told you. I suppose this person may leave the room now?'

It was fated that May Rockett should go through with her purpose and gain her end. But fate alone (which meant in this case the subtlest preponderance of one impulse over another) checked her on the point of a burst of passion which would have startled Lady Shale and Miss Hilda out of their cold-blooded complacency. In the silence May's blood gurgled at her ears, and she tottered with dizziness.

'You may go,' said Lady Shale.

But May could not move. There flashed across her the terrible thought that perhaps she had humiliated herself for nothing.

'My lady – I hope – will your ladyship please to forgive my father and mother? I entreat you not to send them away. We shall all be so grateful to your ladyship if you will overlook—'

'That will do,' said Lady Shale decisively. 'I will merely say that the sooner you leave the lodge the better; and that you will do well never again to pass the gates of the Hall. You may go.'

Miss Rockett withdrew. Outside, the footman was awaiting her. He looked at her with a grin, and asked in an undertone, 'Any good?' But May, to whom this was the last blow, rushed past him, lost herself in corridors, ran wildly hither and thither, tears streaming from her eyes, and was at length guided by a maidservant into the outer air. Fleeing she cared not whither, she came at length into a still corner of the park, and there, hidden amid trees, watched only by birds and rabbits, she wept out the bitterness of her soul.

By an evening train she returned to London, not having confessed to her family what she had done, and suffering still from some uncertainty as to the result. A day or two later Betsy wrote to her the happy news that the sentence of expulsion was withdrawn, and peace reigned once more in the ivy-covered lodge. By that time Miss Rockett had all but recovered her self-respect, and was so busy in her secretaryship that she could only scribble a line of congratulation. She felt that she had done rather a meritorious thing, but, for the first time in her life, did not care to boast of it.

A Warrior's Daughter

In the afternoon shadow of a large tepee, with red-painted smoke lapels, sat a warrior father with crossed shins. His head was so poised that his eye swept easily the vast level land to the eastern horizon line.

He was the chieftain's bravest warrior. He had won by heroic deeds the privilege of staking his wigwam within the great circle of tepees.

He was also one of the most generous gift givers to the toothless old people. For this he was entitled to the red-painted smoke lapels on his cone-shaped dwelling. He was proud of his honours. He never wearied of rehearsing nightly his own brave deeds. Though by wigwam fires he prated much of his high rank and widespread fame, his great joy was a wee black-eyed daughter of eight sturdy winters. Thus as he sat upon the soft grass, with his wife at his side, bent over her bead work, he was singing a dance song, and beat lightly the rhythm with his slender hands.

His shrewd eyes softened with pleasure as he watched the easy movements of the small body dancing on the green before him.

Tusee is taking her first dancing lesson. Her tightly braided hair curves over both brown ears like a pair of crooked little horns which glisten in the summer sun.

With her snugly moccasined feet close together, and a wee hand at her belt to stay the long string of beads which hang from her bare neck, she bends her knees gently to the rhythm of her father's voice.

Now she ventures upon the earnest movement, slightly upward and sidewise, in a circle. At length the song drops into a closing cadence, and the little woman, clad in beaded deerskin, sits down beside the elder one. Like her mother, she sits upon her feet. In a brief moment the warrior repeats the last refrain. Again Tusee springs to her feet and dances to the swing of the few final measures.

Just as the dance was finished, an elderly man, with short, thick hair loose about his square shoulders, rode into their presence from the rear, and leaped lightly from his pony's back. Dropping the rawhide rein to the ground, he tossed himself lazily on the grass. 'Hunhe, you have returned soon,' said the warrior, while extending a hand to his little daughter.

Quickly the child ran to her father's side and cuddled close to him, while he tenderly placed a strong arm about her. Both father and child, eyeing the figure on the grass, waited to hear the man's report.

'It is true,' began the man, with a stranger's accent. 'This is the night of the dance.'

'Hunha!' muttered the warrior with some surprise.

Propping himself upon his elbows, the man raised his face. His features were of the Southern type. From an enemy's camp he was taken captive long years ago by Tusee's father. But the unusual qualities of the slave had won the Sioux warrior's heart, and for the last three winters the man had had his freedom. He was made real man again. His hair was allowed to grow. However, he himself had chosen to stay in the warrior's family.

'Hunha!' again ejaculated the warrior father. Then turning to his little daughter, he asked, 'Tusee, do you hear that?'

'Yes, father, and I am going to dance tonight!'

With these words she bounded out of his arm and frolicked about in glee. Hereupon the proud mother's voice rang out in a chiding laugh.

'My child, in honour of your first dance your father must give a generous gift. His ponies are wild, and roam beyond the great hill. Pray, what has he fit to offer?' she questioned, the pair of puzzled eyes fixed upon her.

'A pony from the herd, mother, a fleet-footed pony from the herd!' Tusee shouted with sudden inspiration.

Pointing a small forefinger toward the man lying on the grass, she cried, 'Uncle, you will go after the pony tomorrow!' And pleased with her solution of the problem, she skipped wildly about. Her childish faith in her elders was not conditioned by a knowledge of human limitations, but thought all things possible to grown-ups.

'Hähob!' exclaimed the mother, with a rising inflection, implying by the expletive that her child's buoyant spirit be not weighted with a denial.

Quickly to the hard request the man replied, 'How! I go if Tusee tells me so!'

This delighted the little one, whose black eyes brimmed over with light. Standing in front of the strong man, she clapped her small, brown hands with joy.

'That makes me glad! My heart is good! Go, uncle, and bring a handsome pony!' she cried. In an instant she would have frisked away, but an impulse held her tilting where she stood. In the man's own tongue, for he had taught her many words and phrases, she exploded, 'Thank you, good uncle, thank you!' then tore away from sheer excess of glee.

The proud warrior father, smiling and narrowing his eyes, muttered approval, 'Howo! Hechetu!'

Like her mother, Tusee has finely pencilled eyebrows and slightly extended nostrils; but in her sturdiness of form she resembles her father.

A loyal daughter, she sits within her tepee making beaded deerskins for her father, while he longs to stave off her every suitor as all unworthy of his old heart's pride. But Tusee is not alone in her dwelling. Near the entrance way a young brave is half reclining on a mat. In silence he watches the petals of a wild rose growing on the soft buckskin. Quickly the young woman slips the beads on the silvery sinew thread, and works them into the pretty flower design. Finally, in a low, deep voice, the young man begins:

'The sun is far past the zenith. It is now only a man's height above the western edge of land. I hurried hither to tell you tomorrow I join the war party.'

He pauses for reply, but the maid's head drops lower over her deerskin, and her lips are more firmly drawn together. He continues:

'Last night in the moonlight I met your warrior father. He seemed to know I had just stepped forth from your tepee. I fear he did not like it, for though I greeted him, he was silent. I halted in his pathway. With what boldness I dared, while my heart was beating hard and fast, I asked him for his only daughter.

'Drawing himself erect to his tallest height, and gathering his loose robe more closely about his proud figure, he flashed a pair of piercing eyes upon me.

'"Young man," said he, with a cold, slow voice that chilled me to the marrow of my bones, "hear me. Naught but an enemy's scalp-lock, plucked fresh with your own hand, will buy Tusee for your wife." Then he turned on his heel and stalked away.'

Tusee thrusts her work aside. With earnest eyes she scans her lover's face.

'My father's heart is really kind. He would know if you are brave and true,' murmured the daughter, who wished no ill-will between her two loved ones.

Then rising to go, the youth holds out a right hand. 'Grasp my hand once firmly before I go, Hoye. Pray tell me, will you wait and watch for my return?'

Tusee only nods assent, for mere words are vain.

At early dawn the round campground awakes into song. Men and women sing of bravery and of triumph. They inspire the swelling breasts of the painted warriors mounted on prancing ponies bedecked with the green branches of trees.

Riding slowly around the great ring of cone-shaped tepees, here and there, a loud-singing warrior swears to avenge a former wrong, and thrusts a bare brown arm against the purple east, calling the Great Spirit to hear his vow. All having made the circuit, the singing war-party gallops away southward.

Astride their ponies laden with food and deerskins, brave elderly women follow after their warriors. Among the foremost rides a young woman in elaborately beaded buckskin dress. Proudly mounted, she curbs with the single rawhide loop a wild-eyed pony.

It is Tusee on her father's warhorse. Thus the war-party of Indian men and their faithful women vanish beyond the southern skyline.

A day's journey brings them very near the enemy's borderland. Nightfall finds a pair of twin tepees nestled in a deep ravine. Within one lounge the painted warriors, smoking their pipes and telling weird stories by the firelight, while in the other watchful women crouch uneasily about their centre fire.

By the first grey light in the east the tepees are banished. They are gone. The warriors are in the enemy's camp, breaking dreams with their tomahawks. The women are hid away in secret places in the long thicketed ravine.

The day is far spent, the red sun is low over the west.

At length straggling warriors return, one by one, to the deep hollow. In the twilight they number their men. Three are missing. Of these absent ones two are dead; but the third one, a young man, is a captive to the foe.

'He-he!' lament the warriors, taking food in haste.

In silence each woman, with long strides, hurries to and fro, tying large bundles on her pony's back. Under cover of night the war-party must hasten homeward. Motionless, with bowed head, sits a woman in her hiding-place. She grieves for her lover.

In bitterness of spirit she hears the warriors' murmuring words. With set teeth she plans to cheat the hated enemy of their captive. In the meanwhile low signals are given, and the war-party, unaware of Tusee's absence, steal quietly away. The soft thud of pony hoofs grows fainter and fainter. The gradual hush of the empty ravine whirrs noisily in the ear of the young woman. Alert for any sound of footfalls nigh, she holds her breath to listen. Her right hand rests on a long knife in her belt. Ah, yes, she knows where her pony is hid, but not yet has she need of him. Satisfied that no danger is nigh, she prowls forth from her place of hiding. With a panther's tread and pace she climbs the high ridge beyond the low ravine. From thence she spies the enemy's campfires.

Rooted to the barren bluff the slender woman's figure stands on the pinnacle of night, outlined against a starry sky. The cool night breeze wafts to her burning ear snatches of song and drum. With desperate hate she bites her teeth.

Tusee beckons the stars to witness. With impassioned voice and uplifted face she pleads:

'Great Spirit, speed me to my lover's rescue! Give me swift cunning for a weapon this night! All-powerful Spirit, grant me my warrior-father's heart, strong to slay a foe and mighty to save a friend!'

In the midst of the enemy's campground, underneath a temporary dance-house, are men and women in gala-day dress. It is late in the night, but the merry warriors bend and bow their nude, painted bodies before a bright centre fire. To the lusty men's voices and the rhythmic throbbing drum, they leap and rebound with feathered headgears waving.

Women with red-painted cheeks and long, braided hair sit in a large half-circle against the willow railing. They, too, join in the singing, and rise to dance with their victorious warriors.

Amid this circular dance arena stands a prisoner bound to a post, haggard with shame and sorrow. He hangs his dishevelled head.

He stares with unseeing eyes upon the bare earth at his feet. With jeers and smirking faces the dancers mock the Dakota captive. Rowdy braves and small boys hoot and yell in derision.

Silent among the noisy mob, a tall woman, leaning both elbows on the round willow railing, peers into the lighted arena. The dancing centre fire shines bright into her handsome face, intensifying the night in her dark eyes. It breaks into myriad points upon her beaded dress. Unmindful of the surging throng jostling her at either side, she glares in upon the hateful, scoffing men. Suddenly she turns her head. Tittering maids whisper near her ear:

'There! There! See him now, sneering in the captive's face. 'Tis he who sprang upon the young man and dragged him by his long hair to yonder post. See! He is handsome! How gracefully he dances!'

The silent young woman looks toward the bound captive. She sees a warrior, scarce older than the captive, flourishing a tomahawk in the Dakota's face. A burning rage darts forth from her eyes and brands him for a victim of revenge. Her heart mutters within her breast, 'Come, I wish to meet you, vile foe, who captured my lover and tortures him now with a living death.'

Here the singers hush their voices, and the dancers scatter to their various resting-places along the willow ring. The victor gives a reluctant last twirl of his tomahawk, then, like the others, he leaves the centre ground. With head and shoulders swaying from side to side, he carries a high-pointing chin toward the willow railing. Sitting down upon the ground with crossed legs, he fans himself with an outspread turkey wing.

Now and then he stops his haughty blinking to peep out of the corners of his eyes. He hears someone clearing her throat gently. It is unmistakably for his ear. The wing-fan swings irregularly to and fro. At length he turns a proud face over a bare shoulder and beholds a handsome woman smiling.

'Ah, she would speak to a hero!' thumps his heart wildly.

The singers raise their voices in unison. The music is irresistible. Again lunges the victor into the open arena. Again he leers into the captive's face. At every interval between the songs he returns to his resting-place. Here the young woman awaits him. As he approaches she smiles boldly into his eyes. He is pleased with her face and her smile.

Waving his wing-fan spasmodically in front of his face, he sits with his ears pricked up. He catches a low whisper. A hand taps him lightly on the shoulder. The handsome woman speaks to him in his own tongue. 'Come out into the night. I wish to tell you who I am.'

He must know what sweet words of praise the handsome woman has for him. With both hands he spreads the meshes of the loosely woven willows, and crawls out unnoticed into the dark.

Before him stands the young woman. Beckoning him with a slender hand, she steps backward, away from the light and the restless throng of onlookers. He follows with impatient strides. She quickens her pace. He lengthens his strides. Then suddenly the woman turns from him and darts away with amazing speed. Clinching his fists and biting his lower lip, the young man runs after the fleeing woman. In his maddened pursuit he forgets the dance arena.

Beside a cluster of low bushes the woman halts. The young man, panting for breath and plunging headlong forward, whispers loud, 'Pray tell me, are you a woman or an evil spirit to lure me away?'

Turning on heels firmly planted in the earth, the woman gives a wild spring forward, like a panther for its prey. In a husky voice she hisses between her teeth, 'I am a Dakota woman!'

From her unerring long knife the enemy falls heavily at her feet. The Great Spirit heard Tusee's prayer on the hilltop. He gave her a warrior's strong heart to lessen the foe by one.

A bent old woman's figure, with a bundle like a grandchild slung on her back, walks round and round the dance-house. The wearied onlookers are leaving in twos and threes. The tired dancers creep out of the willow railing, and some go out at the entrance way, till the singers, too, rise from the drum and are trudging drowsily homeward. Within the arena the centre fire lies broken in red embers. The night no longer lingers about the willow railing, but, hovering into the dance-house, covers here and there a snoring man whom sleep has overpowered where he sat.

The captive in his tight-binding rawhide ropes hangs in hopeless despair. Close about him the gloom of night is slowly crouching. Yet the last red, crackling embers cast a faint light upon his long black hair, and, shining through the thick mats, caress his wan face with undying hope.

Still about the dance-house the old woman prowls. Now the embers are grey with ashes.

The old bent woman appears at the entrance way. With a cautious, groping foot she enters. Whispering between her teeth a lullaby for her sleeping child in her blanket, she searches for something forgotten.

Noisily snore the dreaming men in the darkest parts. As the lisping old woman draws nigh, the captive again opens his eyes.

A forefinger she presses to her lip. The young man arouses himself from his stupor. His senses belie him. Before his wide-open eyes the old bent figure straightens into its youthful stature. Tusee herself is beside him. With a stroke upward and downward she severs the cruel cords with her sharp blade. Dropping her blanket from her shoulders, so that it hangs from her girdled waist like a skirt, she shakes the large bundle into a light shawl for her lover. Quickly she spreads it over his bare back.

'Come!' she whispers, and turns to go; but the young man, numb and helpless, staggers nigh to falling.

The sight of his weakness makes her strong. A mighty power thrills her body. Stooping beneath his outstretched arms grasping at the air for support, Tusee lifts him upon her broad shoulders. With half-running, triumphant steps she carries him away into the open night.

The Wedding Feast

And everywhere Kate went her gown was being talked about – the gown she was to be married in, a grey silk that had been bought at a rummage sale. They were all at her, and so persistently that she had begun to feel she was being driven into a trap, and on the morning of her wedding turned round to ask her sister if she thought she ought to marry Peter. Julia thought it would be a pity if she didn't, for her dress would be wasted, and Kate threw a look down the skirt that boded no good.

'I hate the both of them – the priest and that old waddling sow of a mother-in-law of mine, or what is to be.'

After this speech Julia expected to hear Peter's name, but Kate was not thinking of him then nor did she think of him once during the ceremony; she seemed all the time to be absent from herself; and it was not till he got up beside her on the car that she remembered they were now one flesh. But Peter did not notice that she shrank from him; nor did the others. The distribution occupied all their attention. The fat were set beside the lean,[1] and the bridal party drove away, amid a great waving of hands and hullabaloo.

And when the last car passed out of sight, Mrs M'Shane returned home like a goose, waddling slowly, a little overcome by the thought of the happiness that awaited her son. There would be no more lonely evenings in the cabin; Kate would be with him now, and later on there would be some children, and she waddled home thinking of the cradle, and the joy it would be to her to take her grandchildren upon her knee. Passing in at the door, she sat down, so that she might dream over her happiness a little longer. But she had not been sitting long when she had a thought of the work before her – the cabin to be cleaned from end to end, the supper to be cooked, and she did not pause in her work till the pig's head was on the table, and the sheep's tongues also; till the bread was baked and the barrel of porter rolled up in a corner. As she stood with her arms akimbo, expecting the piper every minute, thinking of the great evening it would be, she remembered that her old friend, Annie Connex, had refused to come to Peter's wedding, and that all the village was saying that Kate wouldn't have married Peter if she hadn't been driven to it by the priest and her mother.

'Poor boy!' she thought, 'his heart is so set upon her that he has no ears for any word against her. And aren't people ill-natured to be talking ill of a girl on her wedding day, and Annie Connex preventing her son from coming to the dance? If she won't come herself, she might let Pat come round for an hour.' And if Annie would do this, all the gossips would have their tongues tied. Anyhow, she might try to persuade her. She locked her door and waddled up the road.

'I came round, Annie, to tell you they're married.'

'Well, come in, Mary,' she said, 'if you have the time.'

'If I have the time,' Mrs M'Shane repeated to herself as she passed into the comfortable kitchen, with sides of bacon and home-cured hams hanging from the rafters. She had not prospered like Mrs Connex, and she knew she would never have a beautiful closed range, but an open hearth, till the end of her days. She would never have a nice dresser with a pretty carved top. The dresser in her kitchen was deal, and had no nice shining brass knobs on it. She would never have a parlour, and this parlour had in it a mahogany table and a grandfather's clock that would show you the moon on it just the same as it was in the sky, and there was a glass over the fireplace. And this was Annie Connex's own parlour. The parlour on the other side of the house was even better furnished, for in the summer months Mrs Connex bedded and boarded her lodgers for one pound or one pound five shillings a week.

'So she was married today, and Father Maguire married her after all. I never thought he would have brought her to it. Well, I'm glad she's married.' It rose to Mary's lips to say, 'You are glad she didn't marry your son,' but she put back the words. 'It comes upon me as a bit of surprise, for sure and all I could never see her settling down in the parish.'

'Them that are the wildest before marriage are often the best after, and I think it will be like that with Kate.'

'I hope so,' said Annie. 'And there is reason why it should be like that. She must have liked Peter better than we thought; you will never get me to believe that it was the priest's will or anybody's will but her own that brought Kate to do what she did.'

'I hope she'll make my boy a good wife.'

'I hope so, too,' said Annie, and the women sat over the fire thinking it out.

Annie Connex held the Kavanagh family in abomination; they got two shillings a week off the rates, though every Saturday evening they bought a quarter barrel of porter, and Annie Connex could not believe in the future of a country that would tolerate such a thing. If her son had married a Kavanagh her life would have come to an end, and the twenty years she had worked for him would have been wasted years. Alert as a bee she sprang from her chair, for she was thinking of the work that was waiting for her as soon as she could rid herself of that bothering old slut Mary, who'd just as lief sit here all the morning talking of the Kavanaghs.

'You know Julia is doing well with her lace-making?'

'Selling it, I haven't a doubt, above its market value.'

'She sells it for what she can get. Why shouldn't she?'

'And it looking like as if it was cut out of paper!'

To sell above the market value was abominable in Annie Connex's eyes. Her idea of life was order and administration. And Mary M'Shane seemed to her the very picture of the thriftless, idle village in which they lived.

'We never had anyone like Kate Kavanagh in the village before. I hear she turned round to her sister Julia, who was dressing her, and said, "Now am I to marry him, or shall I go to America?" And she putting on her grey dress at the time.'

'She looked fine in that grey dress; there was lace on the front of it, and there isn't a man in the parish that wouldn't be in Pether's place today if he only dared.'

'I don't catch your meaning, Mary.'

'Well, perhaps I oughtn't to have said it now that she's my own daughter, but I think many would have been a bit afraid of her after what she said to the priest three days ago.'

'She did have her tongue on him. People are telling all ends of stories.'

' 'Tis said that Father Maguire was up at the Kavanaghs' three days ago, and I heard that she hunted him. She called him a policeman, and a tax collector, and a landlord, and if she said this she said more to a priest than anyone ever said before, for there is plenty in the parish who believe he could turn them into rabbits if he liked, though I don't take it on myself to say if it be truth or lie. But I know for a fact that Patsy Rogan had promised to vote for the Unionist[2] to please his landlord, but the priest had been to see his wife, who was going to be confined, and didn't he tell her that if Patsy voted for the wrong man there would be horns on the new baby, and Mrs Rogan was so frightened that she wouldn't let her husband go when he came in that night till he had promised to vote as the priest wished.'

'Patsy Rogan is an ignorant man,' said Annie; 'there are many like him even here.'

'Ah, sure there will be always some like him. Don't we like to believe the priest can do all things?'

'Anyhow she's married, and there will be an end to all the work that has been going on.'

'That's true for you, Annie, and that's just what I came to talk to you about. I think now she's married we ought to give her a chance. Every girl ought to get her chance, and the way to put an end to all this talk about her will be for you to come round to the dance tonight.'

'I don't know that I can do that. I am not friends with the Kavanaghs, though I always bid them the time of day when I meet them on the road.'

'If you come in for a few minutes, or if Pat were to come in for a few minutes. If Pether and Pat aren't friends they'll be enemies.'

'Maybe they'd be worse enemies if I don't keep Pat out of Kate's way. She's married Pether; but her mind isn't settled yet.'

'Yes, Annie, I've thought of all that; but they'll be meeting on the road, and, if they aren't friends, there will be quarrelling, and some bad deed may be done.'

Annie did not answer, and, thinking to convince her, Mary said:

'You wouldn't like to see a corpse right over your window.'

'It ill becomes you, Mary, to speak of corpses after the blow that Pether gave Pat with his stick at Ned Kavanagh's wedding. And I must stand by my son, and keep him out of the low Irish, and he won't be safe until I get him a good wife.'

'The low Irish! Indeed, it ill becomes you, Annie, to be talking in that way of your neighbours. Is it because none of us have brass knockers on our doors? I have seen this pride growing up in you, Annie Connex, this long while. There isn't one in the village that you've any respect for, except the grocer, that black Protestant,[3] who sits behind his counter and makes money, and knows no enjoyment in life at all.'

'That's your way of looking at it; but it isn't mine. I set my face against my son marrying Kate Kavanagh, and you should have done the same.'

'Something will happen to you for the cruel words you have spoken to me this day.'

'Mary, you came to ask me to your son's wedding, and I had to tell you—'

'Yes, and you've told me that you won't come, and that you hate the Kavanaghs, and you've said all you could against them. I oughtn't to have listened to all you said; if I did, 'tis because we have known each other these twenty years. But don't I remember well the rags you'd on your back when you came to this village? It ill becomes—'

Annie followed her to the gate.

The sounds of wheels and hoofs were heard; it was the wedding party going by, and on the first car whom should they see but Kate sitting between Pat and Peter.

'Goodbye, Annie, and good luck to you. I see that Pat's coming to our dance after all,' and she could not speak for want of breath when she got to her door.

They were all there, Pat and the piper, and Kate and Peter, and all their friends: but she couldn't speak, and hadn't the strength to find the key, for she could only think of the black look that had come over Annie's face when she saw Pat sitting by Kate on the car, and Mrs M'Shane laughed as she searched for the key, thinking how quickly her punishment had come.

And all the while they were telling her how they had met Pat at Michael Dunne's.

'When he saw us he tried to sneak into the yard; but I went after him. And don't you think I did right?' Kate was heard to say; and as soon as they were inside she said: 'Now I'll get the biggest jug of porter, and Pether shall drink one half and Pat the other.'

Peter was fond of jugs, and there were large and small on the dresser: some white and brown, and some were gilt, with pink flowers.

'Now, Pether, you'll say something nice.'

'I'll say, then,' said Peter, 'this is the happiest day of my life, as it should be, indeed: for haven't I got the girl that I wanted, and hasn't Pat forgiven me for the blow I struck him? For he knows well I wouldn't hurt a hair of his head. Weren't we boys together? But I had a cross drop in me at the time, and that was how it was.'

Catching sight of Kate's black hair and rosy cheeks, which were all the world to him, he stopped speaking and stood looking at her, unheedful of everything; and at that moment he looked so good and foolish that more than one woman thought it would be a weary thing to live with him.

'Now, Pat, you must make a speech, too,' said Kate.

'I haven't any speech in me,' he said. 'I'm glad enough to be sitting here; but I'm sore afraid my mother saw me on the car, and I think I had better be going home and letting you finish this marriage.'

'What's that you're saying?' said Kate. 'You won't go out of this house till you've danced a reel with me, and now sit down at the table next to me; and, Pether, you sit on the other side of him, so that he won't run away to his mother.'

Her eyes were as bright as coals of fire, and she calling to her father, who was at the end of the table, to have another slice of pig's head, and to the piper, who was having his supper in the window, to have a bit more; and then turning to Pat, who said never a word, and laughing at him for having nothing to say.

It was afterwards they remembered that Kate had seemed to put Pat out of her mind suddenly, and had stood talking to her husband, saying he must dance with her, though it was no amusement to a girl to dance opposite Peter. It was afterwards that Mary, Ned's wife, remembered how Kate, though she had danced with Peter in the first reel, had not been able to keep her eyes from the corner where Pat sat sulking, and that, sudden-like, she had grown weary of Peter. Mary remembered, too, she had seen a wild look pass in Kate's eyes, and that she had gone over to Pat and pulled him out for a dance. And why shouldn't she? for it was a pleasure for a girl to dance opposite to Pat, so cleverly did his feet move to the pipes. Everyone was admiring them when Pat cried out:

'I'm going home. I bid you all goodnight here; finish this wedding as you like.'

And before anyone could stop him he had run out of the house.

'Pether, go after him,' Kate said; 'bring him back. It would be ill luck on our wedding night for anyone to leave us like that.'

Peter went out of the door, and was away some time; but he came back without Pat.

'The night is that dark, I lost him,' he said.

Then Kate didn't seem to care what she said. Her black hair fell down, and she told Peter he was a fool, and that he should have run faster. And her mother said it was the porter that had been too much for her; but she said it was the priest's blessing, and this frightened everyone. But, after saying all this, she went to her husband, saying that he was very good to her, and she had no fault to find with him. But no sooner were the words out of her mouth than her mind seemed to wander, and everyone had expected her to run out of the house. But she went into the other room instead, and shut the door behind her. Everyone knew then there would be no more dancing that night; the piper packed up his pipes, and the wedding party left Peter by the fire, who seemed to be crying like. And they were all sorry to leave him like this; and, so that he might not remember what had happened, Ned drew a big jug of porter, and put it by him.

He took a sup out of it, but seemed to forget everything, and the jug fell out of his hand.

'Never mind the pieces, Pether,' his mother said. 'You can't put them together; and it would be better for you not to drink any more porther. Go to your bed. There's been too much drinking this night, I'm thinking.'

'Mother, I want to know why she said I didn't run fast enough after Pat. And didn't she know that if I hit Pat so hard it was because there were knobs on his stick; and didn't I pick up his stick by mistake for my own?'

'Sure, Peter, it wasn't your fault; we all know that, and Kate knows it too. Now let there be no more talking or drinking. No, Pether, you've had enough porther for tonight.'

He looked round the kitchen, and seeing that Kate was not there, he said:

'She's in the other room, I think; mother, you'll be wantin' to go to your bed.'

And Peter got on his feet and stumbled against the wall, and his mother had to help him towards the door.

'Is it drunk I am, mother? Will you open the door for me?'

But Mrs M'Shane couldn't open the door, and she said:

'I think she's put a bit of stick in it.'

'A bit of stick in the door? And didn't she say that she didn't want to marry me? Didn't she say something about the priest's blessing?'

And then Peter was sore afraid that he would not get sight of his wife that night, and he said:

'Won't she acquie-esh-sh?'

And Kate said:

'No, I won't.'

And then he said:

'We were married in church – today, you acquieshed.'

And she said:

'I'll not open the door to you. You're drunk, Pether, and not fit to enter a decent woman's room.'

'It isn't because I've a drop too much in me that you should have fastened the door on me; it is because you're thinking of the blow I gave Pat. But, Kate, it was because I loved you so much that I struck him. Now will you open – the door?'

'No, I'll not open the door tonight,' she said. 'I'm tired and want to go to sleep.'

And when he said he would break open the door, she said:

'You're too drunk, Pether, and sorra bit of good it will do you. I'll be no wife to you tonight, and that's as true as God's in heaven.'

'Pether,' said his mother, 'don't trouble her tonight. There has been too much dancing and drinking.'

'It's a hard thing . . . shut out of me wife's room.'

'Pether, don't vex her tonight. Don't hammer her door any more.'

'Didn't she acquie-esh? Mother, you have always been agin me. Didn't she acquie-esh?'

'Oh, Pether, why do you say I'm agin you?'

'Did you hear her say that I was drunk? If you tell me I'm drunk I'll say no more. I'll acquie-esh.'

'Pether, you must go to sleep.'

'Yes, go to sleep . . . I want to go to sleep, but she won't open the door.'

'Pether, never mind her.'

'It isn't that I mind; I'm getting sleepy, but what I want to know, mother, before I go to bed, is if I'm drunk. Tell me I'm not drunk on my wedding night, and, though Kate — and I'll acquie-esh in all that may be put upon me.'

He covered his face with his hands and his mother begged him not to cry. He became helpless, she put a blanket under his head and covered him with another blanket, and went up the ladder and lay down in the hay. She asked herself what had she done to deserve this trouble, and cried a great deal. And the poor, hapless old woman was asleep in the morning when Peter stumbled to his feet and found his way into the yard. As soon as he had dipped his head in a pail of water, he remembered the horses were waiting for him in the farm, and walked off to his work, staggering a little. Kate must have been watching for his going, for as soon as he was gone she drew back the bolt of the door and came into the kitchen.

'I'm going, mother,' she called up to the loft.

'Wait a minute, Kate,' said Mrs M'Shane, and she was halfway down the ladder when Kate said:

'I can't wait, I'm going.' And she walked up the road to her mother's – all the chairs were out in the pathway, for the rector was coming down that afternoon, and she wanted to show him how beautifully clean she kept the cabin.

'I've come, mother, to give you this,' and she took the wedding ring off her finger and threw it on the ground. 'I shut the door on him last night, and I'm going to America today. You see how well the marriage that you and the priest made up together has turned out.'

'Going to America,' said Mrs Kavanagh. 'Now, is Pat going with you? and for pity sake —'

Kate stood looking at the bushes that grew between their cottage and the next one, remembering that elder-flower water is good for the complexion.

'I'm going,' she said suddenly, 'there's nothing more to say. Goodbye.'

And her mother said, 'She's going with Pat Connex.' But Kate had no thought of going to America with him or of seeing him that day. But she met him at the crossroads, out with one of his carts, and she thought he looked a nice boy; but her second thoughts were, 'He's better suited to Ireland.' And on this thought he and the country she had lived in always seemed to escape from her like a dream.

'I'm going to America, Pat.'

'You were married yesterday.'

'Yes, that was the priest's doing and mother's, and I thought they knew best. But I'm thinking one must go one's own way, and there's no judging for oneself here. That's why I'm going. You'll find some other girl, Pat.'

'There's not another girl like you in the village. We're a dead and alive lot. You stood up to the priest.'

'I didn't stand up to him enough. You're waiting for someone. Who are you waiting for?'

'I don't like to tell you, Kate.'

She pressed him to answer her, and he told her he was waiting for the priest. His mother had said he must marry, and the priest was coming to make up a marriage for him.

'Everything's mother's.'

'That's true, Pat, and you'll give a message for me. Tell my mother-in-law that I've gone.'

'She'll be asking me questions, and I'll be sore set for an answer.'

She looked at him steadily, but she left him without speaking, and he stood thinking.

He had had good times with her, and all such times were ended for him for ever. He was going to be married and he didn't know to whom. Suddenly he remembered he had a message to deliver, and went down to the M'Shanes' cabin.

'Ah, Mrs M'Shane, it was a bad day for me when she married Pether. But this is a worse one, for we've both lost her.'

'My poor boy will feel it sorely.'

And when Peter came in for his dinner his mother said:

'Pether, she's gone, she's gone to America, and you're well rid of her.'

'Don't say that, mother, I am not well rid of her, for there's no other woman in the world for me except her that's gone. Has she gone with Pat Connex?'

'No, he said nothing about that, and it was he who brought the message.'

'I've no one to blame but myself, mother. Wasn't I drunk last night, and how could she be letting a drunken fellow like me into her bed?'

And out he went into the back yard, and didn't his mother hear him crying there till it was time for him to go back to work?

EDITH WHARTON

The Reckoning

I

'The marriage law of the new dispensation[1] will be: *Thou shalt not be unfaithful – to thyself.*'

A discreet murmur of approval filled the studio, and through the haze of cigarette smoke Mrs Clement Westall, as her husband descended from his improvised platform, saw him merged in a congratulatory group of ladies. Westall's informal talks on 'The New Ethics' had drawn about him an eager following of the mentally unemployed – those who, as he had once phrased it, liked to have their brain-food cut up for them. The talks had begun by accident. Westall's ideas were known to be 'advanced', but hitherto their advance had not been in the direction of publicity. He had been, in his wife's opinion, almost pusillanimously careful not to let his personal views endanger his professional standing. Of late, however, he had shown a puzzling tendency to dogmatize, to throw down the gauntlet, to flaunt his private code in the face of society; and the relation of the sexes being a topic always sure of an audience, a few admiring friends had persuaded him to give his after-dinner opinions a larger circulation by summing them up in a series of talks at the Van Sideren studio.

The Herbert Van Siderens were a couple who subsisted, socially, on the fact that they had a studio. Van Sideren's pictures were chiefly valuable as accessories to the *mise en scène* which differentiated his wife's 'afternoons' from the blighting functions held in long New York drawing rooms, and permitted her to offer their friends whisky-and-soda instead of tea. Mrs Van Sideren, for her part, was skilled in making the most of the kind of atmosphere which a lay figure and an easel create; and if at times she found the illusion hard to maintain, and lost courage to the extent of almost wishing that Herbert could paint, she promptly overcame such moments of weakness by calling in some fresh talent, some extraneous re-enforcement of the 'artistic' impression. It was in quest of such aid that she had seized on Westall, coaxing him, somewhat to his wife's surprise, into a flattered participation in her fraud. It was vaguely felt, in the Van Sideren circle, that all the audacities were artistic, and that a teacher who pronounced marriage immoral was somehow as distinguished as a painter who depicted purple grass and a green sky. The Van Sideren set were tired of the conventional colour-scheme in art and conduct.

Julia Westall had long had her own views on the immorality of marriage; she might indeed have claimed her husband as a disciple. In the early days of their union she had secretly resented his disinclination to proclaim himself a follower of the new creed; had been inclined to tax him with moral cowardice, with a failure to live up to the convictions for which their marriage was supposed to stand. That was in the first burst of propagandism, when, womanlike, she wanted to turn her disobedience into a law. Now she felt differently. She could hardly account for the change, yet being a woman who never allowed her impulses to remain unaccounted for, she tried to do so by saying that she did not care to have the articles of her faith misinterpreted by the vulgar. In this connection, she was beginning to think that almost everyone was vulgar; certainly there were few to whom she would have cared to entrust the defence of so esoteric a doctrine. And it was precisely at this point that Westall, discarding his unspoken principles, had chosen to descend from the heights of privacy, and stand hawking his convictions at the street corner!

It was Una Van Sideren who, on this occasion, unconsciously focused upon herself Mrs Westall's wandering resentment. In the first place, the girl had no business to be there. It was 'horrid' – Mrs Westall found herself slipping back into the old feminine vocabulary – simply 'horrid' to think of a young girl's being allowed to listen to such talk. The fact that Una smoked cigarettes and sipped an occasional cocktail did not in the least tarnish a certain radiant innocency which made her appear the victim, rather than the accomplice, of her parents' vulgarities. Julia Westall felt in a hot helpless way that something ought to be done – that someone ought to speak to the girl's mother. And just then Una glided up.

'Oh, Mrs Westall, how beautiful it was!' Una fixed her with large limpid eyes. 'You believe it all, I suppose?' she asked with seraphic gravity.

'All – what, my dear child?'

The girl shone on her. 'About the higher life – the freer expansion of the individual – the law of fidelity to one's self,' she glibly recited.

Mrs Westall, to her own wonder, blushed a deep and burning blush.

'My dear Una,' she said, 'you don't in the least understand what it's all about!'

Miss Van Sideren stared, with a slowly answering blush. 'Don't *you*, then?' she murmured.

Mrs Westall laughed. 'Not always – or altogether! But I should like some tea, please.'

Una led her to the corner where innocent beverages were dispensed. As Julia received her cup she scrutinized the girl more carefully. It was not such a girlish face, after all – definite lines were forming under the rosy haze of youth. She reflected that Una must be six-and-twenty, and wondered why she had not married. A nice stock of ideas she would have as her dower! If *they* were to be a part of the modern girl's trousseau—

Mrs Westall caught herself up with a start. It was as though someone else had been speaking – a stranger who had borrowed her own voice: she felt herself the dupe of some fantastic mental ventriloquism. Concluding suddenly that the room was stifling and Una's tea too sweet, she set down her cup and looked about for Westall: to meet his eyes had long been her refuge from every uncertainty. She met them now, but only, as she felt, in transit; they included her parenthetically in a larger flight. She followed the flight, and it carried her to a corner to which Una had withdrawn – one of the palmy nooks to which Mrs Van Sideren attributed the success of her Saturdays. Westall, a moment later, had overtaken his look, and found a place at the girl's side. She bent forward, speaking eagerly; he leaned back, listening, with the depreciatory smile which acted as a filter to flattery, enabling him to swallow the strongest doses without apparent grossness of appetite. Julia winced at her own definition of the smile.

On the way home, in the deserted winter dusk, Westall surprised his wife by a sudden boyish pressure of her arm. 'Did I open their eyes a bit? Did I tell them what you wanted me to?' he asked gaily.

Almost unconsciously, she let her arm slip from his. 'What *I* wanted—?'

'Why, haven't you – all this time?' She caught the honest wonder of his tone. 'I somehow fancied you'd rather blamed me for not talking more openly – before—. You almost made me feel, at times, that I was sacrificing principles to expediency.'

She paused a moment over her reply; then she asked quietly: 'What made you decide not to – any longer?'

She felt again the vibration of a faint surprise. 'Why – the wish to please you!' he answered, almost too simply.

'I wish you would not go on, then,' she said abruptly.

He stopped in his quick walk, and she felt his stare through the darkness.

'Not go on—?'

'Call a hansom, please. I'm tired,' broke from her with a sudden rush of physical weariness.

Instantly his solicitude enveloped her. The room had been infernally hot – and then that confounded cigarette smoke – he had noticed once or twice that she looked pale – she mustn't come to another Saturday. She felt herself yielding, as she always did, to the warm influence of his concern for her, the feminine in her leaning on the man in him with a conscious intensity of abandonment. He put her in the hansom, and her hand stole into his in the darkness. A tear or two rose, and she let them fall. It was so delicious to cry over imaginary troubles!

That evening, after dinner, he surprised her by reverting to the subject of his talk. He combined a man's dislike of uncomfortable questions with an almost feminine skill in eluding them; and she knew that if he returned to the subject he must have some special reason for doing so.

'You seem not to have cared for what I said this afternoon. Did I put the case badly?'

'No – you put it very well.'

'Then what did you mean by saying that you would rather not have me go on with it?'

She glanced at him nervously, her ignorance of his intention deepening her sense of helplessness.

'I don't think I care to hear such things discussed in public.'

'I don't understand you,' he exclaimed. Again the feeling that his surprise was genuine gave an air of obliquity to her own attitude. She was not sure that she understood herself.

'Won't you explain?' he said with a tinge of impatience.

Her eyes wandered about the familiar drawing room which had been the scene of so many of their evening confidences. The shaded lamps, the quiet-coloured walls hung with mezzotints, the pale spring flowers scattered here and there in Venice glasses and bowls of old Sèvres, recalled, she hardly knew why, the apartment in which the evenings of her first marriage had been passed – a wilderness of rosewood and upholstery, with a picture of a Roman peasant above the mantelpiece, and a Greek slave in 'statuary marble' between the folding doors of the back drawing room. It was a room with which she had never been able to establish any closer relation than that between a traveller and a railway station; and now, as she looked about at the surroundings which stood for her deepest affinities – the room for which she had left that other room – she was startled by the same sense of strangeness and unfamiliarity. The prints, the flowers, the subdued tones of the old porcelains, seemed to typify a superficial refinement which had no relation to the deeper significances of life.

Suddenly she heard her husband repeating his question.

'I don't know that I can explain,' she faltered.

He drew his armchair forward so that he faced her across the hearth. The light of a reading lamp fell on his finely drawn face, which had a kind of surface-sensitiveness akin to the surface-refinement of its setting.

'Is it that you no longer believe in our ideas?' he asked.

'In our ideas—?'

'The ideas I am trying to teach. The ideas you and I are supposed to stand for.' He paused a moment. 'The ideas on which our marriage was founded.'

The blood rushed to her face. He had his reasons, then – she was sure now that he had his reasons! In the ten years of their marriage, how often had either of them stopped to consider the ideas on which it was founded? How often does a man dig about the basement of his house to examine its foundation? The foundation is there, of course – the house rests on it – but one lives above-stairs and not in the cellar. It was she, indeed, who in the beginning had insisted on reviewing the situation now and then, on recapitulating the reasons which justified her course, on proclaiming, from time to time, her adherence to the religion of personal independence; but she had long ceased to feel the want of any such ideal standards, and had accepted her marriage as frankly and naturally as though it had been based on the primitive needs of the heart, and required no special sanction to explain or justify it.

'Of course I still believe in our ideas!' she exclaimed.

'Then I repeat that I don't understand. It was a part of your theory that the greatest possible publicity should be given to our view of marriage. Have you changed your mind in that respect?'

She hesitated. 'It depends on circumstances – on the public one is addressing. The set of people that the Van Siderens get about them don't care for the truth or falseness of a doctrine. They are attracted simply by its novelty.'

'And yet it was in just such a set of people that you and I met, and learned the truth from each other.'

'That was different.'

'In what way?'

'I was not a young girl, to begin with. It is perfectly unfitting that young girls should be present at – at such times – should hear such things discussed—'

'I thought you considered it one of the deepest social wrongs that such things never *are* discussed before young girls; but that is beside the point, for I don't remember seeing any young girl in my audience today—'

'Except Una Van Sideren!'

He turned slightly and pushed back the lamp at his elbow.

'Oh, Miss Van Sideren – naturally—'

'Why naturally?'

'The daughter of the house – would you have had her sent out with her governess?'

'If I had a daughter I should not allow such things to go on in my house!'

Westall, stroking his moustache, leaned back with a faint smile. 'I fancy Miss Van Sideren is quite capable of taking care of herself.'

'No girl knows how to take care of herself – till it's too late.'

'And yet you would deliberately deny her the surest means of self-defence?'

'What do you call the surest means of self-defence?'

'Some preliminary knowledge of human nature in its relation to the marriage tie.'

She made an impatient gesture. 'How should you like to marry that kind of a girl?'

'Immensely – if she were my kind of girl in other respects.'

She took up the argument at another point.

'You are quite mistaken if you think such talk does not affect young girls. Una was in a state of the most absurd exaltation—' She broke off, wondering why she had spoken.

Westall reopened a magazine which he had laid aside at the beginning of their discussion. 'What you tell me is immensely flattering to my oratorical talent – but I fear you overrate its effect. I can assure you that Miss Van Sideren doesn't have to have her thinking done for her. She's quite capable of doing it herself.'

'You seem very familiar with her mental processes!' flashed unguardedly from his wife.

He looked up quietly from the pages he was cutting.

'I should like to be,' he answered. 'She interests me.'

2

If there be a distinction in being misunderstood, it was one denied to Julia Westall when she left her first husband. Everyone was ready to excuse and even to defend her. The world she adorned agreed that John Arment was 'impossible', and hostesses gave a sigh of relief at the thought that it would no longer be necessary to ask him to dine.

There had been no scandal connected with the divorce: neither side had accused the other of the offence euphemistically described as 'statutory'.[2] The Arments had indeed been obliged to transfer their allegiance to a State which recognized desertion as a cause for divorce, and construed the term so liberally that the seeds of desertion were shown to exist in every union. Even Mrs Arment's second marriage did not make traditional morality stir in its sleep. It was known that she had not met her second husband till after she had parted from the first, and she had, moreover, replaced a rich man by a poor one. Though Clement Westall was acknowledged to be a rising lawyer, it was generally felt that his fortunes would not rise as rapidly as his reputation. The Westalls would probably always have to live quietly and go out to dinner in cabs. Could there be better evidence of Mrs Arment's complete disinterestedness?

If the reasoning by which her friends justified her course was somewhat cruder and less complex than her own elucidation of the matter, both explanations led to the same conclusion: John Arment was impossible. The only difference was that, to his wife, his impossibility was something deeper than a social disqualification. She had once said, in ironical defence of her marriage, that it had at least preserved her from the necessity of sitting next to him at dinner; but she had not then realized at what cost the immunity was purchased. John Arment was impossible; but the sting of his impossibility lay in the fact that he made it impossible for those about him to be other than himself. By an unconscious process of elimination he had excluded from the world everything of which he did not feel a personal need: had become, as it were, a climate in which only his own requirements survived. This might seem to imply a deliberate selfishness; but there was nothing deliberate about Arment. He was as instinctive as an animal or a child. It was this childish element in his nature which sometimes for a moment unsettled his wife's estimate of him. Was it possible that he was simply undeveloped, that he had delayed, some-what longer than is usual, the laborious process of growing up? He had the kind of sporadic shrewdness which causes it to be said of a dull man that he is 'no fool'; and it was this quality that his wife found most trying. Even to the naturalist it is annoying to have his deductions disturbed by some unforeseen aberrancy of form or function; and how much more so to the wife whose estimate of herself is inevitably bound up with her judgement of her husband!

Arment's shrewdness did not, indeed, imply any latent intellectual power; it suggested, rather, potentialities of feeling, of suffering, perhaps, in a blind rudimentary way, on which Julia's sensibilities naturally declined to linger. She so fully understood her own reasons for leaving him that she disliked to think they were not as comprehens-ible to her husband. She was haunted, in her analytic moments, by the look of perplexity, too inarticulate for words, with which he had acquiesced in her explanations.

These moments were rare with her, however. Her marriage had been too concrete a misery to be surveyed philosophically. If she had been unhappy for complex reasons, the unhappiness was as real as though it had been uncomplicated. Soul is more bruisable than flesh, and Julia was wounded in every fibre of her spirit. Her husband's personality seemed to be closing gradually in on her, obscuring the sky and cutting off the air, till she felt herself shut up among the decaying bodies of her starved hopes. A sense of having been decoyed by some world-old conspiracy into this bondage of body and soul filled her with despair. If marriage was the slow lifelong acquittal of a debt contracted in ignorance, then marriage was a crime against human nature. She, for one, would have no share in maintaining the pretence of which she had been a victim: the pretence that a man and a woman, forced into the narrowest of personal relations, must remain there till the end, though they may have outgrown the span of each other's natures as the mature tree outgrows the iron brace about the sapling.

It was in the first heat of her moral indignation that she had met Clement Westall. She had seen at once that he was 'interested', and had fought off the discovery, dreading any influence that should draw her back into the bondage of conventional relations. To ward off the peril she had, with an almost crude precipitancy, revealed her opinions to him. To her surprise, she found that he shared them. She was attracted by the frankness of a suitor who, while pressing his suit, admitted that he did not believe in marriage. Her worst audacities did not seem to surprise him: he had thought out all that she had felt, and they had reached the same conclusion. People grew at varying rates, and the yoke that was an easy fit for the one might soon become galling to the other. That was what divorce was for: the readjustment of personal relations. As soon as their necessarily transitive nature was recognized they would gain in dignity as well as in harmony. There would be no further need of the ignoble concessions and connivances, the perpetual sacrifice of personal delicacy and moral pride, by means of which imperfect marriages were now held together. Each partner to the contract would be on his mettle, forced to live up to the highest standard of self-development, on pain of losing the other's respect and affection. The low nature could no longer drag the higher down, but must struggle to rise, or remain alone on its inferior level. The only necessary condition to a harmonious marriage was a frank recognition of this truth, and a solemn agreement between the contracting parties to keep faith with themselves, and not to live together for a moment after complete accord had ceased to exist between them. The new adultery was unfaithfulness to self.

It was, as Westall had just reminded her, on this understanding that they had married. The ceremony was an unimportant concession to social prejudice: now that the door of divorce stood open, no marriage need be an imprisonment, and the contract therefore no longer involved any diminution of self-respect. The nature of their attachment placed them so far beyond the reach of such contingencies that it was easy to discuss them with an open mind; and Julia's sense of security made her dwell with a tender insistence on Westall's promise to claim his release when he should cease to love her. The exchange of these vows seemed to make them, in a sense, champions of the new law, pioneers in the forbidden realm of individual freedom: they felt that they had somehow achieved beatitude without martyrdom.

This, as Julia now reviewed the past, she perceived to have been her theoretical attitude toward marriage. It was unconsciously, insidiously, that her ten years of happiness with Westall had developed another conception of the tie; a reversion, rather, to the old instinct of passionate dependency and possessorship that now made her blood revolt at the mere hint of change. Change? Renewal? Was that what they had called it, in their foolish jargon? Destruction, extermination rather – this rending of a myriad fibres interwoven with another's being! Another? But he was not other! He and she were one, one in the mystic sense which alone gave marriage its significance. The new law was not for them, but for the disunited creatures forced into a mockery of union. The gospel she had felt called on to proclaim had no bearing on her own case . . . She sent for the doctor and told him she was sure she needed a nerve tonic.

She took the nerve tonic diligently but it failed to quiet her fears. She did not know what she feared; but that made her anxiety the more pervasive. Her husband had not reverted to the subject of his Saturday talks. He was unusually kind and considerate, with a softening of his quick manner, a touch of shyness in his consideration, that sickened her with new fears. She told herself that it was because she looked badly – because he knew about the doctor and the nerve tonic – that he showed this deference to her wishes, this eagerness to screen her from moral draughts; but the explanation simply cleared the way for fresh inferences.

The week passed slowly, vacantly, like a prolonged Sunday. On Saturday the morning post brought a note from Mrs Van Sideren. Would dear Julia ask Mr Westall to come half an hour earlier than usual, as there was to be some music after his 'talk'? Westall was just leaving for his office when his wife read the note. She opened the drawing-room door and called him back to deliver the message.

He glanced at the note and tossed it aside. 'What a bore! I shall have to cut my game of racquets. Well, I suppose it can't be helped. Will you write and say it's all right?'

Julia hesitated a moment, her hand stiffening on the chair back against which she leaned.

'You mean to go on with these talks?' she asked.

'I – why not?' he returned; and this time it struck her that his surprise was not quite unfeigned. The perception helped her to find words.

'You said you had started them with the idea of pleasing me—'

'Well?'

'I told you last week that they didn't please me.'

'Last week? Oh—' He seemed to make an effort of memory. 'I thought you were nervous then; you sent for the doctor the next day.'

'It was not the doctor I needed; it was your assurance—'

'My assurance?'

Suddenly she felt the floor fail under her. She sank into the chair with a choking throat, her words, her reasons slipping away from her like straws down a whirling flood.

'Clement,' she cried, 'isn't it enough for you to know that I hate it?'

He turned to close the door behind them; then he walked toward her and sat down. 'What is it that you hate?' he asked gently.

She had made a desperate effort to rally her routed argument.

'I can't bear to have you speak as if – as if – our marriage – were like the other kind – the wrong kind. When I heard you there, the other afternoon, before all those inquisitive gossiping people, proclaiming that husbands and wives had a right to leave each other whenever they were tired – or had seen someone else—'

Westall sat motionless, his eyes fixed on a pattern of the carpet.

'You *have* ceased to take this view, then?' he said as she broke off. 'You no longer believe that husbands and wives *are* justified in separating – under such conditions?'

'Under such conditions?' she stammered. 'Yes – I still believe that – but how can we judge for others? What can we know of the circumstances—?'

He interrupted her. 'I thought it was a fundamental article of our creed that the special circumstances produced by marriage were not to interfere with the full assertion of individual liberty.' He paused a moment. 'I thought that was your reason for leaving Arment.'

She flushed to the forehead. It was not like him to give a personal turn to the argument.

'It was my reason,' she said simply.

'Well, then – why do you refuse to recognize its validity now?'

'I don't – I don't – I only say that one can't judge for others.'

He made an impatient movement. 'This is mere hair-splitting. What you mean is that, the doctrine having served your purpose when you needed it, you now repudiate it.'

'Well,' she exclaimed, flushing again, 'what if I do? What does it matter to us?'

Westall rose from his chair. He was excessively pale, and stood before his wife with something of the formality of a stranger.

'It matters to me,' he said in a low voice, 'because I do *not* repudiate it.'

'Well—?'

'And because I had intended to invoke it as—'

He paused and drew his breath deeply. She sat silent, almost deafened by her heartbeats.

—'as a complete justification of the course I am about to take.'

Julia remained motionless. 'What course is that?' she asked.

He cleared his throat. 'I mean to claim the fulfilment of your promise.'

For an instant the room wavered and darkened; then she recovered a torturing acuteness of vision. Every detail of her surroundings pressed upon her: the tick of the clock, the slant of sunlight on the wall, the hardness of the chair arms that she grasped, were a separate wound to each sense.

'My promise—' she faltered.

'Your part of our mutual agreement to set each other free if one or the other should wish to be released.'

She was silent again. He waited a moment, shifting his position nervously; then he said, with a touch of irritability: 'You acknowledge the agreement?'

The question went through her like a shock. She lifted her head to it proudly. 'I acknowledge the agreement,' she said.

'And – you don't mean to repudiate it?'

A log on the hearth fell forward, and mechanically he advanced and pushed it back.

'No,' she answered slowly, 'I don't mean to repudiate it.'

There was a pause. He remained near the hearth, his elbow resting on the mantel shelf. Close to his hand stood a little cup of jade that he had given her on one of their wedding anniversaries. She wondered vaguely if he noticed it.

'You intend to leave me, then?' she said at length.

His gesture seemed to deprecate the crudeness of the allusion.

'To marry someone else?'

Again his eye and hand protested. She rose and stood before him.

'Why should you be afraid to tell me? Is it Una Van Sideren?'

He was silent.

'I wish you good luck,' she said.

3

She looked up, finding herself alone. She did not remember when or how he had left the room, or how long afterward she had sat there. The fire still smouldered on the hearth, but the slant of sunlight had left the wall.

Her first conscious thought was that she had not broken her word, that she had fulfilled the very letter of their bargain. There had been no crying out, no vain appeal to the past, no attempt at temporizing or evasion. She had marched straight up to the guns.

Now that it was over, she sickened to find herself alive. She looked about her, trying to recover her hold on reality. Her identity seemed to be slipping from her, as it disappears in a physical swoon. 'This is my room – this is my house,' she heard herself saying. Her room? Her house? She could almost hear the walls laugh back at her.

She stood up, a weariness in every bone. The silence of the room frightened her. She remembered, now, having heard the front door close a long time ago: the sound suddenly re-echoed through her brain. Her husband must have left the house, then – her *husband*? She no longer knew in what terms to think: the simplest phrases had a poisoned edge. She sank back into her chair, overcome by a strange weakness. The clock struck ten – it was only ten o'clock! Suddenly she remembered that she had not ordered dinner . . . or were they dining out that evening? *Dinner – dining out –* the old meaningless phraseology pursued her! She must try to think of herself as she would think of someone else, a someone dissociated from all the familiar routine of the past, whose wants and habits must gradually be learned, as one might spy out the ways of a strange animal . . .

The clock struck another hour – eleven. She stood up again and walked to the door: she thought she would go upstairs to her room. *Her* room? Again the word derided her. She opened the door, crossed the narrow hall and walked up the stairs. As she passed, she noticed Westall's sticks and umbrellas: a pair of his gloves lay on the hall table. The same stair-carpet mounted between the same walls; the same old French print, in its narrow black frame, faced her on the landing. This visual continuity was intolerable. Within, a gaping chasm; without, the same untroubled and familiar surface. She must get away from it before she could attempt to think. But, once in her room, she sat down on the lounge, a stupor creeping over her . . .

Gradually her vision cleared. A great deal had happened in the interval – a wild marching and countermarching of emotions, arguments, ideas – a fury of insurgent impulses that fell back spent upon themselves. She had tried, at first, to rally, to organize these chaotic forces. There must be help somewhere, if only she could master the inner tumult. Life could not be broken off short like this, for a whim, a fancy; the law itself would side with her, would defend her. The law? What claim had she upon it? She was the prisoner of her own choice: she had been her own legislator, and she was the predestined victim of the code she had devised. But this was grotesque, intolerable – a mad mistake, for which she could not be held accountable! The law she had despised was still there, might still be invoked . . . invoked, but to what end? Could she ask it to chain Westall to her side? *She* had been allowed to go free when she claimed her freedom – should she show less magnanimity than she had exacted? Magnanimity? The word lashed her with its irony – one does not strike an attitude when one is fighting for life! She would threaten, grovel, cajole . . . she would yield anything to keep her hold on happiness. Ah, but the difficulty lay deeper! The law could not help her – her own apostasy could not help her. She was the victim of the theories she renounced. It was as though some giant machine of her own making had caught her up in its wheels and was grinding her to atoms . . .

It was afternoon when she found herself out of doors. She walked with an aimless haste, fearing to meet familiar faces. The day was radiant, metallic: one of those searching American days so calculated to reveal the shortcomings of our street cleaning and the excesses of our architecture. The streets looked bare and hideous; everything stared and glittered. She called a passing hansom, and gave Mrs Van Sideren's address. She did not know what had led up to the act; but she found herself suddenly resolved to speak, to cry out a warning. It was too late to save herself – but the girl might still be told. The hansom rattled up Fifth Avenue; she sat with her eyes fixed, avoiding recognition. At the Van Siderens' door she sprang out and rang the bell. Action had cleared her brain, and she felt calm and self-possessed. She knew now exactly what she meant to say.

The ladies were both out . . . the parlour maid stood waiting for a card. Julia, with a vague murmur, turned away from the door and lingered a moment on the sidewalk. Then she remembered that she had not paid the cab-driver. She drew a dollar from her purse and handed it to him. He touched his hat and drove off, leaving her alone in the long empty street. She wandered away westward, toward strange thoroughfares, where she was not likely to meet acquaintances. The feeling of aimlessness had returned. Once she found herself in the afternoon torrent of Broadway, swept past tawdry shops and flaming theatrical posters, with a succession of meaningless faces gliding by in the opposite direction . . .

A feeling of faintness reminded her that she had not eaten since morning. She turned into a side street of shabby houses, with rows of ash barrels behind bent area railings. In a basement window she saw the sign *Ladies' Restaurant:* a pie and a dish of doughnuts lay against the dusty pane like petrified food in an ethnological museum. She entered, and a young woman with a weak mouth and a brazen eye cleared a table for her near the window. The table was covered with a red-and-white cotton cloth and adorned with a bunch of celery in a thick tumbler and a salt cellar full of greyish lumpy salt. Julia ordered tea, and sat a long time waiting for it. She was glad to be away from the noise and confusion of the streets. The low-ceilinged room was empty, and two or three waitresses with thin pert faces lounged in the background staring at her and whispering together. At last the tea was brought in a discoloured metal teapot. Julia poured a cup full and drank it hastily. It was black and bitter, but it flowed through her veins like an elixir. She was almost dizzy with exhilaration. Oh, how tired, how unutterably tired she had been!

She drank a second cup, blacker and bitterer, and now her mind was once more working clearly. She felt as vigorous, as decisive, as when she had stood on the Van Siderens' doorstep – but the wish to return there had subsided. She saw now the futility of such an attempt – the humiliation to which it might have exposed her . . . The pity of it was that she did not know what to do next. The short winter day was fading, and she realized that she could not remain much longer in the restaurant without attracting notice. She paid for her tea and went out into the street. The lamps were alight, and here and there a basement shop cast an oblong of gas-light across the fissured pavement. In the dusk there was something sinister about the aspect of the street, and she hastened back toward Fifth Avenue. She was not used to being out alone at that hour.

At the corner of Fifth Avenue she paused and stood watching the stream of carriages. At last a policeman caught sight of her and signed to her that he would take her across. She had not meant to cross the street, but she obeyed automatically, and presently found herself on the farther corner. There she paused again for a moment; but she fancied the policeman was watching her, and this sent her hastening down the nearest side street . . . After that she walked a long time, vaguely . . . Night had fallen, and now and then, through the windows of a passing carriage, she caught the expanse of an evening waistcoat or the shimmer of an opera cloak . . .

Suddenly she found herself in a familiar street. She stood still a moment, breathing quickly. She had turned the corner without noticing whither it led; but now, a few yards ahead of her, she saw the house in which she had once lived – her first husband's house. The blinds were drawn, and only a faint translucence marked the windows and the transom above the door. As she stood there she heard a step behind her, and a man walked by in the direction of the house. He walked slowly, with a heavy middle-aged gait, his head sunk a little between the shoulders, the red crease of his neck visible above the fur collar of his overcoat. He crossed the street, went up the steps of the house, drew forth a latch key and let himself in . . .

There was no one else in sight. Julia leaned for a long time against the area rail at the corner, her eyes fixed on the front of the house. The feeling of physical weariness had returned, but the strong tea still throbbed in her veins and lit her brain with an unnatural clearness. Presently she heard another step draw near, and moving quickly away, she too crossed the street and mounted the steps of the house. The impulse which had carried her there prolonged itself in a quick pressure of the electric bell – then she felt suddenly weak and tremulous, and grasped the balustrade for support. The door opened and a young footman with a fresh inexperienced face stood on the threshold. Julia knew in an instant that he would admit her.

'I saw Mr Arment going in just now,' she said. 'Will you ask him to see me for a moment?'

The footman hesitated. 'I think Mr Arment has gone up to dress for dinner, madam.'

Julia advanced into the hall. 'I am sure he will see me – I will not detain him long,' she said. She spoke quietly, authoritatively, in the tone which a good servant does not mistake. The footman had his hand on the drawing-room door.

'I will tell him, madam. What name, please?'

Julia trembled: she had not thought of that. 'Merely say a lady,' she returned carelessly.

The footman wavered and she fancied herself lost; but at that instant the door opened from within and John Arment stepped into the hall. He drew back sharply as he saw her, his florid face turning sallow with the shock; then the blood poured back to it, swelling the veins on his temples and reddening the lobes of his thick ears.

It was long since Julia had seen him, and she was startled at the change in his appearance. He had thickened, coarsened, settled down into the enclosing flesh. But she noted this insensibly: her one conscious thought was that, now she was face to face with him, she must not let him escape till he had heard her. Every pulse in her body throbbed with the urgency of her message.

She went up to him as he drew back. 'I must speak to you,' she said.

Arment hesitated, red and stammering. Julia glanced at the footman, and her look acted as a warning. The instinctive shrinking from a 'scene' predominated over every other impulse, and Arment said slowly: 'Will you come this way?'

He followed her into the drawing room and closed the door. Julia, as she advanced, was vaguely aware that the room at least was unchanged: time had not mitigated its horrors. The contadina still lurched from the chimney-breast, and the Greek slave obstructed the threshold of the inner room. The place was alive with memories: they started out from every fold of the yellow satin curtains and glided between the angles of the rosewood furniture. But while some subordinate agency was carrying these impressions to her brain, her whole conscious effort was centred in the act of dominating Arment's will. The fear that he would refuse to hear her mounted like fever to her brain. She felt her purpose melt before it, words and arguments running into each other in the heat of her longing. For a moment her voice failed her, and she imagined herself thrust out before she could speak; but as she was struggling for a word, Arment pushed a chair forward, and said quietly: 'You are not well.'

The sound of his voice steadied her. It was neither kind nor unkind – a voice that supended judgement, rather, awaiting unforeseen developments. She supported herself against the back of the chair and drew a deep breath.

'Shall I send for something?' he continued, with a cold embarrassed politeness.

Julia raised an entreating hand. 'No – no – thank you. I am quite well.'

He paused midway toward the bell, and turned on her. 'Then may I ask—?'

'Yes,' she interrupted him. 'I came here because I wanted to see you. There is something I must tell you.'

Arment continued to scrutinize her. 'I am surprised at that,' he said. 'I should have supposed that any communication you may wish to make could have been made through our lawyers.'

'Our lawyers!' She burst into a little laugh. 'I don't think they could help me – this time.'

Arment's face took on a barricaded look. 'If there is any question of help – of course—'

It struck her, whimsically, that she had seen that look when some shabby devil called with a subscription-book. Perhaps he thought she wanted him to put his name down for so much in sympathy – or even in money . . . The thought made her laugh again. She saw his look change slowly to perplexity. All his facial changes were slow, and she remembered, suddenly, how it had once diverted her to shift that lumbering scenery with a word. For the first time it struck her that she had been cruel. 'There *is* a question of help,' she said in a softer key; 'you can help me; but only by listening . . . I want to tell you something . . .'

Arment's resistance was not yielding. 'Would it not be easier to – write?' he suggested.

She shook her head. 'There is no time to write . . . and it won't take long.' She raised her head and their eyes met. 'My husband has left me,' she said.

'Westall—?' he stammered, reddening again.

'Yes. This morning. Just as I left you. Because he was tired of me.'

The words, uttered scarcely above a whisper, seemed to dilate to the limit of the room. Arment looked toward the door; then his embarrassed glance returned to Julia.

'I am very sorry,' he said awkwardly.

'Thank you,' she murmured.

'But I don't see—'

'No – but you will – in a moment. Won't you listen to me? Please!' Instinctively she had shifted her position, putting herself between him and the door. 'It happened this morning,' she went on in short breathless phrases. 'I never suspected anything – I thought we were – perfectly happy . . . Suddenly he told me he was tired of me . . . there is a girl he likes better . . . He has gone to her . . .' As she spoke, the lurking anguish rose upon her, possessing her once more to the exclusion of every other emotion. Her eyes ached, her throat swelled with it and two painful tears ran down her face.

Arment's constraint was increasing visibly. 'This – this is very unfortunate,' he began. 'But I should say the law—'

'The law?' she echoed ironically. 'When he asks for his freedom?'

'You are not obliged to give it.'

'You were not obliged to give me mine – but you did.'

He made a protesting gesture.

'You saw that the law couldn't help you – didn't you?' she went on. 'That is what I see now. The law represents material rights – it can't go beyond. If we don't recognize an inner law . . . the obligation that love creates . . . being loved as well as loving . . . there is nothing to prevent our spreading ruin unhindered . . . is there?' She raised her head plaintively, with the look of a bewildered child. 'That is what I see now . . . what I wanted to tell you. He leaves me because he's tired . . . but *I* was not tired; and I don't understand why he is. That's the dreadful part of it – the not understanding: I hadn't realized what it meant. But I've been thinking of it all day, and things have come back to me – things I hadn't noticed . . . when you and I . . .' She moved closer to him, and fixed her eyes on his with the gaze which tries to reach beyond words. 'I see now that *you* didn't understand – did you?'

Their eyes met in a sudden shock of comprehension: a veil seemed to be lifted between them. Arment's lip trembled.

'No,' he said, 'I didn't understand.'

She gave a little cry, almost of triumph. 'I knew it! I knew it! You wondered – you tried to tell me – but no words came . . . You saw your life falling in ruins . . . the world slipping from you . . . and you couldn't speak or move!'

She sank down on the chair against which she had been leaning. 'Now I know – now I know,' she repeated.

'I am very sorry for you,' she heard Arment stammer.

She looked up quickly. 'That's not what I came for. I don't want you to be sorry. I came to ask you to forgive me . . . for not understanding that *you* didn't understand . . . That's all I wanted to say.' She rose with a vague sense that the end had come, and put out a groping hand toward the door.

Arment stood motionless. She turned to him with a faint smile.

'You forgive me?'

'There is nothing to forgive—'

'Then will you shake hands for goodbye?' She felt his hand in hers: it was nerveless, reluctant.

'Goodbye,' she repeated. 'I understand now.'

She opened the door and passed out into the hall. As she did so, Arment took an impulsive step forward; but just then the footman, who was evidently alive to his obligations, advanced from the background to let her out. She heard Arment fall back. The footman threw open the door, and she found herself outside in the darkness.

VIRGINIA WOOLF

Phyllis and Rosamond

In this very curious age, when we are beginning to require pictures of people, their minds and their coats, a faithful outline, drawn with no skill but veracity, may possibly have some value.

Let each man, I heard it said the other day, write down the details of a day's work; posterity will be as glad of the catalogue as we should be if we had such a record of how the doorkeeper at the Globe, and the man who kept the Park gates passed Saturday March 18th in the year of our Lord 1568.

And as such portraits as we have are almost invariably of the male sex, who strut more prominently across the stage, it seems worthwhile to take as model one of those many women who cluster in the shade. For a study of history and biography convinces any right-minded person that these obscure figures occupy a place not unlike that of the showman's hand in the dance of the marionettes; and the finger is laid upon the heart. It is true that our simple eyes believed for many ages that the figures danced of their own accord, and cut what steps they chose; and the partial light which novelists and historians have begun to cast upon that dark and crowded place behind the scenes has done little as yet but show us how many wires there are, held in obscure hands, upon whose jerk or twist the whole figure of the dance depends. This preface leads us then to the point at which we began; we intend to look as steadily as we can at a little group, which lives at this moment (the 20th June, 1906); and seems for some reasons which we will give, to epitomize the qualities of many. It is a common case, because after all there are many young women, born of well-to-do, respectable, official parents; and they must all meet much the same problems, and there can be, unfortunately, but little variety in the answers they make.

There are five of them, all daughters they will ruefully explain to you: regretting this initial mistake it seems all through their lives on their parents' behalf. Further, they are divided into camps: two sisters oppose themselves to two sisters; the fifth vacillates equally between them. Nature has decreed that two shall inherit a stalwart pugnacious frame of mind, which applies itself to political economy and social problems successfully and not unhappily; while the other two she has made frivolous, domestic, of lighter and more sensitive temperaments. These two then are condemned to be what in the slang of the century is called 'the daughters at home'. Their sisters deciding to cultivate their brains, go to College, do well there and marry Professors. Their careers have so much likeness to those of men themselves that it is scarcely worthwhile to make them the subject of special enquiry. The fifth sister is less marked in character than any of the others; but she marries when she is twenty-two so that she scarcely has time to develop the individual features of young ladydom which we set out to describe. In the two 'daughters at home' Phyllis and Rosamond, we will call them, we find excellent material for our enquiry.

A few facts will help us to set them in their places, before we begin to investigate. Phyllis is twenty-eight, Rosamond is twenty-four. In person they are pretty, pink cheeked, vivacious; a curious eye will not find any regular beauty of feature; but their dress and demeanour give them the effect of beauty without its substance. They seem indigenous to the drawing room, as though, born in silk evening robes, they had never trod a rougher earth than the Turkey carpet, or reclined on harsher ground than the armchair or the sofa. To see them in a drawing room full of well-dressed men and women, is to see the merchant in the Stock Exchange, or the barrister in the Temple.[1] This, every motion and word proclaims, is their native air; their place of business, their professional arena. Here, clearly, they practise the arts in which they have been instructed since childhood. Here, perhaps, they win their victories and earn their bread. But it would be as unjust as it would be easy to press this metaphor till it suggested that the comparison was appropriate and complete in all its parts. It fails; but where it fails and why it fails it will take some time and attention to discover.

You must be in a position to follow these young ladies home, and to hear their comments over the bedroom candle. You must be by them when they wake next morning; and you must attend their progress throughout the day. When you have done this, not for one day but for many days then you will be able to calculate the values of those impressions which are to be received by night in the drawing room.

This much may be retained of the metaphor already used; that the drawing-room scene represents work to them and not play. So much is made quite clear by the scene in the carriage going home. Lady Hibbert is a severe critic of such performances; she has noted whether her daughters looked well, spoke well, behaved well; whether they attracted the right people and repelled the wrong; whether on the whole the impression they left was favourable. From the multiplicity and minuteness of her comments it is easy to see that two hours' entertainment is, for artists of this kind, a very delicate and complicated piece of work. Much it seems, depends upon the way they acquit themselves. The daughters answer submissively and then keep silence, whether their mother praises or blames: and her censure is severe. When they are alone at last, and they share a modest-sized bedroom at the top of a great ugly house; they stretch their arms and begin to sigh with relief. Their talk is not very edifying; it is the 'shop' of businessmen; they calculate their profits and their losses and have clearly no interest at heart except their own. And yet you may have heard them chatter of books and plays and pictures as though these were the things they most cared about; to discuss them was the only motive of a 'party'.

Yet you will observe also in this hour of unlovely candour something which is also very sincere, but by no means ugly. The sisters were frankly fond of each other. Their affection has taken the form for the most part of a freemasonship which is anything but sentimental; all their hopes and fears are in common; but it is a genuine feeling, profound in spite of its prosaic exterior. They are strictly honourable in all their dealings together; and there is even something chivalrous in the attitude of the younger sister to the elder. She, as the weaker by reason of her greater age, must always have the best of things.

There is some pathos also in the gratitude with which Phyllis accepts the advantage. But it grows late, and in respect for their complexions, these businesslike young women remind each other that it is time to put out the light.

In spite of this forethought they are fain to sleep on after they are called in the morning. But Rosamond jumps up, and shakes Phyllis.

'Phyllis we shall be late for breakfast.'

There must have been some force in this argument, for Phyllis got out of bed and began silently to dress. But their haste allowed them to put on their clothes with great care and dexterity, and the result was scrupulously surveyed by each sister in turn before they went down. The clock struck nine as they came into the breakfast room: their father was already there, kissed each daughter perfunctorily, passed his cup for coffee, read his paper and disappeared. It was a silent meal. Lady Hibbert breakfasted in her room; but after breakfast they had to visit her, to receive her orders for the day, and while one wrote notes for her the other went to arrange lunch and dinner with the cook. By eleven they were free, for the time, and met in the schoolroom where Doris the youngest sister, aged sixteen, was writing an essay upon the Magna Charter in French. Her complaints at the interruption – for she was dreaming of a first class[2] already – met with no honour. 'We must sit here, because there's nowhere else to sit,' remarked Rosamond. 'You needn't think we want your company,' added Phyllis. But these remarks were spoken without bitterness, as the mere commonplaces of daily life.

In deference to their sister, however, Phyllis took up a volume of Anatole France, and Rosamond opened the 'Greek Studies' of Walter Pater.[3] They read for some minutes in silence; then a maid knocked, breathless, with a message that 'Her Ladyship wanted the young ladies in the drawing room.' They groaned; Rosamond offered to go alone; Phyllis said no, they were both victims; and wondering what the errand was they went sulkily downstairs. Lady Hibbert was impatiently waiting them.

'O there you are at last,' she exclaimed. 'Your father has sent round to say he's asked Mr Middleton and Sir Thomas Carew to lunch. Isn't that troublesome of him! I can't think what drove him to ask them, and there's no lunch – and I see you haven't arranged the flowers, Phyllis; and Rosamond I want you to put a clean tucker in my maroon gown. O dear, how thoughtless men are.'

The daughters were used to these insinuations against their father: on the whole they took his side, but they never said so.

They silently departed now on their separate errands: Phyllis had to go out and buy flowers and an extra dish for lunch; and Rosamond sat down to her sewing.

Their tasks were hardly done in time for them to change for lunch; but at 1.30 they came pink and smiling into the pompous great drawing room. Mr Middleton was Sir William Hibbert's secretary; a young man of some position and prospects, as Lady Hibbert defined him; who might be encouraged. Sir Thomas was an official in the same office, solid and gouty, a handsome piece on the board, but of no individual importance.

At lunch then there was some sprightly conversation between Mr Middleton and Phyllis, while their elders talked platitudes, in sonorous deep voices. Rosamond sat rather silent, as was her wont; speculating keenly upon the character of the secretary, who might be her brother-in-law; and checking certain theories she had made by every fresh word he spoke. By open consent, Mr Middleton was her sister's game; she did not trespass. If one could have read her thoughts, while she listened to Sir Thomas's stories of India in the Sixties, one would have found that she was busied in somewhat abstruse calculations; Little Middleton, as she called him, was not half a bad sort; he had brains; he was, she knew, a good son, and he would make a good husband. He was well-to-do also, and would make his way in the service. On the other hand her psychological acuteness told her that he was narrow-minded, without a trace of imagination or intellect, in the sense she understood it; and she knew enough of her sister to know that she would never love this efficient active little man, although she would respect him. The question was should she marry him? This was the point she had reached when Lord Mayo was assassinated;[4] and while her lips murmured ohs and ahs of horror, her eyes were telegraphing across the table, 'I am doubtful.' If she had nodded her sister would have begun to practise those arts by which many proposals had been secured already. Rosamond, however, did not yet know enough to make up her mind. She telegraphed merely 'Keep him in play.'

The gentlemen left soon after lunch, and Lady Hibbert prepared to go and lie down. But before she went she called Phyllis to her.

'Well my dear,' she said, with more affection than she had shown yet, 'did you have a pleasant lunch? Was Mr Middleton agreeable?' She patted her daughter's cheek, and looked keenly into her eyes.

Some petulancy came across Phyllis, and she answered listlessly. 'O he's not a bad little man; but he doesn't excite me.'

Lady Hibbert's face changed at once; if she had seemed a benevolent cat playing with a mouse from philanthropic motives before, she was the real animal now in sober earnest.

'Remember,' she snapped, 'this can't go on for ever. Try and be a little less selfish, my dear.' If she had sworn openly, her words could not have been less pleasant to hear.

She swept off, and the two girls looked at each other, with expressive contortions of the lips.

'I couldn't help it,' said Phyllis, laughing weakly. 'Now let's have a respite. Her Ladyship won't want us till four.'

They mounted to the schoolroom, which was now empty; and threw themselves into deep armchairs. Phyllis lit a cigarette, and Rosamond sucked peppermints, as though they induced to thought.

'Well, my dear,' said Phyllis at last, 'what do we decide? It is June now; our parents give me till July: little Middleton is the only one.'

'Except –' began Rosamond.

'Yes, but it is no good thinking of him.'

'Poor old Phyllis! Well, he's not a bad man.'

'Clean sober, truthful industrious. O we should make a model pair! You should stay with us in Derbyshire.'

'You might do better,' went on Rosamond; with the considering air of a judge. 'On the other hand, they won't stand much more.' 'They' intimated Sir William and Lady Hibbert.

'Father asked me yesterday what I could do if I didn't marry. I had nothing to say.'

'No, we were educated for marriage.'

'*You* might have done something better. Of course I'm a fool so it doesn't matter.'

'And I think marriage the best thing there is – if one were allowed to marry the man one wants.'

'O I know: it is beastly. Still there's no escaping facts.'

'Middleton,' said Rosamond briefly. 'He's the fact at present. Do you care for him?'

'Not in the least.'

'Could you marry him?'

'If her Ladyship made me.'

'It might be a way out, at any rate.'

'What d'you make of him now?' asked Phyllis, who would have accepted or rejected any man on the strength of her sister's advice. Rosamond, possessed of shrewd and capable brains, had been driven to feed them exclusively upon the human character and as her science was but little obscured by personal prejudice, her results were generally trustworthy.

'He's very good,' she began; 'moral qualities excellent: brains fair: he'll do well of course: not a scrap of imagination or romance: he'd be very just to you.'

'In short we would be a worthy pair: something like our parents!'

'The question is,' went on Rosamond; 'is it worthwhile going through another year of slavery, till the next one comes along? And who is the next? Simpson, Rogers, Leiscetter.'[5]

At each name her sister made a face.

'The conclusion seems to be: mark time and keep up appearances.'

'O let's enjoy ourselves while we may! If it weren't for you, Rosamond, I should have married a dozen times already.'

'You'd have been in the divorce court my dear.'

'I'm too respectable for that, really. I'm very weak without you. And now let's talk of your affairs.'

'My affairs can wait,' said Rosamond resolutely. And the two young women discussed their friends' characters, with some acuteness and not a little charity till it was time to change once more. But two features of their talk are worth remark. First, that they held intellect in great reverence and made that a cardinal point in their enquiry;

secondly that whenever they suspected an unhappy home life, or a disappointed attachment, even in the case of the least attractive, their judgements were invariably gentle and sympathetic.

At four they drove out with Lady Hibbert to pay calls. This performance consisted in driving solemnly to one house after another where they had dined or hoped to dine, and depositing two or three cards in the servant's hand. At one place they entered and drank a cup of tea, and talked of the weather for precisely fifteen minutes. They wound up with a slow passage through the Park, making one of the procession of gay carriages which travel at a foot's pace at that hour round the statue of Achilles.[6] Lady Hibbert wore a permanent and immutable smile.

By six o'clock they were home again and found Sir William entertaining an elderly cousin and his wife at tea. These people could be treated without ceremony, and Lady Hibbert went off to lie down; and left her daughters to ask how John was, and whether Milly had got over the measles. 'Remember; we dine out at eight, William,' she said, as she left the room.

Phyllis went with them; the party was given by a distinguished judge, and she had to entertain a respectable KC; her efforts in one direction at least might be relaxed; and her mother's eye regarded her with indifference. It was like a draught of clear cold water, Phyllis reflected, to talk with an intelligent elderly man upon impersonal subjects. They did not theorize, but he told her facts and she was glad to realize that the world was full of solid things, which were independent of her life.

When they left she told her mother that she was going on to the Tristrams, to meet Rosamond there. Lady Hibbert pursed up her mouth, shrugged her shoulders and said 'very well', as though she would have objected if she could have laid her hands on a sufficiently good reason. But Sir William was waiting, and a frown was the only argument.

So Phyllis went separately to the distant and unfashionable quarter of London where the Tristrams lived. That was one of the many enviable parts of their lot. The stucco fronts, the irreproachable rows of Belgravia and South Kensington seemed to Phyllis the type of her lot; of a life trained to grow in an ugly pattern to match the staid ugliness of its fellows. But if one lived here in Bloomsbury, she began to theorize waving with her hand as her cab passed through the great tranquil squares, beneath the pale green of umbrageous trees, one might grow up as one liked. There was room, and freedom, and in the roar and splendour of the Strand she read the live realities of the world from which her stucco and her pillars protected her so completely.

Her cab stopped before some lighted windows which, open in the summer night, let some of the talk and life within spill out upon the pavement. She was impatient for the door to open which was to let her enter, and partake. When she stood, however, within the room, she became conscious of her own appearance which, as she knew by heart, was on these occasions, like that of ladies whom Romney painted.[7] She saw herself enter into the smoky room where people sat on the floor, and the host wore a shooting jacket, with her arch little head held high, and her mouth pursed as though for an epigram. Her white silk and her cherry ribbons made her conspicuous. It was with some feeling of the difference between her and the rest that she sat very silent scarcely taking advantage of the openings that were made for her in the talk. She kept looking round at the dozen people who were sitting there, with a sense of bewilderment. The talk was of certain pictures then being shown, and their merits were discussed from a somewhat technical standpoint. Where was Phyllis to begin? She had seen them; but she knew that her platitudes would never stand the test of question and criticism to which they would be exposed. Nor, she knew, was there any scope here for those feminine graces which could veil so much. The time was passed; for the discussion was hot and serious, and no one of the combatants wished to be tripped by illogical devices. So she sat and watched, feeling like a bird with wings pinioned; and more acutely, because more genuinely, uncomfortable than she had ever been at ball or play. She repeated to herself the little bitter axiom that she had fallen between two stools; and tried meanwhile to use her brains soberly upon what was being said. Rosamond hinted from across the room that she was in the same predicament.

At last the disputants dissolved, and talk became general once more; but no one apologized for the concentrated character it had borne, and general conversation, the Miss Hibberts found, if it did occupy itself with more trivial subjects, tended to be scornful of the commonplace, and knew no hesitation in saying so. But it was amusing; and Rosamond acquitted herself creditably in discussing a certain character which came into question; although she was surprised to find that her most profound discoveries were taken as the starting point of further investigations, and represented no conclusions.

Moreover, the Miss Hibberts were surprised and a little dismayed to discover how much of their education had stuck to them. Phyllis could have beaten herself the next moment for her instinctive disapproval of some jest against Christianity which the Tristrams uttered and applauded as lightly as though religion was a small matter.

Even more amazing to the Miss Hibberts however was the manner in which their own department of business was transacted; for they supposed that even in this odd atmosphere 'the facts of life'[8] were important. Miss Tristram, a young woman of great beauty, and an artist of real promise, was discussing marriage with a gentleman who might easily as far as one could judge, have a personal interest in the question. But the freedom and frankness with which they both explained their views and theorized upon the whole question of love and matrimony, seemed to put the whole thing in a new and sufficiently startling light. It fascinated the young ladies more than anything they had yet seen or heard. They had flattered themselves that every side and view of the subject was known to them; but this was something not only new, but unquestionably genuine.

'I have never yet had a proposal; I wonder what it feels like,' said the candid considering voice of the younger Miss Tristram; and Phyllis and Rosamond felt that they ought to produce their experiences for the instruction of the company. But then they could not adopt this strange new point of view, and their experiences after all were of a different quality entirely. Love to them was something induced by certain calculated actions; and it was cherished in ballrooms, in scented conservatories, by glances of the eyes, flashes of the fan and faltering suggestive accents. Love here was a robust, ingenuous thing which stood out in the daylight, naked and solid, to be tapped and scrutinized as you thought best. Even were they free to love as they chose, Phyllis and Rosamond felt very doubtful that they could love in this way. With the rapid impulse of youth they condemned themselves utterly, and determined that all efforts at freedom were in vain: long captivity had corrupted them both within and without.

They sat thus, unconscious of their own silence, like people shut out from some merrymaking in the cold and the wind; invisible to the feasters within. But in reality the presence of these two silent and hungry-eyed young women was felt to be oppressive by all the people there; although they did not exactly know why; perhaps they were bored. The Miss Tristrams, however, felt themselves responsible; and Miss Sylvia Tristram, the younger, as the result of a whisper, undertook a private conversation with Phyllis. Phyllis snatched at it like a dog at a bone; indeed her face wore a gaunt ravenous expression, as she saw the moments fly, and the substance of this strange evening remained beyond her grasp. At least, if she could not share, she might explain what forbade her. She was longing to prove to herself that there were good reasons for her impotence; and if she felt that Miss Sylvia was a solid woman in spite of her impersonal generalizations, there was hope that they might meet some day on common ground. Phyllis had an odd feeling, when she leant forward to speak, of searching feverishly through a mass of artificial frivolities to lay hands on the solid grain of pure self which, she supposed lay hid somewhere.

'O Miss Tristram,' she began, 'you are all so brilliant. I do feel frightened.'

'Are you laughing at us,' asked Sylvia.

'Why should I laugh? Don't you see what a fool I feel?'

Sylvia began to see, and the sight interested her.

'Yours is such a wonderful life; it is so strange to us.'

Sylvia who wrote and had a literary delight in seeing herself reflected in strange looking-glasses, and of holding up her own mirror to the lives of others, settled herself to the task with gusto. She had never considered the Hibberts as human beings before; but had called them 'young ladies'. She was all the more ready now therefore to revise her mistake; both from vanity and from real curiosity.

'What do you do?' she demanded suddenly, in order to get to business at once.

'What do I do?' echoed Phyllis. 'O order dinner and arrange the flowers!'

'Yes, but what's your trade,' pursued Sylvia, who was determined not to be put off with phrases.

'*That's* my trade; I wish it wasn't! Really Miss Tristram, you must remember that most young ladies are slaves; and you mustn't insult me because you happen to be free.'

'O do tell me,' broke forth Sylvia, 'exactly what you mean. I want to know. I like to know about people. After all you know, the human soul is the thing.'

'Yes,' said Phyllis, anxious to keep from theories. 'But our life's so simple and so ordinary. You must know dozens like us.'

'I know your evening dresses,' said Sylvia; 'I see you pass before me in beautiful processions, but I have never yet heard you speak. Are you solid all through?' It struck her that this tone jarred upon Phyllis: so she changed.

'I daresay we are sisters. But why are we so different outside?'

'O no, we're not sisters,' said Phyllis bitterly; 'at least I pity you if we are. You see, we are brought up just to come out in the evening and make pretty speeches, and well, marry I suppose, and of course we might have gone to college if we'd wanted to; but as we didn't we're just accomplished.'

'We never went to college,' said Sylvia.

'And you're not accomplished? Of course you and your sister are the real thing, and Rosamond and I are frauds: at least I am. But don't you see it all now and don't you see what an ideal life yours is?'

'I can't see why you shouldn't do what you like, as we do,' said Sylvia, looking round the room.

'Do you think we could have people like this? Why, we can never ask a friend, except when our parents are away.'

'Why not?'

'We haven't a room, for one thing: and then we should never be allowed to do it. We are daughters, until we become married women.'

Sylvia considered her a little grimly. Phyllis understood that she had spoken with the wrong kind of frankness about love.

'Do you want to marry?' asked Sylvia.

'Can you ask? You are an innocent young thing! – but of course you're quite right. It should be for love, and all the rest of it. But,' continued Phyllis, desperately speaking the truth, 'we can't think of it in that way. We want so many things, that we can never see marriage alone as it really is or ought to be. It is always mixed up with so much else. It means freedom and friends and a house of our own, and oh all the things you have already! Does that seem to you very dreadful and very mercenary?'

'It does seem rather dreadful; but not mercenary I think. I should write if I were you.'

'O there you go again, Miss Tristram!' exclaimed Phyllis in comic despair. 'I cannot make you understand that for one thing we haven't the brains; and for another, if we had them we couldn't use them. Mercifully the Good Lord made us fitted for our station. Rosamond might have done something; she's too old now.'

'My God,' exclaimed Sylvia. 'What a Black Hole! I should burn, shoot, jump out of the window; at least do something!'

'What?' asked Phyllis sardonically. 'If you were in our place you might; but I don't think you could be. O no,' she went on in a lighter and more cynical tone, 'this is our life, and we have to make the best of it. Only I want you to understand why it is that we come here and sit silent. You see, this is the life we should like to lead; and now I rather doubt that we can. You,' she indicated all the room, 'think us merely fashionable minxes; so we are, almost. But we might have been something better. Isn't it pathetic?' She laughed her dry little laugh.

'But promise me one thing, Miss Tristram: that you will come and see us, and that you will let us come here sometimes. Now Rosamond, we must really go.'

They left, and in the cab Phyllis wondered a little at her outburst; but felt that she had enjoyed it. They were both somewhat excited; and anxious to analyse their discomfort, and find out what it meant. Last night they had driven home at this hour in a more sullen but at the same time in a more self-satisfied temper; they were bored by what they had done, but they knew they had done it well. And they had the satisfaction of feeling that they were fit for far better things. Tonight they were not bored; but they did not feel that they had acquitted themselves well when they had the chance. The bedroom conference was a little dejected; in penetrating to her real self Phyllis had let in some chill gust of air to that closely guarded place; what did she really want, she asked herself? What was she fit for? to criticize both worlds and feel that neither gave her what she needed. She was too genuinely depressed to state the case to her sister; and her fit of honesty left her with the conviction that talking did no good; and if she could do anything, it must be done by herself. Her last thoughts that night were that it was rather a relief that Lady Hibbert had arranged a full day for them tomorrow: at any rate she need not think; and river parties were amusing.

Leves Amores[1]

I can never forget the Thistle Hotel. I can never forget that strange winter night.

I had asked her to dine with me, and then go to the Opera. My room was opposite hers. She said she would come but – could I lace up her evening bodice, it was hooks at the back. Very well.

It was still daylight when I knocked at the door and entered. In her petticoat bodice and a full silk petticoat she was washing, sponging her face and neck. She said she was finished, and I might sit on the bed and wait for her. So I looked round at the dreary room. The one filthy window faced the street. She could see the choked, dust-grimed window of a wash house opposite. For furniture, the room contained a low bed, draped with revolting, yellow, vine-patterned curtains, a chair, a wardrobe with a piece of cracked mirror attached, a washstand. But the wallpaper hurt me physically. It hung in tattered strips from the wall. In its less discoloured and faded patches I could trace the pattern of roses – buds and flowers – and the frieze was a conventional design of birds, of what genus the good God alone knows.

And this was where she lived. I watched her curiously. She was pulling on long, thin stockings, and saying 'damn' when she could not find her suspenders. And I felt within me a certainty that nothing beautiful could ever happen in that room, and for her I felt contempt, a little tolerance, a very little pity.

A dull, grey light hovered over everything; it seemed to accentuate the thin tawdriness of her clothes, the squalor of her life; she, too, looked dull and grey and tired. And I sat on the bed, and thought: 'Come, this Old Age. I have forgotten passion, I have been left behind in the beautiful golden procession of Youth. Now I am seeing life in the dressing room of the theatre.'

So we dined somewhere and went to the Opera. It was late, when we came out into the crowded night street, late and cold. She gathered up her long skirts. Silently we walked back to the Thistle Hotel, down the white pathway fringed with beautiful golden lilies, up the amethyst shadowed staircase.

Was Youth dead? . . . *Was* Youth dead?

She told me as we walked along the corridor to her room that she was glad the night had come. I did not ask why. I was glad, too. It seemed a secret between us. So I went with her into her room to undo those troublesome hooks. She lit a little candle on an enamel bracket. The light filled the room with darkness. Like a sleepy child she slipped out of her frock and then, suddenly, turned to me and flung her arms round my neck. Every bird upon the bulging frieze broke into song. Every rose upon the tattered paper budded and formed into blossom. Yes, even the green vine upon the bed curtains wreathed itself into strange chaplets and garlands, twined round us in a leafy embrace, held us with a thousand clinging tendrils.

And Youth was not dead.

KATHERINE MANSFIELD

The Tiredness of Rosabel

At the corner of Oxford Circus Rosabel bought a bunch of violets, and that was practically the reason why she had so little tea – for a scone and a boiled egg and a cup of cocoa at Lyons[1] are not ample sufficiency after a hard day's work in a millinery establishment. As she swung on to the step of the Atlas bus, grabbed her skirt with one hand and clung to the railing with the other, Rosabel thought she would have sacrificed her soul for a good dinner – roast duck and green peas, chestnut stuffing, pudding with brandy sauce – something hot and strong and filling. She sat down next to a girl very much her own age who was reading *Anna Lombard*[2] in a cheap, paper-covered edition, and the rain had tear-spattered the pages. Rosabel looked out of the windows; the street was blurred and misty, but light striking on the panes turned their dullness to opal and silver, and the jewellers' shops seen through this, were fairy palaces. Her feet were horribly wet, and she knew the bottom of her skirt and petticoat would be coated with black, greasy mud. There was a sickening smell of warm humanity – it seemed to be oozing out of everybody in the bus – and everybody had the same expression, sitting so still, staring in front of them. How many times had she read these advertisements – 'Sapolio Saves Time, Saves Labour' – 'Heinz's Tomato Sauce' – and the inane, annoying dialogue between doctor and judge concerning the superlative merits of 'Lamplough's Pyretic Saline'.[3] She glanced at the book which the girl read so earnestly, mouthing the words in a way that Rosabel detested, licking her first finger and thumb each time that she turned the page. She could not see very clearly; it was something about a hot, voluptuous night, a band playing and a girl with lovely, white shoulders. Oh, heavens! Rosabel stirred suddenly and unfastened the two top buttons of her coat . . . she felt almost stifled. Through her half-closed eyes the whole row of people on the opposite seat seemed to resolve into one fatuous, staring face . . .

And this was her corner. She stumbled a little on her way out and lurched against the girl next her. 'I beg your pardon,' said Rosabel, but the girl did not even look up. Rosabel saw that she was smiling as she read.

Westbourne Grove looked as she had always imagined Venice to look at night, mysterious, dark, even the hansoms were like gondolas dodging up and down, and the lights trailing luridly – tongues of flame licking the wet street – magic fish swimming in the Grand Canal. She was more than glad to reach Richmond Road, but from the corner of the street until she came to No. 26 she thought of those four flights of stairs. Oh, why four flights! It was really criminal to expect people to live so high up. Every house ought to have a lift, something simple and inexpensive, or else an electric staircase like the one at Earl's Court – but four flights! When she stood in the hall and saw the first flight ahead of her and the stuffed albatross head on the landing, glimmering ghost-like in the light of the little gas jet, she almost cried. Well, they had to be faced; it was very like bicycling up a steep hill, but there was not the satisfaction of flying down the other side . . .

Her own room at last! She closed the door, lit the gas, took off her hat and coat, skirt, blouse, unhooked her old flannel dressing-gown from behind the door, pulled it on, then unlaced her boots – on consideration her stockings were not wet enough to change. She went over to the washstand. The jug had not been filled again today. There was just enough water to soak the sponge, and the enamel was coming off the basin – that was the second time she had scratched her chin.

It was just seven o'clock. If she pulled the blind up and put out the gas it was much more restful – Rosabel did not want to read. So she knelt down on the floor, pillowing her arms on the window sill . . . just one little sheet of glass between her and the great wet world outside!

She began to think of all that had happened during the day. Would she ever forget that awful woman in the grey mackintosh who had wanted a trimmed motor-cap – 'something purple with something rosy each side' – or the girl who had tried on every hat in the shop and then said she would 'call in tomorrow and decide definitely'. Rosabel could not help smiling; the excuse was worn so thin . . .

But there had been one other – a girl with beautiful red hair and a white skin and eyes the colour of that green ribbon shot with gold they had got from Paris last week. Rosabel had seen her electric brougham at the door; a man had come in with her, quite a young man, and so well dressed.

'What is it exactly that I want, Harry?' she had said, as Rosabel took the pins out of her hat, untied her veil and gave her a hand mirror.

'You must have a black hat,' he had answered, 'a black hat with a feather that goes right round it and then round your neck and ties in a bow under your chin, and the ends tuck into your belt – a decent-sized feather.'

The girl glanced at Rosabel laughingly. 'Have you any hats like that?'

They had been very hard to please; Harry would demand the impossible, and Rosabel was almost in despair. Then she remembered the big, untouched box upstairs.

'Oh, one moment, Madam,' she had said. 'I think perhaps I can show you something that will please you better.' She had run up, breathlessly, cut the cords, scattered the tissue paper, and yes, there was the very hat – rather large, soft, with a great, curled feather, and a black velvet rose, nothing else. They had been charmed. The girl had put it on and then handed it to Rosabel.

'Let me see how it looks on you,' she said, frowning a little, very serious indeed.

Rosabel turned to the mirror and placed it on her brown hair, then faced them.

'Oh, Harry, isn't it adorable,' the girl cried, 'I must have that!' She smiled again at Rosabel. 'It suits you beautifully.'

A sudden, ridiculous feeling of anger had seized Rosabel. She longed to throw the lovely, perishable thing in the girl's face, and bent over the hat, flushing.

'It's exquisitely finished off inside, Madam,' she said. The girl swept out to her brougham, and left Harry to pay and bring the box with him.

'I shall go straight home and put it on before I come out to lunch with you,' Rosabel heard her say.

The man leant over her as she made out the bill, then, as he counted the money into her hand – 'Ever been painted?' he said.

'No,' said Rosabel shortly, realizing the swift change in his voice, the slight tinge of insolence, of familiarity.

'Oh, well you ought to be,' said Harry. 'You've got such a damned pretty little figure.'

Rosabel did not pay the slightest attention. How handsome he had been! She had thought of no one else all day; his face fascinated her; she could see clearly his fine, straight eyebrows, and his hair grew back from his forehead with just the slightest suspicion of crisp curl, his laughing, disdainful mouth. She saw again his slim hands counting the money into hers . . . Rosabel suddenly pushed the hair back from her face, her forehead was hot . . . if those slim hands could rest one moment . . . the luck of that girl!

Suppose they changed places. Rosabel would drive home with him, of course they were in love with each other, but not engaged, very nearly, and she would say – 'I won't be one moment.' He would wait in the brougham while her maid took the hatbox up the stairs, following Rosabel. Then the great, white and pink bedroom with roses everywhere in dull silver vases. She would sit down before the mirror and the little French maid would fasten her hat and find her a thin, fine veil and another pair of white suède gloves – a button had come off the gloves she had worn that morning. She had scented her furs and gloves and handkerchief, taken a big muff and run downstairs. The butler opened the door, Harry was waiting, they drove away together . . . *That* was life, thought Rosabel! On the way to the Carlton they stopped at Gerard's, Harry bought her great sprays of Parma violets,[4] filled her hands with them.

'Oh, they are sweet!' she said, holding them against her face.

'It is as you always should be,' said Harry, 'with your hands full of violets.'

(Rosabel realized that her knees were getting stiff; she sat down on the floor and leant her head against the wall.) Oh, that lunch! The table covered with flowers, a band hidden behind a grove of palms playing music that fired her blood like wine – the soup, and oysters, and pigeons, and creamed potatoes, and champagne, of course, and afterwards coffee and cigarettes. She would lean over the table fingering her glass with one hand, talking with that charming gaiety which Harry so appreciated. Afterwards a matinée, something that gripped them both, and then tea at the 'Cottage'.

'Sugar? Milk? Cream?' The little homely questions seemed to suggest a joyous intimacy. And then home again in the dusk, and the scent of the Parma violets seemed to drench the air with their sweetness.

'I'll call for you at nine,' he said as he left her.

The fire had been lighted in her boudoir, the curtains drawn, there were a great pile of letters waiting her – invitations for the Opera, dinners, balls, a weekend on the river, a motor tour – she glanced through them listlessly as she went upstairs to dress. A fire in her bedroom, too, and her beautiful, shining dress spread on the bed – white tulle over silver, silver shoes, silver scarf, a little silver fan. Rosabel knew that she was the most famous woman at the ball that night; men paid her homage, a foreign Prince desired to be presented to this English wonder. Yes, it was a voluptuous night, a band playing, and *her* lovely white shoulders . . .

But she became very tired. Harry took her home, and came in with her for just one moment. The fire was out in the drawing room, but the sleepy maid waited for her in her boudoir. She took off her cloak, dismissed the servant and went over to the fireplace, and stood peeling off her gloves; the firelight shone on her hair, Harry came across the room and caught her in his arms – 'Rosabel, Rosabel, Rosabel . . .' Oh, the haven of those arms, and she was very tired.

(The real Rosabel, the girl crouched on the floor in the dark, laughed aloud, and put her hand up to her hot mouth.)

Of course they rode in the park next morning, the engagement had been announced in the *Court Circular*, all the world knew, all the world was shaking hands with her . . .

They were married shortly afterwards at St George's, Hanover

Square, and motored down to Harry's old ancestral home for the honeymoon; the peasants in the village curtseyed to them as they passed; under the folds of the rug he pressed her hands convulsively. And that night she wore again her white and silver frock. She was tired after the journey and went upstairs to bed . . . quite early . . .

The real Rosabel got up from the floor and undressed slowly, folding her clothes over the back of a chair. She slipped over her head her coarse, calico nightdress, and took the pins out of her hair – the soft, brown flood of it fell round her, warmly. Then she blew out the candle and groped her way into bed, pulling the blankets and grimy 'honeycomb' quilt closely round her neck, cuddling down in the darkness . . .

So she slept and dreamed, and smiled in her sleep, and once threw out her arm to feel for something which was not there, dreaming still.

And the night passed. Presently the cold fingers of dawn closed over her uncovered hand; grey light flooded the dull room. Rosabel shivered, drew a little gasping breath, sat up. And because her heritage was that tragic optimism, which is all too often the only inheritance of youth, still half asleep, she smiled, with a little nervous tremor round her mouth.

EVELYN SHARP

Filling the War Chest

As a passer-by, I had known that spot in a busy street all my life; or rather, I thought I knew it. It was only when I took my courage in both hands and a money-box in one of them, and went to stand there every day for a week, that I discovered how wide a gulf it is that separates the passer-by from those who are passed by.

It was all right as long as the sun shone and sent charming sidelights across the bunches of colour in the flower-lady's basket, and put gay and human feelings into the heart of the public so that it lingered and bought daffodils and pink newspapers[1] and ephemeral air-balls from my companions of the gutter, and even sometimes gave me a coin as well as an amused smile. One liked it almost as well when the wind blew up unimportant showers, so hurriedly and unexpectedly that the rain seemed almost out of breath when it came; for this turned the bit of western sky that blocked the end of the street into a fine country sky, that ought to have swept across a moor instead of scudding past a London Tube station. But when it snowed, or rained long and uncompromisingly, and when the wind blew swift and cold without blowing up anything interesting with it, there were no street effects and no smiles, and the public shut its impressionable heart against colour and pink news and polemics, and everything else we were hawking; and one learned suddenly the meaning of being passed by. Perhaps it was worth learning – one of those odd, disagreeable experiences that are worth gathering up by the way when you stand on the edge of a London pavement, helping to fill a war chest for rebel women. Certainly I might not otherwise have reached the heart of my fellows in the gutter.

'It's a 'ard life, ain't it?' said the flower-lady sympathetically. I had known her in the past, too – the past that seemed so long ago and yet dated back only to last week – had sometimes bought flowers of her because she looked cold, and had generally found her unprepossessing and much inclined to grumble. I thought I knew now, as I stamped my feet to keep warm, and shook my box invitingly in front of cold and distant people who refused to be invited, how very much she might have had to grumble at. The queer part of it was that she was not grumbling now; she had ceased to grumble, in fact, for the very reason that made me understand for the first time why she should grumble. Standing there beside her, in God's rain that knew no respect of persons, I was no longer a client out of whom another penny might with tact be wheedled; I was just a boon companion, bent like herself on wheedling that penny from a miserly public that eternally hurried by. So she gave me her pity, though I wore a fur coat and she only a threadbare shawl, and the same biting wind bit at us both.

The newspaper sellers at first held aloof; so did the girl who sold air-balls.

'I haven't took a bloomin' copper all the afternoon,' she complained, looking pointedly after the lady who had just dropped a shilling in my box. I considered the wisdom of explaining that what I was doing was going to help her in the long run, but decided that under similar circumstances I should prefer a more practical and immediate evidence of goodwill from any one who offered me such an explanation. For the worst of the long run, mean this what it may, is that it never, never runs.

Luckily for our future relations, a gust of wind carried off a blue air-ball, and in the chase that followed I came off victorious, and was able to hand it to the owner with a disarming smile. She unbent slightly in return.

'Dessay you find it chilly out here, not bein' used to it,' she suggested, pulling the knot in the string tighter with her teeth.

'What are they doin' it for? That's what I arst! What are they doin' it for?' said the lame newsboy in a slightly peevish tone.

My agility in capturing the air-ball had made him sore, I think, though he had no reason to feel any envy on that score. Seeing the alertness and speed with which he dragged his useless limb after him when he came to show me anything uncomplimentary about the Suffragettes that happened to appear in his pink newspaper, I could but marvel at the thought of what he might have accomplished on two legs. One could only suppose that his agility, like the flower-lady's sympathy, was the result of a lifelong evasion of difficulties.

The elderly gentleman who sold the penny Conservative paper[2] knew why we were doing it. He never failed to wink joyously to his friends if a male elector stopped to argue across my money-box about the cause for which I was shaking it.

'Doin' it to git theirselves 'usbands, that's what they're doin' it for,' he would say conclusively, in denial of the usual contention of the anti-suffragist, that we are doing it because of our distaste for husbands.

When the enemy attacked, my fellow-hawkers waited with grim anticipation for my replies.

'Is not this a terrible condescension on your part?' asked one disapproving lady, putting up her lorgnette to read the inscription on the box. 'Oh, I quite believe in your cause, but why do this sort of thing? How much better to get round the men another way!'

She looked gently pained when I explained rather obviously that I should consider that a condescension, and so would the right sort of man; and my companions looked with puzzled eyes after the retreating lady who seemed to belong to a strange world out of their ken, in which helplessness had a market value. It was pleasantly illuminating to find, however, as the week wore on, that they had come to accept me as an equal, not because I could hold my own against the passer-by, but because they saw me, like themselves, exposed to all the discomforts of being passed by. That, I am sure, is why the elderly paper-seller gave me so much friendly information about goloshes, and why the lame boy observed so sympathetically, one wet evening, that I had had a quiet day.

'Yes; nice and quiet, wasn't it?' I answered gladly, being a militant suffragist of many and strenuous experiences that would not generally be called either nice or quiet. It was only when I caught his astonished expression that I understood him to be referring, not to political passions, but to trade.

Even when you are filling the war chest at the edge of the pavement it is not impossible, I find, to spare a little pity for those who pass as well as for those who are passed by. '*L'homme oisif tue le temps; le temps tue l'homme oisif*',[3] as it is expressed by the nation that knows better than any other, possibly, how to kill time gracefully. Time seemed to be killing a good many idle people, I thought, during the week of days that I stood outside that Tube station. The habitual hawker, of course, was a loiterer by profession; so was the friendly constable who remarked, 'Well, you ladies do have to face somethink, you do!' referring, I imagine, to the snow, which was soft and soothing compared to some of the street witticisms I had to face in the course of business. The real waster was rather the person who stood at the entrance of the station, sometimes for hours, waiting, not for something to happen, or even in most cases for somebody to come, but just waiting.

Sometimes the idler was a man. For one whole afternoon it was a man with a pale and purposeless blue eye that stamped him at once as being one of those who, in killing time, are being gradually killed by it. He said something about the weather to the policeman, something about the winners to the boy who sold pink information about winners; but he did not spend a halfpenny on the information, nor did he look as though he had spent a halfpenny on information in the whole of his life. Even when a motor car broke down opposite, he did not cross the road to look at it. You have to be really interested in life, I suppose, to form one of a street crowd.

Most of the women loiterers seemed to be the victims, either of their small unearned incomes, or of somebody else's unpunctuality. One of these, after stamping her feet in unison with mine for more than half an hour, asked me if I had seen a lady in a green hat. I think I had seen hundreds, which was not very helpful; but the enquiry made an opening, and I shook my box gently and seductively in her direction. She was quite affable, told me she had believed in woman suffrage all her life, and thought it an excellent idea for other people to stand out in the rain collecting money for it.

'It gives you a pinched look, and then people throw you something before they see what it is for,' she added genially.

Evidently my complexion had not taken her unawares in this way, for she made no effort to support the cause in which she had believed all her life. She had so many claims, she said. I understood what she meant when one of the claims, wearing a mountainous hat in emerald-green straw, bore down upon her with torrential apologies for being late, and carried her off to the shops.

'It's for something to do up my every-evening black, and you have such a good eye for colour,' was the cryptic remark I overheard, as they went. In about half an hour they were back again, and the girl in the green mountain was dropping twopence in my box. She smiled rather nicely, and on a sudden impulse I asked her what she had bought for the every-evening black.

She stared, laughed a little, and ended on a sigh. 'Nothing,' she confessed. 'Isn't it tragic?'

'It must be,' I tried to agree. I suppose I succeeded in sounding a human note, for she still lingered.

'I hope you'll get your vote soon, and not have to go on wasting your time like this,' she said.

'It isn't my vote particularly, or my waste of time,' I called after her. But she was gone, her ridiculous hat bobbing up and down in the crowd like a Chinese lantern on a stick; and I wondered if she would some day make a truce with time and save her soul alive.

Time, though a deadly murderer, does not succeed in killing all the people who are trying so hard to kill him; and hope, even for a serious cause, lurked sometimes in that stream of bored and idle passers-by, who seemed so bent on cheating their nature out of everything it demanded of them. It was always a pleasant shock when women and girls, wearing the most preposterous hats and the most fearsome of purple-spotted veils, slid something into my hand and hurried on, trying to look as if they had done nothing of the kind. And my knowledge of things human played me entirely false over the expensive dowager in sable and velvet.

She had stood in front of the nearest shop window for some minutes, discussing with a patient companion the rival qualities of jet trimming[4] and gold braid. 'Jet lasts,' she observed ponderously.

'It does last,' agreed the companion.

'Perhaps that gold edging would look handsomer,' proceeded the old lady, assailed by sudden doubts.

'Oh, yes, it might,' said the companion hastily, adapting her tone.

'You are looking at the wrong one,' said the old lady bluntly. 'It isn't likely I should put a four-three edging on my best satin between-wrap.' Then she veered round and saw me.

Naturally I expected something very cutting, the more so that a kindly supporter threw me a shilling just then from the top of an omnibus, and, a money-box not being so handy as a tambourine, I spent the next few seconds grovelling in the snow at the lady's feet. When I came up again, successful but apprehensive, I found her smiling blandly.

'If I were ten years younger I should be out in the street fighting with you,' was the astonishing remark that accompanied a handsome donation to the war chest.

'Do come, all the same,' I urged, caught by the fighting gleam in her little grey eye. But she shook her head and returned to the jet and the gold edging – a wicked waste of a warlike grey eye!

So the week drew to an end, and I was no longer to be numbered among those who are passed by at the edge of the pavement. In my foolishness I thought it would be easy to remain on friendly terms with my fellow-hawkers of yesterday; and with that idea in my mind I took an early opportunity of returning to the spot and buying a half-penny pink paper and a penny white paper and a blue air-ball and a bunch of daffodils.

I met with a chilly civility from them all, with the exception of the flower-lady, who shamelessly overcharged me for the daffodils.

'Yes, lady, they are dear this morning; cost me that in the market, they did – thank you, lady, much obliged, I'm sure. Yes, it is cold for a body, sitting out here all day.'

That was all – from the friend and sister who had almost offered me her shawl, a week ago, because she saw me shivering.

The sun was shining, and the snow had gone, and I suppose the patch of sky at the western end of the street was all right. But I had been put back in my place as a passer-by; and neither sun nor sky belonged to me any longer.

The Game that wasn't Cricket

Down the alley where I happen to live, playtime draws a sharp line between the sexes. It is not so noticeable during working hours, when girls and boys, banded together by the common grievance of compulsory education, trot off to school almost as allies, even hand-in-hand in those cases where protection is sought from the little girl by the little boy who raced her into the world and lost – or won – by half a length. But when school is over sex antagonism, largely fostered by the parent, immediately sets in. Knowing the size of the average back yard in my neighbourhood, I have plenty of sympathy for the mother who wishes to keep it clear of children. But I always want to know why, in order to secure this privacy, she gives the boy a piece of bread-and-dripping and a ball, while the girl is given a piece of bread-and-dripping and a baby. And I have not yet decided which of the two toys is the more destructive of my peace.

Every evening during the summer, cricket is played just below my window in the hour preceding sunset. Cricket, as played in my alley, is less noisy than football, in which anything that comes handy as a substitute for the ball may be used, preferably an old, jagged salmon-tin. But cricket lasts longer, the nerves of the parents whose windows overlook the cricket-ground being able to stand it better. As the best working hour of my day is destroyed equally by both, I have no feeling either way, except that the cricket, as showing a more masterly evasion of difficulties, appeals to me rather more. It is comparatively easy to achieve some resemblance to a game of football even in a narrow strip of pavement bordered by houses, where you can place one goal in the porch of the model dwellings at the blind end of the alley, and the other goal among the motor traffic at the street end. But first-class cricket is more difficult of attainment when the field is so crowded as to make it hard to decide which player out of three or four has caught you out, while your only chance of not being run out first ball is to take the wicket with you – always a possibility when the wicket is somebody's coat that has a way of getting mixed up with the batsman's feet.

In spite of obstacles, however, the cricket goes on every evening before sunset; and all the while, the little girl who tripped to school on such a gay basis of equality with her brother only a few hours back, sits on the doorstep minding the baby. I do not say that she actively objects to this; I only know with acute certainty that the baby objects to it, and for a long time I felt that it would be at least interesting to see what would happen if the little girl were to stand up at the wicket for a change while her brother dealt with the baby.

And the other evening this did happen. A mother, making one of those sorties from the domestic stronghold, that in my alley always have the effect of bringing a look of guilt into the faces of the innocent, shouted something I did not hear, picked up the wicket, cuffed somebody's head with it and made him put it on, gave the baby to a brother, and sent his sister off to the oil-shop with a jar in one hand and a penny tightly clasped in the other. The interruption over, the scattered field re-formed automatically, somebody else's jacket was made into a mound and cricket was resumed with the loss of one player, who, by the way, showed an astonishing talent for minding the baby.

Then the little girl came back from the oil-shop. I know not what spirit of revolt entered suddenly her small, subdued soul; perhaps the sight of a boy minding the baby suggested an upheaval of the universe that demanded her instant co-operation; perhaps she had no distinct idea in her mind beyond a wish to rebel. Whatever her reasons, there she stood, hat in hand, waiting for the ball, while the baby crowed delightedly in the unusual embrace of a boy who, by all the laws of custom, was unsexing himself.

Another instant, and the air was rent with sound and fury. In front of the wicket stood the Spirit of Revolt, with tumbled hair and defiant eyes, breathless with much running, intoxicated with success; around

347

her, an outraged cricket team, strong in the conventions of a lifetime, was protesting fiercely.

What had happened was quite simple. Grasping in an instant of time the only possible way of eluding the crowd of fielders in the narrow space, the little impromptu batswoman had done the obvious thing and struck the ball against the wall high over their heads, whence it bounded into the open street and got lost in the traffic. Then she ran till she could run no more. Why wasn't it fair? she wanted to know.

''Cause it ain't – there!' was one illuminating reply.

''Cause we don't never play that way,' was another upon which she was quick to pounce.

'You never thought of it, that's why! ' she retorted shrewdly.

She was desperately outnumbered. It was magnificent, but it wasn't cricket; moreover, her place was the doorstep, as she was speedily reminded when the door reopened and avenging motherhood once more swooped down upon the scene. A shake here, a push there – and the boy was back again at the wicket, while a weeping baby lay unheeded on the lap of a weeping Spirit of Revolt.

And the queer thing is that the innovation made by the small batswoman in her one instant of wild rebellion has now been adopted by the team that plays cricket down my alley, every evening before sunset.

CHARLOTTE PERKINS GILMAN

Turned

In her soft-carpeted, thick-curtained, richly furnished chamber, Mrs Marroner lay sobbing on the wide, soft bed.

She sobbed bitterly, chokingly, despairingly; her shoulders heaved and shook convulsively; her hands were tight-clenched; she had forgotten her elaborate dress, the more elaborate bedcover; forgotten her dignity, her self-control, her pride. In her mind was an overwhelming, unbelievable horror, an immeasurable loss, a turbulent, struggling mass of emotion.

In her reserved, superior, Boston-bred life she had never dreamed that it would be possible for her to feel so many things at once, and with such trampling intensity.

She tried to cool her feelings into thoughts; to stiffen them into words; to control herself – and could not. It brought vaguely to her mind an awful moment in the breakers at York Beach, one summer in girlhood, when she had been swimming under water and could not find the top.

In her uncarpeted, thin-curtained, poorly furnished chamber on the top floor, Gerta Petersen lay sobbing on the narrow, hard bed.

She was of larger frame than her mistress, grandly built and strong; but all her proud, young womanhood was prostrate now, convulsed with agony, dissolved in tears. She did not try to control herself. She wept for two.

If Mrs Marroner suffered more from the wreck and ruin of a longer love – perhaps a deeper one; if her tastes were finer, her ideals loftier; if she bore the pangs of bitter jealousy and outraged pride, Gerta had

349

personal shame to meet, a hopeless future, and a looming present which filled her with unreasoning terror.

She had come like a meek young goddess into that perfectly ordered house, strong, beautiful, full of good will and eager obedience, but ignorant and childish – a girl of eighteen.

Mr Marroner had frankly admired her, and so had his wife. They discussed her visible perfections and as visible limitations with that perfect confidence which they had so long enjoyed. Mrs Marroner was not a jealous woman. She had never been jealous in her life – till now.

Gerta had stayed and learned their ways. They had both been fond of her. Even the cook was fond of her. She was what is called 'willing', was unusually teachable and plastic; and Mrs Marroner, with her early habits of giving instruction, tried to educate her somewhat.

'I never saw anyone so docile,' Mrs Marroner had often commented. 'It is perfection in a servant, but almost a defect in character. She is so helpless and confiding.'

She was precisely that; a tall, rosy-cheeked baby; rich womanhood without, helpless infancy within. Her braided wealth of dead-gold hair, her grave blue eyes, her mighty shoulders, and long, firmly moulded limbs seemed those of a primal earth spirit; but she was only an ignorant child, with a child's weakness.

When Mr Marroner had to go abroad for his firm, unwillingly, hating to leave his wife, he had told her he felt quite safe to leave her in Gerta's hands – she would take care of her.

'Be good to your mistress, Gerta,' he told the girl that last morning at breakfast. 'I leave her to you to take care of. I shall be back in a month at latest.'

Then he turned, smiling, to his wife. 'And you must take care of Gerta, too,' he said. 'I expect you'll have her ready for college when I get back.'

This was seven months ago. Business had delayed him from week to week, from month to month. He wrote to his wife, long, loving, frequent letters; deeply regretting the delay, explaining how necessary, how profitable it was; congratulating her on the wide resources she had; her well-filled, well-balanced mind; her many interests.

'If I should be eliminated from your scheme of things, by any of those "acts of God" mentioned on the tickets, I do not feel that you would be an utter wreck,' he said. 'That is very comforting to me. Your life is so rich and wide that no one loss, even a great one, would wholly cripple you. But nothing of the sort is likely to happen, and I shall be home again in three weeks – if this thing gets settled. And you will be looking so lovely, with that eager light in your eyes and the changing flush I know so well – and love so well! My dear wife! We shall have to have a new honeymoon – other moons come every month, why shouldn't the mellifluous kind?'

He often asked after 'little Gerta', sometimes enclosed a picture postcard to her, joked his wife about her laborious efforts to educate 'the child'; was so loving and merry and wise—

All this was racing through Mrs Marroner's mind as she lay there with the broad, hemstitched border of fine linen sheeting crushed and twisted in one hand, and the other holding a sodden handkerchief.

She had tried to teach Gerta, and had grown to love the patient, sweet-natured child, in spite of her dullness. At work with her hands, she was clever, if not quick, and could keep small accounts from week to week. But to the woman who held a Ph.D., who had been on the faculty of a college, it was like babytending.

Perhaps having no babies of her own made her love the big child the more, though the years between them were but fifteen.

To the girl she seemed quite old, of course; and her young heart was full of grateful affection for the patient care which made her feel so much at home in this new land.

And then she had noticed a shadow on the girl's bright face. She looked nervous, anxious, worried. When the bell rang she seemed startled, and would rush hurriedly to the door. Her peals of frank laughter no longer rose from the area gate as she stood talking with the always admiring tradesmen.

Mrs Marroner had laboured long to teach her more reserve with men, and flattered herself that her words were at last effective. She suspected the girl of homesickness; which was denied. She suspected her of illness, which was denied also. At last she suspected her of something which could not be denied.

For a long time she refused to believe it, waiting. Then she had to believe it, but schooled herself to patience and understanding. 'The poor child,' she said. 'She is here without a mother – she is so foolish and yielding – I must not be too stern with her.' And she tried to win the girl's confidence with wise, kind words.

But Gerta had literally thrown herself at her feet and begged her with streaming tears not to turn her away. She would admit nothing, explain nothing; but frantically promised to work for Mrs Marroner as long as she lived – if only she would keep her.

Revolving the problem carefully in her mind, Mrs Marroner thought she would keep her, at least for the present. She tried to repress her sense of ingratitude in one she had so sincerely tried to help, and the cold, contemptuous anger she had always felt for such weakness.

'The thing to do now,' she said to herself, 'is to see her through this safely. The child's life should not be hurt any more than is unavoidable. I will ask Dr Bleet about it – what a comfort a woman doctor is! I'll stand by the poor, foolish thing till it's over, and then get her back to Sweden somehow with her baby. How they do come where they are not wanted – and don't come where they are wanted!' And Mrs Marroner, sitting alone in the quiet, spacious beauty of the house, almost envied Gerta.

Then came the deluge.

She had sent the girl out for needed air toward dark. The late mail came; she took it in herself. One letter for her – her husband's letter. She knew the postmark, the stamp, the kind of typewriting. She impulsively kissed it in the dim hall. No one would suspect Mrs Marroner of kissing her husband's letters – but she did, often.

She looked over the others. One was for Gerta, and not from Sweden. It looked precisely like her own. This struck her as a little odd, but Mr Marroner had several times sent messages and cards to the girl. She laid the letter on the hall table and took hers to her room.

'My poor child,' it began. What letter of hers had been sad enough to warrant that?

'I am deeply concerned at the news you send.' What news to so concern him had she written? 'You must bear it bravely, little girl. I shall be home soon, and will take care of you, of course. I hope there is no immediate anxiety – you do not say. Here is money, in case you need it. I expect to get home in a month at latest. If you have to go, be sure to leave your address at my office. Cheer up – be brave – I will take care of you.'

The letter was typewritten, which was not unusual. It was unsigned, which was unusual. It enclosed an American bill – fifty dollars. It did not seem in the least like any letter she had ever had from her husband, or any letter she could imagine him writing. But a strange, cold feeling was creeping over her, like a flood rising around a house.

She utterly refused to admit the ideas which began to bob and push about outside her mind, and to force themselves in. Yet under the pressure of these repudiated thoughts she went downstairs and brought up the other letter – the letter to Gerta. She laid them side by side on a smooth dark space on the table; marched to the piano and played, with stern precision, refusing to think, till the girl came back. When she came in, Mrs Marroner rose quietly and came to the table. 'Here is a letter for you,' she said.

The girl stepped forward eagerly, saw the two lying together there, hesitated, and looked at her mistress.

'Take yours, Gerta. Open it, please.'

The girl turned frightened eyes upon her.

'I want you to read it, here,' said Mrs Marroner.

'Oh, ma'am— No! Please don't make me!'

'Why not?'

There seemed to be no reason at hand, and Gerta flushed more deeply and opened her letter. It was long; it was evidently puzzling to her; it began 'My dear wife.' She read it slowly.

'Are you sure it is your letter?' asked Mrs Marroner. 'Is not this one yours? Is not that one – mine?'

She held out the other letter to her.

'It is a mistake,' Mrs Marroner went on, with a hard quietness. She had lost her social bearings somehow; lost her usual keen sense of the proper thing to do. This was not life, this was a nightmare.

'Do you not see? Your letter was put in my envelope and my letter was put in your envelope. Now we understand it.'

But poor Gerta had no antechamber to her mind; no trained forces to preserve order while agony entered. The thing swept over her, resistless, overwhelming. She cowered before the outraged wrath she expected; and from some hidden cavern that wrath arose and swept over her in pale flame.

'Go and pack your trunk,' said Mrs Marroner. 'You will leave my house tonight. Here is your money.'

She laid down the fifty-dollar bill. She put with it a month's wages. She had no shadow of pity for those anguished eyes, those tears which she heard drop on the floor.

'Go to your room and pack,' said Mrs Marroner. And Gerta, always obedient, went.

Then Mrs Marroner went to hers, and spent a time she never counted, lying on her face on the bed.

But the training of the twenty-eight years which had elapsed before her marriage; the life at college, both as student and teacher; the independent growth which she had made, formed a very different background for grief from that in Gerta's mind.

After a while Mrs Marroner arose. She administered to herself a hot bath, a cold shower, a vigorous rubbing. 'Now I can think,' she said.

First she regretted the sentence of instant banishment. She went upstairs to see if it had been carried out. Poor Gerta! The tempest of her agony had worked itself out at last as in a child, and left her sleeping, the pillow wet, the lips still grieving, a big sob shuddering itself off now and then.

Mrs Marroner stood and watched her, and as she watched she considered the helpless sweetness of the face; the defenceless, unformed character; the docility and habit of obedience which made her so attractive – and so easily a victim. Also she thought of the mighty force which had swept over her; of the great process now working itself out through her; of how pitiful and futile seemed any resistance she might have made.

She softly returned to her own room, made up a little fire and sat by it, ignoring her feelings now, as she had before ignored her thoughts.

Here were two women and a man. One woman was a wife; loving, trusting, affectionate. One was a servant; loving, trusting, affectionate: a young girl, an exile, a dependant; grateful for any kindness; untrained, uneducated, childish. She ought, of course, to have resisted temptation; but Mrs Marroner was wise enough to know how difficult temptation is to recognize when it comes in the guise of friendship and from a source one does not suspect.

Gerta might have done better in resisting the grocer's clerk; had, indeed, with Mrs Marroner's advice, resisted several. But where respect was due, how could she criticize? Where obedience was due, how could she refuse – with ignorance to hold her blinded – until too late?

As the older, wiser woman forced herself to understand and extenuate the girl's misdeed and foresee her ruined future, a new feeling rose in her heart, strong, clear and overmastering; a sense of measureless condemnation for the man who had done this thing. He knew. He understood. He could fully foresee and measure the consequences of his act. He appreciated to the full the innocence, the ignorance, the grateful affection, the habitual docility, of which he deliberately took advantage.

Mrs Marroner rose to icy peaks of intellectual apprehension, from which her hours of frantic pain seemed far indeed removed. He had done this thing under the same roof with her – his wife. He had not frankly loved the younger woman, broken with his wife, made a new marriage. That would have been heartbreak pure and simple. This was something else.

That letter, that wretched, cold, carefully guarded, unsigned letter: that bill – far safer than a cheque – these did not speak of affection. Some men can love two women at one time. This was not love.

Mrs Marroner's sense of pity and outrage for herself, the wife, now spread suddenly into a perception of pity and outrage for the girl. All that splendid, clean young beauty, the hope of a happy life, with marriage and motherhood; honourable independence, even – these were nothing to that man. For his own pleasure he had chosen to rob her of her life's best joys.

He would 'take care of her' said the letter? How? In what capacity?

And then, sweeping over both her feelings for herself, the wife, and Gerta, his victim, came a new flood, which literally lifted her to her feet. She rose and walked, her head held high. 'This is the sin of man against woman,' she said. 'The offence is against womanhood. Against motherhood. Against – the child.'

She stopped.

The child. His child. That, too, he sacrificed and injured – doomed to degradation.

Mrs Marroner came of stern New England stock. She was not a Calvinist, hardly even a Unitarian, but the iron of Calvinism was in her soul: of that grim faith which held that most people had to be damned 'for the glory of God'.[1]

Generations of ancestors who both preached and practised stood behind her; people whose lives had been sternly moulded to their highest moments of religious conviction. In sweeping bursts of feeling they achieved 'conviction', and afterward they lived and died according to that conviction.

When Mr Marroner reached home, a few weeks later, following his letters too soon to expect an answer to either, he saw no wife upon the pier, though he had cabled; and found the house closed darkly. He let himself in with his latchkey, and stole softly upstairs, to surprise his wife.

No wife was there.

He rang the bell. No servant answered it.

He turned up light after light; searched the house from top to bottom; it was utterly empty. The kitchen wore a clean, bald, unsympathetic aspect. He left it and slowly mounted the stair, completely dazed. The whole house was clean, in perfect order, wholly vacant.

One thing he felt perfectly sure of – she knew.

Yet was he sure? He must not assume too much. She might have been ill. She might have died. He started to his feet. No, they would have cabled him. He sat down again.

For any such change, if she had wanted him to know, she would have written. Perhaps she had, and he, returning so suddenly, had missed the letter. The thought was some comfort. It must be so. He turned to the telephone, and again hesitated. If she had found out – if she had gone – utterly gone, without a word – should he announce it himself to friends and family?

He walked the floor; he searched everywhere for some letter, some word of explanation. Again and again he went to the telephone – and always stopped. He could not bear to ask: 'Do you know where my wife is?'

The harmonious, beautiful rooms reminded him in a dumb, helpless way of her; like the remote smile on the face of the dead. He put out the lights; could not bear the darkness; turned them all on again.

It was a long night –

In the morning he went early to the office. In the accumulated mail was no letter from her. No one seemed to know of anything unusual. A friend asked after his wife – 'Pretty glad to see you, I guess?' He answered evasively.

About eleven a man came to see him; John Hill, her lawyer. Her cousin, too. Mr Marroner had never liked him. He liked him less now, for Mr Hill merely handed him a letter, remarked, 'I was requested to deliver this to you personally,' and departed, looking like a person who is called on to kill something offensive.

'I have gone. I will care for Gerta. Goodbye. Marion.'

That was all. There was no date, no address, no postmark; nothing but that.

In his anxiety and distress he had fairly forgotten Gerta and all that. Her name aroused in him a sense of rage. She had come between him and his wife. She had taken his wife from him. That was the way he felt.

At first he said nothing, did nothing; lived on alone in his house, taking meals where he chose. When people asked him about his wife he said she was travelling – for her health. He would not have it in the newspapers. Then, as time passed, as no enlightenment came to him, he resolved not to bear it any longer, and employed detectives. They blamed him for not having put them on the track earlier, but set to work, urged to the utmost secrecy.

What to him had been so blank a wall of mystery seemed not to embarrass them in the least. They made careful enquiries as to her 'past', found where she had studied, where taught, and on what lines; that she had some little money of her own, that her doctor was Josephine L. Bleet, MD, and many other bits of information.

As a result of careful and prolonged work, they finally told him that she had resumed teaching under one of her old professors; lived quietly, and apparently kept boarders; giving him town, street and number, as if it were a matter of no difficulty whatever.

He had returned in early spring. It was autumn before he found her.

A quiet college town in the hills, a broad, shady street, a pleasant house standing in its own lawn, with trees and flowers about it. He had the address in his hand, and the number showed clear on the white gate. He walked up the straight gravel path and rang the bell. An elderly servant opened the door.

'Does Mrs Marroner live here?'

'No, sir.'

'This is number twenty-eight?'

'Yes, sir.'

'Who does live here?'

'Miss Wheeling, sir.'

Ah! Her maiden name. They had told him, but he had forgotten. He stepped inside. 'I would like to see her,' he said.

He was ushered into a still parlour, cool and sweet with the scent of flowers, the flowers she had always loved best. It almost brought tears to his eyes. All their years of happiness rose in his mind again; the exquisite beginnings; the days of eager longing before she was really his; the deep, still beauty of her love.

Surely she would forgive him – she must forgive him. He would humble himself; he would tell her of his honest remorse – his absolute determination to be a different man.

Through the wide doorway there came in to him two women. One like a tall Madonna, bearing a baby in her arms.

Marion, calm, steady, definitely impersonal; nothing but a clear pallor to hint of inner stress.

Gerta, holding the child as a bulwark, with a new intelligence in her face, and her blue, adoring eyes fixed on her friend – not upon him.

He looked from one to the other dumbly.

And the woman who had been his wife asked quietly:

'What have you to say to us?'

KATHERINE MANSFIELD

The Advanced Lady

'Do you think we might ask her to come with us,' said Fräulein Elsa, re-tying her pink sash ribbon before my mirror. 'You know, although she is so intellectual, I cannot help feeling convinced that she has some secret sorrow. And Lisa told me this morning, as she was turning out my room, that she remains hours and hours by herself, writing; in fact Lisa says she is writing a book! I suppose that is why she never cares to mingle with us, and has so little time for her husband and the child.'

'Well, *you* ask her,' said I. 'I have never spoken to the lady.'

Elsa blushed faintly. 'I have only spoken to her once,' she confessed. 'I took her a bunch of wild flowers to her room, and she came to the door in a white gown, with her hair loose. Never shall I forget that moment. She just took the flowers, and I heard her – because the door was not quite properly shut – I heard her, as I walked down the passage, saying "Purity, fragrance, the fragrance of purity and the purity of fragrance!" It was wonderful!'

At the moment Frau Kellermann knocked at the door.

'Are you ready?' she said, coming into the room and nodding to us very genially. 'The gentlemen are waiting on the steps, and I have asked the Advanced Lady to come with us.'

'Na, how extraordinary!' cried Elsa. 'But this moment the gnädige Frau and I were debating whether—'

'Yes, I met her coming out of her room and she said she was charmed with the idea. Like all of us, she has never been to Schlingen.[1] She is downstairs now, talking to Herr Erchardt. I think we shall have a delightful afternoon.'

'Is Fritzi waiting too?' asked Elsa.

'Of course he is, dear child – as impatient as a hungry man listening for the dinner bell. Run along!'

Elsa ran, and Frau Kellermann smiled at me significantly. In the past she and I had seldom spoken to each other, owing to the fact that her 'one remaining joy' – her charming little Karl – had never succeeded in kindling into flame those sparks of maternity which are supposed to glow in great numbers upon the altar of every respectable female heart; but, in view of a premeditated journey together, we became delightfully cordial.

'For us,' she said, 'there will be a double joy. We shall be able to watch the happiness of these two dear children, Elsa and Fritz. They only received the letters of blessing from their parents yesterday morning. It is a very strange thing, but whenever I am in the company of newly engaged couples I blossom. Newly engaged couples, mothers with first babies and normal deathbeds have precisely the same effect on me. Shall we join the others?'

I was longing to ask her why normal deathbeds should cause anyone to burst into flower, and said, 'Yes, do let us.'

We were greeted by the little party of 'cure guests'[2] on the pension steps, with those cries of joy and excitement which herald so pleasantly the mildest German excursion. Herr Erchardt and I had not met before that day, so, in accordance with strict pension custom, we asked each other how long we had slept during the night, had we dreamed agreeably, what time had we got up, was the coffee fresh when we had appeared at breakfast and how had we passed the morning. Having toiled up these stairs of almost national politeness we landed, triumphant and smiling, and paused to recover breath.

'And now,' said Herr Erchardt, 'I have a pleasure in store for you. The Frau Professor is going to be one of us for the afternoon. Yes,' nodding graciously to the Advanced Lady. 'Allow me to introduce you to each other.'

We bowed very formally, and looked each other over with that eye which is known as 'eagle' but is far more the property of the female than that most unoffending of birds. 'I think you are English?' she said. I acknowledged the fact. 'I am reading a great many English books just now – rather, I am studying them.'

'Nu,' cried Herr Erchardt. 'Fancy that! What a bond already! I have made up my mind to know Shakespeare in his mother tongue before I die, but that you, Frau Professor, should be already immersed in those wells of English thought!'

'From what I have read,' she said, 'I do not think they are very deep wells.'

He nodded sympathetically.

'No,' he answered, 'so I have heard . . . But do not let us embitter our excursion for our little English friend. We will speak of this another time.'

'Nu, are we ready?' cried Fritz, who stood, supporting Elsa's elbow in his hand, at the foot of the steps. It was immediately discovered that Karl was lost.

'Ka-rl, Karl-chen!' we cried. No response.

'But he was here one moment ago,' said Herr Langen, a tired, pale youth, who was recovering from a nervous breakdown due to much philosophy and little nourishment. 'He was sitting here, picking out the works of his watch with a hairpin!'

Frau Kellermann rounded on him. 'Do you mean to say, my dear Herr Langen, you did not stop the child!'

'No,' said Herr Langen; 'I've tried stopping him before now.'

'Da, that child has such energy; never is his brain at peace. If he is not doing one thing, he is doing another!'

'Perhaps he has started on the dining-room clock now,' suggested Herr Langen, abominably hopeful.

The Advanced Lady suggested that we should go without him. 'I never take my little daughter for walks,' she said. 'I have accustomed her to sitting quietly in my bedroom from the time I go out until I return!'

'There he is – there he is,' piped Elsa, and Karl was observed slithering down a chestnut tree, very much the worse for twigs.

'I've been listening to what you said about me, mumma,' he confessed while Frau Kellermann brushed him down. 'It was not true about the watch. I was only looking at it, and the little girl never stays in the bedroom. She told me herself she always goes down to the kitchen, and—'

'Da, that's enough!' said Frau Kellermann.

We marched *en masse* along the station road. It was a very warm afternoon, and continuous parties of 'cure guests', who were giving their digestions a quiet airing in pension gardens, called after us, asked if we were going for a walk and cried 'Herr Gott – happy journey' with immense ill-concealed relish when we mentioned Schlingen.

'But that is eight kilometres,' shouted one old man with a white beard, who leaned against a fence, fanning himself with a yellow handkerchief.

'Seven and a half,' answered Herr Erchardt shortly.

'Eight,' bellowed the sage.

'Seven and a half!'

'Eight!'

'The man is mad,' said Herr Erchardt.

'Well, please let him be mad in peace,' said I, putting my hands over my ears.

'Such ignorance must not be allowed to go uncontradicted,' said he, and turning his back on us, too exhausted to cry out any longer, he held up seven and a half fingers.

'Eight!' thundered the greybeard, with pristine freshness.

We felt very sobered, and did not recover until we reached a white signpost which entreated us to leave the road and walk through the field path – without trampling down more of the grass than was necessary. Being interpreted, it meant 'single file', which was distressing for Elsa and Fritz. Karl, like a happy child, gambolled ahead, and cut down as many flowers as possible with the stick of his mother's parasol – followed the three others – then myself – and the lovers in the rear. And above the conversation of the advance party I had the privilege of hearing these delicious whispers.

Fritz: 'Do you love me?' Elsa: 'Nu – yes.' Fritz passionately: 'But how much?' To which Elsa never replied – except with 'How much do *you* love *me?*'

Fritz escaped that truly Christian trap by saying, 'I asked you first.'

It grew so confusing that I slipped in front of Frau Kellermann – and walked in the peaceful knowledge that she was blossoming and I was under no obligation to inform even my nearest and dearest as to the precise capacity of my affections. 'What right have they to ask each other such questions the day after letters of blessing have been received?' I reflected. 'What right have they even to question each other? Love which becomes engaged and married is a purely affirmative affair – they are usurping the privileges of their betters and wisers!'

The edges of the field frilled over into an immense pine forest – very pleasant and cool it looked. Another signpost begged us to keep to the broad path for Schlingen and deposit waste paper and fruit peelings in wire receptacles attached to the benches for the purpose. We sat down on the first bench, and Karl with great curiosity explored the wire receptacle.

'I love woods,' said the Advanced Lady, smiling pitifully into the air. 'In a wood my hair already seems to stir and remember something of its savage origin.'

'But speaking literally,' said Frau Kellermann, after an appreciative pause, 'there is really nothing better than the air of pine trees for the scalp.'

'Oh, Frau Kellermann, please don't break the spell,' said Elsa.

The Advanced Lady looked at her very sympathetically. 'Have you, too, found the magic heart of Nature?' she said.

That was Herr Langen's cue. 'Nature has no heart,' said he, very bitterly and readily, as people do who are overphilosophized and underfed. 'She creates that she may destroy. She eats that she may spew up and she spews up that she may eat. That is why we, who are forced to eke out an existence at her trampling feet, consider the world mad, and realize the deadly vulgarity of production.'

'Young man,' interrupted Herr Erchardt, 'you have never lived and you have never suffered!'

'Oh, excuse me – how can you know?'

'I know because you have told me, and there's an end of it. Come back to this bench in ten years' time and repeat those words to me,' said Frau Kellermann, with an eye upon Fritz who was engaged in counting Elsa's fingers with passionate fervour – and bring with you your young wife, Herr Langen, and watch, perhaps, your little child playing with—' She turned towards Karl, who had rooted an old illustrated paper out of the receptacle and was spelling over an advertisement for the enlargement of Beautiful Breasts.

The sentence remained unfinished. We decided to move on. As we plunged more deeply into the wood our spirits rose – reaching a point where they burst into song – on the part of the three men – 'O Welt, wie bist du wunderbar!'[3] – the lower part of which was piercingly sustained by Herr Langen, who attempted quite unsuccessfully to infuse satire into it in accordance with his – 'world outlook'. They strode ahead and left us to trail after them – hot and happy.

'Now is the opportunity,' said Frau Kellermann. 'Dear Frau Professor, do tell us a little about your book.'

'Ach, how did you know I was writing one?' she cried playfully.

'Elsa, here, had it from Lisa. And never before have I personally known a woman who was writing a book. How do you manage to find enough to write down?'

'That is never the trouble,' said the Advanced Lady – she took Elsa's arm and leaned on it gently. 'The trouble is to know where to stop. My brain has been a hive for years, and about three months ago the pent-up waters burst over my soul, and since then I am writing all day until late into the night, still ever finding fresh inspirations and thoughts which beat impatient wings about my heart.'

'Is it a novel?' asked Elsa shyly.

'Of course it is a novel,' said I.

'How can you be so positive?' said Frau Kellermann, eyeing me severely.

'Because nothing but a novel could produce an effect like that.'

'Ach, don't quarrel,' said the Advanced Lady sweetly. 'Yes, it is a novel – upon the Modern Woman. For this seems to me the woman's hour. It is mysterious and almost prophetic, it is the symbol of the true advanced woman: not one of those violent creatures who deny their sex and smother their frail wings under . . . under—'

'The English tailor-made?'[4] from Frau Kellermann.

'I was not going to put it like that. Rather, under the lying garb of false masculinity!'

'Such a subtle distinction!' I murmured.

'Whom then,' asked Fräulein Elsa, looking adoringly at the Advanced Lady – 'whom then do you consider the true woman?'

'She is the incarnation of comprehending Love!'

'But my dear Frau Professor,' protested Frau Kellermann, 'you must remember that one has so few opportunities for exhibiting Love within the family circle nowadays. One's husband is at business all day, and naturally desires to sleep when he returns home – one's children are out of the lap and in at the university before one can lavish anything at all upon them!'

'But Love is not a question of lavishing,' said the Advanced Lady. 'It is the lamp carried in the bosom touching with serene rays all the heights and depths of—'

'Darkest Africa,' I murmured flippantly.

She did not hear.

'The mistake we have made in the past – as a sex,' said she, 'is in not realizing that our gifts of giving are for the whole world – we are the glad sacrifice of ourselves!'

'Oh!' cried Elsa rapturously, and almost bursting into gifts as she breathed – 'how I know that! You know ever since Fritz and I have been engaged, I share the desire to give to everybody, to share everything!'

'How extremely dangerous,' said I.

'It is only the beauty of danger, or the danger of beauty,' said the Advanced Lady – 'and there you have the ideal of my book – that woman is nothing but a gift.'

I smiled at her very sweetly. 'Do you know,' I said, 'I, too, would like to write a book on the advisability of caring for daughters, and taking them for airings and keeping them out of kitchens!'

I think the masculine element must have felt these angry vibrations: they ceased from singing, and together we climbed out of the wood, to see Schlingen below us, tucked in a circle of hills, the white houses shining in the sunlight, 'for all the world like eggs in a bird's nest,' as Herr Erchardt declared. We descended upon Schlingen and demanded sour milk with fresh cream and bread at the Inn of the Golden Stag, a most friendly place, with tables in a rose garden where hens and chickens ran riot – even flopping upon the disused tables and pecking at the red checks on the cloths. We broke the bread into the bowls, added the cream and stirred it round with flat wooden spoons, the landlord and his wife standing by.

'Splendid weather!' said Herr Erchardt, waving his spoon at the landlord, who shrugged his shoulders.

'What! you don't call it splendid!'

'As you please,' said the landlord, obviously scorning us.

'Such a beautiful walk,' said Fräulein Elsa, making a free gift of her most charming smile to the landlady.

'I never walk,' said the landlady; 'when I go to Mindelbau⁵ my man drives me – I've more important things to do with my legs than walk them through the dust!'

'I like these people,' confessed Herr Langen to me. 'I like them very, very much. I think I shall take a room here for the whole summer.'

'Why?'

'Oh, because they live close to the earth, and therefore despise it.'

He pushed away his bowl of sour milk and lit a cigarette. We ate, solidly and seriously, until those seven and a half kilometres to Mindelbau stretched before us like an eternity. Even Karl's activity became so full fed that he lay on the ground and removed his leather waist-belt. Elsa suddenly leaned over to Fritz and whispered, who on hearing her to the end and asking her if she loved him, got up and made a little speech.

'We – we wish to celebrate our betrothal by – by – asking you all to drive back with us in the landlord's cart – if – if it will hold us!'

'Oh, what a beautiful, noble idea!' said Frau Kellermann, heaving a sigh of relief that audibly burst two hooks.

'It is my little gift,' said Elsa to the Advanced Lady, who by virtue of three portions almost wept tears of gratitude.

Squeezed into the peasant cart and driven by the landlord, who showed his contempt for mother earth by spitting savagely every now and again, we jolted home again, and the nearer we came to Mindelbau the more we loved it and one another.

'We must have many excursions like this,' said Herr Erchardt to me, 'for one surely gets to know a person in the simple surroundings of the open air – one *shares* the same joys – one feels friendship. What is it your Shakespeare says? One moment, I have it. "The friends thou hast, and their adoption tried – grapple them to thy soul with hoops of steel!" '⁶

'But,' said I, feeling very friendly towards him, 'the bother about my soul is that it refuses to grapple anybody at all – and I am sure that the dead weight of a friend whose adoption it had tried would kill it immediately. Never yet has it shown the slightest sign of a hoop!'

He bumped against my knees and excused himself and the cart.

'My dear little lady, you must not take the quotation literally. Naturally, one is not physically conscious of the hoops; but hoops there are in the soul of him or her who loves his fellow men . . . Take this afternoon, for instance. How did we start out? As strangers you might almost say, and yet – all of us – how have we come home?'

'In a cart,' said the only remaining joy, who sat upon his mother's lap and felt sick.

We skirted the field that we had passed through, going round by the cemetery. Herr Langen leaned over the edge of the seat and greeted the graves. He was sitting next to the Advanced Lady – inside the shelter of her shoulder. I heard her murmur: 'You look like a little boy with your hair blowing about in the wind.' Herr Langen, slightly less bitter, watched the last graves disappear. And I heard her murmur: 'Why are you so sad? I, too, am very sad sometimes – but – you look young enough for me to dare to say this – I – too – know of much joy!'

'What do you know?' said he.

I leaned over and touched the Advanced Lady's hand. 'Hasn't it been a nice afternoon?' I said questioningly. 'But you know, that theory of yours about women and Love – it's as old as the hills – oh, older!'

From the road a sudden shout of triumph. Yes, there he was again – white beard, silk handkerchief and undaunted enthusiasm.

'What did I say? Eight kilometres – it is!'

'Seven and a half!' shrieked Herr Erchardt.

'Why, then, do you return in carts? Eight kilometres it must be.'

Herr Erchardt made a cup of his hands and stood up in the jolting cart while Frau Kellermann clung to his knees. 'Seven and a half!'

'Ignorance must not go uncontradicted!' I said to the Advanced Lady.

George Lloyd[1]

A Humorous Sketch

There never was such a boy. He could do almost anything. He polished the boots and the silver, waited at table, played with the children and had even been found surreptitiously nursing the baby. It showed, said Mrs Partington, the inherent superiority of the male to the female. To be sure, she had had other boys in whom the virtues of George Lloyd had not seemed to inhere, but that, according to Mrs Partington, did not affect the argument. And how fortunate it was that he had entered her service at an important juncture; that is to say, shortly before she expected a visit from her first cousin, once removed, who was in the Cabinet. She had not seen much of the cousin since greatness had been thrust upon him. He was *so* much engaged, she told her friends. But now, in response to her sixth invitation, he had at last arranged to spend a night at her house on his way north. And just a week before the visit, when Charles Jones had been summarily dismissed for offences connected with a jam pot, George Lloyd had offered his services.

Mrs Partington took to him at once; he had such a nice face, such clean hands and such a neat figure, and he assured her that he never had and never would put his fingers in the jam. The only thing she didn't quite like was his name; it suggested, somehow, the idea of a Cabinet Minister upside down, which was an idea which Mrs Partington shrank from contemplating. Even at the best it savoured somewhat of presumption.

'You were not called George because your name, being Lloyd – not after – er—'

'Oh, no, ma'am,' said George Lloyd, who was very quick at the uptake, 'my grandfather.'

It was not uppishness, then. Mrs Partington engaged him.

And then came the preparations for the coming of the Cabinet Minister. Such rubbing up of silver, such cleaning of windows, such airing of the best bed had never been seen in Mrs Partington's establishment, correctly as that establishment was usually run. Mrs Partington herself was in a flutter of expectation, mingled with horrid fears; for were there not, in the path and in train of all members of the Government, those unspeakable Suffragettes? They followed them, she knew – the brazen creatures – everywhere, literally, my dear, everywhere, and the responsibility of entertaining eminent men nowadays was really – don't you agree? – overwhelming.

My dear agreed, and so did all the other dears to whom Mrs Partington confided the doubts which sat upon her bosom, and so did George Lloyd, on whom the urgency of super-careful carefulness had to be impressed.

'The iron gates must be locked at dusk, George' (it was better to call him George than Lloyd) 'at dusk, do you understand?'

Oh, yes, he understood. And not to be opened, he supposed, till the morning.

Certainly not. Mrs Partington hoped she could trust him, hoped he would do his utmost to secure the safety and comfort of the Cabinet Minister. George Lloyd assured her that he would see to the Cabinet Minister – no fear.

'If any of those Suffragettes were to get in I should never get over it,' said Mrs Partington.

'They do say they squeeze through anything,' observed George.

'They won't squeeze through my iron railings,' answered Mrs Partington, and George said he supposed not.

George and the parlourmaid together laid the table with the best glass and put the drawing room in an order which the term apple-pie is inadequate to express.

The arrival of the guest was a complete success; there were *no* Suffragettes about the iron gates, and Mrs Partington breathed freely. The dinner went off beautifully. Cook was a member of the local anti-Suffrage society, of which her mistress was president, and had done her utmost; and the way George passed the vegetables and saw that the Minister did not want for bread consolidated the good opinion that Mrs Partington had formed of him. The only disturbing thing – and very curious – that happened was, that on the drawing-room table after dinner, staring guest and hostess in the face, was a copy of *Votes for Women*. The guest thought that the hostess took it, and was a little affronted; the hostess thought the guest had bought it, and was a little surprised. Then when it was discovered that neither would look at anything so vile, consternation supervened. *How* did it get there? *How?* Mrs Partington was overwhelmed with annoyance, crossed with confusion. George Lloyd, summoned by fierce bell-ringing, poured oil on the troubled waters by suggesting that it might have been sent by mistake with the evening papers, and, beholding the relief caused by his words, departed with a gentle smile, while Mrs Partington still asseverated her regrets at the occurrence, for she *had* hoped that dear Jumbo (it was the Minister's pet name) would have found her little home a haven of peace.

Peaceful it was through the still night hours. The iron gates were locked, the key in Mrs Partington's keeping, and in the calm silence the Minister slept the sleep of those who cannot see beyond their noses. Locked gates, barred doors, police on guard. How, then, did it happen that on every door of every room next morning hung a poster bearing the shameless words, 'Votes for Women'? The bell-ringing of the evening was nothing to the bell-ringing of the morning. (In the afternoon the battery had to be recharged.) Every servant was summoned, every soul in the house questioned and requestioned. Nobody knew anything, nobody could suggest anything, except George Lloyd, who repeated his assertion of the previous day: 'They do say they can squeeze through anything.' He also said he had heard a noise in the night, but thought it might be rats. The police could find no clue and could offer no advice, except that the Minister should depart by an earlier train than had been intended, in case an outrage was contemplated at the station; and by twelve o'clock Mrs Partington was guestless, sadly depressed and further discomposed by the appear-ance of George Lloyd, who announced that his grandfather was ill and desired the presence of his namesake.

He went, never to return, and never has Mrs Partington had another boy displaying such inherent superiority to female servants. He went, taking all his possessions with him, including a pamphlet presented to him by Mrs Partington, entitled 'Why Women Do Not Want the Vote'. Two things only he left behind. One was the half-crown given him by the Cabinet Minister, the other was a letter found by the housemaid at the back of a drawer; and the extraordinary thing about the letter was that, though the envelope was directed to Master George Lloyd, it began inside, 'My dear Annie'.

The housemaid wondered and the housemaid pondered. Then she pocketed the half-crown and burned the letter.

GERTRUDE COLMORE

The Woman in the Corner

She was quite a nice-looking woman, and well dressed; not showily, but in clothes of good material. She sat in the corner of a second-class compartment of a suburban train, a train which arrived at Waterloo between seven o'clock and half-past, a train which brought many suburban residents to the London theatres.

There were six other people in the compartment; a young man and woman, evidently husband and wife; two middle-aged women; a Member of Parliament, a man about fifty, in a tail coat and tall hat; and a clergyman of the Church of England. The husband and wife talked about plays, occasionally addressing a remark to the Member of Parliament, who answered somewhat perfunctorily; the middle-aged ladies discussed the latest enormity of the Suffragettes, in terms of reprobation; the clergyman and the woman in the corner sat silent. The clergyman read an evening paper; the woman listened to the scraps of conversation.

'You're not going to anything so frivolous as a theatre, I suppose?' said the wife, turning to the Member of Parliament.

He had taken from his pocketbook a slip of paper on which were notes which he was studying with the aid of an eyeglass. 'No,' he said, 'no, not a theatre.' He shook his head solemnly.

'Oh, no, my dear lady.'

'The House, I suppose. Oh, no, of course it doesn't sit tonight.'

'I am going, if you wish to know, to speak at a meeting – a public meeting, on the White Slave Traffic.'[1]

The young woman's face fell. 'Oh, really!' Then, tentatively, 'You think it – it really goes on?'

'Undoubtedly, to some extent – to some extent.'

'Exaggerated, no doubt,' said the young husband. 'When women take up a subject like that – and women are taking a tremendous part—'

'The daughter of one of my parishioners disappeared a month ago,' said the clergyman, 'and we have failed to trace her.'

'Perhaps – some girls are so giddy,' suggested one of the middle-aged ladies.

'If those Suffragettes would devote themselves to rescue work—' said the other, and left the rest of the sentence to the imagination of the company.

'I have heard it said,' remarked the husband, 'that it's this White Slavery that's at the back of the Suffrage business.'

'And so it is,' said the woman in the corner.

It was the first time she had spoken, and everybody turned and looked at her.

The lady next her edged a little away. 'Are you, may I enquire,' she said, in a tone of insolent politeness, 'are you a Suffragette?'

'Oh, dear no. But I know something of the White Slave Traffic.'

'Indeed?' said the Member of Parliament, looking from his corner, over his eyeglasses, to the corner where the woman sat. 'You have made a study of the question?'

'A practical study – yes,' she said.

'And you think—?'

'I should like to hear *your* views as to how it should be dealt with.'

'Well – er – there is legislation – the Bill before the House; it is on that Bill that the meeting is to be tonight; and – er – with the flogging clauses, it ought to be – er – well, adequate.'

'You think the Bill – with the flogging clauses, will put an end to it?' The woman half smiled; a curious smile. 'Do you suppose the law, when it is passed, will be administered?'

'Of course, madam, of course. The laws of England are the best administered laws in the world.'

'I daresay. But isn't there a law now against abducting girls under sixteen? Who pays any attention to it? No white slave trader that I have ever heard of.'

'You are quite right, madam,' said the clergyman. 'Laws without religion are, comparatively speaking, useless. We must train our girls according to the teaching of St Paul[2] —'

'Just so,' murmured one of the ladies—

'– and our young men in the fear of the Lord.'

'I should advise you,' said the woman, 'to start with the young men. It will take some time, judging from what you've done so far.'

The clergyman looked at her with drawn brows. 'Do you doubt the power of religion?' he asked.

'And rescue work,' suggested one of the ladies.

The woman shrugged her shoulders. 'Rescue work and religious teaching, you can lump 'em both together, and the white slave trader don't care that for them.' She made a gesture of snapping her fingers with a well-gloved hand.

'Then may I ask,' said the Member of Parliament, 'since neither law, nor religion, nor rescue work can have any effect, may I ask what you, who profess to have studied the question, would recommend?'

'As to recommending,' the woman answered quietly, 'that's not my business; but if you want to know what's the only thing that's got a chance of stopping the traffic, I'll tell you. It's putting women on a level with men; putting them where men won't look upon them as animals to be used and played with; it's letting them have a chance to look after themselves; it's giving them the vote.'

'But I thought' – the words came in a sort of chorus, 'I thought you were against the suffrage?'

The train was slowing as it ran alongside the platform of Waterloo Station. The woman put her hand upon the handle of the door. 'So I am,' she said, 'dead against it. I hate it and I fear it; because I know.'

The train had stopped, and she stepped out on to the platform, then turned and spoke into the compartment.

'I'm a procuress, and *I know*.'

MARY SAMUEL DANIEL

Jimmy's Afternoon

At five o'clock the operating surgeon passed through the entrance door, and, with a friendly, if rather preoccupied, nod to the porter who opened it, stood for a contemplative moment at the top of the stone steps leading up to the hospital, glancing at, without seeing, the pair of gloves held in one hand, and aware somewhere near the bottom step of a gleam of yellow daffodils.

The westering April sun caught the flower-seller's basket in a golden glory, and fell with mellowing touches on the dull walls of the houses in the long, irregular street, where cottages with ancient gables and windows dedicated to those public favourites, the pig's trotter and the British bun, stood wedged between large modern emporiums flaunting tawdry cheap apparel and ornately adulterated food.

'That's it!' said Dr Graham to himself. 'A cup of tea with Aunt Leebie. I can do with a little optimism this afternoon.'

Yet optimism was not a quality in which by his co-workers Dr Graham was considered lacking. Jimmy, the small patient who had been operated on that day, though he would not have expressed it in those words, thought him extremely optimistic, basing his opinion on a flow of unfailingly cheerful conversation combined with air-ships that flew over your bed. The little ward-maid, who proudly boasted as her special prorogative the doctor's white operating coats, which he gave her to cut up into aprons 'long afore they was worn out', agreed with Jimmy, infusing into the agreement a demonstrative warmth from which Jimmy manfully abstained.

The surgeon passed down the hospital steps and took the short cut to the Green, beyond which lay Maitland Road and Miss Elizabeth Sampson's neat and cheerful villa. Miss Elizabeth's choice of Maitland

Road as a place of residence had been subconsciously determined by its nearness to her nephew's hospital; consciously, the matter had been placed 'unreservedly' in the hands of an overruling Providence, strengthened incidentally by those of approving, authoritative Scottish relatives.

The appearance of the flower-seller suggested, unpleasantly, Jimmy's mother, towards whom in the clean sunshine of this April's afternoon he felt a not unreasonable grudge for having produced that sorry addition to the race – Jimmy. (He must get him a new air-ship for convalescence – if ever those days were reached.) Certainly, and this reflection further upset the world for him, a quite diabolically-tangled web of contradictory causes had combined to produce that God-forsaken slip of wretchedness whose pitiful offspring had lain stark and mute today on the operating table, while several highly-skilled workers put forth their finest efforts to save if possible one deplorable little body rotten with disease. To what end? What was likely to be the end of Jimmy, who, in his own words, 'hadn't got no father'? The lump was gone from his shoulder, and it seemed rather more than likely the arm might have to follow, and Jimmy – doubtful subject for thankfulness – was alive still. Why, anyway, were Jimmies allowed to come into this already overcrowded corner of a rotten world? – a world, nevertheless, which produced daffodils golden in April sunshine, and in which the blades of grass were springing emerald green after April rain. He had obviously overpaid the flower-seller for these daffodils, but they would help to brighten up the corners of the cosy room at Maitland Road, particularly if it was Joan Marchment he saw putting them into bowls where the light would find them.

Would she have run in from her studio this afternoon to see Aunt Leebie? Her face painted itself for him as he strode across the Green. Joan, with her hazel-grey eyes and the lashes curling upwards, her gold-brown hair with the wavy tendrils on temples, her serious mouth so sweet in the dimpled corners; Joan with her ridiculous devotion to work and independence and – causes. Why, she could have her studio just the same if – yes, and paint as many pictures as she liked. As to causes? Yes, of course; he couldn't separate Joan from causes, and he wouldn't if he could. Causes were necessary evils; Jimmy and his mother were pretty clear proofs of that. For Jimmy's was a common cause, the old, old story of a bad man and his prey;[1] and the man, as usual, had escaped all punishment. He hated the thought of Joan and Jimmy's mother as two aspects of one question. Joan and her blossoming face; motherhood, as it so often was and as it might be – Joan and Jimmy's mother – things were damnably mixed up and muddled; but, oh, the Lord preserve her – and him – from hammers and Holloway![2]

Would she be there this afternoon? That 'little more', the muchness of which he realized in a daily increasing vividness; would it be any nearer today? Perhaps the question was too manifestly in his eyes as he presented the flowers. Perhaps it accounted for the sudden readjustment of Joan's, as she held out eager hands for the daffodils and made haste to find bowls for them, and became very busy in corners as Miss Elizabeth marshalled the teacups. There was an almost perceptibly exultant rattle of the little thin silver spoons in their delicate old blue saucers. To hold the fate of the two people you love best in the world poised in the hollow of your hand; to give two havering, foolish bodies one more chance to make an end of folly; to lead Opportunity firmly but discreetly by the fingers – Miss Sampson foresaw the imminent hour when prayer must surely be merged in thanksgiving.

'Eh, Joan, and you'll maybe find a mat,' remarked Aunt Leebie, affecting, with only partial success, an unawareness of the dramatic moment; 'I'm not for water-droppings all over my polished mahogany. And, for any sake, child, come and sit you down in comfort for your tea.'

For answer a pair of arms came round the little low shoulders and a kiss descended on the soft and silvery hair. 'It's just beautiful this afternoon,' said artful Joan. 'I'd give anything to have lovely white hair like yours, Leebie dear.'

'And what'll be the matter with your own, I'm wondering? Alec, you'll find the scones perhaps. And what thirsty work will you have been doing this afternoon?' added Miss Elizabeth, manipulating with a nicety and justness the cream.

'Interfering with Nature's merciful destructiveness,' answered Alec grimly, and Joan's curving eyelashes went up, and a question filled the wide-open, steady grey eyes.

Later, when Aunt Leebie had bustled from the room on absorbing business elsewhere – 'Tell me more about it,' said Joan. 'I know there is more to tell.'

And he told her the plain story of Jimmy. They often talked over the terrible facts of life; they were the best of comrades, these two, though one was very much in love.

'It's horrible,' said Alec, in conclusion. 'The mother was a child, barely sixteen; and for men like the father there is no justice in things as they stand. The law, as made, neither can nor will deal justly with these devils.'

'No,' said Joan. 'The law, as made, is man's law, and – oh, you know, you know . . . *We've* got to get it altered – we women. Women must do it – for women and children – and men. We've got to do it with—'

'Hammers?' put in Alec, whimsically, looking with a curious heart-pang at the tightly-clasped frail-looking hands.

'With violence, apparently – the kingdom of Heaven has to be taken that way, you know, sometimes. With force, certainly, if – if there is no other way. What other way is there?' she added passionately. 'All other ways have been tried – and tried – and tried, for half a hundred years. One instrument, and one alone, will give us power to amend the law; and man's law for men and women has got to be changed. Men will never change it, neither will they give us, without force, that for want of which all our crusades are futile. Therefore' – the voice dropped sadly and very wearily, but not unsteadily; 'therefore we shall use – whatever force is necessary, and some of us, I suppose, will die. No,' she said, as, remonstrating, he tried to take her hand; 'no, I cannot listen now—'

'Yes,' broke in Alex, 'you shall listen. You know I love you, and – I believe you love me. You don't know it, perhaps, yet; but I believe you will. Joan, marry me. I won't hinder your – your work, however mistaken I think its methods. I want you as my wife. Perhaps the world wants us – both. It isn't for nothing a man loves a woman as I love you. Marry me, Joan, and – see.' He had hold of her hands. As they stood facing each other, he felt them tremble, and her slight body sway a little. Then the curved lashes swept up, revealing eyes dim with tears.

He needed her, this valiant lover. She saw his man's need of her; saw, too, as through a widely opened window, a vision of her rightful woman's kingdom, its sweet sanctities of wifehood and motherhood and home. And there he stood, the man who held the key to the treasure-house, who loved her, whom she knew she loved.

'And some of us will die.' Remorselessly her own words echoed in her heart.

Freeing her hands, she retook both of his and held them tightly.

'I love you,' she said. She paused, and her eyes were proud, and glad – and loving. 'But – while men keep barred the door of justice on women; while men can, within the law, shut women up in hell; while motherhood can be – what it is to Jimmy's mother, and men within the law can make it so, I will never marry any man. Go and work for us – for the common cause, women's cause and men's. It is true the world wants us both, and together. Go and help to break down the evil wall of partition. And when the cause is won, on the day that victory is ours – if you still want me —' She kissed his hands as she held them, smiling through tender tears. 'I love you,' she ended. 'I will marry you – *then*.'

SAKI (HECTOR HUGH MUNRO)

The Schartz–Metterklume Method

Lady Carlotta stepped out on to the platform of the small wayside station and took a turn or two up and down its uninteresting length, to kill time till the train should be pleased to proceed on its way. Then, in the roadway beyond, she saw a horse struggling with a more than ample load, and a carter of the sort that seems to bear a sullen hatred against the animal that helps him to earn a living. Lady Carlotta promptly betook her to the roadway, and put rather a different complexion on the struggle. Certain of her acquaintances were wont to give her plentiful admonition as to the undesirability of interfering on behalf of a distressed animal, such interference being 'none of her business'. Only once had she put the doctrine of non-interference into practice, when one of its most eloquent exponents had been besieged for nearly three hours in a small and extremely uncomfortable may tree by an angry boar-pig, while Lady Carlotta, on the other side of the fence, had proceeded with the watercolour sketch she was engaged on, and refused to interfere between the boar and his prisoner. It is to be feared that she lost the friendship of the ultimately rescued lady. On this occasion she merely lost the train, which gave way to the first sign of impatience it had shown throughout the journey, and steamed off without her. She bore the desertion with philosophical indifference; her friends and relations were thoroughly well used to the fact of her luggage arriving without her. She wired a vague non-committal message to her destination to say that she was coming on 'by another train'. Before she had time to think what her next move might be she was confronted by an imposingly attired lady, who seemed to be taking a prolonged mental inventory of her clothes and looks.

'You must be Miss Hope, the governess I've come to meet,' said the apparition, in a tone that admitted of very little argument.

'Very well, if I must I must,' said Lady Carlotta to herself with dangerous meekness.

'I am Mrs Quabarl,' continued the lady; 'and where, pray, is your luggage?'

'It's gone astray,' said the alleged governess, falling in with the excellent rule of life that the absent are always to blame; the luggage had, in point of fact, behaved with perfect correctitude. 'I've just telegraphed about it,' she added, with a nearer approach to truth.

'How provoking,' said Mrs Quabarl; 'these railway companies are so careless. However, my maid can lend you things for the night,' and she led the way to her car.

During the drive to the Quabarl mansion Lady Carlotta was impressively introduced to the nature of the charge that had been thrust upon her; she learned that Claude and Wilfrid were delicate, sensitive young people, that Irene had the artistic temperament highly developed and that Viola was something or other else of a mould equally commonplace among children of that class and type in the twentieth century.

'I wish them not only to be *taught*,' said Mrs Quabarl, 'but *interested* in what they learn. In their history lessons, for instance, you must try to make them feel that they are being introduced to the life-stories of men and women who really lived, not merely committing a mass of names and dates to memory. French, of course, I shall expect you to talk at mealtimes several days in the week.'

'I shall talk French four days of the week and Russian in the remaining three.'

'Russian? My dear Miss Hope, no one in the house speaks or understands Russian.'

'That will not embarrass me in the least,' said Lady Carlotta coldly.

Mrs Quabarl, to use a colloquial expression, was knocked off her perch. She was one of those imperfectly self-assured individuals who are magnificent and autocratic as long as they are not seriously opposed. The least show of unexpected resistance goes a long way towards rendering them cowed and apologetic. When the new governess failed to express wondering admiration of the large newly purchased and expensive car, and lightly alluded to the superior advantages of one or two makes which had just been put on the market, the discomfiture of her patroness became almost abject. Her feelings were those which might have animated a general of ancient warfaring days, on beholding his heaviest battle-elephant ignominiously driven off the field by slingers and javelin throwers.

At dinner that evening, although reinforced by her husband, who usually duplicated her opinions and lent her moral support generally, Mrs Quabarl regained none of her lost ground. The governess not only helped herself well and truly to wine, but held forth with considerable show of critical knowledge on various vintage matters, concerning which the Quabarls were in no wise able to pose as authorities. Previous governesses had limited their conversation on the wine topic to a respectful and doubtless sincere expression of a preference for water. When this one went as far as to recommend a wine firm in whose hands you could not go very far wrong Mrs Quabarl thought it time to turn the conversation into more usual channels.

'We got very satisfactory references about you from Canon Teep,' she observed; 'a very estimable man, I should think.'

'Drinks like a fish and beats his wife, otherwise a very lovable character,' said the governess imperturbably.

'My *dear* Miss Hope! I trust you are exaggerating,' exclaimed the Quabarls in unison.

'One must in justice admit that there is some provocation,' continued the romancer. 'Mrs Teep is quite the most irritating bridge-player that I have ever sat down with; her leads and declarations would condone a certain amount of brutality in her partner, but to souse her with the contents of the only soda-water syphon in the house on a Sunday afternoon, when one couldn't get another, argues an indifference to the comfort of others which I cannot altogether overlook. You may think me hasty in my judgements, but it was practically on account of the syphon incident that I left.'

'We will talk of this some other time,' said Mrs Quabarl hastily.

'I shall never allude to it again,' said the governess with decision.

Mr Quabarl made a welcome diversion by asking what studies the new instructress proposed to inaugurate on the morrow.

'History to begin with,' she informed him.

'Ah, history,' he observed sagely; 'now in teaching them history you must take care to interest them in what they learn. You must make them feel that they are being introduced to the life-stories of men and women who really lived—'

'I've told her all that,' interposed Mrs Quabarl.

'I teach history on the Schartz-Metterklume method,' said the governess loftily.

'Ah, yes,' said her listeners, thinking it expedient to assume an acquaintance at least with the name.

'What are you children doing out here?' demanded Mrs Quabarl the next morning, on finding Irene sitting rather glumly at the head of the stairs, while her sister was perched in an attitude of depressed discomfort on the window seat behind her, with a wolfskin rug almost covering her.

'We are having a history lesson,' came the unexpected reply. 'I am supposed to be Rome, and Viola up there is the she-wolf;[1] not a real wolf, but the figure of one that the Romans used to set store by – I forget why. Claude and Wilfrid have gone to fetch the shabby women.'[2]

'The shabby women?'

'Yes, they've got to carry them off. They didn't want to, but Miss Hope got one of father's fives-bats and said she'd give them a number nine spanking if they didn't, so they've gone to do it.'

A loud, angry screaming from the direction of the lawn drew Mrs Quabarl thither in hot haste, fearful lest the threatened castigation might even now be in process of infliction. The outcry, however, came principally from the two small daughters of the lodgekeeper, who were being hauled and pushed towards the house by the panting and dishevelled Claude and Wilfrid, whose task was rendered even more arduous by the incessant, if not very effectual, attacks of the captured maidens' small brother. The governess, fives-bat in hand, sat negligently on the stone balustrade, presiding over the scene with the cold impartiality of a Goddess of Battles. A furious and repeated chorus of

'I'll tell muvver' rose from the lodge children, but the lodge-mother, who was hard of hearing, was for the moment immersed in the preoccupation of her washtub. After an apprehensive glance in the direction of the lodge (the good woman was gifted with the highly militant temper which is sometimes the privilege of deafness), Mrs Quabarl flew indignantly to the rescue of the struggling captives.

'Wilfrid! Claude! Let those children go at once. Miss Hope, what on earth is the meaning of this scene?'

'Early Roman history; the Sabine women, don't you know? It's the Schartz-Metterklume method to make children understand history by acting it themselves; fixes it in their memory, you know. Of course, if, thanks to your interference, your boys go through life thinking that the Sabine women ultimately escaped, I really cannot be held responsible.'

'You may be very clever and modern, Miss Hope,' said Mrs Quabarl firmly, 'but I should like you to leave here by the next train. Your luggage will be sent after you as soon as it arrives.'

'I'm not certain exactly where I shall be for the next few days,' said the dismissed instructress of youth; 'you might keep my luggage till I wire my address. There are only a couple of trunks and some golf-clubs and a leopard cub.'

'A leopard cub!' gasped Mrs Quabarl. Even in her departure this extraordinary person seemed destined to leave a trail of embarrassment behind her.

'Well, it's rather left off being a cub; it's more than half-grown, you know. A fowl every day and a rabbit on Sundays is what it usually gets. Raw beef makes it too excitable. Don't trouble about getting the car for me, I'm rather inclined for a walk.'

And Lady Carlotta strode out of the Quabarl horizon.

The advent of the genuine Miss Hope, who had made a mistake as to the day on which she was due to arrive, caused a turmoil which that good lady was quite unused to inspiring. Obviously the Quabarl family had been woefully befooled, but a certain amount of relief came with the knowledge.

'How tiresome for you, dear Carlotta,' said her hostess, when the overdue guest ultimately arrived; 'how very tiresome losing your train and having to stop overnight in a strange place.'

'Oh, dear, no,' said Lady Carlotta; 'not at all tiresome – for me.'

CHARLOTTE PERKINS GILMAN

If I were a Man

That was what pretty little Mollie Mathewson always said when Gerald would not do what she wanted him to – which was seldom.

That was what she said this bright morning, with a stamp of her little high-heeled slipper, just because he had made a fuss about that bill, the long one with the 'account rendered', which she had forgotten to give him the first time and been afraid to the second – and now he had taken it from the postman himself.

Mollie was 'true to type'. She was a beautiful instance of what is reverentially called 'a true woman'. Little, of course – no true woman may be big. Pretty, of course – no true woman could possibly be plain. Whimsical, capricious, charming, changeable, devoted to pretty clothes and always 'wearing them well', as the esoteric phrase has it. (This does not refer to the clothes – they do not wear well in the least; but to some special grace of putting them on and carrying them about, granted to but few, it appears.)

She was also a loving wife and a devoted mother; possessed of 'the social gift' and the love of 'society' that goes with it, and, with all these was fond and proud of her home and managed it as capably as – well, as most women do.

If ever there was a true woman it was Mollie Mathewson, yet she was wishing heart and soul she was a man.

And all of a sudden she was!

She was Gerald, walking down the path so erect and square-shouldered, in a hurry for his morning train, as usual, and, it must be confessed, in something of a temper.

Her own words were ringing in her ears – not only the 'last word', but several that had gone before, and she was holding her lips tight shut, not to say something she would be sorry for. But instead of acquiescence in the position taken by that angry little figure on the veranda, what she felt was a sort of superior pride, a sympathy as with weakness, a feeling that 'I must be gentle with her', in spite of the temper.

A man! Really a man; with only enough subconscious memory of herself remaining to make her recognize the differences.

At first there was a funny sense of size and weight and extra thickness, the feet and hands seemed strangely large, and her long, straight, free legs swung forward at a gait that made her feel as if on stilts.

This presently passed, and in its place, growing all day, wherever she went, came a new and delightful feeling of being *the right size*.

Everything fitted now. Her back snugly against the seat-back, her feet comfortably on the floor. Her feet? . . . His feet! She studied them carefully. Never before, since her early school days, had she felt such freedom and comfort as to feet – they were firm and solid on the ground when she walked; quick, springy, safe – as when, moved by an unrecognizable impulse, she had run after, caught and swung aboard the car.

Another impulse fished in a convenient pocket for change – instantly, automatically, bringing forth a nickel for the conductor and a penny for the newsboy.

These pockets came as a revelation. Of course she had known they were there, had counted them, made fun of them, mended them, even envied them; but she never had dreamed of how it *felt* to have pockets.

Behind her newspaper she let her consciousness, that odd mingled consciousness, rove from pocket to pocket, realizing the armoured assurance of having all those things at hand, instantly get-at-able, ready to meet emergencies. The cigar case gave her a warm feeling of comfort – it was full; the firmly held fountain-pen, safe unless she stood on her head; the keys, pencils, letters, documents, notebook, chequebook, bill folder – all at once, with a deep rushing sense of power and pride, she felt what she had never felt before in all her life – the possession of money, of her own earned money – hers to give or to withhold; not to beg for, tease for, wheedle for – hers.

That bill – why if it had come to her – to him, that is, he would have paid it as a matter of course, and never mentioned it – to her.

Then, being he, sitting there so easily and firmly with his money in his pockets, she wakened to his lifelong consciousness about money. Boyhood – its desires and dreams, ambitions. Young manhood – working tremendously for the wherewithal to make a home – for her. The present years with all their net of cares and hopes and dangers; the present moment, when he needed every cent for special plans of great importance, and this bill, long overdue and demanding payment, meant an amount of inconvenience wholly unnecessary if it had been given him when it first came; also, the man's keen dislike of that 'account rendered'.

'Women have no business sense!' she found herself saying, 'and all that money just for hats – idiotic, useless, ugly things!'

With that she began to see the hats of the women in the car as she had never seen hats before. The men's seemed normal, dignified, becoming, with enough variety for personal taste, and with distinction in style and in age, such as she had never noticed before. But the women's—

With the eyes of a man and the brain of a man; with the memory of a whole lifetime of free action wherein the hat, close-fitting on cropped hair, had been no handicap; she now perceived the hats of women.

Their massed fluffed hair was at once attractive and foolish, and on that hair, at every angle, in all colours, tipped, twisted, tortured into every crooked shape, made of any substance chance might offer, perched these formless objects. Then, on their formlessness the trimmings – these squirts of stiff feathers, these violent outstanding bows of glistening ribbon, these swaying, projecting masses of plumage which tormented the faces of bystanders.

Never in all her life had she imagined that this idolized millinery could look, to those who paid for it, like the decorations of an insane monkey.

And yet, when there came into the car a little woman, as foolish as any, but pretty and sweet-looking, up rose Gerald Mathewson and gave her his seat; and, later, when there came in a handsome red-cheeked girl, whose hat was wilder, more violent in colour and eccentric in shape than any other; when she stood near by and her soft curling plumes swept his cheek once and again, he felt a sense of sudden pleasure at the intimate tickling touch – and she, deep down within, felt such a wave of shame as might well drown a thousand hats forever.

When he took his train, his seat in the smoking car, she had a new surprise. All about him were the other men, commuters too, and many of them friends of his.

To her, they would have been distinguished as 'Mary Wade's husband' – 'the man Belle Grant is engaged to' – that rich Mr Shopworth' – or 'that pleasant Mr Beale'. And they would all have lifted their hats to her, bowed, made polite conversation if near enough – especially Mr Beale.

Now came the feeling of open-eyed acquaintance, of knowing men – as they were. The mere amount of this knowledge was a surprise to her; the whole background of talk from boyhood up, the gossip of barber-shop and club, the conversation of morning and evening hours on trains, the knowledge of political affiliation, of business standing and prospects, of character – in a light she had never known before.

They came and talked to Gerald, one and another. He seemed quite popular. And as they talked, with this new memory and new understanding, an understanding which seemed to include all these men's minds, there poured in on the submerged consciousness beneath a new, a startling knowledge – what men really think of women.

Good average American men were there; married men for the most part, and happy – as happiness goes in general. In the minds of each and all there seemed to be a two-storey department, quite apart from the rest of their ideas, a separate place where they kept their thoughts and feelings about women.

In the upper half were the tenderest emotions, the most exquisite ideals, the sweetest memories, all lovely sentiments as to 'home' and 'mother', all delicate admiring adjectives, a sort of sanctuary, where a veiled statue, blindly adored, shared place with beloved yet commonplace experiences.

In the lower half – here that buried consciousness woke to keen distress – they kept quite another assortment of ideas. Here, even in this clean-minded husband of hers, was the memory of stories told at men's dinners, of worse ones overheard in street or car, of base traditions, coarse epithets, gross experiences – known, though not shared.

And all these in the department 'woman', while in the rest of the mind – here was new knowledge indeed.

The world opened before her. Not the world she had been reared in; where Home had covered all the map, almost, and the rest had been 'foreign', or 'unexplored country', but the world as it was, man's world, as made, lived in and seen, by men.

It was dizzying. To see the houses that fled so fast across the car window, in terms of builders' bills, or of some technical insight into materials and methods; to see a passing village with lamentable knowledge of who 'owned it' – and of how its Boss was rapidly aspiring to State power, or of how that kind of paving was a failure; to see shops, not as mere exhibitions of desirable objects, but as business ventures, many mere sinking ships, some promising a profitable voyage – this new world bewildered her.

She – as Gerald – had already forgotten about that bill, over which she – as Mollie – was still crying at home. Gerald was 'talking business' with this man, 'talking politics' with that; and now sympathizing with the carefully withheld troubles of a neighbour.

Mollie had always sympathized with the neighbour's wife before.

She began to struggle violently, with this large dominant masculine consciousness. She remembered with sudden clearness things she had read – lectures she had heard; and resented with increasing intensity this serene masculine preoccupation with the male point of view.

Mr Miles, the little fussy man who lived on the other side of the street, was talking now. He had a large complacent wife; Mollie had never liked her much, but had always thought him rather nice – he was so punctilious in small courtesies.

And here he was talking to Gerald – such talk!

'Had to come in here,' he said. 'Gave my seat to a dame who was bound to have it. There's nothing they won't get when they make up their minds to it – eh?'

'No fear!' said the big man in the next seat, 'they haven't much mind to make up, you know – and if they do, they'll change it.'

'The real danger,' began the Revd Alfred Smythe, the new Episcopal clergyman, a thin, nervous, tall man, with a face several centuries behind the times, 'is that they will overstep the limits of their God-appointed sphere.'

'Their natural limits ought to hold 'em, I think,' said cheerful Dr Jones. 'You can't get around physiology, I tell you.'

'I've never seen any limits, myself, not to what they want, anyhow;' said Mr Miles, 'merely a rich husband and a fine house and no end of bonnets and dresses, and the latest thing in motors, and a few diamonds – and so on. Keeps us pretty busy.'

There was a tired grey man across the aisle. He had a very nice wife, always beautifully dressed, and three unmarried daughters, also beautifully dressed – Mollie knew them. She knew he worked hard too, and looked at him now a little anxiously.

But he smiled cheerfully.

'Do you good, Miles,' he said. 'What else would a man work for? A good woman is about the best thing on earth.'

'And a bad one's the worst, that's sure,' responded Miles.

'She's a pretty weak sister, viewed professionally,' Dr Jones averred with solemnity, and the Revd Alfred Smythe added: 'She brought evil into the world.'

Gerald Mathewson sat up straight. Something was stirring in him which he did not recognize – yet could not resist.

'Seems to me we all talk like Noah,' he suggested drily. 'Or the ancient Hindu scriptures.[1] Women have their limitations, but so do we, God knows. Haven't we known girls in school and college just as smart as we were?'

'They cannot play our games,' coldly replied the clergyman.

Gerald measured his meagre proportions with a practised eye.

'I never was particularly good at football myself,' he modestly admitted, 'but I've known women who could outlast a man in all-round endurance. Besides – life isn't spent in athletics!'

This was sadly true. They all looked down the aisle where a heavy ill-dressed man with a bad complexion sat alone. He had held the top of the columns once, with headlines and photographs. Now he earned less than any of them.

'It's time we woke up,' pursued Gerald, still inwardly urged to unfamiliar speech. 'Women are pretty much *people*, seems to me. I know they dress like fools – but who's to blame for that? We invent all those idiotic hats of theirs, and design their crazy fashions, and, what's more, if a woman is courageous enough to wear common-sense clothes – and shoes – which of us wants to dance with her?

'Yes, we blame them for grafting on us, but are we willing to let our wives work? We are not. It hurts our pride, that's all. We are always criticizing them for making mercenary marriages, but what do we call a girl who marries a chump with no money? Just a poor fool, that's all. And they know it.

'As for those physical limitations, Dr Jones, I guess our side of the house has some responsibility there, too – eh?

'And for Mother Eve – I wasn't there and can't deny the story, but I will say this, if she brought evil into the world we men have had the lion's share of keeping it going ever since – how about that?'

They drew into the city, and all day long in his business, Gerald was vaguely conscious of new views, strange feelings, and the submerged Mollie learned and learned.

APPENDIX I

This story, which has not been republished since 1928, charts a development in Grand's style of writing, from the domestic realism that her novels embraced, and which she maintained to greater or lesser degree in her short stories, to a self-reflexivity much more in keeping with the modernism of its time.

SARAH GRAND

In Search of a Subject

If you have ever been asked to write a little paper on any subject you like, only it must be in by a given date, and have promised to do it if you possibly can, you will understand my dilemma as I sit here at my desk, pen in hand, pressed for time, trying frantically to find something to write about. Concentrating on a given subject is easy enough. Given a title and one's thoughts begin to flow; but choosing for oneself in haste has quite the opposite effect. At the present moment it is just as if my mind were up against a stone wall, with all the subjects I know anything about on the other side of it. Though I am a busy woman, it seemed but a trifle to promise with the date of delivery far ahead. I forgot all the other things that would have to be thought about and attended to first; so it has come to be now or never, and I am not prepared. I have promised to do it if I possibly can. A conditional promise. For a cowardly moment I glance at that loophole of escape. But can I honestly say that it was not possible? No, I cannot without making an effort. Poor Mrs Dombey![1] But I musn't think about poor

Mrs Dombey. What *am* I to think about? As if the question had summoned them, subjects innumerable come crowding into my mind. They make me feel like a child in a toyshop with leave to choose only one toy. The Modern Girl, Brown Bread versus White, The League of Nations, The Parlous Condition of the Land, Journalism as a Career for Women, Are Athletic Sports being overdone? Food, Cooking, Health and Beauty, Fiction, Christmas, Christmas time, Holiday time ... It should be something suitable, seasonable, something cheery—

'Beg pardon, madam, I did knock,' the little maid gasps out of breath. (She will run up those four flights of stairs.) 'Somebody at the telephone.'

'Tell them to hold on.'

And it was only to make sure that I hadn't taken cold last night. Most kindly meant, but O dear! just as I had got it – almost. Where on earth is that paper I was jotting my thoughts down on?

Knock at the door. Cook this time. Apologetic. Knows she's sinning, but can't think what to get for a change that I'll eat. 'Get a bullock and boil it' expresses my feelings. But she is inured to that form of expression on like occasions and, ignoring the interruption, goes on stolidly 'And you didn't eat your breakfast, and if you don't eat—.'

'Oh, do go away, you bold, bad woman! Not another word or I'll eat *you*.'

I am reminded of Carford by the way she takes that (Carford was a great dear too) – that morning when she was brushing my hair, and I woke up out of a reverie, suddenly, because the brushing had ceased, and saw her in the glass standing off with the brush in her hand, in a despairing attitude, patiently waiting till I had done rubbing my head with both hands, a habit I have when I'm thinking hard.

'Won't it do if I brush it?' she meekly remonstrated.

'I should like to throw something at you, Carford,' I exploded.

'Well, do, madam, please, if it's any help,' said Carford, twinkling, and we laughed.

Poor Carford! It was hard to part with her when I went to America, and had to have an 'experienced travelling maid, good packer, hair-dresser, dressmaker' (as per advertisements). Carford was all that, but a bad traveller, and too delicate to stand a strenuous time anywhere. There was no help for it, we had to separate, but it was only to be until my return. I found her a temporary place that appeared to be all that was desirable. The lady was not an acquaintance of mine, but a friend who was intimate with her, and whose judgement I had no reason to doubt, vouched for it that she was extremely nice. Unfortunately, hers was not the kind of niceness that would have considered the health of an obviously delicate maid. She put Carford into a cold, dark room on the ground floor, and kept her there when the floods were out, with the water seeping up through the floor, and the walls streaming with the damp. When at last one of the other servants called in a doctor, he found Carford suffering from rheumatic fever, and ordered her to be moved into a suitable room and kept warm in bed for at least a fortnight. Instead, her mistress packed her off on the spot by train, some hours' journey in the depth of winter, to her home. She survived the exposure, but was crippled for life. When I think of her, I am in sympathy with the pious people who used to look forward to having their bliss in heaven enhanced by a full view of the unregenerate in torment in the other place. There is one woman, at any rate, that I should like to see there.

When the writing mood is not on me, and has to be induced, I find the best way is not to try to think. One's mind has a perverse trick of immediately doing what it is not wanted to do. I sit pen in hand; there is a blank interval; then, on a sudden, there comes an idea, a reflection, a recollection; it is not what I want for my immediate purpose, but I jot it down, because I have often found that a stray thought was a clue. In the same way the letter B may turn out to be a clue when you are trying to remember the name of a flower. If such irrelevant words as battle and burn and bee and brute present themselves to your mind, and you seize on the B as a clue, you are bound to arrive at *begonia* sooner or later, which was the word you wanted . . .

O bother! another interruption! Lady on the telephone, says she must speak to me, most important, won't keep me a minute, is sure I won't mind when I hear who it is. Won't mind! And her minutes as uncertain in length as one of the six days which were devoted to the creation of the universe . . . Back at my writing table. She only wanted to remind me of my promise . . . as if I had no engagement book to refer to, or as if anyone who answered the telephone couldn't have been entrusted with such a message. I shall be frothing with irritation directly. Ah, these talk, talk, talkers! . . . The word acts on my mind like the blotting out of one picture by another on the Cinema screen. The picture now is a close up of a plump little, good little, smiling little woman, wife of the incumbent of a big poverty-stricken parish in a manufacturing town. But oh! how she talked. It was as if, in the absence of the usual receptacle in which thoughts are stored up in silence, she was forced to utter aloud all that occurred to her. And the wonder was that mortal woman had ever been able to talk so incessantly without ever saying anything to anybody's hurt, absent or present. She was a hard worker too, and an intelligent observer. It was she who discovered for me the reason that the mill-girls were better behaved than the fustian cutters. The uproar of the machinery in the mills makes talking impossible, she pointed out; in the fustian cutting rooms the silence promotes conversation, and conversation, led by the more daring spirits in such a company, is far from edifying. The mill-girls and fustian cutters who swarmed about the dear little lady had good reason to bless her. She spared no pains to promote their well-being in every respect, and they were grateful. I was present on the occasion of a presentation they made her. Only on this occasion and in church had I ever seen her sit silent. I thought she would make up for it when it was her turn to speak. There were speeches in her honour overflowing with the milk and honey of praise. She was deeply moved. When at last the time came for her to reply, we had no fears for her fluency, but it was with an obvious effort that she began. 'My dear friends,' she faltered, 'I am a worker, I am not a talker—'. For the next few minutes the hall rocked with shouts of laughter and applause.

Here again the magic word 'talkers' switched my thoughts off to another episode. We were a party of intimate friends sitting down to a schoolroom tea, the kind of people who don't break a party up into bits by talking together in pairs, each on a different subject, instead of listening so that one at a time may speak and be heard, and joining in with a contribution to the topic, when they can, which will help to make the conversation general. As a hostess I want to hear what everybody has to say. It bores me to have my whole attention claimed in turn by the guests on my right and on my left. All my friends but one present that day understood sociability on these occasions as a fair game of give and take. The first remark made was like a ball tossed to us all. It was caught and tossed again by someone at the opposite end of the table who tossed it on. A good hit that time, to judge by the laughter; but I had missed the joke because my guest on the left was babbling confidentially as if she and I were alone together.

'Well, but what is the greatest pleasure in life?' was the next remark that I caught.

'Talk,' I plunged.

Dissentients shot objections at me from all sides. That all the trouble in the world is made by talk was the conclusion at which they were arriving, when someone asked me to define talk. Did I mean conversation?

'I fall between two stools,' I replied. '"Conversation" suggests pedantic discussions, and "talk", as you took it, deserves all the objections you levelled at it. Still, I do mean talk, good talk, sprinkled with wit and humour, laughter-provoking; sweetened with sympathetic insight, heart-expanding; the kind of talk that acts as a tonic, mentally, morally and physically, without being didactic. Talk is the pleasure to ourselves which at the same time gives most pleasure to others; it may be enjoyed from the beginning of life till the end, and it never palls. *The Fine Art of Conversation*—.'

I threw down my pen. There it was, my subject, at last, but too late. No time left for it now. But at least I have an honest excuse for not fulfilling my promise. These notes are a proof that the failure is my misfortune rather than my fault.

APPENDIX 2

In 1913, Charlotte Perkins Gilman wrote a piece in her own magazine, in which she emphasized the personal and didactic elements in her story and noted that through it she achieved her aim of altering medical practice.

CHARLOTTE PERKINS GILMAN

Why I Wrote 'The Yellow Wallpaper'?

Many and many a reader has asked that. When the story first came out, in the *New England Magazine* about 1891, a Boston physician made protest in *The Transcript*. Such a story ought not to be written, he said; it was enough to drive anyone mad to read it.

Another physician, in Kansas I think, wrote to say that it was the best description of incipient insanity he had ever seen, and – begging my pardon – had I been there?

Now the story of the story is this:

For many years I suffered from a severe and continuous nervous breakdown tending to melancholia – and beyond. During about the third year of this trouble I went, in devout faith and some faint stir of hope, to a noted specialist in nervous diseases, the best known in the country. This wise man put me to bed and applied the rest cure, to which a still good physique responded so promptly that he concluded there was nothing much the matter with me, and sent me home with solemn advice to 'live as domestic a life as far as possible', to 'have but two hours' intellectual life a day' and 'never to touch pen, brush or pencil again, as long as I lived'. This was in 1887.

I went home and obeyed those directions for some three months, and came so near the border line of utter mental ruin that I could see over.

Then, using the remnants of intelligence that remained, and helped by a wise friend, I cast the noted specialist's advice to the winds and went to work again – work, the normal life of every human being; work, in which is joy and growth and service, without which one is a pauper and a parasite; ultimately recovering some measure of power.

Being naturally moved to rejoicing by this narrow escape, I wrote 'The Yellow Wallpaper', with its embellishments and additions to carry out the ideal (I never had hallucinations or objections to my mural decorations) and sent a copy to the physician who so nearly drove me mad. He never acknowledged it.

The little book is valued by alienists[1] and as a good specimen of one kind of literature. It has to my knowledge saved one woman from a similar fate – so terrifying her family that they let her out into normal activity and she recovered.

But the best result is this. Many years later I was told that the great specialist had admitted to friends of his that he had altered his treatment of neurasthenia since reading 'The Yellow Wallpaper'.

It was not intended to drive people crazy, but to save people from being driven crazy, and it worked.

NOTES

Original place of publication, and source of text in this volume, if different, given.

Definitions, foreign words and phrases, and places, especially in London, are given in the Glossary.

OSCAR WILDE, *The Sphinx without a Secret*

First published in *World* (25 May 1887), as 'Lady Alroy'

Reproduced from Oscar Wilde, *Lord Arthur Saville's Crime, The Portrait of Mr W. H. and Other Stories* (London: Methuen & Co., 1909)

1. *Café de la Paix*: One of the most famous cafés in Paris, designed by Charles Garnier of the Opéra Garnier; it was part of the Grand Hôtel built in 1867 to welcome VIPs to the Universal Exhibition.
2. *Pentateuch*: First five books of the Old Testament, regarded as a unity.
3. *the Madeleine . . . the Bois*: In 1806, when the building of the Madeleine church was in progress, Napoleon decided it should be a Temple of Glory dedicated to the Great Army, but Louis XVIII, restored to power in 1814, ordered that it be once more a church. The Bois de Boulogne is a fashionable park and area in Paris.
4. *Gioconda*: The smiling lady (Italian), another name for Leonardo da Vinci's *Mona Lisa*.
5. *Morning Post*: London paper with a reputation for recording the doings of the aristocratic and wealthy, and advocating a forward foreign policy. First London daily, early in the nineteenth century, to print notices of plays, operas and concerts.

OLIVE SCHREINER, *The Buddhist Priest's Wife*

First published in *Stories, Dreams and Allegories* (London: T. Fisher Unwin, 1923)

After Schreiner's death, Samuel Cronwright-Schreiner gathered her uncollected and unpublished writings. In the preface, he relates 'The Buddhist Priest's Wife' was written 'at Matjesfontein in 1891 and the following year'. Schreiner wrote of the story: 'it has given me more bliss than anything else I ever wrote' (Schreiner to Cronwright, 4 January 1893, in Richard Rive (ed.), *Oliver Schreiner Letters 1871–1899* (Oxford University Press, 1988), vol. 1, p. 217). Matjesfontein was a fashionable watering-place, attracting wealthy visitors. Schreiner lived in her own cottage there for five years. During the Second South African War, it supported a base hospital.

MONA CAIRD, *The Yellow Drawing Room*

First published in *A Romance of the Moors* (Leipzig: Heinemann and Balestier, 1892)

The title was part of the English Library series; its stated aims were to issue its volumes simultaneously with the appearance of the same works in England and America and to compress works, wherever possible, into one volume. Among its authors were Oscar Wilde, Henry James, Margaret Oliphant, William Dean Howells and Ouida.

1. *Columbine*: Sweetheart of Harlequin in traditional pantomime.

CHARLOTTE PERKINS GILMAN, *The Yellow Wallpaper*

First published in *New England Magazine* (January 1892), 647–56

All Gilman stories are reproduced from *The Yellow Wall-Paper and Other Stories*, ed. Robert Shulman (Oxford: Oxford University Press, 1995)

The magazine began in 1886 as a continuation of *The Bay State Monthly*, and was initially called the *New England Magazine and Bay State Monthly*. It absorbed other publications such as the *Era* magazine from Philadelphia, ceasing publication in 1917.

Shulman notes that the hyphenation of the word 'wall-paper' was inconsistent in *New England Magazine*, and he retained this 'device . . . since it underscores both elements of this central symbol' (p. xxxiii). It has been standardized to 'wallpaper' in this volume.

1. *it sticketh closer than a brother*: 'A man that hath friends must shew himself friendly: and there is a friend that sticketh closer than a brother' (Proverbs 18.24, Authorized Version here and below).

2. *Weir Mitchell*: Silas Weir Mitchell (1829–1914), prominent American neurologist who devised a rest cure for 'neurasthenic' and 'hysterical' women. He treated Gilman in 1887; see Appendix 2.

3. *'debased Romanesque' with delirium tremens*: Somewhat resembling the Roman; loosely applied to all the styles of Western Europe, from the fall of the Western Roman Empire to the appearance of Gothic architecture, and implies that which grew up from the attempts of barbarous people to copy Roman architecture. Literally trembling delirium (Latin); psychotic condition associated with chronic alcoholism, characterized by severe tremor and vivid hallucinations.

4. *improve the shining hours*: From Isaac Watts (1674–1748), *Divine Songs for Children*, 'Against Idleness and Mischief' (1715): 'How doth the little busy bee/Improve each shining hour,/And gather honey all the day/From every opening flower!'

GEORGE EGERTON, *A Cross Line*

First published in *Keynotes* (London: Elkin Mathews and John Lane, 1893)

One of six stories published by John Lane and Elkin Mathews at the Bodley Head publishing firm in Piccadilly, London, under the title of *Keynotes*, in September 1893. The volume sold over 6,000 copies in its first year, was translated into seven languages and was reprinted eight times by 1898. The second edition (1894), was used by Lane to launch his Keynote Series of short stories and one-volume novels; the thirty-four titles included works by Grant Allen, Ella D'Arcy and Henry Harland. John Lane also published the famous *Yellow Book* between 1894 and 1897, a quarterly book-length magazine and the main organ of 1890s aestheticism, edited by Harland and illustrated by Aubrey Beardsley until his dismissal after four issues in the wake of the Wilde trials.

1. *Tanagra*: Town in ancient Boeotia, famous for terracotta figurines of the same name (examples were first found in the late nineteenth century).

2. *speckled red 'fairy hats'*: Foxgloves. The name 'foxglove' is derived from 'Little Folks' Glove', and in fairylore they are believed to be worn by fairies as hats and gloves.

3. *stone loach 'Beardies'*: Type of bottom-feeding freshwater fish. The term 'beardie' alludes to their barbels around the mouth.

4. *Cleopatra sailing down to meet Antony*: See Shakespeare's *Antony and Cleopatra*: 'When she first met Mark Antony, she pursed up his heart, upon the river of Cydnus' (II.ii.188–9).

5. *a Strindberg or a Nietzsche*: August Strindberg (1849–1912), Swedish dramatist and novelist, whose plays include *The Father* (1887) and *Miss Julie* (1888). Friedrich Wilhelm Nietzsche (1844–1900), German philosopher, poet and critic, noted especially for his concept of the superman and his rejection of traditional Christian values. His principal works are the *Birth of Tragedy* (1872), *Thus Spake Zarathustra* (1883–91) and *Beyond Good and Evil* (1886).

6. *qualities . . . to make a Napoleon*: Napoleon Bonaparte (1769–1821), Emperor of France 1804–15, finally defeated at Waterloo. Both an enlightened rationalist and superstitious fatalist, his characteristics included striking determination and self-confidence, authoritarianism and intolerance.

KATE CHOPIN, *Désirée's Baby*

First published in *Vogue* (14 January 1893), and *Bayou Folk* (1894)

All Chopin stories are reproduced from *The Complete Works of Kate Chopin*, ed. Per Seyersted (Baton Rouge: Louisiana State University Press, 1969, 1997)

1. *La Blanche's*: The white woman (French) – the name has been given to the slave on account of her light complexion. Cf. Négrillon (Black Boy), a few paragraphs later.

BORGIA SMUDGITON (OWEN SEAMAN), *She–Notes*

First published in *Punch* (10 and 17 March 1894), 109, 129, with '*Japanese Fan de Siècle Illustrations by Mortarthurio Whiskerley*' (see Introduction)

1. *Norfolk-broad*: The term is deliberately confused here, for humorous effect. A Norfolk jacket is a kind of shooting jacket, with a waistband; a Norfolk suit is a suit of breeches; either can be called Norfolks. The Norfolk Broads are shallow lakes in the east of Norfolk, a low-lying county of East England, on the North Sea and the Wash.

2. *footlights of the Pavillon Rouge*: Pavillion Rouge is a light red wine; Moulin Rouge a Parisian music-hall.

3. KILANYI: Contemporary *tableau vivant* artist (see Glossary).

4. NAPOLEON. NELSON: See note 6 to Egerton's 'A Cross Line'. Horatio, Viscount Nelson (1758–1805), British naval commander during the Revolutionary and Napoleonic Wars. Killed at Trafalgar after defeating Villeneuve's fleet. He was blind in one eye.

5. *heavenly twins*: The title of Sarah Grand's bestselling and sensational novel of 1893, which caused a stir by its open treatment of venereal disease. The twins of the novel, Angelica and Diavolo, subvert the gender stereotypes which their names denote. See also n. 1 to Daniel's 'Jimmy's Afternoon'.

THOMAS HARDY, *An Imaginative Woman*

First published in *Pall Mall Magazine* (April 1894)

Collected in *Wessex Tales* in 1896 before being transferred to the 1912 Wessex Edition (Macmillan) of *Life's Little Ironies*, from which the story is reproduced

Hardy wrote in the Prefatory Note to the Wessex Edition:

Of the following collection the first story, 'An Imaginative Woman', which has hitherto stood in *Wessex Tales*, has been brought into this volume as being more nearly its place, turning as it does upon a trick of Nature, so to speak, a physical possibility that may attach to a wife of vivid imaginings, as is well known to medical practitioners and other observers of such manifestations.

Frank Pinion notes in *A Thomas Hardy Dictionary* (1989) that the story is based on a psychological fantasy Hardy found in Weismann's *Essays on Heredity* (1889), vol. 1, pp. 457–61; 'undoubtedly its imaginings were fanned by Hardy's love of Mrs Henniker, who lived at Southsea'. Pinion also notes that Robert Trewe is 'drawn considerably from the poet Dante Gabriel Rossetti (1828–82), and the idealization of his lady in *The House of Life* (1870)'.

1. *Solentsea in Upper Wessex*: Based on Southsea, Hampshire. Along with the other fictional place names in the story, it forms part of Hardy's 'Wessex', in which all his novels and short stories are set, and in which real places are given fictional names. Budmouth is real-life Weymouth.

2. *lymphatic . . . nervous and sanguine*: Alludes to the four humours correspond-

ing to the four temperaments: bilious, lymphatic, sanguine and nervous. During the early stages of the Renaissance, this concept of disease was attacked violently and discarded by many. But later, new factors came to light that reawakened interest in humoral medicine. Scientific enquiry into its theory revived in 1901.

3. *'a votary of the muse'*: Devoted follower of the goddess that inspires the artist; hence, an artist.

4. *the Island opposite*: The Isle of Wight, across the Solent from Southsea. The 'fashionable town' (p. 92) is Ryde.

5. *symboliste . . . décadent*: Symbolism was a late-nineteenth-century movement beginning in French and Belgian poetry by Mallarmé, Valéry and Verlaine, while the decadent movement, also associated with *fin-de-siècle* France, was characterized by the artificial, and epitomized by Joris Karl Huysmans (1848–1907), *A Rebours* (*Against Nature*) (1884). Social-purity New Women defined their own writings in direct opposition to the French decadent movement, which they saw as masculine and socially irresponsible. Pinion notes that Hardy read an article on these movements in *Revue des Deux Mondes* (1 November 1881).

6. *The mantle of Elijah*: In 1 Kings 19, Elijah puts his cloak on Elisha, who then becomes his disciple.

7. *Green Silesian band*: Brass band from Silesia, region of central Europe around the upper and middle Oder valley, annexed by Prussia in 1742.

8. *'Severed Lives'*: Cf. Rossetti's 'Severed Selves', in *The House of Life*, in *Poems* (1870) and expanded in *Ballads and Sonnets* (1881).

9. *black moustache and imperial . . . slouched hat*: Pinion suggests that Hardy based his description of Trewe on Holman Hunt's portrait of Rossetti 'and the "slouched hat" of his later years'. An imperial is a small tuft of hair growing beneath the lower lip, so called because Emperor Napoleon III wore one.

10. *Shelley's scraps . . . immortality*: Poetic fragments left in notebooks by Percy Bysshe Shelley at his death. Quotation from *Prometheus Unbound* (1820), I, 748–9.

11. *sleeping on a poet's lips*: See 'On a poet's lips I slept/Dreaming like a love-adept', Shelley, *Prometheus Unbound*, I, 737–8.

12. *'Behold, he standeth . . . our land'*: Song of Solomon 2.9, 11–12 (Authorized Version), with a few minor changes. The Song of Solomon, in the form of a collection of love poems, is an allegory or parable either of God's love for Israel, or for the church, or for the soul that loves Him.

13. *God is a jealous God*: Exodus 20.5.

14. *'The hour . . . was barren'*: Rossetti, 'Stillborn Love', sonnet 55, in *The House of Life*.

GEORGE EGERTON, *Virgin Soil*

First published in *Discords* (London and New York: John Lane, 1894)

1. *lint-locked*: Cf. lint-haired: flaxen-haired. See Mathilde Blinde's 'The Dying Dragoman', stanza 11, from *Birds of Passage: Songs of the Orient and Occident* (1895): 'lint-locked babes about her knees / Hark to strange tales of talking trees'.

2. *Alhambra*: Alhambra Palace Music Hall, Britain's first music-hall, opened in 1860 on Charing Cross Road in the West End; by 1875 London housed over three hundred music-halls. See 'At the Alhambra: Impressions and Sensations', *Savoy* 1 (1896), 75–83, by Arthur Symons, decadent, poet and editor of *Savoy*.

SARAH GRAND, *The Undefinable*

First published in *Cosmopolitan* 17 (October 1894), 745–57

Reproduced from *Emotional Moments* (London: Hurst and Blackett, 1908)

1. *'long, long thoughts'*: From Henry Wadsworth Longfellow, 'My Lost Youth' (1858): 'and the thoughts of youth are long, long thoughts'; each of the ten stanzas closes with this line.

2. *Martha troubled about many things*: 'And Jesus answered and said unto her, Martha, Martha, thou art careful and troubled about many things: But one thing is needful: and Mary hath chosen that good part, which shall not be taken away from her' (Luke 10.41–2).

3. *Lot's wife*: God rained down burning sulphur on Sodom and Gomorrah for their wickedness. On leaving, Lot's wife disobeyed God's express command by turning back and became a pillar of salt (Genesis 19.15–17, 24–6). She is cited as an example to demonstrate the fate that will befall those who cannot abandon their lives at the second coming of Christ (Luke 17.28–33).

4. *Tree of Life*: In the Garden of Eden the fruit of this tree had the power of conferring eternal life (Genesis 2.9 and 3.22).

5. *it is my innings*: Metaphor from cricket: it is my turn, opportunity.

6. *Greek – form … wanting the spirit part*: Classical Greek art, with its mathematically proportioned architecture and sculptures of cold white marble, might be thought heartless.

7. *'icily regular, splendidly null'*: From Tennyson's *Maud* (1855), I, 82–3:

> Faultily faultless, icily regular, splendidly null:
> Dead perfection, no more; nothing more.

8. *Melbury Hill . . . London, W.*: Fictitious . . . West London.

9. *Apelles*: Celebrated fourth-century-BC Greek painter.

10. *'the reptile equal . . . to the god'*: Shelley, *Prometheus Unbound* (1820), II, 43.

11. *Sappho . . . Diana*: Sappho, a Greek lyric poet of early fifth century BC famous for her love poetry addressed to a woman. The others are epitomes of agricultural bounty (Ceres), love (Venus) and chaste athleticism (Diana).

12. *Johnson*: Samuel Johnson (1709–84), British poet, essayist and lexicographer, celebrated for his dictionary of 1755, the first standard English dictionary. The statue of him in St Paul's has him wearing a toga.

13. *Homer*: Idealized portraits of Homer (*c.* ninth century BC) showed him with a harp and wearing a laurel wreath. According to tradition he was blind.

14. *Aesculapius*: Greek god of medicine, supposed to have founded the science. On Venus's visit, was Grand thinking of her visits to the mortal Anchises, to whom she bore Aeneas?

15. *sith*: Possibly a misspelling of 'sithe', meaning sigh, thus suggesting the sigh, or rustle, of silk.

16. '*"He is the greatest artist who has the greatest number"*': See 'he is the greatest artist who has embodied, in the sum of his works, the greatest number of the greatest ideas', John Ruskin, *Modern Painters*, vol. 1 (1843), Part 1, ch. 2, sect. 9.

KATE CHOPIN, *The Story of an Hour*

First published in *Vogue* (1894), as 'The Dream of an Hour'

Reproduced from *The Complete Works*

ELLA D'ARCY, *The Pleasure-Pilgrim*

First published in *Monochromes* (London: John Lane, and Boston: Robert Bros., 1895)

1. *'Guten Tag . . . Wie geht's? Und die Herrschaften?* Good day . . . How are you? And the ladies and gentlemen? (German).

2. *Herrick . . . coy*: Robert Herrick (1591–1674), 'To the Virgins, to Make Much of Time' (1648), stanza 1, 13–16:

Then be not coy, but use your time,
And while ye may, go marry;
For having lost just once your prime,
You may for ever tarry.

3. *Shakespeare . . . kissed*: From *Twelfth Night*, II. iii. 51–2: 'Then come kiss me, sweet-and-twenty! Youth's a stuff will not endure.'

4. *Nemesis*: Greek goddess of retribution and vengeance.

5. '*"Wenn ich Dich liebe, was geht's Dich an"'*: If I love you, what's it to do with you? (German).

6. *Bullier's*: Montparnasse dance-hall. In Henry James's *The American* (1877) ch. 17, Madame de Bellegarde tells Newman she wants to go to Bullier's: 'the ball in the Latin Quarter, where the students dance with their mistresses. Don't tell me you have not heard of it.'

7. *prix de Rome . . . Hebe*: Prize awarded annually by the French government to students of the fine arts, which entitles them to four years' study at the Académie de France à Rome. It was instituted by Louis XIV in 1666. Hebe is the Greek goddess of youth.

8. *Heine's poems*: Heinrich Heine (1797–1856), German romantic poet, most famous for emotionally-charged lyric poetry. (The teacher is fictitious).

9. *Halma*: European board game that was developed in the late nineteenth century; it soon began to be played in the United States, and by the 1930s was known as Chinese Checkers. In Mona Caird's *The Daughters of Danaus* (1894), the rebellious Hadria remarks: 'I will ask Mrs Gordon to teach me the spirit of acquiescence, and one of those distracting games – bézique or halma, or some of the other infernal pastimes that heaven decrees for recalcitrant spirits in need of crushing discipline.'

WILLA CATHER, *Tommy the Unsentimental*

First published in *Home Monthly* (Pittsburgh) 6 (August 1896), 6–7

1. *the Divide*: Continental divide – huge mountain range which divides east and west America.

2. *Bohemians*: Inhabitants of Bohemia, former kingdom of central Europe belonging to the Hapsburgs. In the second half of the nineteenth century a sizeable number of Bohemians emigrated to Texas and other central western states.

ALICE MEYNELL, *A Woman in Grey*

First published in *The Colour of Life and Other Essays on Things Seen and Heard* (London: John Lane, and Chicago: Way and Williams, 1896)

1. *'Have you not love . . . you so'*: *Julius Caesar* IV. iii. 119–23.
2. *'If by traduction . . . blood'*: John Dryden, 'To the Pious Memory of the Accomplished Young Lady Mrs Anne Killigrew Excellent in the Two Sister-Arts of Poësy and Painting: An Ode' (1686), 2, 23–6.
3. *winning of Waterloo upon the Eton playgrounds*: The Duke of Wellington is held to have said that the battle of Waterloo was won on the playing fields of Eton.
4. *momentary*: Here, made up of moments.
5. *'Thou art . . . frame thee'*: Shakespeare's *Coriolanus*: V. iii. 63–4 continues: 'Do you know this lady?'

RUDOLPH DIRCKS, *Ellen*

First published in *Savoy* 1 (1896), 103–8

GEORGE EGERTON, *A Nocturne*

First published in *Symphonies* (London and New York: John Lane, 1897)

1. *Cleopatra's Needle*: Egyptian obelisk, originally set up at Heliopolis *c.* 1500 BC, and moved to Thames Embankment in 1878.
2. *Christine Nilsson*: Swedish soprano (1843–1921), who established operatic fame in Paris, London and New York.
3. *Siege of Paris*: Paris was besieged during the Franco-Prussian War of 1870–71.
4. *Aldine classic*: Relating to Aldus Manutius (1450–1515), Italian printer, noted for his fine editions of the classics. (He introduced italic type.)
5. *index expurgatorius*: Authoritative specification of the passages to be expunged or altered in works otherwise permitted to be read by Roman Catholics. The term is frequently used in Britain to cover the 'Index Librorum Prohibitorum', or list of forbidden books.
6. *'Globe'*: The Globe and Traveller (formerly *The Globe* 1803–22), English

newspaper printed and published at the Globe and Traveller Office, London, 1822–1921, then merged in the *Evening Standard*.

7. *turnover*: An article that begins in the last column of a newspaper page and continues overleaf. A series of sketches in the *Globe* were called 'Turnovers'.

KATE CHOPIN, *Miss McEnders*

First published in *Criterion* (USA) (6 March 1897), as 'Miss McEnders. An Episode'

Reproduced from *The Complete Works*

1. *c'est un propre, celui la!*: He's a right one! (French).
2. *Whisky Ring*: A national tax-evasion scheme. Distillers bribed government officials so they could retain the excise taxes they had collected, and the officials used the profits to support political activities (including preventing the reduction of the whisky tax), counter investigations and silence journalists. The corruption was uncovered in 1875, and indictments were brought against eighty-six government officials, including President Grant's private secretary.

KATE CHOPIN, *A Pair of Silk Stockings*

First published in *Vogue* (16 September 1897)

Reproduced from *The Complete Works*

1. *cutting the pages*: Pages in an untrimmed journal needed cutting to separate them.

CLARENCE ROOK, *The Stir Outside the Café Royal*

First published in *Harmsworth Magazine* 3 (September 1898), 319–22

1. *long firm frauds*: Frauds in which the fraudster simply sets up in business as a wholesaler, and places orders with suppliers with the intention of evading payment. Initially payment is prompt in order to establish creditworthiness, but then larger orders are placed and the delivered goods are promptly sold for what they will fetch.
2. *Café Royal*: Established in 1865 by a Parisian wine merchant, this chic

cafe-restaurant in Regent Street was a focus of the literary and artistic worlds at the turn of the century. In 1894 the night-porter, Marius Martin, was shot and killed there.

3. *McKinley tariff*: McKinley Tariff Act, shepherded through Congress by William McKinley, later president of the USA (1896–1901), and passed in October 1890. The measure, designed to protect American manufacturers, led to high protective tariffs and proved widely unpopular.

SARAH GRAND, *When the Door Opened*—

First published in and reproduced from *Idler* (12 January 1898), 708–14. Collected in *Emotional Moments*

1. *Philip IV . . . Velasquez period*: Diego Velázquez (1599–1660), was court painter to Philip IV of Spain. His portraits are remarkable for their realism and their bravura treatment of the rich fabrics of the clothes of his sitters.

KATE CHOPIN, *The Storm*

Written in 1898; first published in *The Complete Works*

'At the 'Cadian Ball' was published in *Bayou Folk* in 1894. It sets the scene for 'The Storm', exploring the sexual attraction between Alcée and Calixta. Clarisse declares her love for her cousin Alcée, and on the same evening the disappointed Calixta agrees, in 'business-like manner', to marry Bobinôt.

1. *Assumption*: Louisiana parish south of Baton Rouge and west of New Orleans.
2. *Biloxi*: City in southern Mississippi, on the Gulf of Mexico.

SARAH GRAND, *A New Sensation*

First published in and reproduced from *Windsor Magazine: An Illustrated Monthly for Men and Women* 2 (December 1899), 144–52. Collected in *Emotional Moments*

Windsor Magazine was published in London, 1895–1939

1. *children's 'bread and cheese'*: The edible young leaves and leaf buds of the hawthorn.

2. *a new heaven and a new earth*: Allusion to 'And I saw a new heaven and a new earth: for the first heaven and the first earth were passed away' (Revelations 21.1).
3. *'Far flickers . . . By the North Sea'*: A meditation (1880), upon spiritual bleakness, in which Algernon Charles Swinburne argues that time has wrecked Christianity as it had destroyed the worship of Venus and Proserpine.
4. *The grand old gardener . . . long descent*: Tennyson, 'Lady Clara Vere de Vere' (1842), stanza 7.

KATE CHOPIN, *An Egyptian Cigarette*

First published in *Vogue* (19 April 1900)

Reproduced from *The Complete Works*

PAULINE HOPKINS, *Talma Gordon*

First published in *Colored American Magazine* (1900)

Reproduced from *American Local Color Writing, 1880–1920*, ed. Elizabeth Ammons and Valerie Rohy (New York: Penguin, 1998)

1. *'There's a divinity . . . we will'*: Shakespeare, *Hamlet*, V. ii. 10–11.
2. *East India*: The Indo-Chinese peninsula, and the Malay archipelago, as opposed to the West Indies, the Caribbean Islands.
3. *New England Puritans . . . 'Mayflower'*: In 1608 a mixed group of adventurers and Puritan emigrants (the 'Pilgrims'), fleeing religious persecution, left England for the Netherlands. They remained there until 1620, when they set sail in the *Mayflower* and landed on Cape Cod in November of that year.
4. *American Academy at Rome*: Founded in 1894 as the American School of Architecture in Rome by Charles F. McKim and enlarged in 1897 with the founding of the American Academy in Rome for students of architecture, sculpture and painting.
5. *'Smiling, frowning . . . Madeline'*: From Tennyson, 'Madeline' (1830), stanza 2, ll. 18–20.
6. *'Whom the gods love die young'*: Classical proverb (Menander, *Dis Exapaton*, fragment 4), quoted by Byron, *Don Juan* (1821), IV, 12.
7. *'all went merry as a marriage bell'*: From Byron, *Childe Harold's Pilgrimage* (1812), III, 21.
8. *'A wet sheet . . . on the lea'*: Poem by Allen Cunningham (1784–1842);

included in his collection *The Songs of Scotland, Ancient and Modern* (1825), it became one of the best known of British sea songs.

9. *suffering all things, enduring all things*: Cf. the love which St Paul describes as patient, kind, not rude, not boastful, 'Beareth all things, believeth all things, hopeth all things, endureth all things' (1 Corinthians 13: 7).

10. *Dumas*: Alexandre Dumas (1802–70), French novelist and playwright, author of *The Three Musketeers* and *The Count of Monte Cristo* (both 1844–5). Through his grandmother, Dumas could claim African descent.

GEORGE GISSING, *A Daughter of the Lodge*

First appeared in *Illustrated London News* (17 August 1901), 235–7

Reproduced from *The House of Cobwebs and Other Stories* (London: Archibald Constable, 1906)

1. *remained childless*: Differential class fertility was a growing concern at this time among the middle and upper classes.
2. *Mudie*: The famous circulating library, the main branch of which was opened in Oxford Street in 1852. The strict moral censure of Charles Edward Mudie (1818–90) caused outrage, and was fought by various writers, notably George Moore.

ZITKALA-ŠA, *A Warrior's Daughter*

First published in *Everybody's Magazine* (USA) (1902), 346–52

GEORGE MOORE, *The Wedding Feast*

First published as 'The Marriage Feast' in the copyright edition of *The Untilled Field* (Leipzig, 1903); revised as 'The Wedding Feast' in the 1914 edition

Reproduced from *The Untilled Field* (Gerrards Cross: Colin Smythe, 1976)

1. *The fat . . . beside the lean*: See Genesis 41. The dream is used to indicate a cycle of lean and fat years; it counsels sensible economy to smooth out the good and bad times.
2. *Unionist*: Supporter (Protestant) of the Union with Britain. The common

religious bond between landlords and tenants and a fair system of tenants' rights produced comparative harmony.

3. *black Protestant*: Term used of Protestant Irish who supported Ulster Rule, or 'Black Ulster'. Some Catholics in Ireland still use 'Black Irish' to describe the Protestant Irish.

EDITH WHARTON, *The Reckoning*

First published in *Harper's Monthly* (New York) 105 (August 1902), 342–55

Reproduced from the first British publication, *The Descent of Man and Other Stories* (London: Macmillan, 1904)

1. *new dispensation*: Note the religious undertones: within a Christian context, a system or code of prescriptions for life and conduct regarded as of divine origin. The implication is that these will differ from the 'old' (Old Testament) dispensation. The 'new' were more forgiving and more case-related than the old, which would lose the spirit for the law. However, in spite of this claim, the new dispensation turns out to differ little from the old.

2. *'statutory'*: Divorce laws varied from state to state, but the main grounds were adultery, desertion and extreme cruelty. In 1813 in New York, where the story is set, the legislature rejected its commission's recommendation that desertion be made a ground for divorce and instead enacted a separation statute for wives – extended to husbands in 1880. In 1827, the legislature rejected habitual drunkenness as grounds for divorce. In 1830 it enacted an annulment statute authorizing annulments for nonage, bigamy, insanity, fraud or force, and physical incapacity.

VIRGINIA WOOLF, *Phyllis and Rosamond*

Holograph draft written in 1906, in the Monks House Papers, University of Sussex Library; first published in *The Complete Shorter Fiction of Virginia Woolf*, ed. Susan Dick (New York: Harcourt Brace & Company, 1989)

1. *Temple*: Building in London that now houses two of the main law societies; it belonged originally to the Templars, the military religious order Knights of the Temple of Solomon, founded by Crusaders in Jerusalem in the twelfth century.

2. *first class*: Highest classification of university degree.

3. *Anatole France . . . Walter Pater*: France (Anatole François Thibault, 1844–1924), writer and critic, was awarded the Nobel Prize for Literature in 1921; Pater (1839–94), writer, critic and aesthete, and author of *Greek Studies: A Series of Essays* (1895).

4. *Lord Mayo was assassinated*: The sixth earl of Mayo, who was appointed Viceroy of India in 1868, was assassinated in the Adaman Islands in 1872.

5. *Leiscetter*: This name is unclear in the draft.

6. *Park . . . statue of Achilles*: Bronze statue of Achilles, in the south-eastern corner of Hyde Park; erected in 1822, it recalls the Duke of Wellington's victories.

7. *ladies whom Romney painted*: The elegant clothing of the women whose portraits George Romney (1734–1802) painted would have been out of place, and date, at the Tristrams' party.

8. *'the facts of life'*: (Stark) realities of existence, brute fact; the colloquial use as a euphemism for 'knowledge of human sexual functions' does not appear to be intended here.

KATHERINE MANSFIELD, *Leves Amores*

First published in Claire Tomalin, *Katherine Mansfield: A Secret Life* (London: Viking, 1987)

All Mansfield stories are reproduced from *The Collected Stories of Katherine Mansfield* (London: Penguin, 1981)

1. *Leves Amores*: Quotation from a medieval Latin love lyric, in which a poet describes the eyes of the beloved: 'There sit Venus, and nimble Cupids, and in the centre Desire herself' (*Oxford Book of Latin Verse*, ed. H. W. Garrod, 1912, no. 324). 'Levis' means light and nimble, but also capricious or fickle; Amor is both love and its personification in Cupid. The phrase, taken out of its original context, is thus ambiguous.

KATHERINE MANSFIELD, *The Tiredness Of Rosabel*

Written in 1908; first published in *Something Childish and Other Stories* (London: Constable, 1924)

Reproduced from *The Collected Stories*

1. *Lyons*: The first of the famous Lyons Corner Houses opened in 1908 in London's West End.

2. *Anna Lombard*: New Woman novel billed as 'the most popular novel of the day' (London: John Lang, 1902), by Victoria Cross [Cory Vivien], author of *The Woman Who Didn't*, a response to Grant Allen's *The Woman Who Did*. Set in India, Anna loves two men at once; *Literature* commented that she was 'so entirely non-moral as to think nothing of living with both. The daughter of a general and the heiress of a thousand conventions, she is sometimes mysteriously Greek, sometimes Oriental, and sometimes Machiavellian. She is generally wicked, and always interesting.' W. T. Stead, in *Review of Reviews*, wrote: 'a novel to get people thinking. It is a bold, brilliant, defiant presentation of a phase of the relations of the sexes which I do not remember ever having seen treated with the same freedom, delicacy and audacity.' (Comments taken from the 1902 edition.)

3. *Sapolio . . . Lamplough's Pyretic Saline*: Popular scouring soap, and Lamplough's Effervescing Pyretic Saline, a medicine to reduce fever, produced in England, and exported to the USA. Cf. 'that comforter of my childhood, Lamplough's pyretic saline', in Fanny Van de Grift and Robert Louis Stevenson's *The Dynamiter* (1885).

4. *Carlton . . . Parma violets*: A luxurious hotel in Haymarket, which opened in 1899. Violets from Parma, city in northern Italy. Cf. Wilde, *The Picture of Dorian Gray* (1891): 'that evening, at half-past eight, dressed in exquisite elegance and with a small bunch of Parma violets in his buttonhole, Dorian Gray was introduced ceremoniously by servants, into the lounge of Lady Narborough'.

EVELYN SHARP, *Filling the War Chest*

First published in *Rebel Women* (London: Women's Freedom League, 1910)

1. *pink newspapers*: Racing papers.

2. *penny Conservative paper*: The *Standard*, a penny morning paper, staunchly supportive of the Conservative party.

3. *'L'homme oisif . . . l'homme oisif'*: The idle person kills time; time kills the idle person (French).

4. *jet trimming*: Jet beads were a popular trimming for women's clothing during the Victorian and Edwardian period. See, for example, Isabel A. Mallon, 'The Woman of Forty', *Ladies' Home Journal* (September 1893): 'the received best dress for the woman past forty was, for a number of years, a very severe black silk one, made without any decoration unless it should be a flat jet trimming'.

EVELYN SHARP, *The Game that wasn't Cricket*

First published in *Rebel Women*

CHARLOTTE PERKINS GILMAN, *Turned*

First published in *Forerunner* 2:9 (September 1911), 1–6

Reproduced from *The Yellow Wall-Paper and Other Stories*

Forerunner began in 1909.

This story makes an interesting comparison with George Eliot's *Romola* (1863). In *Impress* (1 December 1894, p. 5), Gilman praised Eliot, remarking upon 'that sweeping breadth of vision, deep insight, and wide scholarship which make the author of *Romola* so great a power in literature'.

1. *Calvinist . . . of God'*: Follower of Calvinism, a system of theological thought found in the doctrinal expressions of the Reformed and Presbyterian churches, from Calvin's *Institutes of the Christian Religion* (1536). Calvinism flourished in the Puritan culture of New England. *Unitarian*: Believing that God is one being and rejects the doctrine of the Trinity, Unitarians were not perceived to be as strict as Calvinists. *'for the glory of God'*: Samuel Hopkins (1721–1803), New England minister, maintained a heightened sense of God's sovereignty by insisting that people should be willing even 'to be damned for the glory of God'. Hopkins was the leader of an extreme Calvinist movement known as the New Divinity or Hopkinsianism.

KATHERINE MANSFIELD, *The Advanced Lady*

First published in *In a German Pension* (London: Constable, 1911)

Reproduced from *The Collected Stories*

1. *Schlingen*: Village just to the south of the spa-village Wörishofen (Bad Wörishofen from 1920), in southern Bavaria, centre for hydropathy, and famous for the Kneipp-Kur, a water cure developed by the nineteenth-century cleric Sebastian Kneipp (1821–97).
2. *'cure guests'*: Patients at the spa.
3. *'O Welt . . . wunderbar'*: 'O world, how wonderful you are' (German); song unidentified.
4. *tailor-made*: Literally, clothing made by a tailor to fit exactly (British). Here, Frau Kellermann responds again on a literal plane to the Advanced Lady's comments, this time choosing to misinterpret her figurative language, and unsettling her.
5. *Mindelbau*: There is a small village called Mindelau, just to the south-west of Mindelheim, a historical town in southern Bavaria. See also Mansfield's 'At Lehman's', earlier in the series *In a German Pension*, set in Mindelbau.
6. *'The friends thou hast . . . steel'*: *Hamlet*, I. iii. 62–3.

GERTRUDE COLMORE, *George Lloyd*

First published in *Votes for Women* (16 May 1913), 471

1. *George Lloyd*: Allusion to Lloyd George, Chancellor of the Exchequer (1908–15) and Prime Minister (1916–22).

GERTRUDE COLMORE, *The Woman in the Corner*

First published in *Mr Jones and the Governess* (London: Women's Freedom League, 1913)

Votes for Women reviewed *Mr Jones and the Governess* (13 October 1913, p. 5), and chose 'The Woman in the Corner' as the best story, declining to give away the plot.

The Criminal Law Amendment (White Slave Traffic) Bill, later the Criminal Law Amendment Bill (1912), sought to make more effective the Criminal Law Amendment Act of 1885 which had raised the age of consent to 16, and introduced tighter laws against brothel-keeping, in the wake of W. T. Stead's campaign (see, for example, Hansard (1912), vol. 39, cols 571–627, and vol. 45, cols 699–734). Arthur Lee, who proposed the 1912 Bill, emphasized that it was aimed not at prostitutes – 'the unfortunate women who are the victims of commercialized vice' – but at 'those sinister creatures who batten upon commercialized vice, and who make a profitable business out of kidnapping, decoying, and ruining, and subsequently turning into prostitutes, unwilling girls' (Hansard, vol. 39, col. 574). Lee added: 'I feel very strongly as an opponent of Women's Suffrage that we men are under a special obligation to pay heed to the appeal made to us as men by the united voice of women on behalf of the most miserable and unfortunate of their sex' (Ibid.). He emphasized the urgency of the Bill 'during the Christmas shopping, when an unusually large number of young girls are about the streets' (Hansard, vol. 45, col. 705). The House laid out the grounds for punishment by private whipping, in addition to six months' imprisonment, agreeing that nobody would be flogged 'except after trial by jury' (Hansard, vol. 45, col. 733). The liberal Josiah Wedgwood, a staunch supporter of individual autonomy, in the tradition of J. S. Mill, and an ardent opponent of eugenics, objected to the insertion 'if a male', declaring

I should rather like to know whether it is desirable to make this distinction at all between the sexes . . . the crime is just the same in regard to women, and why are we not to flog women also . . . nearly all the stories which we know so well from letters to the papers or in the columns of the sensational Press deal with women. It is the woman who decoys away for ever the girl who assists her when she faints. It is the woman who is waiting in her carriage at Euston station to catch the unwary servant girl, and take her away in her carriage and pair to a brothel in Soho. In all these cases it is the woman who is the villain of the piece. (Hansard, vol. 45, cols. 733–44)

His objection was carried. In the story Colmore points out that women played a central role in luring girls into prostitution. The Bill was given royal consent on 13 December 1912.

1. *White Slave Traffic*: 'White slavery' was commonly used to describe sweated labour; for example, see Introduction, n. 110. However, 'Maiden Tribute of Modern Babylon' by the sex reformer and editor of the *Pall Mall Gazette*, Stead, had referred to pimps and procuresses as 'slave traders' (*Pall Mall Gazette*, 1885) and to the trade in female child prostitutes as a 'slave market'. By the early twentieth century, the phrase 'white slave traffic' was commonly

used to describe the traffic in young prostitutes, and was part of the initial title of the Criminal Law Amendment Bill (see above).

2. *St Paul*: See, for example, 1 Timothy 5. 14: 'I will therefore that the younger women marry, bear children, guide the house, give none occasion to the adversary to speak reproachfully.'

MARY SAMUEL DANIEL, *Jimmy's Afternoon*

First published in *Votes for Women* (10 January 1913), 214

1. *the old, old story of a bad man and his prey*: See, published in the same year, Christabel Pankhurst, *Plain Facts about a Great Evil* (*The Great Scourge and How to End It*) (London: Women's Social and Political Union, 1913). Pankhurst alleged that between 75 and 80 per cent of all men were infected with gonorrhoea; her solution was votes for women and chastity for men. New Women literature was actively engaged in the debates over syphilis and the sexual double standard; see especially Grand's *The Heavenly Twins* and her short story 'Eugenia' (1908). Syphilitic children appear in *The Heavenly Twins*, and Emma Brooke's *A Superfluous Woman* (1894); Hardy's Jude junior in *Jude the Obscure* (1894–5) bears the signs of a syphilitic child, notably premature ageing.

2. *Holloway*: Prison, opened in 1852 – with three wings for men and one for women, became a remand prison at the end of the nineteenth century and by then was for women only.

SAKI (HECTOR HUGH MUNRO), *The Schartz-Metterklume Method*

First published in *Beasts and Super-Beasts* (London: John Lane, 1914)

Reproduced from *The Complete Works of Saki* (London: Penguin, 1982)

1. *she-wolf*: In legend, Romulus and Remus, the founders of Rome, were suckled by a she-wolf after they had been abandoned. A sixth-century BC statue of the wolf, now in the Capitoline Museum in Rome, has become an emblem of the city.

2. *shabby women*: In legend, the early Romans, needing to increase their population, seized a number of women from the Sabines, a tribe living to the north-east of Rome. It was a popular subject for painters; see, for example,

Peter Paul Rubens (1577–1640), *The Rape of the Sabine Women.* in the National Gallery, London.

CHARLOTTE PERKINS GILMAN, *If I were a Man*

First published in *Physical Culture* (July 1914), 31–4

Reproduced from *The Yellow Wall-Paper and Other Stories*

Physical Culture was founded in 1899 by the entrepreneur, body-builder and publisher Bernaar Macfadden. It sold for five cents and was a huge success, preaching the virtues of healthy living, warning readers against tobacco, alcohol and coffee, and advocating sex as natural, healthy and enjoyable. It was heavily informed by developing ideas about fitness.

1. *Noah . . . Hindu scriptures*: Noah serves here as an epitome of 'Old Testament' (ancient, out-of-date) values. While lecturing his brother Bharata on how to govern the kingdom, Lord Rama says women are not to be trusted: *Ramayana* 2:100; see also, for example, *Rig Veda* 10:86:6.

APPENDICES

I SARAH GRAND, *In Search of a Subject*

First published in *Bath College Domestic Subjects* (January 1928), 6–10

The editorial on p. 3 of the old student's magazine reads: 'All members will realize the honour paid to the college by Madame Sarah Grand in contributing the article on page 6 and feel gratefully indebted to her for so very kindly responding to the invitation.'

1. *Poor Mrs Dombey*: The allusion is to the first Mrs Dombey, in Dickens's *Dombey and Son* (1844–6), who appears only in the first chapter, giving birth to her son. Grand's narrator empathizes with Mrs Dombey, who, we repeatedly hear, did not make an effort. In the words of Dr Parker Peps, 'the system of our patient has sustained a shock, from which it can only hope to rally by a great and strong . . . and vigorous effort'. He, the family physician and her sister-in-law Louisa stress that if Mrs Dombey can't make that effort,

she will die. Moments before Mrs Dombey dies, Louisa tells her: 'it's necessary for you to make an effort, and perhaps a great and very painful effort which you are not disposed to make; but this is a world of effort you know, Fanny, and we must never yield, when so much depends upon us.' Mrs Dombey is soon forgotten; like Grand's narrator, she has no story (Penguin, 1985, ch. 1).

2 CHARLOTTE PERKINS GILMAN,
Why I wrote 'The Yellow Wall-paper'?

First published in *Forerunner* 4 (October 1913), 271

Reproduced from *The Yellow Wall-Paper and Other Stories*

1. *alienists*: Persons who practise alienism, the study and treatment of mental illness.

GLOSSARY

afflatus: Inspiration (Latin).
air-balls: Balloons.
antimacassar: Cloth covering the back of a chair, to prevent soiling by hair oil or as decoration.

bean feasts: Parties.
Belgravia: Prestigious neighbourhood situated between Green Park to the east and Hyde Park to the north, near Buckingham Palace.
bistre: Water-soluble brownish-yellow pigment made by boiling the soot of wood, used for pen-and-water drawings.
black letter: see Old German entry.
Bloomsbury: District of central London, contains the British Museum. Home of the Bloomsbury Group, a group of writers, artists and intellectuals in the early decades of the twentieth century.
blue-points: Small oysters.
Bond Street: Opulent shopping street in the centre of London.
bonnes ménagères: Happy housewives (French).
Bonté: Goodness (French).
bouts-rimés: Rhymed endings (French).
brougham: Four-wheeled horse-drawn closed carriage with a raised open driver's seat in front. Named after Henry Peter, Lord Brougham (1788–1868).
Bufo vulgaris: European toad.

cestus: Girdle of Aphrodite (Venus) decorated to incite amorousness.
Cheapside: Street in the City, the oldest part of London, by St Paul's. Originally a market (the name meant marketside), its development as a centre for gold- and silver-smiths was underway by the fourteenth century.
Chene: Abbreviation of *chenapan*, rascal, or scallywag (humorous, affectionate) (French).
cher maître: Good Lord! (French).

chiffonnier: Tall, elegant chest of drawers.

chiton: Ancient Greek tunic.

City: London's financial city, home to the Bank of England and the Stock Exchange.

clairvoyante: Woman who claims to be able to foretell future events (French).

cochon de lait: Piglet (French).

Coleoptera: Beetles.

contadina: Woman of the fields (Italian).

corbeille: Wedding presents (French).

couleur de rose: Rose-coloured (French).

Court Circular: Daily record of the activities, engagements, etc., of the sovereign, Prince of Wales and the court generally, which were published in a national newspaper.

coûte que coûte: At all costs, no matter what (French).

Da: Now (in context on p. 361).

daguerreotype: One of the earliest types of photograph; the image was produced on iodine-sensitized silver and developed in mercury vapour.

'devilled': Practised underpaid 'hack' writing.

Dieu sait: God knows (French).

diggings: Lodgings.

Earl's Court: Situated west of South Kensington. Its 'Empire of India Exhibition' opened in May 1895; a large 'Ferris Wheel' was inaugurated in July of that year, which turned for eleven years.

ewig weibliche: Eternal femininity (German).

famos: Splendid (Italian).

fast: Extravagant in habits; devoted to pleasure; usually implying some immorality.

Fauteuils de balcon: dress circle (French).

fiancé en titre: Officially betrothed (French).

fly: One-horse carriage.

Fraulein: Miss (Fräulein, German).

Freiherr: Baron (German).

frumps: Drab, old-fashioned women.

genre: Type (French).

'gesegnete Mahlzeit': Thanksgiving at mealtime, usually before the meal (German).

gladstone bag: Hand luggage consisting of two equal-sized hinged compartments (named after the British statesman, William Gladstone).

gnädige Frau: Lady, or madam (German).

gooseberry: Unwanted single person in a group of couples, especially a third person with a couple.

grand écart: The splits (French).

gutta percha: White rubbery substance derived from tropical trees, especially *Palaquium gutta*.

Hampstead: North London suburb, north of St John's Wood.

hansom: Two-wheeled one-horse carriage with a fixed hood; the driver sits on a high outside seat at the rear. Typically used to provide a taxi service. Also called hansom cab. Named after J. A. Hansom (1803–1902).

Henry Clays: Brand of Cuban cigar, named after a US politician in the early nineteenth century.

Herr Gott: Good Lord (German, informal).

himation: Greek cloak.

hunter: Pocket watch enclosed in a metal case.

J'vous responds: I give you my word (French).

KC: King's Counsel, a senior barrister.

layette: Baby's clothing (French).

Levée: Public court reception for men, held in the early afternoon (French).

lieber Gott im Himmel: My goodness me (German; literally, dear God in Heaven).

Lord Henry, by the: Mild oath.

Loyalesque: Words formed with the suffix 'esque' are chiefly nonce-words of a jocular character (*OED*). The context suggests something that looks loyal but isn't quite.

ma belle inconnue: My beautiful stranger (French).

Mahlsaal: Dining room (German).

Mais si: Yes, indeed (French).

Marylebone Road . . . Regent's Park . . . Piccadilly: Marylebone Road is a broad, busy street running along the south side of Regent's Park. Opened in 1841, the Park houses London Zoo. Piccadilly runs along the north side of Green Park, between Piccadilly Circus and Hyde Park.

mein lieber: My dear (German).

merveille: Wonderfully (French).

mezzotints: Type of print; copper-plate engravings.

mise en scène: Production, stage effect (French).

muliebre: Female; from Latin *mulier*: woman.

Na: Well (German).

Nu: Now, abbreviation of *nun* (German).

octoroon: Person of one-eighth African ancestry (French).

*old German (*and *black letter)*: Term (esp. British) for Gothic script, the family of heavy script typefaces in use from the fifteenth to eighteenth centuries.

oleosaccharine: Distilled oil mixed with sugar.

Oxford Street: Major central London road running west to east. Its development as a major shopping centre began early in the twentieth century.

packet: Packet boat, vessel ferrying people and goods between two ports.

Park Lane: Joins Oxford Street in the north with Piccadilly in the south. With Hyde Park on its west side, and Mayfair to its east, it is one of London's most fashionable addresses.

peignoir: Robe or dressing gown (French).

perk: To carry oneself in a smart, brisk or jaunty manner (*OED*).

permanent way: The fixed road-bed of a railway.

phthisis: Tuberculosis of the lungs.

Piccadilly: see Marylebone Road entry.

porte-monnaie: Purse (French).

quadroon: Person of one-quarter African ancestry (French).

rates: Taxes.

'redding': Cleaning.

Regent's Park: see Marylebone Road entry.

Regent's Street: Regent Street, broad avenue designed by John Nash as part of the Prince Regent's early-nineteenth-century grand scheme to connect Regent's Park in the north of the city with the Mall in the south.

Richmond Road: Prestigious neighbourhood, in Richmond, town in West Greater London, on the River Thames.

Rittersaal: Trophy room (see D'Arcy, 'The Pleasure-Pilgrim', section 5).

Row: Narrow street.

St George, Hanover Square: Massive baroque church designed by the architect John James, follower of Christopher Wren; built 1712–25.

St John's Wood: North London suburb.

St Paul's: Cathedral in central London, designed by Christopher Wren between 1675 and 1710 to replace an earlier cathedral destroyed by the Great Fire of 1666.

Seigneur Dieu: Lord God! (French).

Sèvres: Fine porcelain manufactured at Sèvres, near Paris, from 1756, characterized by the use of clear colours and elaborate decorative detail.

shirtwaist: A woman's blouse or dress with details as in a man's shirt (USA).

sorra: Dialect or colloquialism for sorry (*OED*).

South Kensington: At the centre of the Victorian cultural complex (including the Natural History and Victoria and Albert museums), funded from the profits of the Great Exhibition of 1851, which was held in Hyde Park.

sovereign: Former British gold coin worth one pound.

street arab: Child of the street.

Tableau Vivant: Representation of a scene, painting, sculpture, etc., by a person or group posed silent and motionless (nineteenth-century French; literally, living picture).

three-cent piece: Minted between 1851 and 1873, 14 mm in diameter.

tubercle-fiend: Tuberculosis.

under stoppages: Docking a soldier's pay in order to buy necessary items or to pay off his debts.

Victoria: Light four-wheeled horse-drawn carriage with a folding hood, two passenger seats and a seat in front for the driver.

vis inertiae: The force of inactivity (Latin).

viveur: Reveller (French).

waist: A bodice, blouse (chiefly USA).

Westbourne Grove: The roots of a cosmopolitan upper-middle-class community were established in this area of London from the mid nineteenth century. Located close to the West End and the Royal Parks, its developing wealth of shops led it to be seen by the close of the century as the Bond Street of the West.

windgalls: Soft swelling in the area of the fetlock joint of a horse.

Zum Beispiel: For example (German).

BIOGRAPHICAL NOTES

MONA CAIRD (1854–1932) (Alice Mona Alison) was born on the Isle of Wight. Her landowning father was an engineer and inventor, and her mother had been born in Schleswig-Holstein. Caird published her first novel, *Lady Hetty*, anonymously when she was seventeen. At the age of twenty-three, she married James Alexander Henryson-Caird, a thirty-one-year-old landowner from an established Scottish family. Their married lives seem to have been largely separate, with James spending most of the year on his estate, and Caird living there one or two months each year, and the rest of the time in London or abroad. They had one son. Caird was a humanitarian feminist who opposed eugenics and vivisection and, more generally, state encroachment on individual freedom. Her most successful novel was *The Daughters of Danaus* (1894); she was the author of seven novels (including *Stones of Sacrifice* (1915), a number of short stories, a travel book, a number of anti-vivisection tracts and several articles on the Woman Question and other social issues. She published her last novel, *The Great Wave*, in 1931.

WILLA CATHER (1873–1947) was born in Virginia. Her father made his living raising sheep on his father's farm, but after the barn burned down in 1883, the family relocated to Nebraska, where her paternal grandparents had established a farm some years earlier. She arrived at the University of Nebraska dressed as William Cather, her twin. In 1896 she moved to Pittsburgh, where she had obtained a job as editor of *Home Monthly*, and then, from 1897, she worked for the Pittsburgh *Leader*. Cather later moved to New York City and worked for *McClure's Magazine* 1906–12, becoming its managing editor. Her published work included *The Troll Garden* (1905), *My Antonia* (1918), *One of Ours* (1922) and *A Lost Lady* (1923). She lived with Edith Lewis in New York for forty years.

KATE CHOPIN (1850–1904) (Katherine O'Flaherty) was born in St Louis, Missouri, of Irish and French ancestry. She graduated from the St Louis

Academy of the Sacred Heart in 1868, married Oscar Chopin two years later and went to live with him in New Orleans. By 1878 they had five sons, and the following year they moved to Cloutierville, a French village in north-west Louisiana where their daughter was born. Following Oscar's death from swamp fever, Chopin ran the plantation to pay off his debts, and had a relationship with a married neighbour. In 1884 she returned to St Louis and began to write to support her children. Her first novel, *At Fault* (1890), was followed by the stories that made her famous, *Bayou Folk* (1894), which drew on her experiences in the Cane River, a swampland region of Louisiana, and *A Night in Acadie* (1897). She wrote over a hundred short stories, poems, essays and reviews, and in 1899 published *The Awakening*, which explores a woman's extramarital desires. The book caused outrage, and her publisher cancelled the third short-story collection, *A Vocation and a Voice*, which was published for the first time by Penguin in 1991.

GERTRUDE COLMORE, English suffragette, was the author of *Suffragettes: A Story of Three Women* (first published as *Suffragette Sally*, 1911), which details the suffragette movement to the Conciliation Bill and beyond.

MARY SAMUEL DANIEL, English suffragette, and author of *Choice* (1914).

ELLA D'ARCY (1851–1939) was born in London of Irish parents and educated in Germany and France. She was assistant editor of *The Yellow Book*, and published short stories in other literary magazines in the 1890s; the stories were collected in two volumes, *Monochromes* (1895), and *Modern Instances* (1898). In 1898 D'Arcy published a novel, *The Bishop's Dilemma*. Although she did not publish further fiction, she translated André Maurois's biography of Shelley, *Ariel*, into English. Most of her later life was spent in Paris.

RUDOLPH DIRCKS, English playwright and art critic. His works include *The Haunted Man and the Ghost's Bargain* (1862), *Retaliation* (1883) (a comedy), *Players of To-day* (1892), *Verisimilitudes* (1897) and *Auguste Rodin* (1904).

GEORGE EGERTON, pseudonym of Mary Chavelita Dunne (1859–1945), was born in Melbourne, Australia, the oldest daughter of an Irish army officer and a Welsh mother. She spent most of her childhood in Ireland, but also travelled to New Zealand, Chile, Wales and Germany. Her mother died when she was fourteen, and the family broke up. Egerton trained as a nurse and in 1887 eloped to Norway with a married man and friend of her father, Henry Higginson. He was violent and nearly always drunk. She left him and returned to England, where she married a Newfoundlander, George Egerton Clairmonte, settled in Ireland and wrote *Keynotes* (1893). Soon after the birth of their son in 1895 their marriage came to an end. They divorced in 1901, when she married Reginald Golding Bright, fifteen years her junior, a literary agent. Egerton became a dramatic agent for, among others, George Bernard Shaw and Somerset Maugham. She wrote a number of collections of short stories (including *Fantasias* (1898)), *The Wheel of God* (1898), a full-length autobiographical novel, and *Rosa Amorosa* (1901), an epistolary novel which celebrated her brief affair with a Norwegian man.

CHARLOTTE PERKINS GILMAN (1860–1935) (Charlotte Anna Perkins) was born in Hartford, Connecticut. Her father deserted the family soon after her birth, leaving the family close to poverty. Her great-aunts were Harriet Beecher Stowe, an abolitionist and author of *Uncle Tom's Cabin*; Catherine Beecher, the prominent advocate of 'domestic feminism'; and Isabella Beecher Hooker, an ardent suffragist. Gilman married Charles Walter Stetson, an artist, in 1884, and gave birth to a daughter the following year, then suffered depression, for which she took the rest cure prescribed by Silas Weir Mitchell. Travelling to California without her husband in 1885 improved her health, and she decided to separate from him. When he married her friend, the author Grace Ellery Channing, she sent their daughter to live with them. She began writing feminist essays and fiction, and in 1898 she published *Women and Economics*, which made her famous on both sides of the Atlantic. In 1900 she married her first cousin, George Houghton Gilman, a lawyer who supported her feminist activities. She was a widely sought-after public lecturer between 1900 and 1915, and ran her own monthly magazine, the *Forerunner* (1909–16). Gilman met George Bernard Shaw and the Webbs on a trip to England, and espoused Fabian socialism. In 1935 she published her autobiography, *The Living of Charlotte Perkins Gilman* and, suffering from cancer, and mourning her husband's death the previous year, took her own life.

GEORGE ROBERT GISSING (1857–1903) was born in Wakefield, the oldest of five children. His father, a pharmacist, died when he was thirteen. In 1872 Gissing won a scholarship to Owens College, Manchester, but in 1876 he was expelled for stealing from the college cloakroom, and imprisoned for a month. He had intended to use the money to help a young prostitute, Nell Harrison. He then left for America where he began publishing short stories. Returning to England in 1877 he lived with Nell and married her in 1879, but the marriage was unhappy and they separated. After her death, Gissing married another working-class woman, Edith Underwood, in 1891. This marriage was also unhappy, and in 1898 Gissing met the French translator, Gabielle Fleury, with whom he lived, mainly in France, for the rest of his life. Writing to survive, and influenced by Dickens and Zola, Gissing made poverty his lifelong subject, exploring the degradation of the London poor, the Woman Question and social injustice. His novels include *New Grub Street* (1891) and *The Odd Women* (1893). The author of twenty-two novels and several short stories, he also wrote a critical study of Dickens, a travel book and a collection of partly autobiographical essays, *The Private Papers of Henry Ryecroft* (1903). He died of lung cancer at the age of forty-six in the Pyrenees.

SARAH GRAND, pseudonym of Frances Elizabeth Bellenden (Clark) McFall (1854–1943), was born in Donaghadee, County Down, Northern Ireland, the fourth of five children. Her father was a naval lieutenant then serving in Northern Ireland and her mother, Margaret Bell, was the child of Yorkshire gentry. Following the death of her father, Grand moved to Yorkshire with her mother in 1861 and then attended finishing school in London. Her stepson Haldane claimed Alfred the Great and Lady Godiva numbered among her ancestors. In 1871, when she was sixteen, Grand married David Chambers McFall, thirty-nine, widowed, and an army surgeon. The couple spent the next five years at military stations in the Far East, and had one son. In 1890, Grand left her husband and her career as a writer took off. Her first novel, *Two Dear Little Feet* (1873), had been didactic and, like her later novels, informed by the medical knowledge she had acquired from her husband; *The Heavenly Twins* (1893) was a sensational bestseller, dealing openly with syphilis and the double standard. She also published *Ideala* (1888) and *The Beth Book: Being a Study from the Life of Elizabeth Caldwell Maclure, A Woman of Genius* (1897) and published her last novel, *The Winged Victory*, in 1916. During the last years of the suffrage campaign Grand was President of the Tunbridge Wells Branch of the Women's Constitutional Suffrage Society. She was also President of the Writers' Suffrage League. After the war, she moved to Bath where she was Mayoress for six years.

THOMAS HARDY (1840–1928) was born in Higher Bockhampton, Dorset, where his father was a stonemason. His mother came from a family of small landowners and worked as a servant prior to marriage. He was educated locally and articled to an architect. In 1862 he moved to London and began working for another architect. His first, unpublished novel, *The Poor Man and the Lady*, was rejected by Macmillan in 1868 as 'too socialist, not to say revolutionary'. His first published novel, *Desperate Remedies* (1871), explores a lesbian relationship. Hardy's lifelong engagement with questions of freedom brought him unavoidably and actively into the Woman Question debates. Before his marriage in 1874 to Emma Gifford, he had published four novels and was earning his living as a writer. In 1878 *The Return of the Native* was published and the Hardys moved to London, returning to Dorset in 1885. His novels include *The Mayor of Casterbridge* (1886), *The Woodlanders* (1887), *Tess of the D'Urbervilles* (1891) and *Jude the Obscure* (1895), as well as a great number of poems and short stories. *Jude the Obscure*, with its open criticism of marriage, caused an outrage. In the wake of the storm, Hardy turned to the poetry he had been writing all his life. In 1912 Emma died and in 1914 he married Florence Dugdale, a close friend for several years.

PAULINE ELIZABETH HOPKINS (1859–1930) was born in Portland, Maine, and raised in Boston, Massachusetts. She was a playwright, journalist, novelist, short-story writer, biographer and editor of the *Colored American Magazine*, a pioneering magazine aimed at an African-American audience (1900–1904). In 1877 she wrote a play, *Colored History*, and completed another, *Slaves' Escape; or, The Underground Railroad* in 1879. Hopkins published two series of biographical sketches of African-Americans, 'Famous Women of the Negro Race' and 'Famous Men of the Negro Race'. Her first novel, *Contending Forces: A Romance Illustrative of Negro Life North and South* (1900), dealt with disenfranchisement and lynching.

KATHERINE MANSFIELD (1888–1923) was born in Wellington, New Zealand, and lived for six years in the rural village of Karori. In 1903 she went to London to finish her education, studying at the Queen's College, where she joined the staff of the *College Magazine*. Mansfield led a bohemian life, and after an unhappy marriage to George Bowden, whom she married for a few days in 1909, she toured with a musical company and spent time in Bavaria. During her stay in Germany she wrote sketches of German characters, which were published in 1911 as *In a German Pension*. On returning to London in 1910 she began publishing stories in *New Age*, *Rhythm* and *Blue Review* and met Virginia Woolf and John Middleton Murry, socialist and editor of *Rhythm*. She lived and worked with Murry for several years, and married him in 1918. Mansfield and Murry became closely associated with D. H. Lawrence and his wife Frieda. When Murry had an affair with Princess Bibesco she objected not to the affair but to the Princess's letters. In her last years Mansfield spent much of her time in southern France and in Switzerland, seeking relief from tuberculosis. She died of a pulmonary haemorrhage in January 1923, in Gurdjieff Institute, near Fontainebleau, France.

ALICE MEYNELL (1847–1922) (Alice Thompson) was born in London and spent much of her childhood in Italy. She published a volume of poems, *Preludes* (1875), which was praised by Ruskin and Tennyson. In 1876 she began journalistic work, and was a prolific essayist throughout her life, writing for the *Spectator*, *Saturday Review*, *Art Journal* and other journals. In 1877 she married the writer and critic Wilfrid Meynell and bore eight children. In 1881 the Meynells began editing the *Weekly Register*, a Catholic periodical. Alice was a close friend of Coventry Patmore and George Meredith. In 1901 and 1902, she lectured in New York, Chicago, Los Angeles, Indianapolis and Boston. On her return to England Meynell campaigned for female suffrage, writing, speaking and marching. Her *Collected Poems* (1913) were a huge success, and for the second time her name was mentioned for the Laureateship. Meynell was Vice-President of the Women Writers' Suffrage League in 1913.

GEORGE AUGUSTUS MOORE (1852–1933) was born at the family estate of Moore Hall, County Mayo. He attended the Roman Catholic college of Oscott, near Birmingham (1861–7), and moved to London with his family in 1869, following the election to parliament of his father. Moore wrote a collection of poems, *Flowers of Passion* (1878), *A Modern Lover* (1883) (which affronted circulating libraries), *A Mummer's Wife* (1885), *A Mere Accident* (1887), *Confessions of a Young Man* (1888) and *Vain Fortune* (1891). In *Literature at Nurse; or Circulating Morals* (1885), Moore attacked the moral censorship of circulating libraries, which banned his novels. His realist novel, *Esther Waters* (1894), which charts the life of a single mother who turns down multiple offers of marriage, was hugely popular and led to these libraries being forced to alter their regulations to allow such works to be borrowed. In 1899 Moore became director of the Irish Literary Theatre, and he settled in Dublin in 1901. He wrote two 'psychological novels', *Evelyn Innes* (1898) and *Sister Teresa* (1901), and became involved with Irish language drama and writing. His stories for the *New Irish Review* in 1902 were published in *The Untilled Field* (1903); many of these had also appeared in Irish translation. Both this collection and his novel *The Lake* (1905) express an ambivalence about Ireland and Catholicism.

CLARENCE ROOK was the English author of *Hooligan Nights* (1899).

SAKI, pseudonym of Hector Hugh Munro (1870–1916), was born in Burma, the son of a senior official in the Burma police. He was brought up in Devon and went to school in Exmouth and at Bedford Grammar School before his father retired and took over his education by travelling in Europe with him. Saki joined the Burma police but resigned on grounds of ill health and began his writing career with political sketches for the *Westminster Gazette* before working as a foreign correspondent for the *Morning Post* in the Balkans, Russia and Paris. The first of his collections of short stories, *Reginald*, appeared in 1904. In 1913 he published *When William Came*, a pro-war fantasy of England under German occupation. In 1914 he enlisted, refusing a commission, and was killed at Beaumont Hamel.

OLIVE SCHREINER (1855–1920) was born in Cape Colony, South Africa. Her mother was English, her father a German Methodist minister. In 1880 she came to London and in 1883 her first novel, *The Story of an African Farm*, was published under the pseudonym 'Ralph Iron'. In 1897 she published her fictional attack on Cecil Rhodes, *Trooper Peter Halket of Mashonaland*. In London she became friends with Eleanor Marx, and fell in love with Karl Pearson, founder of the Men and Women's Club. She returned to South Africa in 1889, marrying Samuel Cronwright, an ostrich farmer, in 1894. The following year she gave birth to their daughter, who died shortly afterwards. In 1899, when the second Anglo-Boer War broke out, she published her pro-Boer anti-war tract, *An English South African's View of the Situation*, causing offence to her brother, Prime Minister of the Cape Colony. In addition to her novels and short stories, she published *Woman and Labour* in 1911, and *Stories, Dreams and Allegories* and *Thoughts on South Africa* were published posthumously in 1923.

EVELYN SHARP (1869–1955) was born in London, the youngest of nine children. She left school at sixteen, and published a story in *The Yellow Book* in 1894. Her novel *At the Relton Arms* was published the following year. Sharp was a committed suffragette, and in 1912 she was assistant editor, then editor, of *Votes for Women*. Twice imprisoned in connection with the suffrage campaign, she wrote numerous articles and stories campaigning for legal improvements for working-class women. A selection of her short stories was published in *Rebel Women* (1910). Once female suffrage was achieved, Sharp began relief work in Germany and Russia. She supported the Labour Party, the National Council for Civil Liberties, the Council for the Abolition of the Death Penalty and the English Folk Dance and Song Society, which her brother, Cecil Sharp, had started. In 1933 she married her friend of many years, Henry Nevinson, and published an autobiography, *An Unfinished Adventure: Selected Reminiscences*. She wrote the libretto for Ralph Vaughan Williams's opera *The Poisoned Kiss* (1936).

BORGIA SMUDGITON, pseudonym of Owen Seaman (1861–1936), son of a Suffolk dressmaker. Graduating in Classics from Cambridge, he became a schoolmaster at Rossall (1884), Professor of Literature at Durham College of Science, Newcastle-upon-Tyne (1890–1903) and a barrister of the Inner Temple (1897). Seaman had a talent for light verse, and wrote a number of parodies of older and contemporary poets, many of which are collected in *The Battle of the Bays* (1896), as well as more serious, political verse, particularly during the First World War. In 1897 he joined the staff of *Punch*, becoming assistant editor in 1902 and then editor (1906–32). In 1914 he was knighted, and in 1933 he was created a baronet.

EDITH WHARTON (1862–1937) was born in New York City and travelled widely in Europe as a child. In 1885 she began an unhappy marriage to Teddy Wharton. In 1907 he was diagnosed as neurasthenic, and the following year he stole fifty thousand dollars from her trust fund and set up his mistress in a flat in Boston; Wharton divorced him in 1913. She began a three-year relationship with Paris journalist Morton Fullerton in 1908. Wharton spent much of her later life in France, devoting herself to war work during the First World War. She published ten collections of short stories, twenty novels and several works of non-fiction. In 1921 she won the Pulitzer Prize with her novel *The Age of Innocence*, and in 1935 her novella, *The Old Maid*, was performed and she won the Pulitzer Prize for drama. In 1932, Wharton was the first woman to receive an honorary degree from Yale University.

OSCAR WILDE (1854–1900) was born in Dublin, the son of an eminent surgeon. He went to Trinity College, Dublin, and then Magdalen College, Oxford. In 1881 he published *Poems*, and the following year lectured in America. He married Constance Lloyd in 1884, and they had two sons. Wilde was editor of *Woman's World* from 1887 to 1889. In 1889 'The Decay of Lying' appeared in the *Nineteenth Century*, and 'The Soul of Man under Socialism' in the *Fortnightly Review* in 1891. The same year he published *The Picture of Dorian Gray*. In 1892 *Lady Windermere's Fan* was performed, followed by *A Woman of No Importance* in 1893. In 1895 *An Ideal Husband* and *The Importance of Being Earnest* ran simultaneously. In 1895 Wilde brought a libel action against the Marquess of Queensberry; he lost the case and was sentenced to two years' imprisonment with hard labour for committing homosexual acts. In prison he wrote *The Ballad of Reading Gaol* (1898), and his health broke down. The first unabridged edition of *De Profundis*, which he had also written in prison, was published in 1949.

VIRGINIA WOOLF (1882–1941) (Adeline Virginia Stephen) was born in Kensington, the daughter of Leslie Stephen, founding editor of the *Dictionary of*

National Biography. She had a busy social life in London, campaigned for female suffrage and began writing short essays and reviews for the London journals in 1905. She married Leonard Woolf in 1912. Her first novel, *The Voyage Out*, appeared in 1915. Her novels include *Night and Day* (1919), *Jacob's Room* (1922), *Mrs Dalloway* (1925), *Orlando* (1928), *To the Lighthouse* (1927), *The Waves* (1931), *The Years* (1937) and *Between The Acts* (1941); her other works include *The Common Reader* (1925; second series, 1932), *A Room of One's Own* (1929) and *The Three Guineas* (1938). Her stories and sketches were collected for the first time in 1989. Woolf suffered recurrent bouts of depression and in March 1941 drowned herself.

ZITKALA-ŠA (1876–1938) (Gertrude Simmons), a Sioux, was born on the Yankton Reservation in South Dakota. Her father (surname Felkner) abandoned the family before she was born and her mother gave her the surname of her second husband, Simmons. At eight she went to study at White's Manual Institute in Wabash, Indiana, and then at Earlham College in Richmond, Indiana. In 1896 she won second place in the Indiana State Oratorical Contest. She gave herself the name Zitkala-Ša, Red Bird, after the wife of her half-brother asked her to give up the family name Simmons, which she shared with him. Angry that she had insisted on getting an education, the sister-in-law argued that Zitkala-Ša had deserted home, and called into question her rights to the name. In 1901 she published a collection of Sioux tales, *Old Indian Legends*, and the following year she married Raymond T. Bonnin, a Sioux, and moved with him to the Uintah and Ouray reservation in Utah. Their son was born in 1903. In 1916, now known as Gertrude Bonnin, she was elected secretary of the Society of the American Indian, and the family moved to Washington, D.C. When the Society dissolved in 1920 Zitkala-Ša worked for the General Federation of Women's Clubs, and campaigned for an Indian Welfare Committee, which was established in 1921. In 1926 she founded the National Council of American Indians, of which she remained president until her death.